Springer Japan KK

Q. Jin, J. Li, N. Zhang, J. Cheng,
C. Yu, S. Noguchi (Eds.)

Enabling Society with
Information Technology

With 100 Figures

 Springer

Qun Jin
The University of Aizu
Aizu-Wakamatsu, Fukushima 965-8580, Japan

Jie Li
University of Tsukuba
Tsukuba, Ibaraki 305-8573, Japan

Nan Zhang
Hiroshima Shudo University
Hiroshima 731-3195, Japan

Jingde Cheng
Saitama University
Saitama 338-8570, Japan

Clement Yu
University of Illinois at Chicago
Chicago, IL 60612, USA

Shoichi Noguchi
Sendai Foundation for Applied Information Sciences
Sendai, Miyagi 983-0852, Japan

ISBN 978-4-431-66981-4

Library of Congress Cataloging-in-Publication Data

Enabling society with information technology / Q. Jin ... [et al.].
    p. cm.
Includes bibliographical references and index.
  ISBN 978-4-431-66981-4   ISBN 978-4-431-66979-1 (eBook)
  DOI 10.1007/978-4-431-66979-1
  1. Information technology--Congresses. I. Jin, Q. (Qun), 1962-
  T58.5 .E53 2001
  303.48'33--dc21

                                2001054977

Printed on acid-free paper

© Springer Japan 2002
Originally published by Springer-Verlag Tokyo Berlin Heidelberg New York in 2002
Softcover reprint of the hardcover 1st edition 2002

Typesetting: Camera-ready by the editors and authors

SPIN: 10854736

Preface

Throughout society the explosion of information technologies is changing how we work and live. This volume focuses on emerging technologies and their impact on people and organizations in the early years of the new century.

This book contains a collection of 36 papers selected from more than 110 high-quality presentations at the 2000 International Conference on the Information Society in the 21st Century (IS2000). The conference was held November 5–8, 2000, in Aizu-Wakamatsu, Japan. IS2000 featured lively exchanges of ideas and opinions on the impact of emerging technologies on our society among international participants from academic and industrial organizations.

The chapters in this book are grouped under the following six headings: Information and Knowledge Management Towards an Intelligent Society; Collaborative Internet, Multimedia, and Electronic Commerce; Intelligent Robots and Auditory Interfaces; New Models and Approaches for a Knowledge Economic Society; IT-Based Innovative Education Systems and Strategies; and Emerging Technologies for the Information Society in the New Century. The papers offer excellent perspectives on advances in the various fields and provide a framework for the development of improvements in technologies that hold promise for enhancing our lives in the new century.

Special thanks are due to the University of Aizu and the Telecommunications Advancement Foundation for providing grants to support IS2000 and the publication of this volume. We also would like to thank all the authors for their excellent work in assuring the high quality of the contents.

The Editors

August 2001

Contents

Part III Intelligent Robots and Auditory Interfaces

Part IV New Models and Approaches for a Knowledge Economic Society

Part V IT-Based Innovative Education Systems and Strategies

Part VI Emerging Technologies for the Information Society in the New Century

Part I

Information and Knowledge Management

Towards an Intelligent Society

Information and Knowledge Management: Dilemmas and Directions

Albert Bokma

Centre for Electronic Commerce, University of Sunderland
St. Peter's Campus, SCET - Room 306, Sunderland, SR6 0DD, United Kingdom
E-mail: albert.bokma@sunderland.ac.uk

Abstract. As the amount of information that individuals and organisations have to deal with on a day-by-day basis increases dramatically, new ways of information management are needed. This need manifests itself both in the need of the individual to effectively manage large collections of information and associated knowledge that builds up around these collections as well as the need to effectively share these collections of information and the knowledge with others in a collaborative environment. Current information management strategies in our view tend to be search-based and are inadequate for more intuitive browsing of information and knowledge. The paper introduces the dilemmas and presents an innovative approach to the management of documents and associated knowledge. The paper will present the use case and sketches a solution that will provide an intuitive, user-oriented solution and the benefits resulting.

1 Introduction

Rapid information growth and changes in organisational patterns: An almost exponential proliferation of information, evident in recent times, is starting to cause considerable problems both for individuals and organisations. As a consequence there is both a need to effectively manage existing collections of information and access and import new information relevant to a particular task. While document management solutions and information retrieval techniques and systems do exist to alleviate some of the problems associated with collections of documents, they provide little assistance for the individual user to create their own maps and pathways through this information and that allows them to manage collections of documents and the knowledge they incrementally build up around these documents. In addition, in collaborative situations there is also a need to effectively share this with others in the organisation.

Emerging changes in organisational practice including the increased use of flexible, project-based modes of working, as well as teleworking and virtual enterprises are rapidly eroding a common culture and common understanding that traditionally significantly helped the effective collaboration between individuals. Thus there is a need for effective communication and sharing approaches to manage shared collections of information and key knowledge to support increased productivity.

The need for integrated information and knowledge management: In the process of working with these documents and information sources, knowledge about these and their relations is being created and which is essential for engaging with these collections and in the process of generating new documents and other records. Detailed knowledge is often quickly forgotten when the user does not continuously engage with the documents in question and if recorded this will both help the individual user to speed up their tasks and if shared will help to increase the productivity of their collaborators. There is a lack of solutions that do allow the user to intuitively navigate such collections of information and understand the relationships between individual documents/records as well as effectively communicating associated knowledge in a context-sensitive fashion. We therefore argue that effective solutions that are more user-centered and user-friendly in the future remains a challenge to the IT community.

2   An Information and Knowledge Management Use Case

The case for associative approaches: As argued by Tan [1], amongst philosophers and psychologists it has long been recognised that human memory is associative. It has been concluded by [2] that human beings tend to understand and manage domains by devising abstract models and classifications and which are used to interpret their observations and categorise them. Accordingly, information and associated knowledge should be categorised in a conceptual fashion and where relations amongst items of information (documents and their components in this case) and any knowledge associated with them can be recorded.

It is therefore vital to maintain the context in which these documents fit in order to ensure their correct interpretation by the owner and/or those these documents are shared with. The issue of context is particularly significant for items of knowledge that typically build on information and cannot easily be taken out of its context and disassociated from its author. Therefore the connections and the interpretations that can be put on them need to be recorded. This lesson is increasingly becoming evident in the field of knowledge management as can be seen from Sellens et al. [3].

The shortcomings of search based approaches: When trying to locate documents in a shared environment (be it web-based or otherwise), the user either has to already know likely locations where to find document. This requires to understand how the collection of documents are organised and may involve looking in several candidate locations. Alternatively, the user may have to take recourse to searching tools and in some cases search-based access is the only available strategy where no filing structures are available. Though search-based retrieval techniques have their uses, it often depends on the skill of the user to correctly locate and retrieve documents. One cannot help but feeling that this is analogous to geologists drilling for oil, who, while being able to rely on some scanning techniques, in the end also need a bit of luck to hit on a productive site. Website searching facilities are a typical example of this problem and who frequently provide bad and patchy results leaving the more ingenious user to navigate the site manually in order to get to the documents he knows to be there. Though this is not to denigrate the sound basis of the search techniques themselves, their competent application is often less than satisfactory. What seems to be missing in this respect (in addition to the use of searching techniques) are ways to make collections of information more intuitively navigable.

Inadequacy of filing hierarchies: Filing hierarchies as an information organising principle are usually a combination of thematic and organisational categories, but few users are able to devise failsafe hierarchies that allow them subsequently to effortless locate documents. The filing hierarchy also suffers from the fact that it invariably allows the user to create only a single categorisation of the entire set of files. What is frequently needed is a set of alternative strategies, where a particular document is classified by subject (what it is about), organisational context (i.e. the project it originated in) and by author, to name but a few. In this way the user could find their document thematically by browsing the subject hierarchy, or find it by looking in the organisational hierarchy and the project it is associated with, or just look at only their documents by following the "people" viewpoint. Another advantage of such a strategy is that it potentially allows the user also to see other documents that fall under the same category and thus to find related documents.

While a multiple filing hierarchies can also be achieved with conventional tools involving the use of links to make the same document available in different categorisations, this requires strict discipline by the users to ensure that each document is correctly classified in all available dimensions and therefore needs to be enforceable. As there is a need to go a step further and explicitly allow connections to be made between documents to express their relationships and to associate records containing knowledge about these documents a filing hierarchy alone will not suffice. Also, in order to manage documents in a more intuitive fashion, there is a need to go beyond considering documents in isolation and to represent the context in which these documents fit. This would allow both direct access to any associated materials as well as making explicit any relations between them. The resulting framework is therefore able also to convey the context in which documents and records of knowledge fit and which is vital for their correct interpretation in a shared environment.

Multi-viewpoint modelling: Consequently, it is proposed that the information and knowledge management strategies of the future should follow conceptual principles and allow the user to catalogue and access in a conceptual and graphical way. This requires a model of the organisation and of the respective domain and to associate documents with elements in this model. In this way the context in which the documents fit and how they relate to other documents can be expressed.

A conceptual framework solution: Work is currently under way for an experimental platform that supports integrated information and knowledge management [4]. The following diagram shows a taxonomy at the top, which the user uses to categorise new items of information (documents, designs, diagrams, records, etc.) by linking them to one or more of the concepts provided. For the purposes of simplicity only the subject taxonomy is used but there could be multiple taxonomies such as for organisational divisions to associate the document with originating departments or specific project for instance. The core ontology can then be used as a cataloguing system for information contained in documents stored elsewhere. The user can also add reference links to other items in the system and to which the new item is related, such as to indicate another document containing background information or the design that relates to the specification and so on. Alternatively, the user can record annotations containing knowledge about any item and which can represent a critical appraisal, rationale for the item in question or any additional knowledge about the item and its use for a particular purpose. The authorship will be made browseable by linking the document to the user. When looking for a specific document the user will progress through the taxonomy using those keywords that match the content of the document or through the projects they are associated with to locate and retrieve relevant documents.

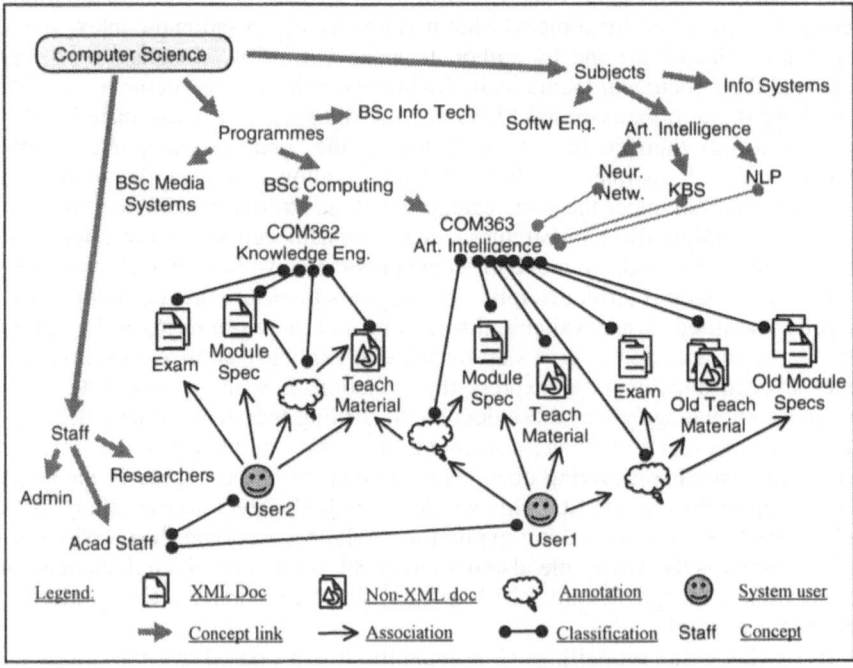

Fig 1: A Sample Knowledge Management

The need for graphical browsing: In this context, the user will be able to browse and explore this conceptual structure via a graphical browser, by progressing through nodes and arcs. When looking for a specific document the user can go through the subject hierarchy using those concepts that match the content of the document or alternatively through the organisational hierarchy to access the projects they are associated with. In figure 1, User1 is associated with a number of documents indicated by arrows relating to COM362 and it's associated module specification, exam papers and teaching materials. The lines with bullet ends indicate the semantic association with concepts in the core ontology. User1's reflections about previous module specifications and teaching materials is indicated by a thought-bubble. In addition, the module specification is in part based on a critique of the Teaching Materials for the related COM362 by User2. User2 is associated with a set of documents and an annotation containing the retionale for the Module Spec and Course content for COM362. The documents themselves are stored in separate files and a reference being stored in the conceptual framework top be able to locate them. The knowledge management system will record additional information about items in this structure that can be inspected. There are three major categorisations shown in this example, namely users, programmes and a subject hierarchy to allow access to items via different routes. Icons are used to graphically indicate the nature of the item and different types of connecting lines to denote different types of links. The user will be able to navigate through a point-and-click interface and inspect the properties of items.

3   The Use of Ontology Based Solutions

Current research in related fields: In recent years there has been a growing community working in the field of ontology and conceptual graph research and there have been some interesting developments which, in our view, can usefully contribute to a solution to the type of problem outlined. Ontologies, as used in AI circles, are conceptualisations of a domain, which allow the user to build a model and reason about it [5]. Formal models of a domain can be derived in this way and can be shared amongst users. A number of ontology-based approaches have been developed (see amongst others [6], [7], [8]) where the main motivation has been to support the sharing and reuse of bodies of knowledge in a computational form [9].

  Suitability of ontologies for the proposed domain: Ontologies tend to be used to develop a detailed model of a chosen domain (fine grained), whereas we would like to use them in a more schematic fashion (coarse grained) and which should result in a much smaller overall size of the ontology and the resulting conceptual structure whose complexity could otherwise get out of hand. We also propose to develop sets of smaller ontologies to represent viewpoints such as the subject hierarchy, and the organisational hierarchy and which will offer alternative access paths to documents and items of knowledge. The resulting ontology will serve as a document organisation principle and as a model to represent the world of the organisation. Some work in this direction is already under way in the KA2 Initiative that likewise develops a number of ontologies used for annotation of documents amongst a research community [10]. While that approach will offer an ontology-based information and knowledge management functionality the connection between ontologies and related documents and knowledge is not available in a persistent graphical browseable form, but where connections need to be made by an intelligent web-crawler following a user query. Again this is query-based whereas we propose to allow users to create maps/webs of information and associated knowledge and make this available in this form to other users in a shared environment. At the same time, ontology-based approaches are in principle appropriate for the purposes of developing organisational specific or domain specific classifications and could be used to categorise and associate items of information and knowledge. For our purposes it is important to be able to create arbitrary connections between items to represent relations between these, which can be annotated by the user. This should be supported by a graphical navigation capability where the user can browse the information and knowledge space so the user can browse the information and knowledge space so created by navigating a graph-like structure rather than by conventional searching techniques and presentation of results in tabular form.

The role of ontologies in the conceptual framework: The general problem for the average user is that the formalisms are rather technical assuming familiarity with frame-based approaches. Using ontologies to devise detailed models of in a fine-grained form will require specific training and a logic/formal mindset to develop and will be impracticable for the average use case. They are intended for a level of detail that goes beyond what we believe is strictly required for the task at hand, and which will be too laborious to build up and maintain. We therefore suggest a solution that operates at a higher level, operating at document level rather than individual propositions. We propose to use a pre-specified custom ontology, developed for a domain or enterprise, and which provides a suitable core taxonomy to which the user can attach items of information and annotations containing knowledge (knowledge objects), linked to the documents they relate to and likewise attached to the core taxonomy.

The use of ontologies has originally been driven by the motivation to jointly develop definitive global and detailed conceptualisation of a common problem space. The achievability of this is being questioned by some such as [11] and who propose to allow the development of personal, evolving ontologies and that allows the user to not only make changes but annotate these with the rationale behind the changes. APECKS [11] provides the user with tools for the incremental building of this type of ontology. We agree with that philosophy and suggest the use of extendable taxonomies as a basis for categorisation of items and which allows the user to correctly classify any new items of information and to annotate them with any reflections, criticisms or knowledge gained. The taxonomies should include a standard repertoire of cross-referenced organisational and subject based categorisations. This common taxonomy should be capable of being browsed graphically by the users to allow exploration and interaction. The common taxonomy will also provide for a sharing strategy between users, who are familiar with the taxonomy and thus able to easily explore the taxonomy and associated information and knowledge of their colleagues. Knowledge from colleagues can then be browsed on a subject-basis or by association with specific projects/organisational units.

Using ontologies as an information and knowledge organising principle: We favour the use of a core enterprise taxonomy as opposed to a fully fledged ontology based system. This is not to say that a full-scale ontology-based system would be wholly inappropriate at some point. A distinction needs to be made between using a core ontology or taxonomy (coarse-grained) for the purpose of cataloguing from the use of ontologies of a detailed conceptualisation of a large domain (fine-grained) and which would be unworkable for the majority of users in an average organisation as envisaged here. For information management purposes it is also important that the conceptualisation is not isolated from the domain it is modelling, to allow the user to manage a set of information sources. Though it could be argued that the resulting framework is in its totality an ontology we prefer to make a distinction between those parts of the conceptual framework that are used by the user for the classification of items from the items, their interrelations and associated knowledge objects. While the former fulfil the role of an abstract model in which to order items in the universe of discourse the latter are not abstract and normative but real and descriptive and are arbitrarily connected by the user and thus of a different type and would appear to be reasonable to keep that distinction.

4   Conclusion

Departure from current paradigms: Managing information is not just a question of searching for it. In the case of information contained in documents it requires the user to be able to put order into the collection from a number of different viewpoints and which serve to correctly categorise and "shelve" the information for future reference. As users start to actively engage with such a collection of documents and create new documents in their activities, the results of investigations from existing documents filter through to these new documents. As a consequence, the user starts to build a understanding of these documents, how they relate and where there are connections and where parts of documents are used as a source for other documents. This knowledge about these documents and their interrelation usually resides solely in the brain of the user and frequently gets lost as time progresses. The proposed solution aims at allowing the user to externalise this understanding both for personal use, to be able to retrace their thoughts and share them selectively with other users in the organisation so that colleagues can browse through this cognitive network. This will ultimately allow everyone to benefit from the collective understanding and shared documents and speed up work. Knowledge management implementations frequently rely on incentives to encourage users to use the system, and usually requires (what is perceived to be) additional effort. Our philosophy is instead to find a solution that is so useful to the individual user in their tasks that they will want to use it anyway because it makes their job easier. The envisaged architecture will provide the user with human-centred intuitive information access strategies that pays attention to the need for understanding the context of the information retrieved and is essential for its correct interpretation.

The **proposed benefits:** The information and knowledge management needs of the future will require solutions that are predicated on the needs of the user rather the convenience of easy computation. While other approaches and techniques have their benefits we believe that the proposed solution is superior in many respects and will users to:
- Categorise documents and knowledge in different viewpoints (multi-dimensional)
- Usefully externalise their understanding of documents for future reference
- Easily record associated knowledge
- Preserve the context required for correct interpretation
- Make explicit the inter-relation of documents
- Allow to easily find related information and knowledge whilst browsing
- Share information and knowledge with colleagues in an intuitive fashion

We think that this is a convincing list of benefits that speak for themselves. It is in our view vital to look for new avenues for information and knowledge management in the future and the proposed approach we believe provides a positive step in this direction. Undoubtedly, there are other aspects of information and knowledge management not covered by this approach and which will require their own solution but the present problem domain is nevertheless significant and a problem that is faced by a considerable number of users.

Work in progress: Work is currently under way to develop such a platform as part of a collaborative research project called Burma-X and which is funded by the European Commission. The project is concerned with supporting business relations in the extended enterprise and where the approach presented in this paper will be applied to support the knowledge management functionality of a business relationship management portal.

The use case outlined in section 2 requires in essence a meta-level that needs to be built on top of, and related to the collection of information. As with most applications of this type the project will develop a web-based implementation and which leaves a number of implementation issues to be resolved. As already mentioned there are a number of ontology building environments that can be used for the generation of the ontology and which are capable of producing output in RDF that is currently emerging as a standard for meta-level modelling associated with the web. An example of the use case described in section 2 in this format can be found at (http://vega.sunderland.ac.uk/CogNet/CogNetTest.rdf   and http://vega.sunderland.ac.uk/CogNet/CogNetTest.rdfs). Although this uses a web-oriented representation it still leaves a number of issues unresolved. Thus, most web applications of any significant size – as in this case – use databases at the back end to hold the data of which there is in this case two different types, namely the ontology itself that is used for the classification of items and the items themselves. While the latter can be managed in terms of a basic document management system or standard database entries, the representation is more difficult. Given that instances of an ontology are stored in a database the ontology would essentially determine the set up of tables and fields corresponding to classes and slots (properties of classes). This correspondence between the ontology and the underlying database structure is significant as it is needed to support the subsequent retrieval of information. The problem starts when the ontology is not static over the life of the system. As organisations change it is likely that the ontology needed to support this type of information and knowledge management. will need to change and which consequently will require the database structure to change and the existing content to be mapped into the new structure. This is particularly difficult if ontology editing functionality is to be supported on-line. While it is easy to add or delete items such as documents and annotations as it amounts only to adding or deleting entries in a database changing the database structure is more complicated. On the other hand the ontology itself also needs to be stored and which can be done in terms of a separate database. The otology specifies a set of classes and subclasses together with their relations and properties, where the possible instances of the ontology and their properties determine the structure of the database needed to support their storage. Work is currently under way to build an ASP based implementation supported by a database to store and manipulate the ontology and where the instances (documents and annotations in this case) are stored in a dynamic database. The user will access the resources through the ontology, which will make the available resources available to the user eventually with the help of graphical navigation techniques. The users should also be able to edit the ontology dynamically although this functionality may be supported at a later stage. As users will need to use the functionality for their personal information and knowledge management needs as well as sharing in a collaborative environment there is a need for a distributed architecture where a central server will hold the shared components.

The outlined solution currently does not provide for a sophisticated graphical navigation capability that could take the form of 3D or virtual reality approaches. Ongoing work in particular in visualising complex interacting systems by [12] may provide the answer to this current limitation and relevant results in this area will be included in subsequent versions.

References

1. Tan TC, "The Development of an Intelligent Conceptual Storage and Retrieval System", PhD Thesis, University of Sunderland, UK, 1993
2. Bokma A., "A Source Modelling System and its Use for Uncertainty Management", PhD Thesis, University of Durham, UK, March 1993
3. Sellens C. & Wilson O., "The CMG Knowledge Intranet", Proc of the 2nd Int. Conf. On Practical Aspects of Knowledge Management (PAKM98), Basel Switzerland, 29-30 Oct 1998
4. Bokma A, "Ontologies and Conceptual Graphs for Individual and Corporate Knowledge Management", Occasional Paper Series, Report SCET-01-2000, University of Sunderland Library, Sunderland, UK, March 2000
5. Guarino N, "Understanding, Building and Using Ontologies – a Commentary to 'Using Explicit Ontologies in KBS Development' by van Heijst, Wielinga and Schreiber" Int. Journal of Human and Computer Studies 46(3/4), pp 293-310, 1997
6. Farquhar A, Fikes R, Pratt W & Rice J, "Collaborative Ontology Construction for Information Integration", Res. Report No. 63, Knowledge System Laboratory, Stanford University, USA, (ftp://kls.stanford.edu/pub/KSL-95-63.ps)
7. Dominique J, "Tadzebao and WebOnto: Discussing, Browsing and Editing Ontologies on the Web", Proc. of the 11th Knowledge Acquisition Workshop KAW'98, Banff, Alberta Canada, April 1998
8. Erikson H, Ferguson R, Shahar Y & Musen M, "Automatic Generation of Ontology Editors", Proc. of the Knowledge Acquisition Workshop KAW'99, Banff, Alberta, Canada http://ksi.cpsc.ucalgary.ca/KAW/KAW99/
9. Duineveld A, Stoter R, Weiden M, Kenepa B & Benjamins V, "Wondertools? A Comparative Study of Ontological Engineering Tools", Proc. of the 12th Knowledge Acquisition Workshop (KAW'99), Banff, Alberta, Canada, 16-22 October 1999
10. Benjamins VR, Fensel D & Gomez-Perez A, "Knowledge Management Through Ontologies", In Proc. of the 2nd Int. Conf. on Practical Aspects of Knowledge Management (PAKM'98), Basel, Switzerland, October 1998.
11. Tennison J and Shadbolt N, "APECKS: A Tool to Support Living Ontologies, Proc. of the 11th Knowledge Acquisition Workshop KAW'98, Banff, Alberta Canada, April 1998

12   Albert Bokma

12. Drew N & Hendley B, "Visualising Complex Interacting Systems", Proc. of CHI'95, ACM Press, 1995, http://www.acm.org/sigchi/chi95/

Similarity-Based Queries for Time Series Databases

Fei Wu, Véronique Plihon and Georges Gardarin

PRiSM Laboratory, University of Versailles, 45 Avenue des Etats-Unis
78035 Versailles Cedex, France
E-mail: fei.wu@prism.uvsq.fr

Abstract. We consider the similarity problem in time series databases. Given a set of sequences, we are interested in finding those sequences whose behaviors are similar. Several methods have been proposed so far to solve this problem. Among them, [AFS93] mapped a time sequence to the frequency domain using the Discrete Fourier Transformation (DFT), and kept only first few coefficients. The similarity of two sequences is determined by the Euclidean distance between their coefficients. [ALS+95] (hereafter referred to as ALS approach) introduced a new model. Two time-series are said to be similar if they have enough non-overlapping time-ordered pairs of subsequences that are similar. Different from the ALS approach, [DGM97] used another method to find the longest common subsequence. The idea is, given a set of transformation functions, to try to find a linear function $y=ax+b$ such that two subsequences X, Y are ε-similar. However no paper up to now, as to our knowledge, had compared these algorithms on the same benchmark. This paper discusses and compares these three popular methods. By overcoming the drawbacks of these algorithms, a new algorithm is proposed. Experiments are conducted on the Nasdaq-100 market.

1 Introduction

Time-series data are of importance in many database applications, such as data mining [DLM+98], [HDY99], [KJF97], [Man97] or data warehousing. A time-series is a sequence of numbers, where each number is associated with a timestamp. The sequence could represent stock values, exchange rates, weather data, sales and etc. Similarity queries in time-series database are the most frequent.

To measure the similarity between two time-series, many approaches have been proposed in the literature. As time sequences are sometimes very long, computing the Euclidean distance of two sequences is time consuming. To solve this problem, [AFS93] and [FRM94] mapped a time sequence to the frequency domain using the Discrete Fourier Transformation (**DFT**) and kept only first few coefficients. These coefficients are stocked in an R^+-tree. The Euclidean distance between the coefficients is calculated to measure the similarity of two sequences. Some approaches worked on the longest similar subsequences. [ALS+95] considered two sequences to be similar if they have enough non-overlapping time-ordered pairs of subsequences that are similar. [DGM97] tried to find the longest common subsequence by finding a linear transformation. We refer to this algorithm as **LCSS** approach.

We evaluated and compared the algorithms **DFT**, **ALS** and **LCSS** on the Nasdaq data. To the best of our knowledge, this is the first work that compares these different methods on the same data set.

The notations used in this paper are summarized in Table 1. S and T are two sequences.

Table 1. Notations

Notations	Meaning
$Len(S)$	the length of S
s_i	the ith entry of S
$\bar{S}$	the mean of S
$D(s_i, t_i)$	the distance between the ith entry of S and the ith entry of T
$first(S)$	the first element in S
$last(S)$	the last element in S
$s_i < s_j (i < j)$	s_j occurs after s_i
$S < T$	$first(S) < first(T)$
$N(s_i)$	Neighbor points of an entry s_i. They are points s_{i-1} and s_{i+1}

The rest of this paper is organized as follows. Section 2 reviews the **DFT**, **ALS** and **LCSS** algorithms. Section 3 compares these three methods, and reports experimental results. A new algorithm is introduced in Section 4. Finally section 5 concludes the paper.

2   Related Work

This section reviews the three algorithms compared in this paper: **DFT**, **ALS** and **LCSS** approaches. The DFT family is based on the Discrete Fourier Transform (**DFT**). **ALS** and **LCSS** are focused on finding the longest common subsequences.

2.1   Discrete Fourier Transform

In [AFS93], the authors used the Discrete Fourier Transform (**DFT**) to map a time sequence to the frequency domain, and the first n frequencies of this sequence are kept. Each sequence is then regarded as an n-dimension point and is inserted into either an R^+-tree [SRF87] or an R*-tree [BKS+90]. The similarity of two sequence is determined by the Euclidean distance of their coefficients. Finding all simila sequences to a given sequence becomes a range query problem. [FRM94] extende this idea to support subsequence matching.

A great problem of this kind of approach is that the user has no control ove the meaning of similarity other than providing a threshold. The results ar sometimes inexplicable.

2.2   Longest Common Subsequence

This kind of methods focuses on finding the longest similar subsequences. We introduce two approaches here. The first one is **ALS** approach proposed by [ALS+95]. The other one is **LCSS** approach presented in [DGM97].

2.2.1   ALS Approach

Since the **DFT** family uses the Euclidean distance to calculate the similarity of two sequences, the measurement can be quite sensitive to a few outliers. [ALS+95] introduced a new model of similarity of time sequences. Two sequences are said to be similar if they have enough non-overlapping time-ordered pairs of subsequences that are similar. The model is illustrated as follows. Suppose two sequences S and T. Let $S_1, \ldots, S_m$ and $T_1, \ldots, T_m$ be their non-overlapping similar subsequences such that $S_i < S_j$ and $T_i < T_j$ for $1 \le i < j \le m$. S and T are said to be ξ-similar if

$$\frac{\sum_{i=1}^{m} Len(S_i) + \sum_{i=1}^{m} Len(T_i)}{Len(S) + Len(T)} \ge \xi .$$ That means they are similar if the fraction of

the subsequences match length to the total length is above a given threshold ξ.

Their search algorithm for discovering all similar sequences in a set of sequences is composed of three steps:
- Find all pairs of similar "atomic" subsequences (*windows*) of length w.
- Stitch these similar windows to form pairs of long similar subsequences.
- Find the longest similar sequences.

For supporting amplitude scaling and offset translation, they normalized the sequence values within each window to a range $(-1, 1)$ using the formula

$$\widetilde{W}_i = \frac{W_i - \frac{W_{min} + W_{max}}{2}}{\frac{W_{max} - W_{min}}{2}} ,$$ where W_{min} and W_{max} are the minimum and maximum

values in the window W. The similarity is defined with respect to a user-defined ε distance in $L\infty$ norm. Two normalized windows W_1 and W_2 are ε-similar if $\forall i$, $| \widetilde{W}_{1[i]} - \widetilde{W}_{2[i]} | \le \varepsilon$. They considered each normalized window of length w as a point in a w-dimension space and stored these windows in an R^+-tree. A self-join algorithm is applied to retrieve all pairs of matching windows.

This approach has some limitations. First, the similarity model does not allow outliers within windows, i.e., intra-gaps. The gaps they considered are gaps between two windows, i.e., inter-gaps.

Another problem is that the similarity of two windows varies in the length of window size. Let us give an example. Suppose $\varepsilon = 0.4$. We extracted 11 closing values of CSCO and MSFT stock data (see Table 2). When the window size ω is set to 10, the corresponding normalized values of CSCO and MSFT and the $L\infty$ distances of their elements are calculated in Table 3. Table 4 gives the results when the window size is set to 11. The unqualified points are presented in bold. When the window size ω is equal to 10, the distances between the first 10 elements of CSCO and MSFT are all less than ε. These two windows are similar. By adding the 11th element, i.e., ω is turned to 11, four elements (the 1st 6th, 7th and 9th) are found not similar. Thus these two windows are not similar. Notice that the distance between the 7th element of CSCO and MSFT increases even from 0.0362 to 0.4332! This is because of the fact that W_{max} in the new MSFT 11-window is changed from the 7th element (80.906) to the 11[h] element (82.938), while the new CSCO 11-window keeps unchanged. That is why the first similar 10 elements are no more regarded as similar. That means the similarity of two points depends on which window contains them, not on their own behaviors.

Table 2. Part of CSCO MSFT data

	CSCO	MSFT
	49.719	75.875
2	47.844	74.281
3	47.563	74.813
4	49.125	76.125
5	50.406	77.469
6	52.281	79.5
	52.656	80.906
8	52.188	80.688
9	52.75	80.719
10	51.625	80.094
11	52.5	82.938

Table 3. Normalization of CSCO and MSFT ($\omega = 10$)

	CSCO Norm.	MSFT Norm.	Distance
1	-0.1687	-0.5188	0.3501
2	-0.8917	-1	0.1083
3	-1	-0.8394	0.1606
4	-0.3977	-0.4433	0.0456
5	0.0962	-0.0376	0.1338
6	0.8192	0.5755	0.2436
7	0.9638	1	0.0362
8	0.7833	0.9342	0.1509
9	1	0.9435	0.0565
10	0.5662	0.7549	0.1886

Table 4. Normalization of CSCO and MSFT ($\omega = 11$)

	CSCO Norm.	MSFT Norm.	Distance
1	**-0.1687**	**-0.6317**	**0.4631**
2	-0.8917	-1	0.1083
3	-1	-0.8771	0.1229
4	-0.3977	-0.5740	0.1763
5	0.0962	-0.2635	0.3597
6	**0.8192**	**0.2057**	**0.6134**
7	**0.9638**	**0.5306**	**0.4332**
8	0.7833	0.4802	0.3031
9	**1**	**0.4874**	**0.5126**
10	0.5662	0.3430	0.2233
11	0.9036	1	0.0964

2.2.2 LCSS Approach

To determine the similarity of two sequences, [DGM97] tried to find the longest common subsequence, instead of a set of the longest similar subsequences. The idea is, given a set F of transformation functions, to try to find a linear function $f \in F$ such that two subsequences X, Y of length δ are ε-similar, i.e.,

$$\forall k, \ 1 \leq i \leq k < i + \delta \leq n, \ y_i/(1+\varepsilon) \leq ax_k + b \leq y_{k_i} 1 + \varepsilon).$$

where n is the total length of a sequence. To find the candidate pairs of (a, b), the authors used some statistical arguments to compute the bounds for possible values of a and b. They also used a grid to sample the area defined by the bounds.

The similarity Sim(X,Y) defined in [BDG+97] is *lcss/n*, where *lcss* represents the length of the longest common subsequence satisfying the above inequality, and n is the total length of the sequence.

One of the main drawbacks of this approach is that the distance measurement is not symmetric. The similarity *Sim(X, Y)* can be different from the similarity *Sim(Y, X)*. [BDG+97] suggested to take the maximum similarity: {*Max(Sim(Y,X), Sim(X,Y))*}.

3   Comparison of the Similarity Approaches and A New Algorithm

To the best of the authors' knowledge, no work had been done on comparing these different approaches on the same benchmark. We implemented these three methods in JAVA 1.2, and applied them to the Nasdaq-100[1]. The data set consists of 100 stocks for 5 years. Each stock contains 1200 values. All experiments are done on a PC running Windows NT workstation 4.0 with Pentium II 300M Hz, 64M memory. The experiment consisted of two parts. The first part studies the behavior of these three algorithms by tuning their parameters. The second part compares their execution cost.

3.1   Similarity Results

We extracted the closing prices from January to October 1999 for each stock. Each stock contains 200 values. Given the CSCO stock as a query sequence, we want to find similar sequences among 100 stocks.

3.1.1 DFT Results

DFT approach measures the similarity of two sequences by computing the Euclidean distance of their coefficients. Less is the distance, more similar are two sequences. The number of DFT coefficients to keep is the only parameter of this method. Changing this parameter *(coeff)* from 4 to 10, the 5 most similar sequences

---

1 The data can be downloaded from http://www.nasdaq.com

to CSCO are given in Figure 1. The column Sym. represents a stock symbol and the column Dist. is the Euclidean distance between two sequences.

	Sym.	Dist.
1	JDSU	1,1051
2	ADBE	1,5506
3	CNXT	1,6203
4	QCOM	1,6293
5	MCHP	1,9321

coeff = 4

	Sym.	Dist.
1	CNXT	2,3332
2	ALTR	2,3906
3	ERTS	2,4898
4	SUNW	2,6266
5	MXIM	2,7126

coeff = 6

	Sym.	Dist.
1	SUNW	2,6760
2	ERTS	2,7594
3	XLNX	2,7645
4	CNXT	2,8318
5	ADBE	2,8644

coeff = 8

	Sym.	Dist.
1	SUNW	2,7088
2	XLNX	2,7861
3	ERTS	2,8940
4	ADBE	2,9284
5	CNXT	2,9511

coeff = 10

Figure 1. Changing *coeff*

The distance between two sequences augments with *coeff*. This is because more frequencies per sequence are stored and are taken into account. JDSU appears only in the case where *coeff* is small (*coeff* = 3, 4). When the *coeff* is larger than 6, it is SUNW that takes the head. From *coeff* = 8, the results become stable. This is explained by the fact that the energy of a sequence is kept in the first few coefficients. As we mentioned before, the results of the DFT are sometimes difficult to explain. For example we do not know why SUNW is more similar to CSCO than XLNX to CSCO.

3.1.2 ALS Results

The **ALS** algorithm has three parameters: the window size (ω), distance threshold (ε) and gap size (γ). The behavior of this algorithm was studied by changing these three parameters. Fixing ε to 0.4, γ to 4 and changing ω from 8 to 15, the five best results found are shown in Figure 2. Figure 3 varies ε from 0.3 to 0.5 with $\omega = 10$, $\gamma = 4$. Setting $\varepsilon = 0.4$, Figure 4 and 5 study the influence of the gap size by setting ε to 0.4. The Figure 4 sets the window size to 10, while in the Figure 5 the window size is set to 5. The gap size γ in these two figures is changed from 1 to 6. The column % represents the fraction of the subsequence match length to the total

length, i.e., $\% = \dfrac{\sum_{i=1}^{m} Len(S_i) + \sum_{i=1}^{m} Len(T_i)}{Len(S) + Len(T)}$. Figure 6 visualizes two

similar subsequences found by **ALS** between CSCO and SUNW.

From the Figure 2, we observe that in most cases the similarity decreases in augmenting the window size. This is because similar subsequences are often short ones, not very long. We can see the similarity of SUNW to CSCO decrease from 43.2% to 21.36% when increasing the window size from 8 to 15. However not all sequences follow this rule. When the window size is changed from 10 to 12, the similarity of MSFT climbs from 18.93% to 20.87%. As mentioned in Section 2.2.1, when changing the window size, some windows considered similar before are not more similar and some not similar windows are turned to be similar. The similarity between two points varies in the window size.

The Figure 3 shows the impact of ε (error tolerance) on the **ALS** method. By increasing ε, more elements will be matched, so more windows will be said to be similar. This explains why the similarities of all sequences augment.

The Figure 4 and 5 show that when γ augments, so does the fraction. This is because big gaps are omitted and more subsequences are stitched together. When the window size is large (see Figure 4), the only difference of the fraction is MSFT. Its fraction is changed from 18.93% to 20.87% when γ augments from 4 to 5. More such phenomena appear in the Figure 5. When the window size is small, more small windows will be joined. The Figure 4 and 5 show that the gap size has little impact on the behavior of the **ALS** approach.

	Sym.	%
1	SUNW	43.2%
2	TLAB	36.41%
3	AMZN	22.82%
4	MXIM	20.87%
5	ORCL	18.93%

$\omega = 8$

	Sym.	%
1	SUNW	31.07%
2	TLAB	25.73%
3	MXIM	23.79%
4	MSFT	18.93%
5	DELL	16.99%

$\omega = 10$

	Sym.	%
1	SUNW	27.18%
2	MSFT	20.87%
3	JDSU	19.42%
4	MXIM	18.93%
5	LVLT	17.96%

$\omega = 12$

	Sym.	%
1	SUNW	21.36%
2	MSFT	16.5%
3	TLAB	16.5%
4	EFII	16.02%
5	JDSU	16.02%

$\omega = 15$

Figure 2. Changing ω ($\varepsilon = 0.4$, $\gamma = 4$)

	Sym.	%
1	DELL	11.65%
2	SUNW	11.17%
3	CMVT	10.68%
4	BBBY	5.83%
5	ORCL	5.83%

$\varepsilon = 0.3$

	Sym.	%
1	SUNW	31.07%
2	TLAB	25.73%
3	MXIM	23.79%
4	MSFT	18.93%
5	DELL	16.99%

$\varepsilon = 0.4$

	Sym.	%
1	SUNW	52.43%
2	TLAB	51.46%
3	MSFT	45.63%
4	DELL	41.75%
5	INTC	32.04%

$\varepsilon = 0.5$

Figure 3. Changing ε ($\omega = 10$, $\gamma = 4$)

	Sym.	%
1	SUNW	31.07%
2	TLAB	25.73%
3	MXIM	23.79%
4	MSFT	18.93%
5	DELL	16.99%

γ = 2

	Sym.	%
1	SUNW	31.07%
2	TLAB	25.73%
3	MXIM	23.79%
4	MSFT	18.93%
5	DELL	16.99%

γ = 4

	Sym.	%
1	SUNW	31.07%
2	TLAB	25.73%
3	MXIM	23.79%
4	MSFT	20.87%
5	DELL	16.99%

γ = 5

	Sym.	%
1	SUNW	31.07%
2	TLAB	25.73%
3	MXIM	23.79%
4	MSFT	20.87%
5	DELL	16.99%

γ = 6

Figure 4. Changing γ (ω = 10, ε = 0.4)

	Sym.	%
1	SUNW	51.94%
2	TLAB	38.83%
3	DELL	31.07%
4	MXIM	31.07%
5	ATML	30.58%

γ = 2

	Sym.	%
1	SUNW	53.88%
2	TLAB	41.26%
3	DELL	32.52%
4	ATML	32.04%
5	MXIM	31.07%

γ = 4

	Sym.	%
1	SUNW	53.88%
2	TLAB	41.26%
3	DELL	34.47%
4	ATML	33.98%
5	MSFT	32.52%

γ = 5

	Sym.	%
1	SUNW	56.31%
2	TLAB	43.69%
3	DELL	36.89%
4	ATML	36.41%
5	MSFT	32.52%

γ = 6

Figure 5. Changing γ (ω = 5, ε = 0.4)

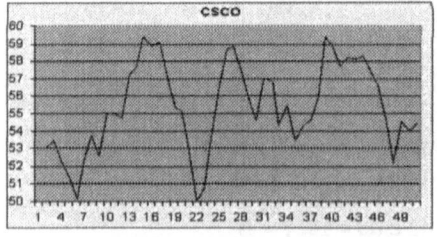 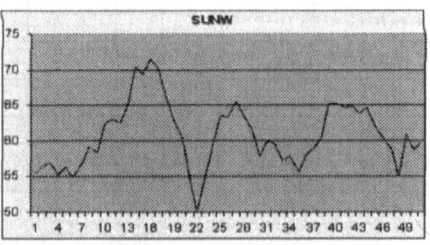

Figure 6. Similar subsequences of CSCO and SUNW found by ALS

3.1.3   LCSS Results

The **LCSS** approach has two parameters: error tolerance ε and the length of the subsequences to be compared (δ). Setting δ to 50, the five most similar sequences returned by changing ε are shown in Figure 7. We fixed ε to 0.08 and varied δ from 10 to 50 and 100, the results are shown in Figure 8. The column % indicates the fraction of the longest common subsequence to the total length (*lcss/n*)

The Figure 7 shows that increasing the error tolerance (ε) also increases the similarity between two sequences. When ε is small, sequences are not well distinguished from each other. BGEN and MSFT and ADBE and BMCS have the same fractions for ε = 0.05. By increasing the error tolerance, these sequences begin to present their difference. For ε = 0.12, the fraction of BGEN is 78.16%, and that of SEBL is 66.99%. When ε is large (ε = 0.15), we find the sequence SUNW is nearly 100% similar to CSCO.

The Figure 8 shows that the similarity degree is not related to δ. When δ augments from 10 to 30, the similarity of MSFT to CSCO decreases from 68.45% to 57.77%, while SUNW increases from 46.12% to 59.22%.

The Figure 9 and 10 compare the linear function $f(x) = ax + b$ and the real y for CSCO-SUNW and CSCO-MSFT. As mentioned in section 2.2.2, the **LCSS** method is not symmetric. The Figure 10 shows the linear transformation on CSCO, and the Figure 11 shows the linear transformation on MSFT. The form $f(x) = ax + b$ and y are not similar. Their values are only close to each other.

	Sym.	%		Sym.	%
1	SANM	26.70%	1	MSFT	65.53%
2	SEBL	26.0%	2	ADBE	65.05%
3	BGEN	25.24%	3	EFII	59.71%
4	MSFT	25.24%	4	SEBL	59.22%
5	ADBE	24.76%	5	LLTC	58.25%
5	BMCS	24.76%			

ε=0.05   ε=0.1

	Sym.	%		Sym.	%
1	SUNW	78.64%	1	MSFT	99.03%
2	BGEN	78.16%	2	CMVT	97.09%
3	EFII	74.27%	3	SUNW	87.86%
4	MSFT	67.48%	4	EFII	84.47%
5	SEBL	66.99%	5	BGEN	83.01%

ε=0.12   ε=0.15

Figure 7. Changing ε (δ=50)

	Sym.	%
1	MSFT	68.45%
2	LLTC	59.22%
3	USAI	58.74%
4	SUNW	46.12%
5	MXIM	44.17%

δ=10

	Sym.	%
1	SUNW	59.22%
2	MSFT	57.77%
3	ALTR	56.80%
4	MCHP	50.00%
5	CMVT	49.03%

δ=30

	Sym.	%
1	MSFT	65.53%
2	ADBE	65.05%
3	EFII	59.71%
4	SEBL	59.22%
5	LLTC	58.25%

δ =50

	Sym.	%
1	JDSU	80.10%
2	SUNW	77.67%
3	ADBE	64.56%
4	PHSY	56.31%
5	MXIM	54.85%

δ =100

Figure 8. Changing δ (ε=0.1)

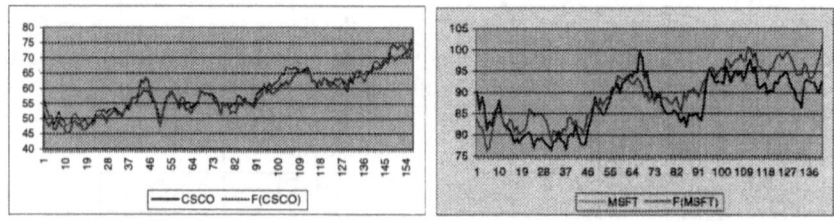

Figure 9. The longest common subsequence found of CSCO-SUNW (f(x)=0,548x+ 24,135).

Figure 10. The longest common subsequence found of CSCO-MSFT (f(x)=0,907x+32,013).

3.2   Execution Time Cost

This section compares the CPU costs of these approaches for sequence matching.

DFT approach needs to transform a sequence into the frequency domain using the DFT which costs $O(coeff * n)$ where *coeff* is the number of coefficients to keep. Inserting points into an R*-tree needs $O(nlogn)$. In total, the time for DFT to construct an index is $O(coeff * n + nlogn)$. To retrieve similar sequence is the problem of a range query which costs $O(nlogn)$.

ALS creates a set of windows then stores these windows as points into an R⁺-tree. Windows creation needs a sequential scanning of data. Time consuming for index constructing is $O(n + nlogn)$. Finding similar sequences needs first to retrieve pairs of matching windows $O(nlogn)$ and then to stitch these windows $O(m^2)$ where *m* is the number of pairs of matching windows found. In our cases *m* is much smaller than *n*.

LCSS does not use index. On the contrary, for each sequence they need to find the subsequences which minimize or maximize the deviation respectively in order to compute bounds for a and b. These operations take a sequential scanning on the data which costs $O(n\text{-}\delta\text{+}1)$ where δ is the length of subsequence to compare. To find the linear function, which maximizes the length of the longest common subsequence, LCSS used a grid to sample points in this bound. The running time for the LCSS is $O(M*n(n\text{-}\delta\text{+}1))$ where M is the number of sampling points. In our implementation, we used 400 points.

For comparing execution times of these algorithms, we must set their parameters first. The parameter *coeff* of the DFT is set to 7. For the ALS, the window size ω is set to 10, the distance threshold ε is set to 0.4 and the gap size γ is set to 4. For the LCSS algorithm, the error tolerance ε is 0.1 and the length of the subsequences to be compared δ is 50. We run these three algorithms on the data of one year, two years, three years, four years and five years data respectively. Each data contains 200, 460, 710, 960 and 1220 values respectively. The CPU costs of DFT, ALS and LCSS are compared in Table 5. Both index constructing cost and similarity query cost are taken into account. The DFT is the least CPU demanding among three algorithms. ALS is close to DFT. The LCSS needs much execution time, and its CPU cost augments almost exponentially.

Table 5. CPU Cost in milliseconds

	One Year	Two Years	Three Years	Four Years	Five Years
DFT	240	501	721	912	1111
ALS	281	521	821	1132	1332
LCSS	2904	6449	10265	12938	16253

From our experimental results, we conclude that the **ALS** approach is the best one among these three algorithms. Its results can be visualized so that user can easily understand why two sequences are considered similar. Furthermore, the execution time cost of **ALS** is not expensive. It is close to the **DFT**.

4   A New Algorithm

Although the **ALS** approach is the best method among the three algorithms compared, it has a main drawback as discussed in the Section 2.2.1. The similarity of two windows is very sensible to the window size. To tackle this problem, we modified the model of **ALS**, and a new corresponding algorithm is also proposed. In financial domain, we hear more often: stock X has climbed 2%; stock Y has drop down 1%, etc. Let us take an example of three stocks. Their normalized forms with the formula $\dfrac{s_i - \bar{s}}{\sqrt{\sum_i (s_i - \bar{s})^2}}$ are depicted in Figure 11. Evidently they are similar each other from the point of the view of the form. However, if we compare their raw values and percentage changes given in Figure 12, the percentage changes of stock3 are similar to stock1 while not that of stock2.

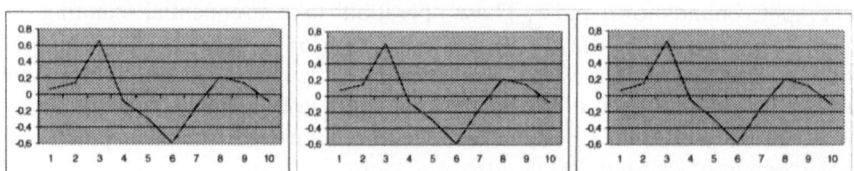

Figure 11. Visualization after normalization

Value	% Change
80	
81	1.25%
88	8.64%
78	-11.36%
75	-3.85%
71	-5.33%
77	8.45%
82	6.49%
81	-1.22%
78	-3.70%

Stock1

Value	% Change
10	
11	10.00%
18	63.64%
8	-55.56%
5	-37.50%
1	-80.00%
7	600.00%
12	71.43%
11	-8.33%
8	-27.27%

Stock2

Value	% Change
200	
203	1.50%
221	8.87%
196	-11.31%
188	-4.08%
178	-5.32%
193	8.43%
205	6.22%
202	-1.46%
194	-3.96%

Stock3

Figure 12. Values and percentage changes of stock1, stock2 and stock3

In most cases, percentage change has totally different signification compared to net change in financial domain for decision-making purpose. Let us take the previous example in the Figure 12. When stock1 increases from $71 to $77, it climbs 8.45%. When stock2 increases from $1 to $7, it grows up to 600%! In this sense, we do not think that stock1 and stock2 have similar behaviors. Certainly, the corresponding decision-making will be different too. Hence it is better to distinguish stock2 from stock1 and stock3. This is the main idea of our new similarity measurement. We say two sequences are similar if they have enough pairs of subsequences that have identical movements and the corresponding percentage changes are within a user defined ε distance in $L\infty$ norm, i.e. $|s_i - t_i| < \varepsilon$. Our similarity measurement is similar to that of the **ALS** except that we considered one point by one point, instead of constructing a set of windows. The similarity of two points is determined by their own percentage changes.

Our algorithm to find similar time series is composed of three steps:
1. Find all pairs of elements in a set of sequences whose trends are identical and their distances are less than ε, i.e. $D(s_i, t_i) < \varepsilon$.
2. Sort these similar points by the timestamp. All neighbor points $N(s_i)$ are joined together in order to construct consecutive similar subsequences.
3. If two subsequences S and T having $last(S) < first(T)$ and $| last(S) - first(T)| \leq \gamma$ (gap size), S and T are stitched into a new long similar subsequence.

Figure 13 shows two long similar subsequences with gaps found by our algorithm between CSCO and SUNW. The light lines indicate the similar subsequences found by the **ALS** method.

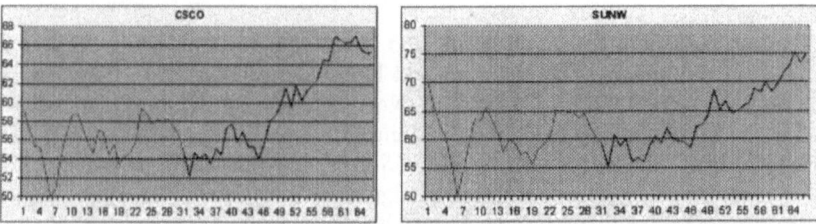

Figure 13. Similar subsequences found by new algorithm

5   Conclusion

This paper compares three similarity models and discusses their limitations for similarity query in time-series databases. According to our experimental results, the **ALS** approach is the best one. Its results are understandable by visualizations and its execution cost is not expensive. However this kind of algorithm is sensible to the window size. A new algorithm is proposed to solve this problem. This new algorithm works on the percentage changes, two sequences are similar if they have enough pairs of subsequences that have identical movements and the similar percentage changes. The result shows that our algorithm is similar to that of **ALS** method. However since we work on points themselves rather than construing a window, we do not suffer from the problem of **ALS**. All experiments are performed on the Nasdaq market.

Future work includes clustering stocks into groups. Most clustering algorithms are based on distance computation. Thus, our similarity measure can be used to cluster time series. The clusters could then be used to forecast the evolution of stocks according to similar events.

References

1.   Rakesh Agrawal, Christos Faloutsos and Arun N. Swami. *Efficient Similarity Search in Sequence Databases*. In Proceedings of 4th Foundations of Data Organization and Algorithms (FODO'93), Chicago, Illinois, USA, October 13-15, 1993, pp: 69-84.
2.   Rakesh Agrawal, King-Ip Lin, Harpreet S. Sawhney and Kyuseok Shim. *Fast Similarity Search in the Presence of Noise, Scaling, and Translation in Time-Series Databases*. In Proceedings of 21th International Conference on Very Large Data Bases, September 11-15, 1995, Zurich, Switzerland, pp 490-501.
3.   Béla Bollobás, Gautam Das, Dimitrios Gunopulos and Heikki Mannila. *Time-Series Similarity Problems and Well Separated Geometric Sets*. Proceedings of the Thirteenth Annual Symposium on Computational Geometry, June 4-6, 1997, Nice, France, pp 454 –456.

4. Norbert Beckmann, Hans-Peter Kriegel, Ralf Schneider and Bernhard Seeger. *The R*-tree: An Efficient and Robust Access Method for Points and Rectangles*. In Proceedings of the 1990 ACM SIGMOD International Conference on Management of Data, Atlantic City, NJ, May 23-25, 1990, pp: 322-331.

5. Gautam Das, Dimitrios Gunopulos and Heikki Mannila. *Finding Similar Time Series*. Principles of Data Mining and Knowledge Discovery, First European Symposium, PKDD '97, Trondheim, Norway, June 24-27, 1997, pp: 88-100.

6. Gautam Das, King-Ip Lin, Heikki Mannila, Gopal Renganathan and Padhraic Smyth. *Rule Discovery from Time Series*. In Proceedings of the Fourth International Conference on Knowledge Discovery and Data Mining (KDD-98), August 27-31, 1998, New York City, New York, USA, pp: 16-22.

7. R. D. Edwards and J. Magee. *Technical Analysis of Stock Trends*. John Magee, Springfield, Massachsetts, 1969.

8. Christos Faloutsos, H. V. Jagadish, Alberto O. Mendelzon and Tova Milo. *A Signature Technique for Similarity-Based Queries*. SEQUENCES 97, Positano-Salerno, Italy June 11-13 1997.

9. Christos Faloutsos, M. Ranganathan and Yannis Manolopoulos. *Fast Subsequence Matching in Time-Series Databases*. In Proceedings of the 1994 ACM SIGMOD International Conference on Management of Data, Minneapolis, Minnesota, May 24-27, 1994, pp: 419-429.

10. Dina Q. Goldin and Paris C. Kanellakis. *On Similarity Queries for Time-Series Data: Constraint Specification and Implementation*. International Conference, CP'95, Cassis, France, September 19-22, 1995, pp 137-153.

11. Jiawei Han, Guozhou Dong and Yiwen Yin. *Efficient Mining of Partial Periodic Patterns in Time Series Database*. In Proceedings of the 15th International Conference on Data Engineering, 23-26 March 1999, Sydney, Australia, pp: 106-115.

12. Flip Korn, H. V. Jagadish and Christos Faloutsos. *Efficient Supporting Ad Hoc Queries in Large Datasets of Time Sequences*. In Proceedings ACM SIGMOD International Conference on Management of Data, May 13-15, 1997, Tucson, Arizona, USA, pp: 289-300.

13. Heikki Mannila. *Methods and Problems in Data Mining*. Database Theory - ICDT '97, 6th International Conference, Delphi, Greece, January 8-10, 1997, pp: 41-55.

14. T.Sellis, N. Roussopoulos, and C. Faloutsos. *The R+-tree: a dynamic index for multidimensional objects*. In Proceedings of the 13th International Conference on VLDB, England, 1987, pp: 507-518.

15. Davood Rafiei. *On Similarity-Based Queries for Time Series Data*. In Proceedings of the 15th International Conference on Data Engineering, 23-26 March 1999, Sydney, Austrialia, pp: 410-417.

16. Byoung-Kee Yi, H. V. Jagadish and Christos Faloutsos. *Efficient Retrieval of Similar Time-Sequences under Time Warping*. In Proceedings of the Fourteenth International Conference on Data Engineering, February 23-27, 1998, Orlando, Florida, USA, pp: 201-208.

Constraints-Based Query Translation across Heterogeneous Sources for Distributed Information Retrieval

Lieming Huang, Ulrich Thiel, Matthias Hemmje and Erich J. Neuhold

GMD-IPSI, Dolivostr. 15, D-64293, Darmstadt, Germany
E-mail: {lhuang, thiel, hemmje, neuhold}@darmstadt.gmd.de

Abstract. In this paper we propose a method for translating queries across heterogeneous information sources with widely varying query forms. First, the query capabilities of specific sources are described while taking into account the information of various constraints. When translating a query from one source to another source, we also sufficiently consider the function and position restrictions of terms, term modifiers and logical operators among the controls in the user interfaces to the underlying sources, so we can utilize the query capabilities of the specific sources as much as possible. In addition, we put forward a two-phase query subsuming mechanism to compensate for the functional discrepancies between sources, in order to make a more accurate query translation.

1   Introduction

The number of queryable information sources on the Internet, such as search engines, search tools, and online repositories, is growing rapidly. The information explosion makes it difficult for even the most powerful search engine to index all web pages (there are innumerable local databases that can only be visited through their query interfaces on the Internet) and to index new and updated pages within a reasonable amount of time. Thus, sometimes it is difficult to satisfy users' information needs by only visiting one source. Efficient information integration systems (IISs, such as meta-search engines, information brokers, agent-based information systems, multi-databases, and so on) will undoubtedly facilitate users in acquiring information. Such systems integrate many distributed, heterogeneous information sources with quite differing query models and user interfaces. In this paper, we focus on automatic query translation across different sources. Considering the great diversity of heterogeneous Internet sources, it is certainly a significant task to design an efficient query mapping mechanism that can sufficiently coordinate the conflicts between sources.

Suppose that a user wants to search for information as follows: Q: ((Author is "Charlie Brown") *AND* ((("Information Integration" in All fields) *AND* (Title contains "query")) *OR* (("Metadata", "XML") in Abstract))), published during the period of 1995 to 1999.

Before discussing how this query can be translated into the formats supported by several concrete sources, we first briefly introduce the method we have used to describe the query interfaces and query capabilities of different information sources.

In Fig. 1, we divide all the controls in the query construction user interface to a source into three groups: (1) classification selection controls, (2) result display controls, and (3) query input controls.

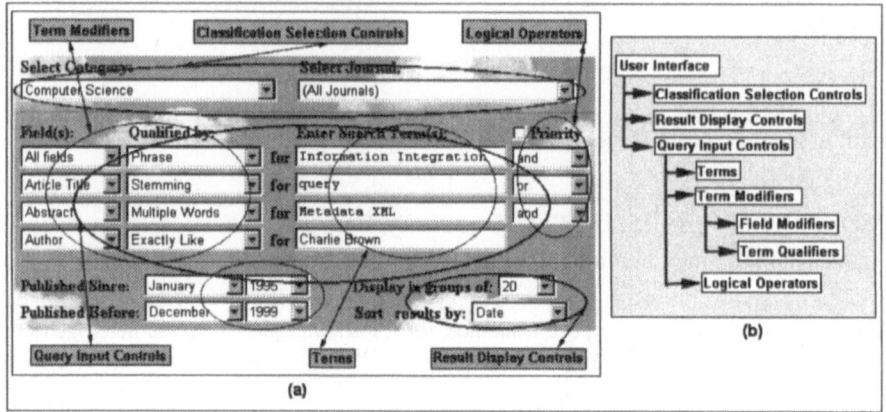

Fig. 1 Classifying the controls in a query form

A classification selection control is a component in the user interface to an information source which allows users to select one or more items in order to limit their information needs to certain domains, subjects, categories, etc.

A result display control can be used by users to control the formats, sizes or sorting methods of the query results. For example, Sorting Criteria = {<Relevance ranking>, <Author>, <Date>, etc.}; Grouping Size = {<10>, <20>, etc.}; Results Description = {<full>, <brief>, <URL>, etc.}.

A query input control is a component in the user interface to a source through which users can express their information needs (queries). Each query input control belongs to one of the three types: (1) TERMS. A *"term"* is the content keyed into an input box in the user interface to a source. This is different from the usual meaning of "term", because a term in our sense can be a single keyword, multiple words, a phrase, or a Boolean expression. In some cases, the input term may support wildcards, truncation, or stemming. It may be case sensitive, and might drop stop-words, hyphens, diacritics and special characters. (2) TERM MODIFIERS. A *"term modifier"* is a control in the user interface to a source that is used to limit the scope, the quality, or the form of a term. For example, we can divide all term modifiers into two groups: (i) field modifiers: {<Title>, <Full-Text>, <Review>, < Keywords>, etc.}, (ii) term qualifiers: {<Exactly Like>, <Multiple Words>, <Using Stem Expansion>, <Phrase>, etc.}. (3) LOGICAL OPERATORS. A *"logical operator"* is a control in the user interface to a source that is used to logically combine two terms to perform a search, the results of which are then evaluated for relevance. For example, there are four logical operators: {AND, OR, NOT, NEAR}.

Based on this classifying method, we can describe the query capabilities of various information sources, especially those with complex, powerful user interfaces, such as search engines with advanced query input forms, digital libraries, etc. In the following, we show how the example query Q is posed in two concrete query interfaces (Figures 2-3) from various sources, thus demonstrating the great diversity in the query models and user interfaces of heterogeneous sources, and illustrating the difficulties involved in translating a query from one source to another.

Search *ALL* bibliographic fields ...

Search for	adata"Information Integratio

Sort results by: date ▼

Search *SPECIFIC* bibliographic fields ...

Author: "Charlie Brown"

Title: query

Abstract: "Information Integration"

Combine fields with ⦿ AND ⦾ OR

Sort results by: date ▼

Fig. 2 NCSTRL

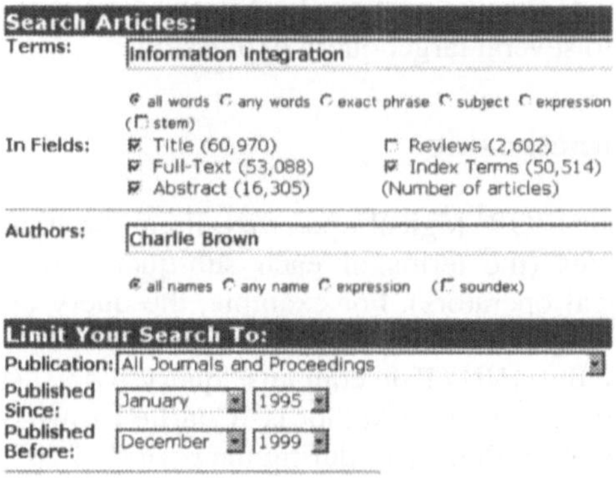

Search Articles:

Terms: Information integration

⦿ all words ⦾ any words ⦾ exact phrase ⦾ subject ⦾ expression
(☐ stem)

In Fields: ☑ Title (60,970)   ☐ Reviews (2,602)
            ☑ Full-Text (53,088)   ☑ Index Terms (50,514)
            ☑ Abstract (16,305)   (Number of articles)

Authors: Charlie Brown

⦿ all names ⦾ any name ⦾ expression (☐ soundex)

Limit Your Search To:

Publication: All Journals and Proceedings ▼

Published Since: January ▼ 1995 ▼

Published Before: December ▼ 1999 ▼

Fig.3 ACM-DL

In Fig. 2, two separate fill-out forms of the NCSTRL search engine are shown. The first form ("Search ALL bibliographic fields ...") contains only one input box and a result-sorting criteria pull-down menu. We can put all words and phrases into the input box. However, the field modifiers (Title, Abstract, Author, etc), term qualifiers (Exactly like, Using stem expansions, etc), and date range cannot be expressed in this form, and the search is likely to retrieve irrelevant results with respect to the original query. The second form ("Search SPECIFIC bibliographic fields ...") contains three input boxes (each input box is associated with a single field modifier: 'Author', 'Title', and 'Abstract'), two radio boxes as logical operators (AND, OR) used to combine the three input boxes, and also a result-sorting criteria pull-down menu. Compared with the first form, the second form can better support the query Q. Fig. 3 shows the query page of the ACM-DL with an input box for users to input keywords (it has several term qualifiers), five check boxes in which users can select field modifiers (title, full-text, abstract, review, article keywords), and one author input box.

From the above two figures, we can see that there is great diversity among the user interfaces and query models of various information sources, and that translating a query across sources is not trivial. An information integration system may integrate hundreds or even thousands of information sources. Depending on some source selection algorithms, the system can choose some sources that are relevant to a user query and then translate the user query into the formats supported by these sources. In the next section, we will discuss how such query translations are carried out.

2   Constraints-Based Query Translation

In this section, we will introduce the process of constraints-based query translation. Section 2.1 introduces how an original query can be disjunctivized into several conjunctive sub-queries. Section 2.2 discusses the translation from a conjunctive query into a single target query and how the common filters and the special filters are generated and how they work. Section 2.3 gives a detailed example to explain this translation method. Finally, section 2.4 briefly discusses the translation from an arbitrary query into several target query expressions.

2.1   Query Disjunctivizing

If a user query contains 'OR' logical operators, it can be transformed into several conjunctive sub-queries (the terms of each sub-query are combined by AND, NEAR, or NOT logical operators). For example, the query Q can be decomposed into 2 sub-queries: Q_1: ((Author is "Charlie Brown") *AND* ("Information Integration" in All fields) *AND* (Title contains "query") *AND* (Published during the period of 1995 to 1999)); and Q_2: ((Author is "Charlie Brown") *AND* (("Metadata", "XML") in Abstract) *AND* (Published during the period of 1995 to 1999)).

In order to explain our query translation method more clearly, we use figures to express the query capabilities of query forms. For example, query Q_1 can be described as Fig. 4 and the query capability of the second form (See Fig. 2) of the NCSTRL search engine can be described as Fig. 5.

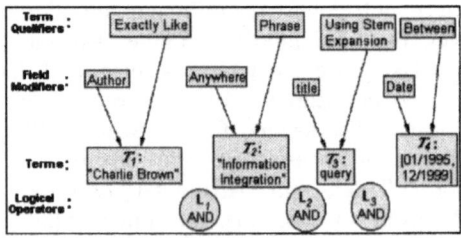

Fig. 4 Description of Q

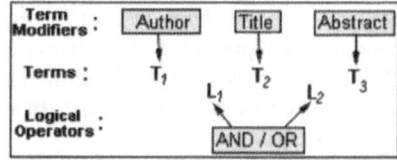

Fig. 5 The second form of NCSTRL

Because each field in Fig. 5 can only be limited by a specific term modifier, when we translate Q_1 into the formats supported by Fig. 5, the second term ("Information Integration" in All fields) in Q_1 can only be mapped into three concrete fields in Fig. 5: <Title>, <Abstract> and <Author>. So Q_1 can be disjunctivized into three sub-expressions: $Q_{1.1}$: (T_1) AND $(T_2$: Title) AND (T_3) AND (T_4); $Q_{1.2}$: (T_1) AND $(T_2$: Abstract) AND (T_3) AND (T_4); and $Q_{1.3}$: (T_1) AND $(T_2$: Author) AND (T_3) AND (T_4). Apparently, the third sub-query $Q_{1.3}$ contains the term (Authors contain "Information Integration") and this query will retrieve nothing.

A query and its disjunctivized sub-queries have the same effects, i.e. the retrieved results of these two situations are same. Sometimes an original disjunctive query can be directly mapped into a target query without being transformed.

2.2   Translation of a conjunctive query into a single target query

Now we discuss the translation of generic query expressions. We suppose that the original query Q^o is a conjunctive query with m (m>0) terms and (m-1) logical operators (can be 'AND', 'NOT', or 'NEAR') and that the target query Q^t is a query with n (n>0) terms and (n-1) logical operators (See Fig. 6).

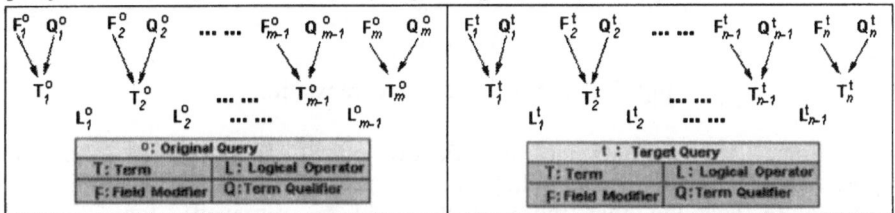

Fig. 6 The original query Q^o and the target query Q^t

When the system translates Q^o into Q^t, one of the following three cases will occur. Fig. 7 illustrates these three cases. Now we discuss these three cases separately and at the same time introduce how the common filters (these kinds of filters occur frequently and most of them can be applied to refine the results, so we call them "Common") and the special filters (these kinds of filters occur not often and most of them cannot be applied to refine the results, so we call them "special") are generated and how they later will be used to post-process the raw results.

Case 1: In this case, each term in Q^o can be put into a certain term in Q^t, and the field modifier and the term qualifier of this term can also be supported by the corresponding term in Q^t. Furthermore, each logical operator in Q^o can also be supported in Q', and the logical value of the new query is equivalent to the original query if some terms exchange their positions. For example, (A AND B AND C NOT D) equals (B AND C AND A NOT D). We call this situation as "Perfect Match" because the results need not be post-processed. In the following we give a more detailed description of this case.

For each term T^o_i in Q^o, if the field modifier of this term is one (or a subset) of the field modifiers of the corresponding term T^t_j in Q', and the term qualifier of T^o_i is one (or a subset) of the term qualifiers of T^t_j, then we consider the following three situations (otherwise, this translation fails): (a) If T^t_j is empty and the logical operator L^t_{j-1} supports L^o_{i-1} (L^t_{j-1} can be set as L^o_{i-1}), then the system can put T^o_i into T^t_j, set the field modifier and term qualifier of T^t_j as the corresponding ones of T^o_i, and set L^t_{j-1} as L^o_{i-1}. (b) Otherwise, if the term qualifier of T^t_j supports <Multiple Words> (the term T^t_j can be several words, but not a phrase) and L^t_{j-1} equals L^o_{i-1}, then put T^o_i into T^t_j. (c) Otherwise, Q^o cannot be translated into Q', and this translation fails.

If all terms in Q^o satisfy situation (a) or situation (b), the translation is successful. Otherwise, this query will be transferred to the next stage (<u>Case 2</u>) of the query translation.

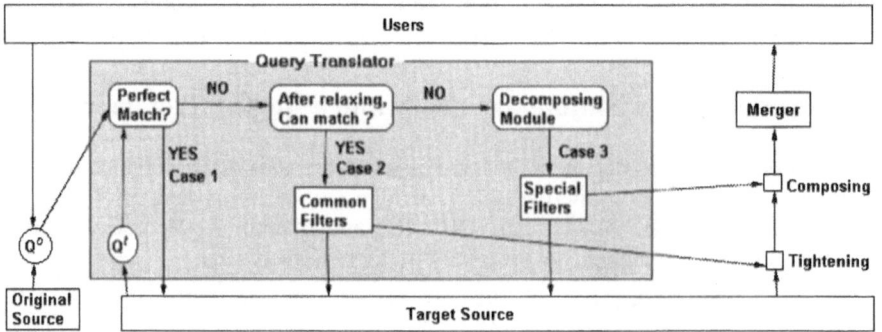

Fig. 7 Three cases of query translation

<u>Case 2</u>: Some field modifiers, term qualifiers or logical operators in Q^o cannot be supported by Q', but after relaxing them (i.e. broadening the scope of the limitation and therefore enabling that more results may be retrieved), for example, 'NEAR'→'AND', <Phrase> → <Multiple Words>, <Title> → <Abstract> → <Full Text>, etc., the newly-generated Q^o can be supported by Q'. In this case, the IIS dispatches the relaxed query, and when the results come, the system then post-processes the results according to the previous relaxing information. For the relaxed field modifiers, term qualifiers and logical operators, the system will use some filters to record such information and later use them to refine the results in order to compensate for the relaxing of constraints. We call such filters "common filters" and call the result refining process as "Tightening" (See Fig. 7). Now we will discuss some common filters: (1)'NEAR'→'AND'. Many sources do not support 'NEAR' logical operators. The system uses "A AND B" to replace "A NEAR B" and generates a new common filter to record this information. After the results are retrieved, the system uses this filter to select those entries in which term A and term B are near each other (e.g. within 5 words). If term A and term B are in the 'Title' field, this post-processing is easy, but if they are in the 'Abstract' field or even in the 'Full-Text' field, the system will consider the cost of analyzing the content of the source file and then decide whether to post-process it. (2) 'Phrase'→'Multiple words'. For this case, the system chooses those results that contain the exact phrase. (3) 'NOT A'. Some sources do not support the 'NOT' logical operator. When translating the original query, the system discards the 'NOT' operator and its term and generates a new common filter to record this information. After the results come, the system uses this filter to remove the results containing the terms that the original query "NOTted".

Case 3: In this case, Q^o cannot be supported by Q^t even after relaxing some modifiers or logical operators. The system will break Q^o into several sub-queries, then translate and dispatch each sub-query separately. We use special filters to record such decomposition information (See Fig. 7). When the corresponding results come, these "special filters" are employed to compose the results. However, in most cases, either because we cannot obtain relevant information from target sources or because post-processing will cost unreasonable CPU-time, it is impossible to post-process broken conjunctive expressions. For example, suppose that a four-term query is (A *AND* B *AND* C *AND* D) and the target query only supports two terms. Now we decompose the original expression into two sub-expressions (A *AND* B) and (C *AND* D). If the four terms are limited to the "Abstract" field or the "Full-Text" field of the publications, we cannot intersect the two result sets from (A *AND* B) and (C *AND* D) because we cannot check whether a term is in such fields. Even if we can get such information (e.g. by analyzing the PS, HTML, or PDF source file), such strenuous work is unnecessary. If the four terms are in the "title" field of the publications, it is possible to check if each entry from the two result sets contains these four terms. If the post-processing costs a lot of time, it is better to directly display the raw results to users.

When translating the original query into the target query, three steps (i.e. disjunctivizing, decomposing, relaxing) need to be accomplished, in which one or more of these steps may be skipped depending on the actual situation. When transferring the results from a source to users, three corresponding steps (i.e. tightening, composing, merging) will be done. The common filters record the relaxing information and later will be used to tighten the results. The special filters record the decomposing information and later will be used to compose the results.

2.3   An Example of Query Translation and Post-processing

Now, we discuss an example of how common filters and special filters are generated and later employed to post-process the results (See Fig. 8). Suppose there is a query six-term query Q^o: (A NEAR B AND C AND D AND E NOT F), term A and term B belong to the 'Abstract' field, term C belongs to the 'Author' field, term D belongs to the 'Title' field, term E belongs to the 'Full-Text' field and term F belongs to the 'Keywords' field. The target query Q^t can only support two terms and each term can only support the 'Author', 'Title', 'Abstract', and 'Keywords' field modifiers, and the 'AND' and 'OR' logical operators.
Because both term A and term B belong to the "Abstract" field, they can be put

together into an input-box of the target source. Because Q^t cannot support the 'NEAR' logical operator, the system generates a new common filter *CF1: "NEAR->AND(A, B)"* and Q^o becomes ((A B) AND C AND D AND E NOT F). In this query expression, the first term is "A B" (because both the term A and term B belong to "Abstract" field, they can be put together in an input-box in the target source. For example, the term A is "XML" and the term B is "RDF", then the new term in the input-box can be regarded as two words: <u>XML RDF</u>, not a phrase "XML RDF".) and the second term is "C"

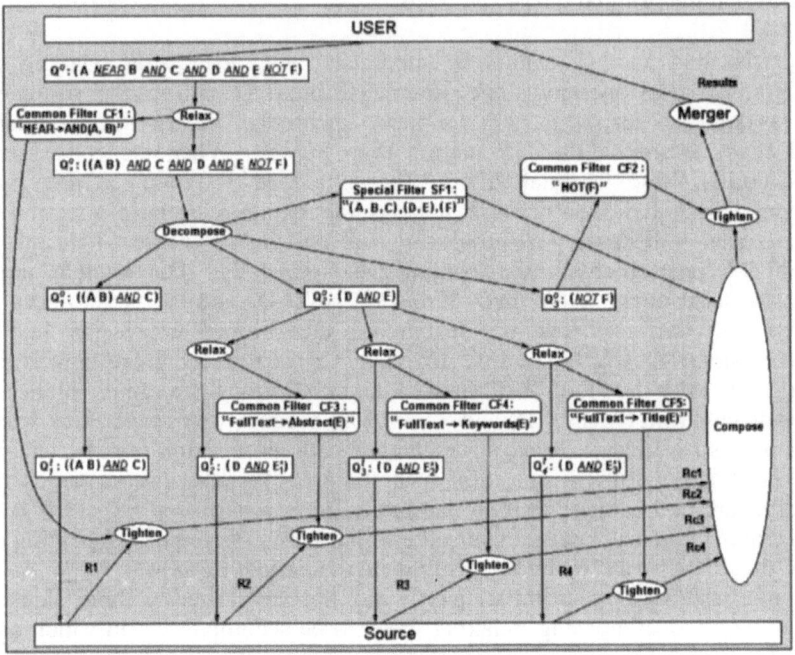

Fig. 8 An example query translation

Because the target source can only support two terms, when the system translates Q^o into Q^t, Q^o will be decomposed (See case 3 in Fig. 7) into three sub-queries: Q^o_1: ((A B) AND C), Q^o_2: (D AND E) and Q^o_3: (NOT F) and a new special filter *SF1: "(A, B, C), (D, E), (F)"* will be generated. Later this special filter will be employed to compose the three result sets of these three sub-queries.

Because the target source cannot support 'NOT' operator, so the sub-query Q^o_3: (NOT F) cannot be sent to the target source. Then a new common filter *CF2: "NOT(F)"* is generated and later this filter will be used to post-process the results. In the following, we will discuss how the system translates Q^o_1 and Q^o_2 into Q^t separately.

Q^o_1 becomes Q^t_1. In this Q^t_1, the first term is "A B" (because both the term A and term B belong to "Abstract" field, they can be put together in an input-box in the target source) and the second term is "C". When the system translates Q^o_2 into Q^i, because Q^i cannot support the 'Full-Text' field modifier, three new common filters $CF3$: *"FullText->Abstract(E)"* , $CF4$: *"FullText->Keywords(E)"* , and $CF5$: *"FullText->Title(E)"* are generated and Q^o_2 is transformed into Q^i_2: (D AND E^*_1), Q^i_3: (D AND E^*_2), and Q^i_4: (D AND E^*_3) repectively. In Q^i_2, the term E^*_1 belongs to the 'Abstract' field; In Q^i_3, the term E^*_2 belongs to the 'Keywords' field; And in Q^i_4, the term E^*_3 belongs to the 'Keywords' field.

After that, the system dispatches Q^i_1, Q^i_2, Q^i_3, and Q^i_4.

When the results of the query Q^i_1 return (R1), the system will use the common filter $CF1$ (*"NEAR->AND(A, B)"*) to refine them as Rc1, i.e. choosing those entries in which term A and term B are near each other within a number of (e.g., 3) words. When the results of the query Q^i_2 come (R2), the system will use the common filter $CF3$ (*"FullText->Abstract(E)"*) to refine them as Rc2 (this filter will be skipped because the <Abstract> can almost be regarded as a subset of <FullText>). The common filters $CF4$, and $CF5$ are the same as $CF3$. Then the system will use the special filter $SF1$ (*"(A, B, C), (D, E),(F)"*) to compose the two results sets Rc1, Rc2, Rc3, and Rc4, i.e. intersecting the two result sets. Finally the system will use the common filter $CF2$ (*"NOT(F)"*) to remove the entries that contain the term F in the 'keyword' field.

2.4 Translation from an arbitrary query into several target queries

In the above we have discussed this situation: the source query is a conjunctive query and the target source allows only one query expression. However, some sources provide more than one fill-out form, thus allowing more than one query expression, for example, NCSTRL supports two forms (See Fig. 2). Sometimes, the system may distribute several sub-queries from a source query into several target query expressions when translating the original query. Sometimes an original query can be directly mapped into the target query without being disjunctivized. Decomposing a query will increase the number of visits to remote sources and reduce efficiency. However, for most information sources, query decomposition is necessary.

3   Related Work and Discussions

With the tremendous development of the Internet and the explosive growth of digital information, distributed information retrieval on the Internet becomes more and more important. The challenge of its difficulties and importance attracts the attention and efforts of many researchers, such as [1-7], to name a few. In the following, some related work will be discussed.

Papers [2, 3] apply user-defined mapping rules to subsume queries for translation between different sources. They describe some problems involved in predicate rewriting, such as the "contains" predicate and word patterns, the "equals" predicate and phrase patterns, proximity operators, etc. Compared with their work, we propose a more generic model for translating arbitrary queries supported by various sources. Our two-phase method for coping with query subsuming (relaxing and decomposing) and post-processing (tightening with common filters and composing with special filters) can well coordinate the great functional discrepancies among heterogeneous information sources. Many papers, such as [5, 6, 7], describe the query capabilities of sources and deal with the query translation problem. They discuss more on context-free, conjunctive queries and do not consider some special constraints, such as the limitations of term modifiers, logical operators and the order of terms. From Figures 2-3, we know there is great diversity among sources. Sometimes even a very subtle difference will render the query translation impossible. Our paper sufficiently describes all kinds of constraints between the query models (as embodied in the user interfaces) of various sources, and therefore can utilize the functionality of each source to the fullest extent. Paper [1] uses Church-Rosser systems to characterize the query capabilities of information sources and uses "Attribute Preference Ordering" to realize query relaxing. Paper [4] proposes a scheme called "GenCompact" for generating capability-sensitive plans for queries on Internet sources. These two papers try to describe the query capabilities of sources and to translate queries across sources in a generic view. However, they do not consider some specific query constraints and do not provide a mechanism to post-process inexact results. We maintain that the heterogeneity of information sources inevitably renders the query mapping inaccurate, and that post-processing of results is necessary to make up for the inaccuracy.

The constraints-based query translation method proposed in this paper can be applied to all kinds of Internet information integration systems, such as digital libraries, meta-search engines (especially for specific-purpose), agent-based information providers, etc.

References

1. S. Adali and C. Bufi. A Flexible Architecture for Query Integration and Mapping. Proc. CoopIS'98, New York. Aug. 1998, pp. 341-353.
2. B. Chidlovskii, U. M. Borghoff, and P.Y. Chevalier. Boolean Query Translation for Brokerage on the Web. Proc. 2nd Int'l Conf. EuroMedia/WEBTEC'98, Leicester, U.K. Jan. 1998, pp. 37-44.
3. C. Chang, H. Garcia-Molina, and A. Paepcke. Predicate Rewriting for Translating Boolean Queries in a Heterogeneous Information System. ACM TOIS 17(1), Jan. 1999, pp. 1-39.
4. H. Garcia-Molina, W. Labio, and R. Yerneni. Capability-Sensitive Query Processing on Internet Sources. Proc. ICDE' 99, Sydney, Australia, Mar. 1999.
5. Levy, A. Rajaraman, and   J. Ordille. Querying Heterogeneneous Information Sources Using Source Descriptions. Proc. 22nd VLDB. Bombay, India, 1996, pp. 251-262.

6. V. Vassalos and Y. Papakonstantinou. Describing and Using Query Capabilities of Heterogeneous Sources. Proc. 23rd VLDB. Athens, Greece, Aug. 1997. pp 256-265.
7. R. Yerneni, C. Li, H. Garcia-Molina, and J. Ullman. Computing Capabilities of Mediators. Proc. SIGMOD, Philadelphia, PA, Jun. 1999, pp. 443-454.

Video Matching Methods Using Spatial Characteristics in MSP Search System

Mei Kodama

Information Media Center, Hiroshima University
1-7-1 Kagamiyama Higashi-hiroshima Hiroshima, 739-8521 Japan
E-mail: mei@hiroshima-u.ac.jp

Abstract. The concept of multimedia communication services had been proposed using multimedia scalability packages, which can provide integrated multimedia information, such as, MPEG and H.26x standards according to functionality and availability for users. This paper shows a video search system based on exchanging data of MSP: Multimedia Scalability Packages. After the system procedure is shown, we use both of spatial and temporal extension methods actually as simple image search schemes, and from the viewpoint of matching precision and processing time, it is indicated that our system is effective.

1 Introduction

Internet has spread to world wide rapidly and network speed remarkably becomes to high, and capacity of storage media is also getting large in computer networks now. So a lot of video compression technologies are adapted to not only storage media but also communication services, such as, TV conference, video distribution system by internet and digital broadcast. Then, we focus on video search as future video communication tools in multimedia communication services. In other words, we would like to present a communication environment that users can efficiently retrieve multimedia information, which they request.

We had proposed MSP communication system [1]. MSP means Multimedia Scalability Packages, and we defined the concept and its data format. Simply speaking, some hierarchical data are made by scalable coding in image, video, sound and so on as media contents. Moreover, their manipulation, action information and additional information are packetized together for communication system. We consider multimedia services with mutual operation by MSP data, for examples, search, edit, process, display, transmission and so on. As MSP data has scalability functions, they can select image quality, such as, image resolution and video coding rate, these structuring methods had been studied [2][3][4][5]. In addition, Image search methods had been examined [6][7]. And as video applications, MPEG-7 Standards are made a progress now.

In this paper, we use temporal extension methods using spatial characteristics for video. Especially, when simple features in video characteristics are used, from the viewpoint of image and video search precision and processing time, the possibility of scalable search methods using spatial characteristics is made clear by experimental results.

In section 2, we explain concept of MSP search system, and outline of MSP data. In next section 3, outline of our search engine and matching methods are indicated. In section 4, simulation experiments are implemented using actual video sequences, which we made. At first, the conditions of them are shown and we evaluate our search engine. Finally, we conclude in section 5.

2 Concept of MSP Search System

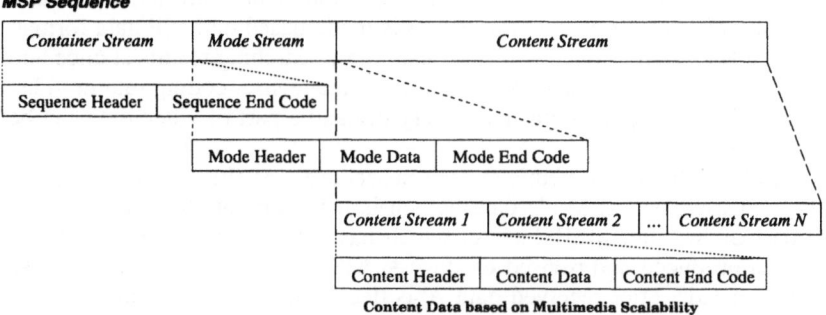

Fig. 2.1. MSP Data Structure

At first, we indicate MSP data structure. MSP data has "content data", such as, image, video, sound, text etc., "mode data", which means manipulation and action information, and "header data", as which there are author, title, date, version, abstract, affiliation, and copyright information and so on. These data are packetized to MSP format in Fig. 2.1.

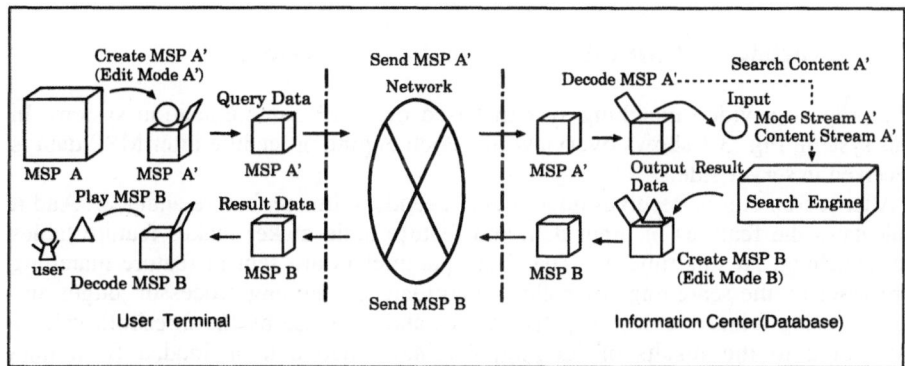

Fig. 2.2. Concept of MSP Information Search System

So we propose MSP search system between client and server terminals in Fig.2.2. In this system, a user get query data in multimedia information and when he request search application, after query data is made in client side, it is sent to multimedia database server. MSP data is decoded in server side and is sent to search engine. Input parameters for searching are described on attached information of MSP contents. After a server receives that, MSP search information, which we call "mode data", and content information are decoded into the matching processor. Output MSP data is made by search system information and searching results in server side and is sent back to user side.

It is the first point that this system uses intelligent package data, MSP. This package data has searching functions, any matching parameter and so on. Second point is that there is an exchange of MSP data each other between client and server terminals. MSP data automatically works in itself in each terminal. For examples, there are calculating image features, judging network environment and watching occupation rate of CPU. Third point is that this system has information search engine using scalability. Off course, these data is made based on MSP data format. Therefore when MSP data is decoded, users can know searching results at once and also use scalability functions, such as, selection of image size, coding rate in video contents. That's because video data size is very big and a part of video data can be used by hierarchical structure.

We explain about the detail of this system procedure. At first, there is original image data A in users' sides. Mode data, which is manipulation data, are made to add to the part of A. After MSP data A', which has MSP header information and content data, is produced and revised by data A, MSP A' is sent to MSP database system. In server side, after received data A' is decoded, MSP stream and content data are retrieved and search engine is worked. Output data are made, such as, system information and matching information, network address and so on as searching results. Finally, new MSP B is made by those data and is sent back to users' terminal. Users can get the searching results and requested data using scalability function based on mode data in MSP B.

3   Video Search Engine

3.1   Procedure of MSP Information Search System

We propose a video matching system based on MSP communication system. In this system, Fig. 3.1 shows overview of search engine procedure after MSP data is received in server side.

After search engine receives query data, it sends to image feature analyzer. And it calculates the features of input data and feature table maker makes feature tables for matching. At this time, the searching parameters are sent to feature matching processor by the searching controller. Then feature matching processor judges any feature using feature tables in query images and database by the threshold values. According to the results of judging, original video data is loaded from data repository, and both of these parameters and results images are packetized as MSP data in order to send back to user side.

In image feature analyzer, values of average of luminance in one frame, variance and number of color space are simply used as spatial characteristics of picture signals in this paper. Query images are compared with database images in matching tables from these matching parameters. Our scalable system is effective in order to gain high matching precision and to decrease processing time.

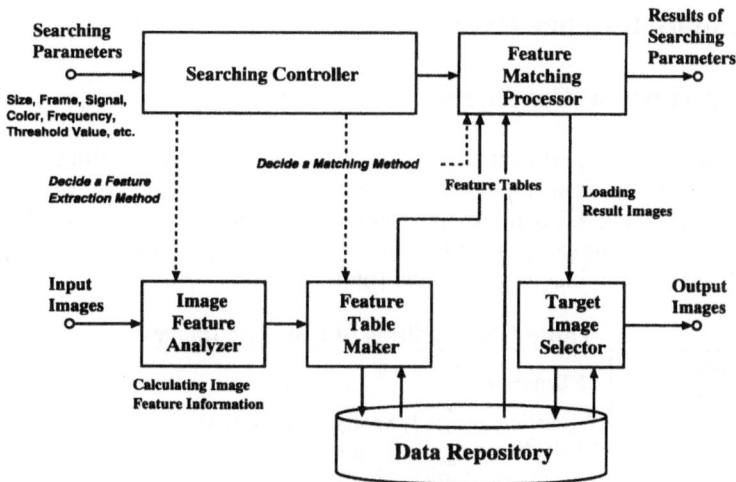

Fig3.1. Overview of Search Engine Procedure

3.2   Matching Method

We propose temporal extension method for video search in MSP search system.

At first, we show a general image matching method by threshold value for still picture. We used equation (3.1) in threshold Th_1, judging that feature between spatial feature in database image and input image.

$$(F_Q - F_{D_i})^2 \leq Th_1 \tag{3.1}$$

Here, F_Q shows the amount of each feature in input images. F_{Di} shows the amount of each feature in database images, and i shows registered frame numbers in the database.

In the same way, if we use temporal extension method, the above method is repeated to temporal domain. If the condition of threshold value is satisfied in a frame, this matching scheme works again in next frame. It shows that spatial characteristics are used to temporal domain as temporal features in moving pictures, and matching frames are distinguished as target images of searching. In other words, we can avoid the fact that the matching precision is low when the quality of query image is down from original image by temporal extension.

$$(F_{Q_m} - F_{D_{(x,n)}})^2 \leq Th_2 \tag{3.2}$$

Here, F_{Qm} shows the amount of each feature in input images and m shows frame numbers in query video and $F_{D(x,n)}$ shows the amount of each feature in database images, and n is frame number in each database video, and x is video number in database.

4   Simulation Experiments

4.1   Experimental Conditions

In our simulation experiments, this search system aims at finding the original frame or video data from input data in data repository effectively. In this section, Table 4.1 and Table 4.2 show experimental conditions for search simulation. The former is database images, and the latter is query images. Down size images are created from original image by average filter.

Table 4.1. Condition of Database Images

Sequence Number	15 Sequence
Sequence Name	Animation, Sports 1, Sports 2, Music 1, Music 2, Move, News, Sports 3, Sports 4, Sports 5, Bus, Flower Garden, Mobile & Calendar, Popl, Table Tennis
Number of Frames	Animation, ..., Sports 5: Each 9000 [Frame] Bus, ..., Table Tennis: Each 150 [Frame] Total 90750 [Frame]
Image Format	ITU-R BT.601, 4:2:0 704[pel] x 480[line], no-compression (Original Size) Return video sequence is MPEG-2 coded data.

Table 4.2. Condition of Query Images

Sequence Number	15 Sequence
Number of Frames	Image Retrieval: 1 [Frame] Video Retrieval: m [Frame] (m = 1,...,150)
Number of Frames and MPEG-2 Coded Rate	Original Image Size: Each 150 [Frame] ITU-R BT.601, 4:2:0: no-compression, 3,6,9 [Mbps] Down Size: Each 150 [Frame] 352[pel] x 240[line]: no-compression, 2.5 [Mbps] 176[pel] x 120[line]: no-compression, 2.0 [Mbps] 88[pel] x 60[line]: no-compression, 0.4 [Mbps]

We calculated the features using the luminance values without the number of color in YCbCr color space. Table 4.1 shows the condition data in database. The maximum difference values are used in 150 frames as threshold in this paper. Here, we simulate the processing time in each schemes, however feature information tables are made from first frame in input data. Moreover, Fujitsu GP7000 SM25 400MHz Ultra SPARC-2 is used for simulation experiments in this paper.

4.2   Simulation Experiments

In this section, we simulate spatial matching method in our search system. We simulated two methods which spatial method and temporal extension method. And three matching methods are used. For example, average value in luminance signal (Ave.), variance value in the same signal (Var.), and number of colors in YCbCr color space are used.

In addition, three matching parameters are picked up, such as, frame size, coded rate, and both of frame size and coded rate. These values are used as matching tables in database images for video search system.

Here, in these simulations, Th_1 is set by equation (4.1). Next Th_2 is given by equation (4.2).

$$Th_1 = \left| F_Q - F_{D_i} \right| \qquad (4.1)$$

$$Th_2 = \max_{i \le i, j \le N} \left| F_{Q_i} - F_{D_j} \right| \qquad (4.2)$$

Where we define that $Y(i,j)$ means luminance value and the horizontal size of image is H, and that the vertical size is V, the average value F_{Ave} is calculated by equation (4.3).

$$F_{Ave} = \frac{1}{V \times H} \sum_{i=1}^{V} \sum_{j=1}^{H} Y(i, j) \qquad (4.3)$$

Next, the variance value F_{Var} is calculated by equation (4.4).

$$F_{Var} = \frac{1}{V \times H} \sum_{i=1}^{V} \sum_{j=1}^{H} \left(Y(i, j) - F_{Ave} \right)^2 \qquad (4.4)$$

Moreover the number of color: F_{col} is given by equation (4.5).

Where
$$S_k = \{(Y_0, Cb_0, Cr_0), (Y_1, Cb_1, Cr_1), \cdots, (Y_k, Cb_k, Cr_k)\}, \qquad (4.5)$$
if $(x, y, z) \notin S_k$ *then*
$(Y_{k+1}, Cb_{k+1}, Cr_{k+1}) = (x, y, z),$
and this process is repeated at n times for all pixels in one frame .

Therefore, F_{col} is given by S_n, but (x, y, z) is value of color space at any pixel.

4.2.1   Spatial Matching Method

As we would like to get one frame or one video sequence from database of 90750 frames, the precision of each matching parameters were simulated. These main results of different parameters in original sizes are shown in Table 4.3 and. Table 4.4. In the case of 704[pel] x480 [line] image size, from the viewpoint of matching precision, the method of using variance value is most effective. After all, these matching parameters are useful to select the query image. In the case of using down size images, the precision is low. Table 4.5 shows that the number of matching frame in each coded frames. It means that the matching precision is also low by error of coding.

Next, Table 4.6 shows the number of matching frames in each coded image size. Both of them mean that the precision is not enough to select the query image. Average parameter is only available. Therefore we use temporal extension method using spatial features in next section.

Table 4.3. Comparison of Matching Frames for each parameter in Original Data [Frame]

Seq.	704x480			Matching Parameters
	Ave.	Var.	Col.	Ave.:Average Value Var.:Variance Value
	$Th_1=0$	$Th_1=0$	$Th_1=0$	Col.:Number of Color
1)	2	1	2	1)Music 2
2)	9	1	1	2)Mobile & Calendar

Table 4.4. Comparison of Matching Frames in each Frame Size [Frame] (No-compression)

Seq.	352x240		176x120		88x60	
	Ave.	Var.	Ave.	Var.	Ave.	Var.
	$Th_1=$ 0.14	$Th_1=$ 401.18	$Th_1=$ 0.04	$Th_1=$ 864.96	$Th_1=$ 0.02	$Th_1=$ 1282.49
1)	46	26873	13	47187	2	56533
2)	227	7079	71	26160	51	47966

Table 4.5. Comparison of Matching Frames in each Coded Rate [Frame]

Seq.	9.0[Mbps]			6.0[Mbps]			3.0[Mbps]		
	Ave.	Var.	Col.	Ave.	Var.	Col.	Ave.	Var.	Col.
	$Th_1=$ 0.08	$Th_1=$ 46.85	$Th_1=$ 10794	$Th_1=$ 0.09	$Th_1=$ 76.85	$Th_1=$ 11878	$Th_1=$ 0.13	$Th_1=$ 148.18	$Th_1=$ 20243
1)	21	4177	31292	22	5596	30692	36	9425	46755
2)	152	370	246	152	653	254	229	1723	339

Table 4.6 Comparison of Matching Frames in each Coded Frame Size [Frame]

Seq.	352x240, 2.5[Mbps]		176x120, 2.0[Mbps]		88x60, 0.4[Mbps]	
	Ave.	Var.	Ave.	Var.	Ave.	Var.
	$Th_1=$ 0.18	$Th_1=$ 456.22	$Th_1=$ 0.07	$Th_1=$ 879.91	$Th_1=$ 0.35	$Th_1=$ 1318.14
1)	59	29177	19	47691	22	57193
2)	308	8604	118	26783	159	51649

4.2.2   Temporal Extension Method

Table 4.7-Table 4.10 show the matching results of the frame number in temporal extension method. By simulation result, this method is more effective than spatial one from matching precision. For example, in Table 4.8 on 704 [pel]x480 [line] size, the query sequence is able to be selected by using maximum two frames maximum. Moreover average value is useful as video matching methods, especially, in the case of small frame size in Table 4.8. But the method using number of color is not effective. That's because it is difference among each image size. On the other hand, values of variance are not often available in each size, but only low frequency image is useful. Because natural image is including high frequency signals, so these values are a large number of differences.

It is more effective using average method than other parameters in 3[Mbps] in Fig. 4.9. Variance value is also useful, but in number of color the matching precision is low, as almost frames are hit by query video. Table 4.10 shows comparison of matching frames in coded and frame size. It means the method using average value is effective until the frame size is 88 [pel] x 60 [line]. Fig.4.1 and Fig.4.2 mainly show comparison of matching frames in temporal extension from each coded rate in average method, variance method. These results show that the number of matching sequence converges in time domain. So we can retrieve the query sequence by temporal extension method.

Table 4.7. Comparison of Matching Frames for each parameter in Original Data [Frame]

Seq.		704x480			FN means frame number when
		Ave.	Var.	Col.	target frame is one, but when it is
		$Th_2=0$	$Th_2=0$	$Th_2=0$	150[frame], target frame is one or
1)	FN	2	1	2	not..
	MN	1	1	1	
2)	FN	2	1	1	MN means Matching Number
	MN	1	1	1	

Table 4.8. Comparison of Matching Frames in each Frame Size [Frame]

Seq.		352x240		176x120		88x60	
		Ave.	Var.	Ave.	Var.	Ave.	Var.
		$Th_2=$ 0.14	$Th_2=$ 1945.06	$Th_2=$ 0.05	$Th_2=$ 2039.83	$Th_2=$ 0.03	$Th_2=$ 2165.04
1)	FN	4	150	3	150	2	150
	MN	1	39715	1	41762	1	43645
2)	FN	9	150	5	150	3	150
	MN	1	26406	1	41117	1	58953

Table 4.9. Comparison of Matching Frames in each Coded Rate [Frame]

Seq.		9.0[Mbps]			6.0[Mbps]			3.0[Mbps]		
		Ave.	Var.	Col.	Ave.	Var.	Col.	Ave	Var.	Col.
		$Th_2=$ 0.36	$Th_2=$ 140.27	$Th_2=$ 20559	$Th_2=$ 0.47	$Th_2=$ 220.20	$Th_2=$ 22407	Th_2 = 0.70	$Th_2=$ 415.56	$Th_2=$ 55144
1)	FN	9	44	150	10	55	150	11	79	150
	MN	1	1	28	1	1	297	1	1	5898
2)	FN	15	150	150	29	150	150	150	150	150
	MN	1	1	1	1	47	2	1	442	151

Table 4.10. Comparison of Matching Frames in each Coded Frame Size [Frame]

Seq.		352x240, 2.5[Mbps] 2.5[Mbps]		176x120, 2.0[Mbps] 2.0[Mbps]		88x60, 0.4[Mbps] 0.4[Mbps]	
		Ave.	Var.	Ave.	Var.	Ave.	Var.
		$Th_2=$ 0.50	$Th_2=$ 1948.22	$Th_2=$ 0.26	$Th_2=$ 2036.44	$Th_2=$ 0.35	$Th_2=$ 2171.81
1)	FN	10	150	6	150	9	150
	M	1	39778	1	41711	1	43780
2)	FN	32	150	14	150	29	150
	M	1	26832	1	40874	1	59208

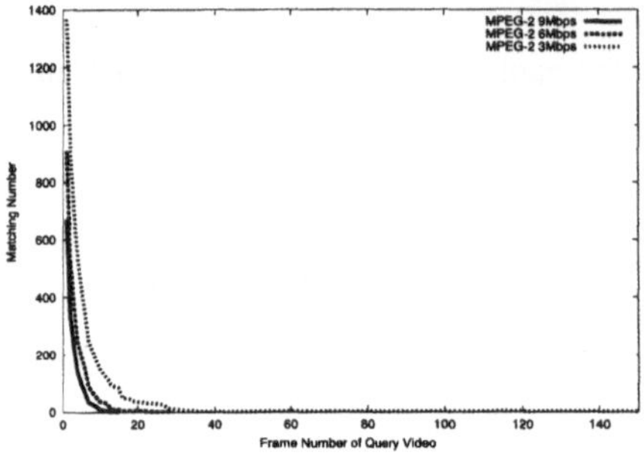

Fig. 4.1. Distribution of Convergence of Matching Number using Average Value

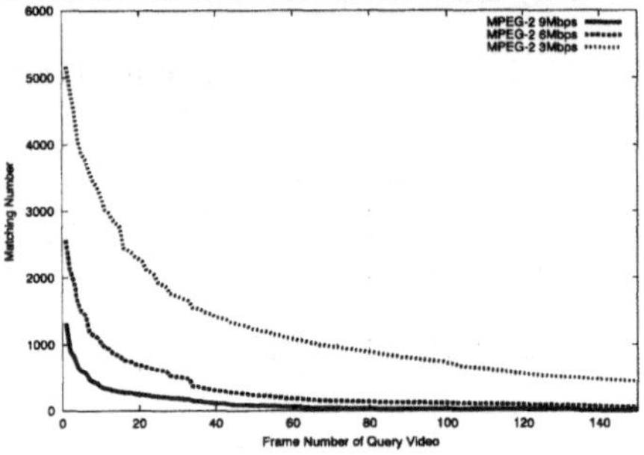

Fig. 4.2. Distribution of Convergence of Matching Number using Variance Value

4.3 Consideration

When the matching precision is kept, making tables for image features and matching time are simulated.

Table 4.12. Calculating Time of Feature Table for each Size per a Frame [s]

Frame Size	Ave.	Var.	Col.
704x480	0.111	0.160	1.828
352x240	0.029	0.045	-
176x120	0.009	0.012	-
88x60	0.004	0.004	-

Table 4.13. Calculating Time of Matching Process

all database(90750) [s]		
Ave.	Var.	Col.
0.385	0.406	0.207
per one frame [$\times 10^{-6}$ s]		
4.242	4.474	2.281

At first, Table 4.12 and 4.13 show calculating times of making feature tables and matching process. By this result, average parameter is simple and useful for making tables. In addition, it shows that smaller images are used, faster the creating time of feature table is. In this case of frame size of 88[pel] x 60[line], it is fastest, and calculating time is about 28 times faster in full size. Average method is about 16 times faster than color scheme. Therefore it means efficiency of using spatial scalability. That's why MSP data is useful. On the other hand, in matching process, it is point that matching time depends on convergence of matching number. After all, even if there are some errors between query images and database images, the mating time is short by using temporal scheme.

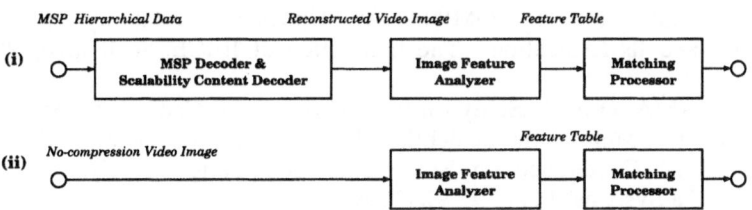

Fig. 4.3. A part of Search System Procedure for Processing Time

Secondly, we consider our search system from processing time by Fig. 4.3. Here, we focus on the processing time from receiving data to finishing searching in server terminal. The case (i) has MPS process and scalability processing is used automatically. The case (ii) is general search system. By simulation results, MSP processing time is 5.03[s] in the case (i). In addition, processing times of image feature analyzer are (i) 4.95[s] and (ii) 17.95[s]. In news sequence, actual matching time is about 0.015[s] for each frame size. By these results, total processing times are (i) 10.00[s] and (ii) 17.97[s]. Our system is about 1.8 times faster than general system. That's because our system uses scalable images.

Finally, our system can answer both a still picture search and video one. So our MSP communication system defines "mode data" and searching parameters are described in this data area according to users' searching requests. As two matching schemes can be selected, it is a flexible search system.

5 Conclusions

In this paper, we proposed temporal extension method using spatial characteristics for video search in MSP search system. As the simulation results, this method was evaluated, and average value is most available as matching parameters. That's because it has error resilience. Even if a feature of one frame is not enough, matching precision is not low using temporal extension method. Moreover, matching time is also short. That's why scalability video data is useful. For example, there are spatial scalability and SNR scalability in MPEG-2 coding standards, the former coding is especially available from the viewpoints of matching processing. Therefore, in MSP search system, it is important that not only server terminal but also client terminal calculates features of query image or video. As proposed search engine is adapted to image search and video one, both image and video search engine could be worked by mode data of MSP data.

We will study the other matching methods and evaluate the matching system in MSP communication system.

Reference

1. M. KODAMA, et al.: "A Study on Multimedia Proceedings and its Image Information Construction based on Scalability", Technical report of IEICE, IN96-122, OFS96-60, pp. 99-106 (1997).

2.   M. KODAMA and H. TOMINAGA: "Updatable Scalability of Moving Pictures and Its Evaluation", The transaction of IEICE,J80-B-I,2,pp.98-105 (1997).
3.   M. KODAMA, et al.: " Study on the Hybrid Image Coding and Structuring Methods for Multimedia Scalability Packages Communication Services", International Conference on Multimedia Computing and Systems, IEEE Multimedia Systems'99, pp. 92-96 (1999).
4.   M. KODAMA, et al.: "The Hierarchical Image Coding and Its Data Description Methods of Video Information Architectures in Multimedia Scalability Packages", PCS'99, pp. 37-40 (1999).
5.   M. KODAMA and T.IKEDA: "Study on the Video Description Methods in MSP Searching System", PV2000 (2000).
6.   Y.SAKAI and R. KATAOKA: "Searching Multimedia Information in Distributed Environment", IEICE transactions on communications, E79-B, 8,pp.989-998 (1996).
7.   K. TAKAHASHI, H. TOMINAGA, et al.: "An Effective Video Retrieval Method Using Video Fingerprint of Peculiar Video", The Journal of IIEEJ, 6,29,pp.818-825 (2000).

Replica Management in Object-Based Systems

Katsuya Tanaka and Makoto Takizawa

Dept. of Computers and Systems Engineering, Tokyo Denki University, Japan
E-mail: katsu@takilab.k.dendai.ac.jp

Abstract. Objects are replicated in order to increase reliability and availability of an object-based system. We discuss how to invoke methods on replicas of objects in a nested manner. If a method t is invoked on multiple replicas and each instance of t on the replicas invokes a method u on another object y, u may be performed multiple times on some replica of y and then the replica gets inconsistent, i.e. redundant invocations. In addition, if each instance of t issues a request to a quorum, more number of the replicas are manipulated than the quorum number of the method u, i.e. quorum explosion. We discuss an invocation protocol to resolve the redundant invocation and quorum explosion. We evaluate the protocol on how many replicas are manipulated and requests are issued.

1 Introduction

Various applications are realized in object-based framework like CORBA [12]. Objects are replicated in order to increase the reliability and availability of object-based systems. The two-phase locking protocol [5] and quorum-based protocol [7] are proposed. *Quorum* numbers N_r and N_w of the replicas are locked for *read* and *write*, respectively, in the quorum-based protocol [7] where $N_r + N_w > a$ for the number a of the replicas. The subset of the replicas is a *quorum*. An object is an encapsulation of data and abstract methods. A pair of methods conflict on an object if the result obtained by performing the methods depends on the computation order. In the papers [13, 14], the quorum concept for read and write is extended to abstract methods. Suppose methods t and u are issued to replicas x_1 and x_2 of an object x. The method t is performed on one replica x_1 and u on x_2 if t and u are compatible. Here, x_1 and x_2 are different but can be the newest ones if u is performed on x_1 and t on x_2. As long as t and u are issued, the methods are performed on replicas in their quorums. If some method v conflicting with t is issued to a replica x_1, every instance of t performed so far is required to be performed on x_1. Even if a replica is updated by t or u, $N_t + N_u \leq a$ only if t and u are compatible.

In the object-based system, methods are invoked in a nested manner. Suppose a method t on an object x invokes a method u on another object y. Let x_1 and x_2 be replicas of the object x. Let y_1 and y_2 be replicas of y. A method t is issued to the replicas x_1 and x_2. We assume that every method is deterministic, i.e. the same computation for t is done on x_1 and x_2. Then,

t invokes the other method u on y_1 and y_2. Here, u is performed twice on each replica although u should be performed only once on each of the replicas y_1 and y_2. Otherwise, y gets inconsistent. This is a *redundant invocation*. In addition, an instance of the method t on x_1 issues a method u to replicas in its own quorum Q_1, and another instance of t on x_2 issues u to replicas in Q_2 where $|Q_1| = |Q_2| = N_u$ but $Q_1 \neq Q_2$. More number of replicas are manipulated than N_u, i.e. $|Q_1 \cup Q_2| \geq N_u$. If the method u furthermore invokes another method, the number of replicas to be manipulated is more increased and eventually all the replicas are manipulated. This is a *quorum explosion*. In order to increase the reliability and availability, a method issued has to be performed on multiple replicas. On the other hand, the replicas may get inconsistent by the redundant invocations and the overhead is increased by the quorum explosion. We discuss how to resolve the redundant invocation and quorum explosion to occur in nested invocations of methods on multiple replicas.

In section 2, we overview the quorum-based protocol for replicas of objects. In sections 3 and 4, we discuss how to resolve the redundant invocation of methods on replicas and the quorum explosion. In section 5, we evaluate the quorum-based protocol.

2   Quorum-based Replication of Object

An object is an encapsulation of data and abstract methods. Let us consider a *counter* object c which supports three types of methods *increment* (*inc*), *decrement* (*dec*), and *display* (*dsp*). Suppose there are four replicas c_1, c_2, c_3, and c_4 of the object c. *inc* and *dec* are considered to be *write* because the state of the object c is changed by the methods. Hence, $N_{inc} + N_{dec} > 4$, $N_{dsp} + N_{inc} > 4$, and $N_{dsp} + N_{dec} > 4$ according to the traditional quorum-based protocols [7]. For example, $N_{inc} = N_{dec} = 3$ and $N_{dsp} = 2$. The quorum concept for *read* and *write* is extended to methods of objects [13, 14].
[Object-based quorum (OBQ) constraint] If a pair of methods t and u conflict, $N_t + N_u > a$ where a is the total number of the replicas. □

It is noted that $N_t + N_u \leq a$ only if t and u are compatible even if t or u is an update type. Every pair of conflicting methods t and u of an object x are performed on at least k ($= N_t + N_u - a$) replicas in the same order. $N_{inc} + N_{dec} \leq 4$, e.g. $N_{inc} = N_{dec} = 2$ because *inc* and *dec* are compatible. Suppose $Q_{inc} = \{c_1, c_2\}$ and $Q_{dec} = \{c_3, c_4\}$. Since either *inc* or *dec* is performed on each replica in the quorums, the states of the replicas in Q_{inc} are different from Q_{dec}. However, if *dec* is performed on c_1 and c_2 and *inc* is performed on c_3 and c_4, all the replicas can be the same. This is an *exchanging procedure* where every method t performed on one replica is sent to other replicas where t has not been performed and only methods compatible with t have been performed. Suppose *dsp* is issued to three replicas c_1, c_2, and c_3 where $Q_{dsp} = \{c_1, c_2, c_3\}$. *dsp* conflicts with *inc* and *dec*. *dsp* cannot be performed on any replica in Q_{dsp} because only *inc* has been performed on c_1 and c_2 and only *dec* on c_3 as shown at step 1 of Figure 1. Before performing *dsp*, *dec* is performed on c_1 and c_2 and *inc* on c_3. *inc* and *dec* can be performed in any order because they are compatible. Here, c_1, c_2, and c_3 get the same at step 2. *dsp* is performed on c_1, c_2, and c_3 at step 3.

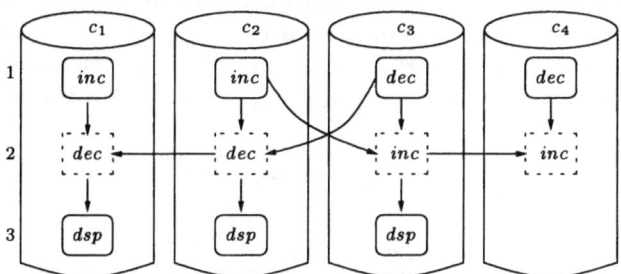

Fig. 1. Exchanging procedure.

3   Redundant Invocation

3.1   Invocation on replicas

In the object-based system, methods are invoked in a nested manner. Suppose a transaction T invokes a method t on an object x and then t invokes a method u on an object y [Figure 2]. Suppose there are multiple replicas $x_1, \ldots, x_a$ of the object x and $y_1, \ldots, y_b$ of the object y.

One way to invoke a method t on replicas is a *primary-secondary* one. First, the transaction T issues a request t to a primary replica x_1. Then, a request u is issued to a primary replica y_1 [Figure 3]. After the method commits, the state of the primary replica is transmitted to the secondary ones. Since only one instance of t invokes u, neither redundant invocation nor quorum explosion occurs. However, this way implies less availability for the fault of primary replica. Since every request is issued to a primary replica, the primary replica is overloaded.

We take another approach where a method is issued to multiple replicas [Figure 4]. Here, a transaction T invokes a method t on multiple replicas of x. Each instance t_i of t on a replica x_i invokes a method u on multiple replicas of y. Even if some replica is faulty, t is performed on other replicas and u is invoked on replicas of y. Suppose that t invokes a method u on an object y. Let Q_{ui} be a set of replicas of y to which an instance t_i on a replica x_i issues a method u. If $|Q_{u1} \cup \cdots \cup Q_{um}| > N_u$, T manipulates more number of replicas of the object y than N_u, i.e. the quorum of u is *exploded*.

A transaction T issues a method t to replicas in the quorum $Q_t = \{x_1, x_2\}$ and $N_t = 2$. Furthermore, t issues a request u to replicas of the object y in the quorum of the method u, say $N_u = 2$. Let t_i be an instance of the method t performed on a replica x_i ($i = 1, 2$). Each instance t_i issues a request u to replicas in a quorum Q_{ui}. Suppose $Q_{u1} = Q_{u2} = \{y_1, y_2\}$. Here, let u_{i1} and u_{i2} show instances of the method u performed on replicas y_1 and y_2, respectively, which are issued by t_i ($i = 1, 2$) [Figure 5]. Suppose the method is "$y = 2*y$", i.e. value of y is multiplied by two. However, the replica y_1 is multiplied by four since two instances u_{11} and u_{21} are performed on y_1. Thus, y_1 gets inconsistent. y_2 also gets inconsistent. This is a *redundant invocation*, i.e. a method on a replica is invoked multiple times by multiple instances of a method. Since every method is deterministic, the same computation of t is performed on the replicas x_1 and x_2. Here, t_1 and t_2 are referred to as *same crone* instances of a method t. u_{11}, u_{12}, u_{21}, and u_{22} are also same crone instances.

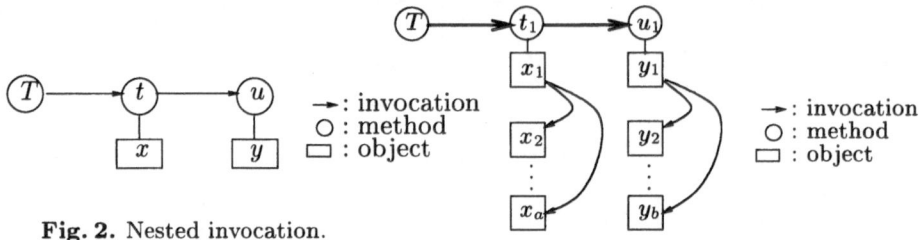

Fig. 2. Nested invocation.

Fig. 3. Primary-secondary replication.

[**Definition**] A pair of instances t_1 and t_2 of a method t are *same crones* if t_1 and t_2 are invoked on replicas by a same instance or by same crones. □

Each replica has to satisfy the following constraint.

[**Invocation constraint**] At most one crone instance of a method invoked in a transaction is performed on each replica. □

[**Theorem**] If every method is invoked on a replica so that the invocation constraint is satisfied, the replica is consistent. □

It is critical to identify whether or not a pair of instances issued to each replica are same crones in order to resolve the redundant invocations.

3.2   Resolution

We discuss how to resolve the redundant invocation in a transaction T so as to satisfy the invocation constraint. In order to resolve the redundant invocation, we have to make clear whether or not every pair of instances issued to a replica are same crones in the transaction. An identifier $id(t_i)$ for each instance t_i invoked on a replica of an object x is composed of a method type t and identifier of the object x, i.e. $id(t_i) = t{:}x$. Each transaction T has a unique identifier $tid(T)$, e.g. thread identifier of T. If T invokes a method t, t is assigned a transaction identifier $tid(t)$ as a concatenation of $tid(T)$ and *invocation sequence number* $iseq(T, t)$ of t in T. $iseq(T, t)$ is incremented by one each time T invokes a method. Suppose an instance t_i on a replica x_i invokes an instance u_k on a replica y_k. $id(t_i) = t{:}x$. The transaction identifier $tid(u_k)$ is $tid(t_i){:}id(t_i){:}iseq(t_i, u_k) = tid(t_i){:}t{:}x{:}iseq(t_i, u_k)$. $id(u_k) = u{:}k$. Thus, $tid(u_k)$ shows an invocation sequence of methods from T to the instance u_k. Suppose $tid(T)$ is assumed to be 6 in Figure 5. Suppose a transaction T

invokes a method t after invoking three methods, i.e. $iseq(T, t_1) = iseq(T, t_2)$ = 4. Since $tid(t_1) = tid(t_2) = tid(T){:}iseq(T, t_1) = tid(T){:}iseq(T, t_2) = 6{:}4$ and $id(t_1) = id(t_2) = t{:}x$, t_1 and t_2 are same crone instances. t invokes another method u after invoking one method. $tid(u_{11}) = tid(u_{12}) = tid(t_1){:}id(t_1){:}2 = 6{:}4{:}t{:}x{:}2$. $tid(u_{21}) = tid(u_{22}) = tid(t_2){:}id(t_2){:}2 = 6{:}4{:}t{:}x{:}2$. Since $tid(u_{11}) = tid(u_{21})$, u_{11} and u_{21} are same crone instances on a replica y_1. Another idea to identify each instance is that $tid(t_i)$ is just a identifier of the transaction T. Every instance invoked in T has same identifier $tid(T)$. Suppose T invokes a method v and then v invokes u. A replica y_i receives a pair of requests of u from different instances of t and u. Here, the instances of u have to be performed on y_i. However, the instances have the same identifier. Thus, if the transaction identifier is taken as tid of each instance, we cannot differentiate crone instances and instances which are invoked by different methods. Hence, we take an identifier which shows an invocation sequence as presented here.

[**Theorem**] Let t_1 and t_2 be instances of a method t. $tid(t_1) = tid(t_2)$ iff t_1 and t_2 are same crone instances of the method t invoked in a transaction. □

Suppose a method t is invoked on a replica x_h. There is a log L_h where information on methods performed on x_h are stored. The method t is performed on x_h as follows:

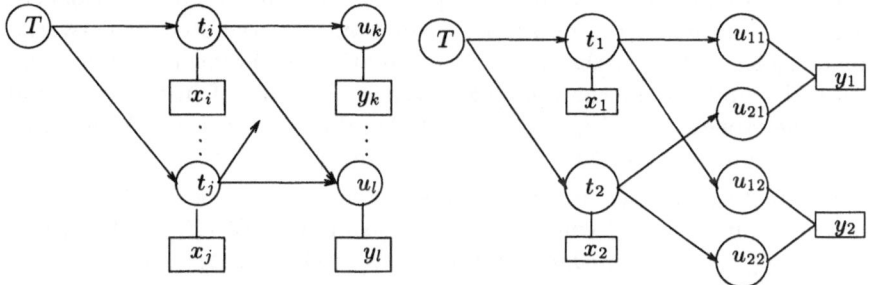

Fig. 4. Invocation on multiple replicas.   **Fig. 5.** Redundant invocation.

1. If the log L_h is empty, an instance t_h is performed and a response res of t is sent back. $\langle t, res, tid(t_h) \rangle$ is stored in the log L_h.
2. If $\langle t, res, tid(t'_h) \rangle$ such that $tid(t_h) = tid(t'_h)$ is found in L_h, the response res of t'_h is sent back as the response of t_h without performing t_h. Otherwise, t is performed on the replica x_h as presented at step 1.

In Figure 5, u_{11} is performed on the replica y_1. $\langle u$, response of u_{11}, $tid(u_{11})\rangle$ is stored in the log L_1. Then, u_{21} is issued. Since $tid(u_{11}) = tid(u_{21})$, u_{11} and u_{21} are same crones. u_{21} is not performed but the response of u_{11} as the response of u_{21} is sent to t_2. By the resolution of the redundant invocation presented here, at most one crone instance is surely performed on each replica. In addition, each method can be performed on some replica even if a replica is faulty.

4   Quorum Explosion

4.1   Basic protocol

In Figure 5, suppose quorums $Q_{u1} = \{y_1, y_2\}$ and $Q_{u2} = \{y_2, y_3\}$ are specified
for invokers t_1 and t_2 of a method u, respectively. The method u is performed
on each replica in a subset $Q = Q_{u1} \cup Q_{u2} = \{y_1, y_2, y_3\}$. Suppose another
transaction manipulates replicas y_3 and y_4 of the object y in the quorum Q_u
through the method u. $|Q_{u1} \cup Q_{u2}| (= 3) \geq N_u (= 2)$. This means that more
number of replicas are manipulated than the quorum number N_u. Then,
the instances of the method u on the replicas in $Q_{u1} \cup Q_{u2}$ issue further
requests to other replicas and more number of replicas are manipulated. This
is *quorum explosion*.

[Definition] A quorum of an object x for a method t is *exploded* in a transaction T if same crone instances of t invoked in T are performed on more
number of replicas of x than the quorum number N_t of t. □

Suppose a method t on an object x invokes a method u on an object y.
Let Q_{uh} be a quorum of the method u invoked by an instance t_h of t on a
replica x_h. In order to resolve the quorum explosion, Q_{uh} and Q_{uk} have to be
the same for every pair of replicas x_h and x_k. If $Q_{uh} = Q_{uk} = Q_u$, only the
same replicas are manipulated for every instance of the method u. If some
method is frequently invoked, the replicas in the quorum are overloaded. In
distributed systems, the quorum information is distributed in networks. If
some replica is faulty, the quorum information including the faulty replica
has to be updated in the networks. $Q_{ui} = Q_{uj}$ only if instances t_i and t_j
are same crones. $Q_{ui} \neq Q_{uj}$ if t_i and t_j are different crones. We introduce a
following function *select* to decide a quorum:

1. A function $select(i, n, a)$ gives a set of n numbers out of $1, \ldots, a$ for a
   same initial value i where $n \leq a$. For example, $select(i, n, a) = \{h \mid h = (i + \lceil \frac{a}{n} \rceil (j - 1)) \bmod a$ for $j = 1, \ldots, n\} \subseteq \{1, \ldots, a\}$.
2. Suppose an instance t_h on a replica x_h invokes a method u.
   $I = select(numb(tid(t_h)), N_u, b)$ is obtained, where N_u is quorum
   number of u and b is a total number of replicas, i.e. $\{y_1, \ldots, y_b\}$.
   Let $tid(t_h)$ be $s_1{:}s_2{:}\cdots{:}s_g$. Here, $numb(tid(t_h))$ is given as $(s_1 + \cdots + s_g)$
   modulo a. $I \subseteq \{1, \ldots, b\}$. Then, $Q_h = \{y_i \mid i \in I\}$.

Every pair of same crone instances have the same transaction identifier
tid as presented in the preceding subsection. Hence, $select(numb(tid(t_h)),$
$N_u, b) = select(numb(tid(t_k)), N_u, b)$ for every pair of crone instances t_h
and t_k. An instance t_h on every replica x_h issues a method u to the same
quorum $Q_{uh} (= Q_u)$. Hence, no quorum explosion occurs [Figure 6].

Some replica may be faulty. Suppose a method t invokes a method u on
replicas of an object y. Let Y be a set $\{y_1, \ldots, y_b\}$ of replicas of the object
y. Here, suppose some replica y_h is faulty. Here, the quorum number N_u can
be decremented by one as far as at most k replicas of y are faulty, i.e. $N_u + N_v - b = k$ for every method v conflicting with u. In one case, an invoker,

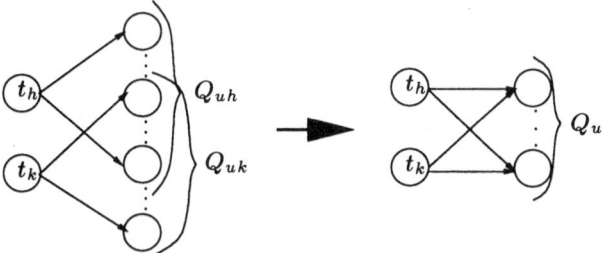

Fig. 6. Resolution of quorum explosion.

say t_i, does not know that y_h is faulty. Here, by using *select*, a quorum Q_{ui} including N_u replicas in Y are selected. In another case, t_i knows y_h is faulty. If $y_h \in Q_{ui}$, y_h is removed from Q_{ui}. Here, $|Q_{ui}| = N_u - 1$. Unless $y_h \in Q_{ui}$, $|Q_{ui}| = N_u$. There is no need u is issued to N_u replicas. The method u is required to be issued to at least $N_u - 1$ replicas. Therefore, one replica y_l is removed from Q_{ui}. For example, a replica y_l where l is the minimum in Q_{ui} is selected and removed from Q_{ui}. If a faulty replica is recovered, *views* on locations and status of the replicas are resynchronized.

4.2 Modified protocol

Each instance t_h on a replica x_h issues a request u to N_u replicas of the object y. Hence, totally $N_t \cdot N_u$ requests are transmitted. We try to reduce the number of requests transmitted in the network. Let Q_u be a quorum $\{y_1, \ldots, y_b\}$ ($b = N_u$) of the method u obtained by the function *select* for each instance t_h. If each instance t_h issues a method u to only a subset $Q_{uh} \subseteq Q_u$, the number of method requests issued to the replicas of the object y can be reduced. Here, $Q_{u1} \cup \ldots \cup Q_{ua} = Q_u$.

In order to tolerate the fault of a replica, each replica y_k in Q_u is required to receive a method request u from more than one instance of the method t. Let r (≥ 1) be a *redundancy factor*, i.e. the number of requests of the method u to be issued to each replica y_k in Q_u. For each instance t_h on a replica x_h in $Q_t = \{x_1, \ldots x_a\}$ where $a = N_t$, Q_{uh} is constructed for the method u as follows ($h = 1, \ldots, a$):

If $a \geq b \cdot r$,
$$Q_{uh} = \begin{cases} \{y_k \mid k = \lceil \frac{hb}{a} \rceil\} & \text{if } h \leq r \cdot b. \\ \phi & \text{otherwise.} \end{cases}$$
If $a < b \cdot r$,
$$Q_{uh} = \{\, y_k \mid (1 + \lfloor \tfrac{(h-1)b}{a} \rfloor) \leq k < [\, 1 + (\lfloor \tfrac{(h+r-1)b}{a} \rfloor - 1)\, mod\ b\,]\}.$$

For example, suppose there are three instances t_1, t_2, and t_3 on replicas x_1, x_2, and x_3 of the object x, respectively. Here, $Q_t = \{x_1, x_2, x_3\}$. Each of the instance issues a request u to replicas y_1, y_2, y_3, and y_4 of the object y. $Q_u = \{y_1, y_2, y_3, y_4\}$. Suppose the redundancy factor r is 2. Hence, Q_{uh}

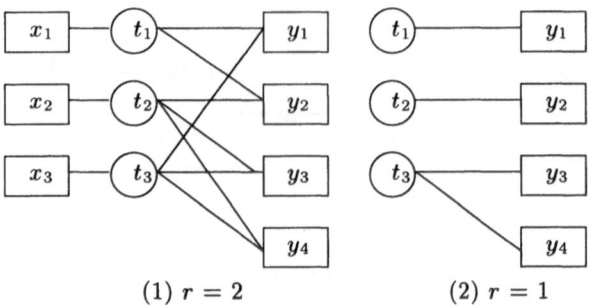

(1) $r = 2$ (2) $r = 1$

Fig. 7. Invocations.

$= \{y_k \mid (1 + (\lfloor \frac{(h-1)4}{3} \rfloor) \leq k \leq (1 + (\lfloor \frac{(h-1)4}{3} \rfloor + \lfloor \frac{8}{3} \rfloor - 1) \; modulo \; 4)\}.$
Hence, $Q_{u1} = \{y_1, y_2\}$, $Q_{u2} = \{y_2, y_3, y_4\}$, and $Q_{u3} = \{y_3, y_4, y_1\}$ for $r = 2$ [Figure 7(1)]. Two requests from the instances of the method t are issued to each replica of the object y. For example, suppose an instance t_1 on the replica x_1 is faulty. Another instance t_2 sends u to the replicas y_2, y_3, and y_4 in Q_{u2} and the other instance t_3 sends u to the replicas in Q_{u3}. Since $Q_{u2} \cup Q_{u3} = \{y_1, y_2, y_3, y_4\}$, u is sent to every replica in Q_u even if t_1 is faulty. $Q_{u1} = \{y_1\}$, $Q_{u2} = \{y_2\}$, and $Q_{u3} = \{y_3, y_4\}$ for $r = 1$ [Figure 7(2)]. Thus, totally $r \cdot N_u$ requests of the method u are issued to the replicas in Q_u. As long as fewer number of instances of the method t than r are faulty, u is performed on N_u replicas of y.

5   Evaluation

We evaluate the QB protocol to resolve the redundant invocation and quorum explosion in nested invocations of methods on replicas in terms of number of replicas manipulated and number of requests issued. We consider three protocols R, Q, and N. In the protocol Q, the redundant invocation is prevented but the quorum explosion is not resolved. The protocol R shows the QB protocol where neither redundant invocation nor quorum explosion occurs. In the protocol N, redundant invocation and quorum explosion may occur.

In the evaluation, we take a simple invocation model where a transaction T first invokes a method t_1 on an object x_1, then t_1 invokes a method t_2 on x_2, $\cdots$ as shown in Figure 8. Here, let a_i be the number of replicas of an object x_i ($i = 1, 2, \ldots$). Let N_i be the quorum number of a method t_i ($N_i \leq a_i$), where i shows a level of invocation. A transaction T first issues N_1 requests of the method t_1 to the replicas of the object x_1. Then, each instance of t_1 on a replica issues N_2 requests of t_2 to the replicas of x_2. In the protocol N, a method t_2 invoked by each instance of t_1 is performed. Here, totally $N_1 \cdot N_2$ requests are performed on the replicas of x_2. In the protocol Q, at most one instance of t_2 is performed on each replica of x_2 by the resolution procedure of the redundant invocation. Since the quorum explosion is not resolved, the expected number QE_2 of replicas where t_2 is performed is $a_2[1$

$- (1 - \frac{N_2}{a_2})^{N_1}]$. Then, each instance of t_2 issues requests of t_3 to N_3 replicas of x_3. Here, $a_3[1 - (1 - \frac{N_3}{a_3})^{N_1 N_2}]$ replicas are manipulated in the protocol N and $QE_3 = a_3[1 - (1 - \frac{N_3}{a_3})^{QE_2}]$ replicas in the protocol Q. In the protocol R, t_2 is performed on only N_2 replicas of the object x_2.

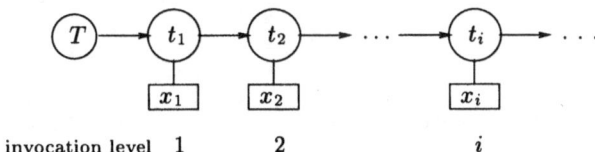

invocation level   1   2   i

Fig. 8. Invocation model.

We assume that each object x_i has the same number of replicas and every method t_i has the same size of quorum, i.e. $a_1 = a_2 = \ldots = a = 10$ and $N_1 = N_2 = \ldots = N$ ($\leq a$). Figure 9 shows the ratios of replicas where a method is performed to the quorum number a ($= 10$) at each invocation level i for $N = 3$. The dotted line with white circles shows the ratio for the protocol R. The straight line indicates the protocol N and the other dotted line with black circles shows the protocol Q. If methods are invoked at a deeper level than two for $N = 3$, all the replicas are manipulated if neither the redundant invocation nor quorum explosion are prevented. In the protocol R, only the quorum number of replicas, i.e. three replicas, in ten replicas are manipulated at any invocation level.

Figure 10 shows the number of request messages transmitted by crone instances of a method t_i for $N = 3$. The vertical axis shows $log(m)$ for the number m of requests issued. In the protocol N, N^i request messages are issued to replicas of the object x_i because N^{i-1} crone instances are performed on replicas of the object x_{i-1}. In the protocol Q, there are $a[1 - (1 - \frac{N}{a})^{QE_{i-2}}]$ replicas of x_{i-1} where crone instances of a method t_{i-1} are performed. Hence, $a[1 - (1 - \frac{N}{a})^{QE_{i-2}}]N$ request messages are transmitted. In the protocol R, we assume the redundancy factor $r = N$ in this evaluation. N^2 request messages are transmitted.

6   Concluding Remarks

In this paper, we discussed how transactions invoke methods on multiple replicas of objects. The object supports abstract methods. In addition, methods are invoked in a nested manner. If methods are invoked on multiple replicas, multiple redundant instances of a same method may be performed on a replica and more number of replicas than the quorum number may be manipulated. We discussed the QB (quorum-based) protocol where redundant invocations and quorum explosions to occur are resolved in systems. By using the QB protocol with the resolution of redundant invocations and quorum explosions, an object-based system including replicas of objects can be efficiently realized.

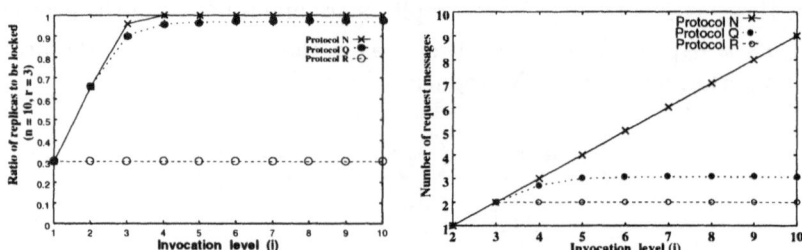

Fig. 9. Ratio of replicas manipulated **Fig. 10.** Number of request messages
($a = 10$ and $N = 3$).   issued ($a = 10$ and $N = 3$).

References

1. Ahamad, M., Dasgupta, P., LeBlanc R., and Wilkes, C. (1987): Fault Tolerant Computing in Object Based Distributed Operating Systems, *Proc. 6th IEEE SRDS*, 115–125.
2. Barrett, P. A., Hilborne, A. M., Bond, P. G., and Seaton, D. T. (1990): The Delta-4 Extra Performance Architecture, *Proc. 20th Int'l Symp. on FTCS*, 481–488.
3. Birman, K. P. and Joseph, T. A. (1987): Reliable Communication in the Presence of Failures, *ACM TOCS*, 5(1), 47–76.
4. Borg, A., Baumbach, J., and Glazer, S. (1983): A Message System Supporting Fault Tolerance, *Proc. 9th ACM Symp. on Operating Sys. Principles*, 27–39.
5. Carey, J. M. and Livny, M. (1991): Conflict Detection Tradeoffs for Replicated Data, *ACM TODS*, 16(4), 703–746.
6. Chevalier, P. -Y. (1992): A Replicated Object Server for a Distributed Object-Oriented System, *Proc. IEEE SRDS*, 4-11.
7. Garcia-Molina, H. and Barbara, D. (1985): How to Assign Votes in a Distributed System, *JACM*, 32(4), 841-860.
8. Gifford, D. K. (1979): Weighted Voting for Replicated Data, *Proc. 7th ACM Symp. on Operating Systems Principles*, 150-159
9. Jing, J., Bukhres, O., and Elmagarmid, A. (1995): Distributed Lock Management for Mobile Transactions, *Proc. IEEE ICDCS-15*, 118-125.
10. Korth, H. F. (1983): Locking Primitives in a Database System, *JACM*, 30(1), 55-79.
11. Powell, D., Chereque, M., and Drackley, D. (1991): Fault-Tolerance in Delta-4, *ACM Operating System Review*, 25(2), 121–125.
12. Silvano, M. and Douglas, C. S. (1997): Constructing Reliable Distributed Communication Systems with CORBA, *IEEE Comm. Magazine*, 35(2), 56–60.
13. Tanaka, K., Hasegawa, K., and Takizawa, M. (2000): Quorum-Based Replication in Object-Based Systems, *Journal of Information Science and Engineering (JISE)*, 16, 317–331.
14. Tanaka, K. and Takizawa, M. (2000): Quorum-Based Replication of Objects, *Proc. 3rd DEXA Int'l Workshop on Network-Based Information Systems (NBIS-3)*, 33–37.

Intelligence in Information Society

Matjaž Gams

Jozef Stefan Institute, Jamova 39, Ljubljana, Slovenia, Europe
E-mail: matjaz.gams@ijs.si

Abstract--Basic properties of the forthcoming information society are analyzed with the emphasis on emerging intelligence. It is claimed that one of the major properties is information overload and intelligent assistants are the best way to fight it. Information society initiated the emergence of primitive network intelligence demonstrated through intelligent assistants agents on the Internet and on PCs. The introduction of intelligent systems, and particularly intelligent agents in Slovenia is analyzed. Finally, the EMA employment agent, one of important intelligent agent applications in Central Europe, is described in detail, especially the feature that enables gathering information from the Internet.

Keywords: information age, Internet, intelligent agents, intelligent assistants, overview.

1   Introduction

We are already in information society and information-technology dominated economy. By 2002, it is predicted that over 80 million Europeans will have access to the Internet, and that 5 % of EU gross domestic product will be affected by the use of digital systems. In 1998, nearly around 9 million American households generated $8 billion sales in USA. In comparison, only $1.2 billion were accounted for online shopping in Europe. Although lagging behind USA, Europe is recently progressing much faster. Forecasts predict that 500.000 e-commerce-related jobs will be created within the next few years. Each year, Web sales to consumers are expected to grow by 70%. This growth is expected to be exponential for several years.

The backbone of the information age is the Internet (Etzioni 1996; http://www.cio.com/WebMaster/metcalfe1.html). Another important improvement is the emergence of network intelligence that represents a natural step in the computational evolution heading towards more helpful, adaptive and creative programs. These programs are essential for humans because without intelligent assistants we cannot cope with information overload. Internet services evolved towards intelligent systems and intelligent agents. Agents are software programs that, with some degree of autonomy, perform operations on behalf of a human user or another program. They help automate a variety of activities, mostly time consuming ones. We identify information society laws in Section 2. In Section 3 we analyse intelligent systems. The first major application of intelligent agents in Slovenia, the EMA employment agent, is described in Section 4.

2 Information Society

Information society laws are described in several publications (Lewis 1998; Metcalfe 1997), particularly in (Metcalf 1999). Here we represent major laws published elsewhere and add a couple of our own:

Moore's Law (http://www.whatis.com/mooresla.htm) describes a constant trend in chip properties. The chip capacity doubles in a time span from 1.5 to 2 years depending on the type of particular performance of a chip. The formula is: Performance(new) = Performance(old)   * 1.5 time where "time" is the number of years.   The basic property of the law - the constant exponential growth - remains unchanged over several decades (Moore 1975, Hamilton 1999).

Metcalfe's Law (http://www.cuug.ab.ca/~branderr/csce/ metcalfe.html) says that the value of a network is proportional to the square of the number of nodes, connected by the network: Value = K   * nodes2. In other words, the bigger the net, the square bigger the value. "K" is a constant.

Sidgemore's Law determines the growth of traffic over nets. The law says that the traffic doubles every three months: Traffic(new) = Traffic(old) * 2(4 time).

Andreesen's   Law says that the cost of bandwidth is dropping exponentially and inversely proportional to Sidgemore's law: Cost(new) = Cost(old) * 1/2 (4 time).

Lewis/Flemig's Law describes the network type of capitalism. It denotes nearly "friction-free economy" in the sense that there is small marginal cost and a huge shelf space. The exponential growth indicates that huge profits will award a genuine new market idea. But in addition to quick rise, an exponential decline is expected when new, more advanced systems appear on the market. The equation describing the law is: MarketShare(time) = 1/(1+ K * B * time) where "K" is a constant. The "B" parameter denotes the learning parameter.

Put on the Internet all your information and information activities. This law means that it is cheaper to put information and information activities on the Web sooner than later (Petrie et al. 1998). Not only it is indeed cheaper and more cost-effective than when done in a standard way, it is also the only way to go along with competition.

The cyber-world doubles fortune. Besides the material world we actually live in, the cyber-copy of our world matures. Since the introduction of the cyber-world in effect tends to double activities and money in circulation, stories of reach youngsters or rich Internet population in the developed countries are well grounded by a general trend. It also guarantees further growth of the developed world despite saturation in other human activities, which are related to classical material world. Another important trend is that our information systems on computers are becoming more and more a cyber-copy of ourselves.

Side effect of information society is information overload. In infosphere we have to cope with more and more information from one month to another in order just to stay competitive. As a consequence, the information overload causes disappearance of free time; it causes the brain overload and decrease in classical human social life.

Information society demands intensive information knowledge for successful leadership. It is commonly accepted that there is a huge gap between existing knowledge of top executives, politicians and other leaders, and the desired knowledge for successful managing and leadership (O'Leary 1997). The gap is higher in Europe than in USA, and higher in Slovenia than in EU.

Information society belongs to all of us. In a democratic society there are several institutions cooperating in the process of governing and creating strategic directions. Among essential institutions of democratic societies are civil institutions (Borenstein 1998). Information society is by definition a civil society although governmental institutions typically implement it. An example would be Clinton's advocating of information highway or several governmental information society projects in Europe; e.g. Bangemann's reports (http://europa.eu.int/comm/dg03/speechba.htm). In countries like Slovenia, lacking richness of civil society structures developed in decades of Western democracy, the introduction of Internet is a major inhibitor of faster progress.

The Internet is the most democratic and free media in the world. This was legally established with the American Supreme Court decisions about pornography and free speech on the Internet. In the simplest way it can be observed as a fact that pornography (inside "reasonable" limits) is allowed on the Internet and not on TV. It also means that anarchy and even criminal organizations can exploit this freedom, but the freedom of speech is accompanied by the fact that in such a case sooner or later we are going to hear things we don't like. Whatever the case, the Internet is the most democratic media humans ever had. While countries differ in their social and economic order, the Internet enhances democracy and civil society regardless of their previous level.

The Internet and information society are our hope for the future. There have been many technological innovations that spurred human progress. For example, we speak of the "iron age" historic period. These days we speak of the "information age" or of the "information society" age. Not only new technology changes the way we live in the technical sense; the changes are essential also in the way society functions (Negroponte 1998). At the same time, the world of computer systems we use is rapidly changing due to the massive introduction of information activities. The trend is towards more user-friendly intelligent systems.

3   Intelligent Systems

Intelligent systems are computer systems aimed at developing advanced user-friendly systems that work in real-life environments (Goonatilake, Treleaven 1995; Bielawski, Lewland 1991). The Internet is the media enabling substantial advantages for intelligent systems (Etzioni 1996; Etzioni 1997). Intelligent systems use a wide variety of artificial intelligence techniques typically implemented on top of classical modules (Bratko, Muggleton 1995): rule-based systems, production systems, expert systems, fuzzy logic systems, neural networks, memory-based reasoning. Advanced systems often combine various methods into one hybrid or integrated system (Gams et al., 1996). The emphasis of intelligent systems design is on combination of AI methods and engineering techniques enabling construction of systems performing practical tasks better than classical systems.

The major application areas of intelligent systems on the Internet are (Levy, Weld 2000):

- User modeling
- Discovery and analysis of remote information systems
- Discovery
- Extraction
- Translation
- Evaluation
- Information integration, and
- Web-site management.

Intelligent agents (Bradshaw 1997; Mueller 1996) are a special branch of intelligent systems, capable of learning, adapting to the environment, to each specific user, and to each specific situation as much as possible. According to Pattie Maes (Maes at al. 1999) intelligent agents are an important step ahead in humanising computers. Intelligent agents represent personal assistants collaborating with the user in the same environment (Maes, 1994; Minsky, 1987; 1991). Intelligent agents are basically intelligent interfaces providing specific utilities of the system while the core of the system is typically an Internet based query or database system. Unlike passive query languages, agents and humans initiate communications, monitor events and perform tasks. The essential properties of agents are autonomy and sociability (Bradshaw 1997; Jennings, Wooldridge 1995; 1997; Etzioni, Weld 1995).

Software agents differ from "traditional" software in their ability to get personalized and social (Gutman et al.1998). Agents are also semi-autonomous and can run continuously. We distinguish four categories of agent functionality:

- Problem-solving (typical research agents; intelligent agents, expert systems)
- User-centric (interaction with user; "intelligent" filtering, user guidance)
- Control (exclusive in multiagent systems, control services for other agents)
- Translation agents (bridge between systems with different data standards).

4   EMA

We have implemented a couple of major intelligent systems in this part of Europe. One example is an intelligent system for controlling quality of the Sendzimir rolling mill emulsion (Gams et al. 1996). Practically all-national production of rolling steel is manufactured through this machine. The application represents one of major national intelligent system in regular industrial use. In addition to this application, the department has in the last ten years designed around 10 intelligent systems now available on the Internet http://turing.ijs.si/Ales/katalog-a/KATALOG-A.html.

In 1993, the first agent was designed in Slovenia - IOI, an Intelligent Operating Interface (Hribovsek 1994; Gams, Hribovsek 1996). The basic task of IOI was correcting typing errors and providing help for users communicating with the VAX/VMS operating systems. IOI is an intelligent agent able to learn, adapt, and communicate in a relatively complex environment with human users. Its most important property is self-learning through observing the user performing tasks in the environment. Later, IOI uses accumulated knowledge through user experience to advise new users. The system thus performs a task similar to MS Office Assistant with the essential difference that knowledge in Assistant is coded in advance while IOI constructs most of its knowledge through user observation.

IOI is implemented as a 2000-line program in Pascal with parts of it written in the VAX/VMS command language. The IOI agent was implemented as a research prototype only, however, its flexibility and adaptability as a personal intelligent agent have shown reasonable improvements over classical systems. The most positive properties as observed by users in the testing period, are: IOI is easy to use, it does not demand specific knowledge, is easy to learn and use, and is very transparent. These favourable properties are typical intelligent-agent properties. Two other major intelligent agents developed in Slovenia are Personal WebWatcher (Mladenic 1998) and Ema (Gams et al. 1998).

The EMA project   (see Figure 1) started seven years ago as an R&D project "An Integrated Information System for Employment in Slovenia" to provide help regarding unemployment problems. The project was partly funded by the Slovenian Ministry of Science and Technology and partly by the Employment Service of Slovenia   (ESS). The system consists of two parts; one is applied at the Employment   Service   of   Slovenia (http://www.ess.gov.si/English/elementi-okvirjev/F-Introduction.htm) where one gets basic information about employment activities in Slovenia, about ESS, and about interesting employment functions. The top part of the system is the EMA agent. For the last three years, the system was further developed as part of the INCO-Copernicus Project: 960154, cooperative research in information infrastructure, CRII (http://www-ai.ijs.si/~ema/proj.html). The intelligent system/agent EMA with a natural language interface consists of several modules.

EMA has four basic functional modules: storing patterns and ordering mails regarding vacant jobs, available workers, it enables storing and observing interesting WEB sites chosen by users, and enables matching jobs and workers. EMA is a "classical" agent providing user-friendly information upon demand or when it notices relevant information for each particular user. The system is a 15.000 lines program written mainly in C, partially in other languages. Together with text and data it occupies 30 M on a disk.

EMA receives data as natural-language Slovenian text and translates it into English. The translation is based on a dictionary consisting of up to four words observed before in the employment data. New combinations are in the worst case translated as direct word-by-word translation and stored for further overview by humans. Stored combinations are sorted by frequency and translated by humans if reasonable. In addition, the translation system looks into the morphology dictionary to capture different forms of the same words. Finally, a spell-checker submodule corrects spelling errors. The translation is currently not yet at the level performed by systems translating between larger European languages, however, it is sufficiently good to enable understanding since the syntax is quite limited.

In the next stage, the text is transformed into appropriate computer readable forms and HTML forms as outputs. Two speech modules transform the data into speech. The English speech system is based on the Microsoft agents. We have designed our own Slovenian speech module (Sef et al. 1998).

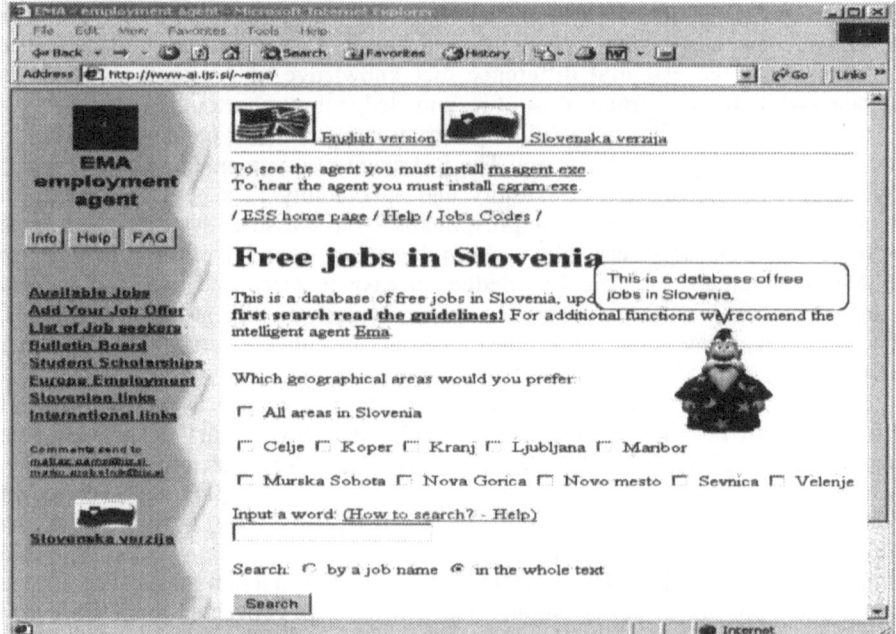

Figure 1: The EMA employment agent was the forth in Europe providing national employment information and among the first in the world to offer over 90% of nationally.

With EMA, we have in a real-life application with hit rate over 300.000 per months tested aspects of intelligent agents and intelligent systems. In particular, we have dealt with

- User modeling when modeling users
- Discovery and analysis of remote information systems when translating data, applying machine learning and data-mining methods when extracting data from data-bases,
- Information integration when integrating information from various sources, from several internal databases as well
- form the Internet HTML files and databases accessed through file wrappers, and
- Web-site management with our real-life application consisting of several 10 WEB pages that constantly changed over the 7-year period.

The EMA agent was and still is among most successful applications of intelligent agents in Slovenia. In the first year of its implementation, our country was the third in Europe to offer national employment·information through the Internet. At that time, we were the first country in the world to provide over 90% of all nationally available jobs on the Internet.

5 Conclusion

We are able to establish general information society laws while specific details and further progress remain enigma to all of us. Intelligent systems and agents through the Internet and partially through PCs form the new software generation, the intelligent systems generation. Especially the Internet provides a gold mine of opportunities for intelligent systems. While current systems still lack true human intelligence and consciousness, the primitive network intelligence emerges consisting of intelligent assistants capable of autonomous and social activities (Munindar 1997; Mylopoulos 1997).

In countries all over the world, information society is perceived as a global phenomenon and as a major technological field, which can bring fortune or stagnation. While globalisation represents a potential threat to less developed countries to push them into information colonies, potential benefits are enormous. The essential question is whether the existing or at least the forthcoming generation of national political and business leaders will fully embrace the information-age rules of the game.

Acknowledgement

Financial support for the EMA project was provided by an international project INCO-Copernicus 960154, Cooperative Research in Information Infrastructure, CRII; by the Ministry of science and technology in Slovenia; and by ESS. We would like to thank the CEO of the Employment Service of Slovenia, Mr. J. Glazer

References

1. L. Bielawski, R. Lewland, Intelligent Systems Design; Integrating Expert systems, Hypermedia and Database Technologies, Wiley, 1991.
2. N. S. Borenstein, "Whose Net is it Anyway", Communications of the ACM, April 1998, pp. 19-21.
3. M. Bradshaw (ed.), Software Agents, AAAI Press/The MIT Press, 1997.
4. I. Bratko, S. Muggleton, "Applications of Inductive Logic Programming", Communications of the ACM, Vol. 38, No. 11, 1995, pp. 65-70.
5. O. Etzioni, D.S. Weld, "Intelligent Agents on the Internet: Fact, Fiction, and Forecast", IEEE EXPERT, Intelligent Systems & Their Applications, Vol. 10, No. 4, 1995, pp. 44-49.
6. O. Etzioni, "The WWW: Quagmire or Gold Mine?", Communications of the ACM, Vol. 39, No. 11, 1996, pp. 65-68.
7. O. Etzioni, "Moving Up the Information Food Chain", AI Magazine, Vol. 18, No. 2, 1997, pp. 11-18.
8. M. Gams, B. Hribovšek, "Intelligent-Personal-Agent Interface for Operating Systems", Applied Artificial Intelligence, Vol. 10, 1996, pp. 353-383.
9. M. Gams, M. Drobniè, N. Karba, "Average-Case Improvements when Integrating ML and KA", Applied Intelligence 6, No. 2, 1996, pp. 87-99.
10. M. Gams, A. Karaliè, M. Drobniè, V. Križman, "EMA - An Intelligent Employment Agent", Proc. of the Forth World Congress on Expert Systems, Mexico, 1998, pp. 57-64.

11. S. Goonatilake, P. Treleaven (eds.), Intelligent Systems for Finance and Business, Wiley, 1995.
12. R. H. Gutmann, A. G. Moukas, P. Maes, Agents as Mediators in Electronic Commerce, Electronic Markets, Vol. 8, No. 1, pp. 22-27, January 1998.
13. S. Hamilton, "Taking Moore's Law into the Next Century", IEEE Computer, Januar 1999, pp. 43-48.
14. B. Hribovsek: Intelligent Interface for VAX/VMS, M. Sc. Thesis (in Slovene).
15. N.R. Jennings, M. Wooldridge, "Intelligent Agents and Multi-Agent Systems", Applied Artificial Intelligence, An International Journal, Vol. 9, 1995, pp. 357-369.
16.   N.R. Jennings, M. Wooldridge, Agent Technology, Springer, 1997.
17. A.Y. Levy, D.S. Weld (eds.), "Special Issue on Intelligent Internet Systems", Artificial Intelligence, Vol. 118, no. 1-2, April 2000.
18. M. Lewis, "Designing for Human-Agent Interaction", AI Magazine, Vol. 19, No. 2, 1998, pp. 67-78.
19. M. Lewis, "Microsoft Rising", IEEE Computer Society, 1999.
20. P. Maes, "Agents that Reduce Work and Information Overload", Communications of the ACM, 37, 1994, pp. 31-40.
21. P. Maes, R.H. Guttman, A. G. Moukas, "Agents That Buy and Sell", Communications of the ACM, Vol. 42, No. 3, 1999, pp. 81-91.
22. B. Metcalfe, "What's Wrong with the Internet", IEEE Internet Computing, 1997, pp. 6-8.
23. M. Minsky, The Society of Mind, Simon and Schuster, New York, 1987.
24. M. Minsky, "Society of mind: a response to four reviews", Artificial Intelligence 48, 1991, pp. 371-396.
25. D. Mladenic, "Turning Yahoo into an Automatic Web-Page Classifier", in Proceedings of the 13th   ECAI'98, 1998, pp. 473-474.
26. G. E. Moore, "Progress in digital integrated electronics", Technical Digest of 1975 International Electronic Devices Meeting 11, 1975.
27. J.P. Mueller, The Design of Intelligent Agents, Springer, 1996.
28. P.S. Munindar, "Agent Communication Languages: Rethink the Principles", Computer, December 1997, pp. 40-47.
29. J. Mylopoulos, "Cooperative Information Systems", IEEE EXPERT, Intelligent Systems & Their Applications, Vol. 12, No. 5,   1997, pp. 28-30.
30. N. Negroponte, "A Wired Worldview", EU RTD info, March 1998, pp. 28-30.
31. D. E. O'Leary, "A Lack of Knowledge at the Top", IEEE Expert, November 1997, p. 2.
32. C. J. Petrie, A. M. Rutkovski, M. Zacks etc., "Dimensioning the Internet", IEEE Internet Computing, April 1998, pp. 8-9.
33. T. Sef, A. Dobnikar and M. Gams, "Improvements in Slovene Text-to-Speech Synthesis",Proceedings ICSLP'98, pp. 2027-2030, 1998, Sydney.

Part II

Collaborative Internet, Multimedia and

Electronic Commerce

The Internet Group Tour via a Shared Web Browser

Jianhua Ma and Runhe Huang

Hosei University, Tokyo 184-8584, Japan
E-mail: jianhua@k.hosei.ac.jp

Abstract. When a group of people would like to visit or access the Internet together, it is necessary to have a shared web browser following the mode of what-you-
see-is-what-I-see (WYSIWIS) that allows all group members to make inputs to the
browser and distributes the results among the all members. This article presents
our design and implementation of such a shared browser using the server-client
model and Java technology. All users who connect to a same server of a shared
browser belong to a same group and see a same web page. Different groups must
run their own browsers'servers. The browser enables a group of users to simultaneously view web documents and synchronously share operations on the browser and
web documents as well. The shared browser is designed to be used practically in
both a standalone mode and a combined mode with other shared applications. We
explains how to the shared browser into another Internet based desktop groupware
system of VCR.

1   Introduction

Both Microsoft Internet Explorer the and Netscape Communicator enables
an individual to load/view web documents in a remote site. However, it is
common in the real world that a group of people travels or visits some places
together. But the current two browsers have no function to enable such group
tour in the web based virtual world. This has motivated us to design and
develop a shared web browser with which multiple remote users can navigate
the virtual world together so long as they have computers connected to the
Internet. Using the shared browser, a group of users share not only web
documents but also operations on the web documents like inputting a new
URL to go to a new corresponding web site, clicking a hyperlink in a HTML
file to jump to another web page, changing a window size, moving the scroll
bar, and etc. The shared browser can be used standalone or jointly used with
other Internet based collaborative tools such as electronic chat, whiteboard,
audio/video conferencing, and some groupware systems like VCR (Virtual
Collaboration Room) [1] [2].

From a distributed computing point of view, the shared web browser can
be generally seen as a shared application which follows the mode of what-
you-see-is-what-I-see (WYSIWIS) that allows all users to make inputs to the
application and distributes the results among the all users [3]. Other types of

the shared applications are shared whiteboard [4],shared simulator [5], shared workspace [6], shared game, and etc. Usually, the data displayed in a shared application is either generated by the application such as typing or drawing in a whiteboard, or rendered/loaded from raw data format such as pasting a graphics/image. Different from the other shared applications, however, data, i.e., a web document to be displayed and operated in the shared browser is made by a third party and stored in remote servers owned by others. Such a difference results in new difficulties in implementing the shared browser.

One difficult is related to Java security restrictions. To be platform independent, our shared browser is implemented using Java technology. We adopt the TCP/IP based server-client model, where the server of the shared browser is a Java application and the client is a Java applet. This makes wider and more powerful applications of the shared browser. Because of security restriction, a Java applet does not allow a direct connection to another host except the host the applet came from [7] [8]. That is to say, written in the Java applet, a shared browser client cannot directly download web documents from other remote hosts. To solve this problem, it is necessary to develop an embedded proxy web server through which clients can access web documents including HTML, image, and other multimedia files in any other remote hosts.

In what follows, we first present user interface and system architecture in the next section, and then describe the proxy server in details in Section 3. Section 4 explains integration of the shared browser into the VCR. Finally, conclusions are drawn and future work is addressed in the last section.

2   User Interface and System Archutecture

The shared browser is designed to be used practically in two modes, standalone and combined use with other shared applications like chat system, whiteboard, realtime audio/video communication system, and other Internet based groupware system. As a standalone system, the server program (Java application) has to be running to wait for connections from the clients before users can use the browser by clicking a hyperlink to load and run the client program (Java applet). A web page with a hyperlink linked to the client program must be also created. When a user accesses the web page and clicks the hyperlink, the client program is downloaded to the user's local machine and starts to run. If the client successfully connects to the server, the shared browser will popped up on the user's screen as shown in Fig. 1.

All users who connect to a same server of a shared browser belong to a same group, and see a same web page. That is, a shared browser's server corresponds to only one group of users. Different groups must run their own browsers' servers in the same server machine with different socket port numbers or different web server's machines. The client program for each group must be connected to its corresponding server's IP address and socket port

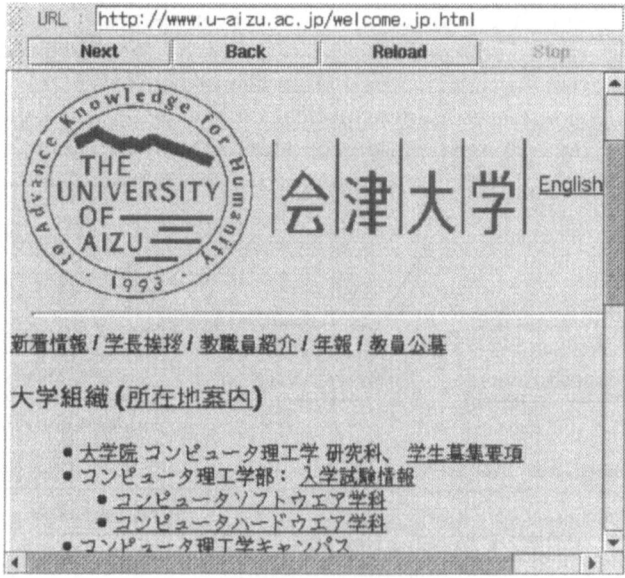

Fig. 1. A snapshot of the shared browser

number. All users in a same group share not only web documents but also operations on the browser and the documents. Our current prototype provides the following shared synchronous operations:

- Entering a URL from a shared text field for going to a new web site.
- Pressing any shared navigation buttons: `Next, Back, Reload` and `Stop`
- Clicking a shared hyperlink in a web page to go to another page/site.
- Changing the shared browser's window size. Moving the shared scroll bars for adjusting visible part of the document.

Before designing a shared web browser, first we have to clarify the requirements of the shared browser system. There are two fundamental requirements: one is the uniform display of any web documents in any other web sites, and the other is the synchronous operations on the browser and any web documents. As stated above, the shared browser client is a Java applet that can only connect to a host the applet came from due to Java security restrictions. A client is not allowed to directly connect any other machines, and it is of course unable to directly access other web documents not resided in the local host. To overcome this problem, a proxy server is required to run within the shared browser server as shown in Fig. 2. The proxy server is software program written in Java application that is familiar with several specific protocols like HTTP and FTP that it relays. A client will make a request through the Internet to the proxy server instead of connecting directly to a remote service, and the proxy server will perform the actual request on

behalf of the client. It can be seen that the proxy server acts as a gateway
between clients and remote web sites. Via the proxy server, remote web sites
become transparent to clients. Apart from the proxy server, there is another
software program written in Java application that receives, dispatchers and
processes the synchronous operation commands from any clients and behaves
as a coordinator to provide services and synchronize events occurred among
clients.

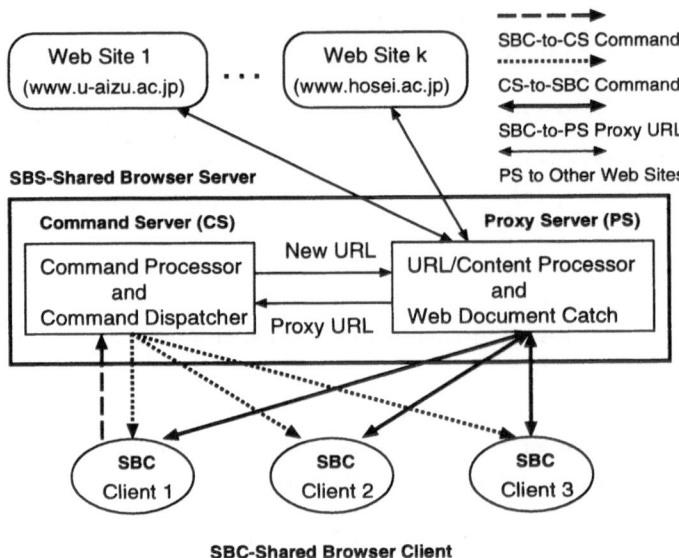

Fig. 2. The architecture of shared browser system

From the system architecture, it can be seen that the shared browser
system consists of the shared browser server (SBS) and the shared browser
client (SBC) and the SBS is composed of the command server (CS) and
the proxy server (PS). The CS is designated for receiving/closing connection
requests, processing navigation related synchronous operation events from
clients such as requesting a new URL, opening the next page, backing to the
previous page, reloading the current page, changing the window size, moving
scrollbars, and sending the corresponding synchronous operation commands
as shown in Tab. 1 to the SBCs. The SBC provides navigation functions and a
user interface where users make URL requests and navigate a web document
by clicking buttons or hyperlinks or resizing the display window as shown in
Fig. 1. Users' requests or navigation events in the SBC are caught and sent
to the SBS for handling.

Table 1. Synchronized commands

Command	Description
INIT	Initialize SBC
OPEN_URL	Open web page
OPEN_TARGET_URL	Open web page into a frame
REQUEST_URL	Request to proxy server
REQUEST_MOVE_REF	Move to #ref
NEXT_OPEN	Open a next history
BACK_OPEN	Open a before history
RELOAD	Reload a current web page
CHANGE_HORIZONTAL	Move horizontal scroll bar
CHANGE_VERTICAL	Move vertical scroll bar
CHANGE_SIZE	Change window size

3   Web Proxy Server

The main task of the proxy server in this context is to receive a requested URL
from a client, access the corresponding remote web server, and download the
requested web documents. The downloaded web documents have to be gone
through a series of necessary processing. The regenerated web documents
after processing are cached in the proxy server under the proxy root directory.
Then all clients navigate the web documents cached in the proxy server. In
this section, we explain the series of necessary processing of web documents
downloaded from the original web site. The necessary processing in the proxy
server includes URL protocol handler, content type handler, content checker,
HTML file parser, web file regenerator, and web document cache as shown
in Fig. 3.

3.1   URL Protocol Handler

The proxy server, being a gateway, is in the intersection of several protocols.
The proxy server has to be able to deal with those protocols commonly used in
web documents. Of course, the primary protocol of a web proxy is HTTP (Hypertext Transfer Protocol) that is use for transferring web documents. However, it handles requests for FTP (File Transfer Protocol) as well as the mailto
protocol. HTTP is a request/response protocol. The client sends a request to
the server and the server sends back a response. HTTP can be easily processed
in Java with java.net.URL.class and java.net.HttpURLConnection.class that
are provided by the Java Development Kit (JDK) [9]. Other protocols such
as FTP and mailto are relatively difficulty to be processed as compared with

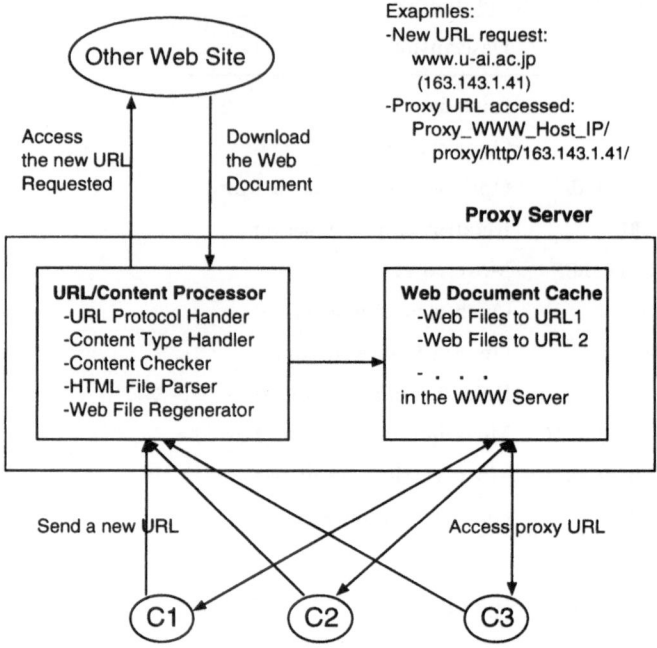

Fig. 3. The proxy sever

HTTP since there is no corresponding API provided by the JDK. Since they are also popular and very useful protocols, they are supported in our shared browser. FTP protocol is uniquely different from HTTP since FTP sessions are long-lived, typically under interactive user supervision and there is an authentication step. Therefore, the proxy server has to take some special cares to handle FTP protocol. For example, the FTP has to be connected to the port number, 21, while running a FTP server. FTP URLs with necessary authentication parameters, such as user name and password, are included in the HTTP request made to the proxy server.

3.2 Content Type Handler

Over the Internet, a variety of media objects are transmitted. The type of web objects is indicated by means of a MIME (Multipurpose Internet Mail Extension) media type. HTTP transmits the media type of the document, whether it is an HTML document, a text file, an image, audio, or video clip, or application-specific data, in the Content-Type: header. From the header, one knows the media type of the contents and encoding method as well if there is any encoding method involved. For example, the content types include text/html (charset=ISO-8859-4), text/plain, image/gif, video/mpeg, etc. The content type handler processes the MIME media type of a web document by reading its Content-Type header and parameter(s) if there is any in the response header from a remote web server. Our shared browser can handles not only text contents, but also multimedia contents by the content type handler.

3.3 Content Checker

When receiving a request to access a web page from a SBC, the content checker in the proxy server checks if the requested web page exists in the requested web site. If it exists, the proxy server downloads it from the requested URL, otherwise the proxy server responds to the SBC with an error code, FILE_NOT_FOUND. Other two error codes are UNKNOWN_PROTOCOL and UNKNOWN ERROR.

3.4 HTML File Parser

With the proxy server, users in fact access the requested web documents in the proxy server rather than in the original web site such that all downloaded web documents have to be modified or regenerated and are stored in the proxy server for users to access. To make all hyperlinks in a web document to be correctly accessible in the proxy server, some hyperlinks in the regenerated HTML files should be modified to match the file hierarchy in the proxy server that is almost same as the file hierarchy in the original web site. In particular, those absolute hyperlinks should be replaced by relative hyperlinks. The task is carried out by the HTML file parser in the proxy server. The HTML File Parser first finds out and identifies tags like <BASE>, <IMG>, <FRAME> and <A> in a web document. Then, it analyses whether any modifications should be made or not. The <BASE> tag is for solving relative hyperlinks. If an <IMG> tag exists in a HTML file, the server has to download image contents. For the <FRAME> tag, its associative contents have to be processed. The <A> tag is for solving frame targets when the <FRAME> tag exists. Finally, the parser generates a new HTML file with modified tag values. Parsing HTML without errors is very difficult because current HTML technical specifications lack uniformity and there are too many HTML tags [10].

3.5 Web Document Cache

Downloaded contents and newly generated HTML files have to be cached in the proxy server so that clients can access them. The proxy server is not an agent. It only downloads and caches requested contents. The web document cache stores regenerated web files in a same file hierarchy in the proxy server as they are in the original web site. The clients in fact access the requested web documents stored in the web document cache in the PS like general proxy servers [11].

4   Integration of the Shared Browser with VCR

The shared browser may become more effective when it is used together
with other shared application systems. The VCR, an Internet based desktop
groupware system, is designed and developed under a framework based on
a room metaphor, i.e., emulating fundamental characteristics of real rooms
and their usages [12] [13]. Like a real room having physical objects for use,
the VCR incorporates many virtual objects, i.e., sharable applications, for
example, whiteboard, chatboard, audio player, video player, voting board,
and aggregate objects in a group case, private drawer and archive. Same as
any other shared applications, the shared browser is integrated into VCR as a
shared object, as shown in the icon `Navigator` in Fig. 4. However, integration

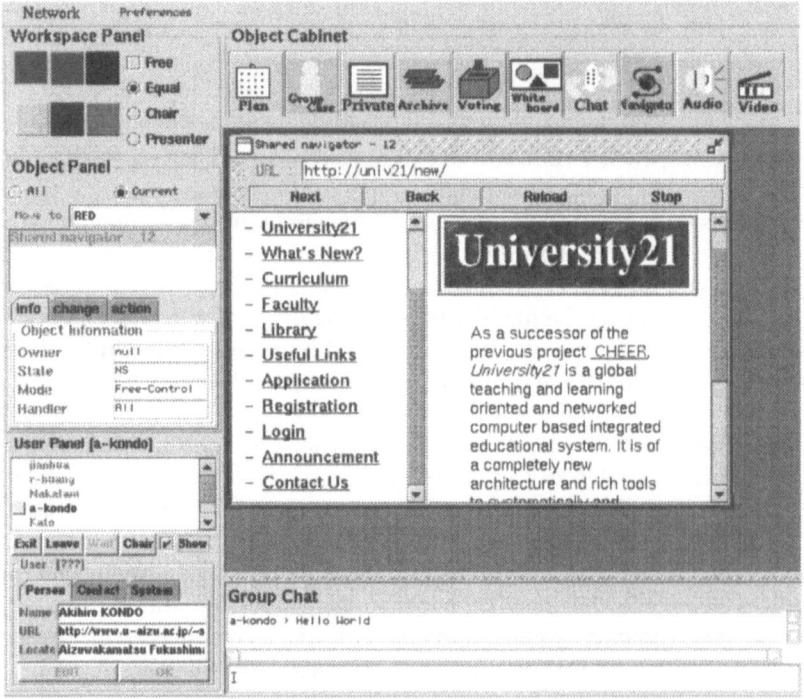

Fig. 4. A shared browser integrated into VCR

of a shared object into VCR is not as simple as just putting a physical object
to a real room. From software engineering viewpoint, performance in terms
of effectiveness and efficiency of the system and consistence after integration
must be taken into considerations. In particular, the shared browser has own
server and client, which is different from other shared applications. This is

because every other shared object only exchanges messages among related clients via a single common VCR room server while the shared browser has to frequently connect to many different web sites other than computers used by group members. Figure 5 presents a diagram that shows how the VCR server and the shared browser server are related and interact each other. As shown in Fig. 5, the request of opening the shared browser is first sent to the VCR server that starts the shared browser server and at the same time informs the VCR client that the SBS is running. The VCR client, therefore, loads the shared browser client applet, makes a connection to the shared browser server, and finally open a browser to all clients as listed steps 1-6. If the shared browser is not used anymore, it can be removed from the workspace in VCR. The removing process is just the reversal process of its creation from step 6 to step 1.

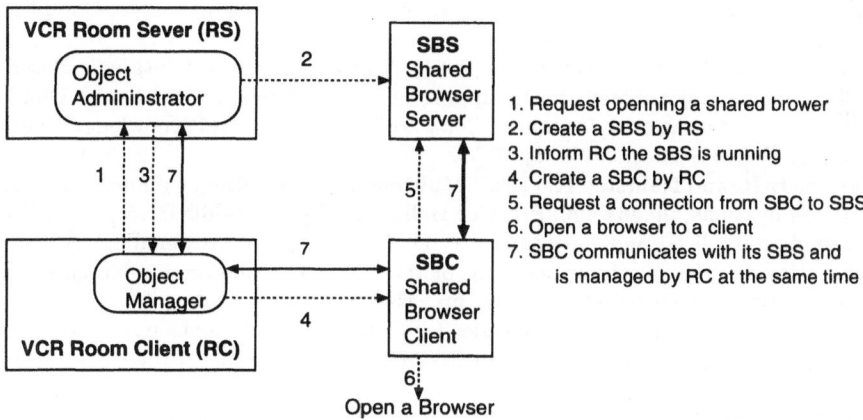

Fig. 5. Servers and clients of VCR and the browser

During the shared browser is being used, the SBC interacts with both its SBS and the VCRC. The interactions and communications between the SBC and the SBS were explained in Section 4. The interactions between the SBC and the VCRC let the object manager in the VCRC to manager the general object physical and social characteristics for the shared browser.

5   Conclusions and Future Work

This article describes our shared web browser with emphasis on the role and implementation of the proxy web server. Different from current popular browsers, our shared web browser enables multi-users to simultaneously view web documents and synchronously share operations on the web documents and the browser as well. The browser can be used as a standalone system

or integrated as a shared object into a sophisticated groupware system like
VCR for reaching its best use and achieving wider ranges of applications.
The future work will be focused on:

- improving the proxy server since it is currently too slow to process a large
  HTML file,
- enhancing HTML file parser so as to process some new HTML specifications,
- keeping history data for late comers, and
- adding more functions to the shared browser.

References

1. Huang R. and Ma, J. (1999) A General Purpose Virtual Collaboration Room, in
   the proceeding of 5th IEEE International Conference on Engineering of Complex
   Computer Systems, Las Vegas
2. Ma J., Huang R. and Nakatani R. (2001): Towards a Natural Internet- Based
   Collaborative Environment with support of Object Physical and Social Characteristics, International Journal of Software Engineering and Knowledge Engineering, World Scientific, No. 1, 37-53.
3. Steinmetz R. and Nahrsted K. (1995) Multimedia: Computing, Communications
   and Applications, pp.384-400, Prentice Hall PTR, Upper Saddle River, NJ 07458
4. Shirmohammadi S. and Georganas N. D. (1997)Jets: a Java-enabled telecol-
   laboration system, in the proceeding of the IEEE International conference on
   Multimedia Computing and System, pp.541-547, Ottawa
5. Beca L. et al. (1997) Web Technologies for Collaborative Visualization and Simulation, in the proceeding of the 8th SIAM Conf. On Parallel Processing, Minneapolis
6. Marsic I. and Dorohonceanu B. (1999)An Application Framework for Synchronous Collaboration Using Java Beans, in the proceeding of the International
   Conference on System Sciences (HICSS-32), Hawaii
7. Harold E. R. (1997) Java Network Programming. CA: O'Reilly and Associates,
   Inc., ISBN 4-900900-56-7
8. Odaka K. (1999) TCP/IP Java network programming for beginner. CA: Ohmsha,
   Inc., ISBN 4-274-06321-6
9. *JAVA 2 SDK DOCUMENTATION*, http://java.sun.com/products/jdk/
10. Watanabe T. (1998) HTML handbook, Softbank Books, Inc., ISBN 4-7973-
    0273-9
11. Luotonen A. (1998) Web Proxy Servers, Prent. Hall RTP, ISBN 0-1368-0612-0
12. Greenberg S. and Roseman M. (1998) Using a Room Metaphor to Ease Transi-
    tions in Groupware, Research report 98/611/02, Department of Computer Sci-
    ence, University of Calgary, Calgary, Alberta, Canada, January
13. Lee J., Prakash A., Jaeger T. and Wu G. (1996) Supporting Multi-user, Multi-
    Applet Workspaces in CBE, in the proceeding of the ACM CSCW'96, pp344-353,
    Cambridge, MA, November

Computer-Supported Online Proofreading in Collaborative Writing

Hiroaki Ogata, Yoshiaki Hada and Yoneo Yano

Dept. of Information Science and Intelligent Systems, Faculty of Engineering, Tokushima University, 2-1, Minamijosanjima, Tokushima 770-8506, Japan
E-mail: ogata@is.tokushima-u.ac.jp

Abstract: This paper describes an online markup-based collaborative writing environment system called **CoCoAJ** (Communicative Collection Assisting System for Java). It allows authors and editors to exchange marked-up documents via Internet, and its environment is very similar to a real world one in which people use pen and paper. In order to record and exchange corrected compositions with marks and comments, this paper proposes XCCML (eXtensible Communicative Correction Mark-up Language), that is based on XML (eXtensible Mark-up Language). XCCML facilitates editors to analyze and reuse the marked-up documents for the instruction.

Keywords: CSCW, collaborative editing, computer assisted language learning, XML, online markup.

1 Introduction

Recently, editor-centered instructional approaches in traditional writing classrooms are replaced with more active and author-centered learning approaches with collaborative writing tools (Bonk et al, 1995). These tools can (1) change the way authors and editors interact; (2) enhance collaborative learning opportunities; (3) facilitate class discussion; and (4) move writing from solitary to more active and social learning. Writing compositions includes various sub-processes such as planning, transcribing, and revising, which do not need to occur in any fixed order (Scardamalia & Berieter 1986). In particular, the review process assisted with computer-based writing tools, has recently received much interest (see as examples (Kehagia & Cox 1997; Coniam 1997)).

Many researchers developed online markup systems employing some markup models. However, it is very difficult to analyze and reuse the marked documents that are collected through the writing classroom because the documents do not have a common structure. Therefore, it is necessary to define the generalized format for encoding and exchanging the marked-up documents in order that online markup systems are used easily and widely.

CoCoA (Communicative Correction Assistant system) has been developed for supporting foreigners and editors to exchange marked-up documents by e-mail (Ogata et al., 1997). Its environment is very similar to a real one in which people use paper and pen. CoCoA allows editors not only to correct the compositions sent from foreigners by E-mail, but also foreigners to see where and why the editor had corrected them. CoCoA improves the opportunities that foreigners have for writing

Japanese compositions and for receiving instructions from editors. CCML (Communicative Correction Mark-up Language) (Ogata et al., 1998) has also been proposed for the representation of marked-up documents, which is based on SGML (Standard Generalized Mark-up Language) (Herwijnen, 1990). With CCML, editors and authors can exchange marked-up documents via e-mail (Ogata et al., 1999, Ogata et al., 2000). In the experimental use of CoCoA, most of users commented that CoCoA was easy for them to understand the mistakes in documents because of the use of marks, and that the optional view of the original, marked or revised text was very useful. However, CoCoA cannot show users a hypermedia document including figures, tables, movies and links because it deals with only text.

This paper tackles how to correct hypermedia documents by the extension of CoCoA. This paper proposes CoCoAJ (CoCoA for Java) to do so. Also this paper describes XCCML (eXtensible CCML) for correcting hypermedia documents, that are based on XML (eXtensible Markup Language). XCCML is combined CCML with HTML (Hyper Text Markup Language) that can represent hypermedia documents including pictures, movies, audios and so on.

We have been investigating technological support for Japanese language learning among overseas authors. For example, CAI systems called Kanji Laboratory (Hayashi & Yano 1994), JUGAME (Yano et al. 1993), GRACILE (Ayala & Yano 1995) and JULLIET (Ochi et al. 1996) were developed to support Japanese language learning. However, an on-line mark-up supporting system for Japanese language learning has not yet been proposed. Usually, in a Japanese writing classroom, editors have to individually review authors' documents using pen and paper (Sato et al. 1994). It takes a lot of time for editors to do this. Therefore, we have implemented CoCoA for writing Japanese composition.

2   Online markup models

There are some editing systems that support editors to review and correct the authors' drafts with online mark-up. Farkas & Poltrock (1995) classified the mark-up models as followings:

1. Silent editing model: This is the simplest model and it requires no special techniques. However, it is very difficult for the author to check the editor's work. This model is destructive because the editor cannot readily recover the original words once he/she has changed it.
2. Comment model: This model employs pop-up notes, temporary footnotes, hidden text, and special symbols placed within the text. This model can work for special groups and ad-hoc situations. A system called XyWrite (Kincade & Oppenheim 1994) was proposed with this model.
3. Edit trace model: In this model, the editor works in the manner of an author, deleting, adding, and moving text as usual. The computer can compare the editor's new version with the original text, and allows the author to view the draft that contains the editor's changes. This model is apt to encourage heavier editing and less regard for the author's original text. Microsoft Word accepts this model.

4. Traditional mark-up model: This adapts the traditional paper mark-up model to the computer screen. The symbols are both familiar and intuitive for editors and authors; for example, deletion, insertion, and move. For instance, Red Pencil allows the editor to apply a complete set of traditional editing symbols directly to a document. The editor uses "digital ink" to mark a traditional editing symbol along with the words. Moreover, MATE (Hardock et al. 1993) allows the editors to use both digital ink and voice command toward pen and voice computing. In this model, authors and editors can interpret the editor's markings much more readily than in the edit trace model.

There are many systems that employ traditional mark-up that allows multiple users to mark-up an electronic document as if they were marking up a printed copy of the document. However, such systems do not globally come into practical and wide use in composition writing classes because of their special format. Moreover, it is very difficult to analyze and reuse the marked documents because the marked documents are unstructured. Therefore, the system should provide a generalized and structured format for encoding and interchanging marked-up documents via the Internet.

3 XCCML

Based on the experimental results, we propose XCCML for exchanging marked-up documents. XCCML is an application of XML, and it supplies a formal notation for the definition of generalized mark-up languages. XML is a device- and system-independent method of representing texts in electronic form. That is to say, XML is a set of mark-up conventions used together for encoding texts. A mark-up language must specify what mark-up is allowed, what mark-up is required, how mark-up is to be distinguished from text and what the mark-up means.

3.1 Features of XCCML

XCCML inherits its features from XML. The main characteristics of XCCML are:
1. Based on the experiment, XCCML presents six marks and annotation XCCML tags.
2. The marks have three degrees of importance levels against respective corrections.
3. The original text is generated by removing all the XCCML tags.
4. The revised text is derived from the XCCML document.
5. Because XCCML documents are text-formated, it is easy to send them by e-mail.
6. CCML documents easily make up a full-text databases.

3.2   XCCML structure

As shown in table 1, XCCML documents consist of three parts: header, body and close. "Header" represents additional information about the document. For instance, "next" tag denotes the next version of the document. The marks for review are shown in the "Body" as XCCML tags. "Close" shows the editor's comments. In one sentence, "insert," "replace" and "delete" marks were used, while "join," "separate" and "move" marks were used over two sentences. The part between the start tag and the end tag denotes the author's mistakes. The "string" attribute represents the revised part of the document.

Table 1: Marks and XCCML tags.

Correction	Mark	Tag
1. Insert	O O O O	<Insert string="text"/>
2. Replace	O O O O	<Replace string="text2"> text </Replace>
3. Delete	O O O O	<Delete> text </Delete>
4. Separate	O O O O	<Separate/>
5. Join	O O O O	<Join/>
6. Move	O O O id	<Movefrom refid="id"/> <Moveto id="id"> text </Moveto>

3.3   Level of marks

We found that the marks do not have the same level of importance. We identify corrections on the following levels:
1. Weak correction: The author does not need to revise the document.
2. Normal correction: The author should correct the document.
3. Strong correction: The author must correct the document.

The strong corrections denote the important part of marks to be revised in the document. Using the importance level that the editor had entered, the system provides the author with the marks he/she wants to see. Therefore, the author can avoid information overload from the reviewed documents. Every tag in table 1 has an attribute "level" that a editor gives a number from one to three. Its default is two as normal correction.

3.4   Level of annotations

It is very important for a editor to annotate the marked text for instruction in composition. For example, PREP Editor (Neuwirth et al, 1996) is a word processor that allows writers and reviewers to create electronic margins, or columns, in which they can write and communicate through their annotations. We identify the following different kinds of annotations:

1. Explanation: This is used for explaining the reason of a correction.
2. Question: This is used for asking the author a question; e.g., what do you want to write?
3. Comment: This shows the educational view of the editor with respect to the document.

4   CoCoAJ

CoCoAJ consists of CoCoAJ_Editor and CoCoAJ_Viewer. An editor corrects the document of authors with CoCoAJ_Editor and the system saves the marked document in XCCML format. CoCoAJ_Viewer interprets the XCCML document, and shows the author the marked document.

4.1   Collaborative writing processes using CoCoAJ

By using CoCoAJ, an author receives instruction about a Japanese composition from a editor with the following processes:

1. The author writes an original text with his/her familiar editor.
2. The author sends the document to his/her editor with his/her own e-mail tool.
3. CoCoAJ_Editor makes the document double-spaced. The editor corrects the document with online marks and annotations. Then, the system allows the editor to set the importance level to the marks in the document.
4. After CoCoAJ_Editor saves the marked text as a XCCML document, the editor sends it to the author by e-mail.
5. CoCoAJ_Viewer provides the author with the marked text after interpreting the XCCML document. Then, the system allows the author to select the importance level to see the important part of the marked text.
6. CoCoAJ_Viewer automatically generates both the original text and the revised one from the XCCML document. After editing the revised text, the author can send it again to the editor and continue refining the text.
7. CoCoAJ maintains the version of the document, if the author wants to revise the same document.

4.2   System configuration

Figure 1 depicts the system configuration of CoCoAJ.

1. XCCML parser: This module analyzes XCCML documents using the XCCML parser after reading them through the file management module. Then, it provides the results of correction according to the level of importance of marks.
2. Correction module: This module inserts XCCML tags into the author's document, according to the revision of the editor. After saving the marked text, the editor sends it by e-mail to the author.

3. Original text display module: This module generates the original text from the XCCML document by removing all the XCCML tags.

4. Revised text display module: This module generates the revised text by applying XCCML tags.

5. File management module: This module manages the versions of the documents. When the author sends the editor the revised document, the system creates a new XCCML document, inserts the "next" tag into the old XCCML document, and also enters the "previous" tag into the new XCCML document.

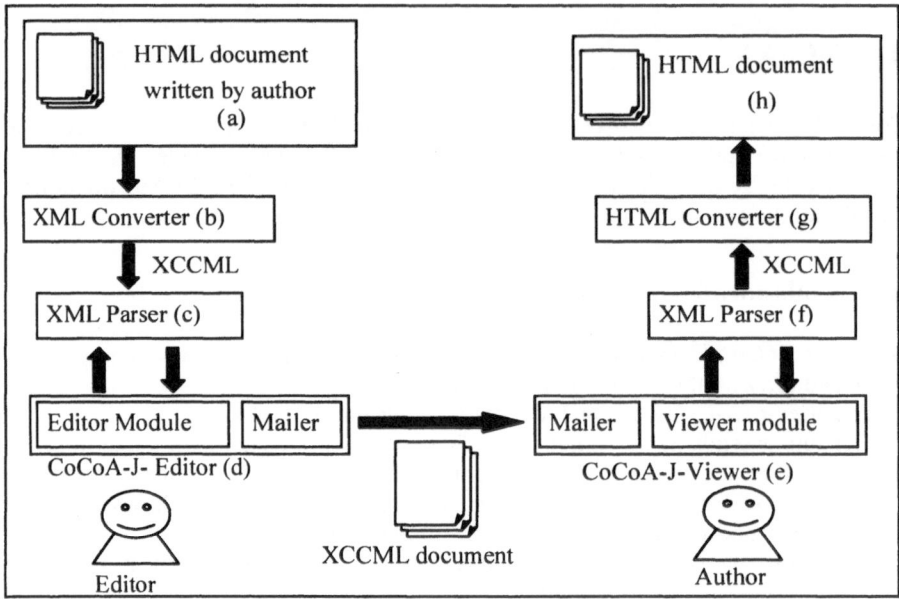

Figure 1: System configuration of CoCoAJ.

4.3   User interface

Figure 2 shows the screen snapshot of CoCoAJ-Editor. First, the author writes compositions with a word processor and saves the document as HTML format. After that, the author sends the document to the editor by e-mail. By selecting a mark from the mark palette shown in the upper window, the editor can revise the document. Moreover, the editor can annotate the document using the annotation palette, and he/she can classify the marks according to the level of importance. The user can see the correcting document at the left side in the window and "*" means the user inserted the comment. The user can see the comments for the correction at the right side in the window. In this figure, the editor substitutes "allow" with "allows" and gives a comment "*2". Also the editor can see the original document and revised one by selecting window tag. After saving the marked document as a XCCML (see appendix A), the editor can send it to the author by e-mail. Using

CoCoAJ-Viewer, the author obtains the same marked text that the editor revised. By selecting the level of importance, CoCoAJ_Viewer provides only the marks over the level. The author can reply to the editor's comments and collaboratively write compositions with the editor.

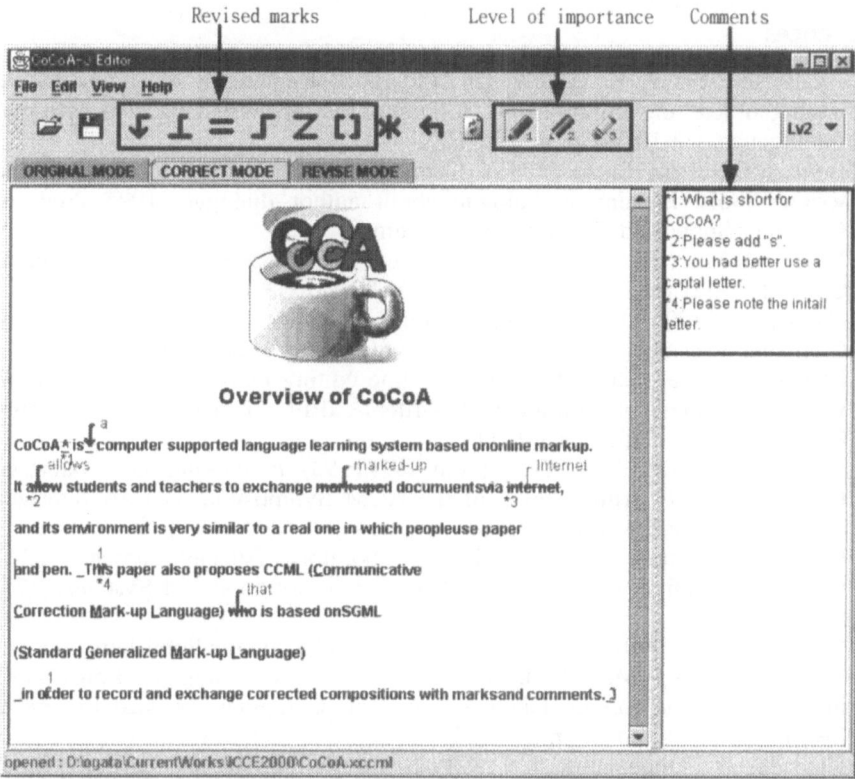

Figure 2: Screen snapshots of CoCoAJ_Editor.

5   Conclusions

This paper proposed a computer-mediated collaborative-writing system called CoCoAJ and XCCML for exchanging electronic marked-up documents. Now we are trying to propose XCCML to W3C (World Wide Web Consortium), and to show an XCCML document into Web browsers. After that, CoCoAJ will be able to be used for writing any language. In our future research, we will investigate how to classify users' writing errors in their drafts, and how to assist a review process with AI technologies.

Acknowledgment

This research was supported in part by the Grant-in-Aid for Scientific Research No.12558011, No.11878032, and No.13780121from the Ministry of Education, Science, Sports and Culture in Japan.

References

1. Ayala, G., Yano, Y. (1995). GRACILE: A framework for collaborative intelligent learning environments, Journal of the Japanese Society of Artificial Intelligence, vol.10. no. 6. pp.156-170.
2. Bonk, J.C., King, S. K. (1995). Computer conferencing and collaborative writing tools: Starting a dialogue about author dialogue, 1995 Proc. of Computer Supported Collaborative Learning.
3. Brock, N.M. (1995). Computerised text analysis: Roots and research, Computer Assisted Language Learning, vol.8, no.2-3, pp.227-258.
4. Coniam, D. (1997) A computerised English language proofing cloze program, Computer Assisted Language Learning, vol. 10, no. 1, pp.83-97.
5. Farkas K.D., Poltrock, E.S. (1995). Online editing mark-up models, and the workspace lives of editors and writers, IEEE Trans. in Professional Communication, 38(2), pp.110-117.
6. Hardock, G., Kurtecbach, G., Buxton, W. (1993). A marking based interface for collaborative writing, Proc. of the ACM Symposium on User Interface Software Techonogy, pp.259-266.
7. Hayashi, T., Yano, Y. (1994). Kanji Laboratory: An environmental ICAI system for Kanji learning, IEICE Trans. on Information and Systems, E77-D(1), pp.80-88.
8. Herwijnen, E. (1990). Practical SGML, Kluwer Academic Publishers.
9. Kehagia, O., Cox, M. (1997). Revision changes when using word processors in an English as foreign languages context, Computer Assisted Language Learning, vol. 10, no. 3, pp.239-253.
10. Kincade, D., Oppenheim, L (1994) Marking it up as we go along: Into editorial production's electronic future, Journal of Scholarly Publishing, Vol. 25, No. 3, pp.233-242.
11. Matsumoto, Y, Kitauchi, A., Yamashita, T., Hirano, Y., Imaichi, O. Imamura, T. (1997) Japanese Morphological Analysis System ChaSen Manual, Nara Institute of Science and Technology Technical Report NAIST-IS-TR 97007. (in Japanese)
12. Neuwirth, M.C., Wojahn, G.P. (1996). Learning to write: Computer support for a cooperative process, CSCL: Theory and practice of an emerging paradigm, Koshmann, T. (Ed.), Lawrence Erlbaum Associates, Publishers, pp.147-170.
13. Ochi, Y., Yano, Y., Hayashi, T. (1996). JULLIET: Interactive learning environment for Kanji compounds learning, Proc. of Educational Multimedia and Hypermedia 1996, pp.539-544.
14. Ogata, H., Yano, Y. (1997). CoCoA: Communicative Correction Assisting System for Composition Studies, Proc. of ICCE 97, pp.461-468.

15. Ogata, H., Yano, Y., Wakita, R. (1998). CCML: Exchanging Marked-up Documents in a Networked Writing Classroom, International Journal of Computer Assisted Language Learning, Vol.11, No.2, pp.201-214.
16. Ogata, H., Feng, C., Hada, Y., Yano, Y. (1999). Computer Supported Proofreading Exercise in a Networked Writing Classroom, Proc. of ICCE 99, Vol.1, pp.414-417.
17. Ogata, H., Feng, C., Hada, Y. Yano, Y. (2000). Online Markup Based Language Learning Environment, International Journal of Computers Education, Vol.34, No.1, pp.51-66.
18. Sato, M., Kano, C., Tanabe, K., Nishimura, Y. (1994). Practical Japanese Compositions, Bonjin-sya. (in Japanese)
19. Scardamalia, M., Bereiter, C. (1986). Research on written composition, M. Wittrock (Ed.), Handbook of research on teaching (third ed.), Macmilian, pp.778-801.
20. Schwind, B.C. (1995) Error analysis and explanation in knowledge based language tutoring, Computer Assisted Language Learning, vol.8, no.4, pp.295-324.
21. Shimano, H. (1986). Handbook of proofreading, Miki Publishers, Japan, in Japanese.
22. Yano, Y., Miyoshi, K., Hayashi, T. (1993). Development of a game style environmental ICAI system for Kanji idiom learning, Proc. of International Conference on Computers in Education '93, pp.411-413.
23. Yano, Y., Ogata, H., Sakakibara, R., Wakita R. (1997). CoCoA: Communicative correction assisting system for learning Japanese compositions, Transactions of Japanese Society for Information and Systems in Education, vol. 14, no.3, pp.21-28. (in Japanese)

Appendix A: XCCML document in figure 4.

```
<?xml version="1.0" encoding="Shift_JIS"?>
<!DOCTYPE XCCML SYSTEM "XCCML.dtd">
<XCCML>
<HEAD>
<Title string="Overview of CoCoA"/>
<Editor name="Hiroaki Ogata" email="ogata@is.tokushima-u.ac.jp"/>
<Author name="Yoshiaki Hada" email="hada@is.tokushima-u.ac.jp"/>
</HEAD>
<BODY>
<CENTER><IMG width="128" height="128"
   src="image001.gif"/></CENTER><CENTER><H2>Overview of
   CoCoA</H2></CENTER> <H4> CoCoA <Annotate level="3"
   comment="What is short for CoCoA?"/> is<Insert string="a" level="3"/>
   computer supported language learning system based ononline markup.<BR/>
It<Replace string="allows" level="3" comment="Please add &#34;s&#34;.">
   allow </Replace> authors and editors to exchange<Replace string="marked-
   up" level="3"> mark-uped</Replace> document via <Replace
   string="Internet" level="1" comment="You had better use a captal letter.">
   internet</Replace>,<BR/> and its environment is very similar to a real one in
   which people use paper<BR/> and pen. <MoveTo fromid="1" level="2"
   comment="Please note the initail letter."/>This paper also proposes CCML
   (<U>C</U>ommunicative<BR/> <U>C</U>orrection <U>M</U>ark-up
   <U>L</U>angua<Replace string="that" level="3">ge)</Replace> who is
   based on SGML<BR/>
(<U>S</U>tandard <U>G</U>eneralized <U>M</U>ark-up
   <U>L</U>anguage)<BR/>
<MoveFrom toid="1" level="2">in order to record and exchange corrected
   compositions with marks and comments.</MoveFrom></H4></BODY>
<CLOSE>
<Comment/></CLOSE>
</XCCML>
```

Design of Satellite-Based Multimedia Content Distribution Systems and Metrics for Systems Evaluation

Yukari Shirota[1], Takako Hashimoto[2][3] and Atsushi Iizawa[2][3]

[1]   Faculty of Economics, Gakushuin University, Tokyo, Japan
      E-mail: yukari.shirota@gakushuin.ac.jp

[2]   Information Broadcasting Laboratories, Inc., Tokyo, Japan
      E-mail: {takako, izw }@ibl.co.jp

[3]   Software Research Center, Ricoh Company Ltd., Tokyo, Japan
      E-mail: {takako, izw }@src.ricoh.co.jp

Abstract. The growth of the Internet is placing severe demands on the existing telecommunications infrastructure. Especially, the growth of download accesses of movie-type contents has made Web traffic highly bursty, and this has become a significant problem for Internet users. In this paper, to solve the multimedia content download problem, we propose a new satellite digital broadcasting service system to provide global distribution of multimedia contents. New scheduling algorithms called *Local Optimization (LO)* and its varieties and new performance metrics called *total sales amount* and *successful reception ratio* are also proposed. Furthermore, we present a detailed performance evaluation of the proposed scheduling algorithm and of some typical existing scheduling algorithms with various traffic and access patterns using computer simulation.

1   Introduction

The exponential growth of the Internet is placing severe demands on the telecommunications infrastructure. Especially, the percentage of download accesses of movie-type contents requiring wide bandwidth resources has been increasing, which has made the Internet more and more congested. Satellite broadcasting was proposed to solve the multimedia content download problem and has been put to good use for Internet communications. The broadcast nature of satellites is highly suitable for the distribution of multimedia content because satellite broadcasting can cover a global area and the distribution cost is fixed even if the number of users increases. In addition, because the download access pattern is asymmetrical in that the content server needs much more bandwidths than the clients, we can make good use of satellite bandwidths.

Digital broadcasting using satellites has rapidly spread throughout the world. With digital TV sets, users at home will be able to receive the satellite broadcasting content directly, rather than via some Internet provider's access point, and they will be able to store the content on a home video server. TV viewing habits will be drastically changed as a user can watch stored TV programs of his or her choosing at any time.

Considering both the spread of the Internet and of digital broadcasting, during the new millennium, satellite systems will play a significant role in supporting a wide range of broadcasting services to end users. In this paper, to solve the multimedia content download problem, we propose a new satellite digital broadcasting service system to provide global distribution of multimedia contents. New scheduling algorithms called *Local Optimization (LO)* and its varieties and new performance metrics called *total sales amount* and *successful reception ratio* are also proposed. Furthermore, we present a detailed performance evaluation of the proposed scheduling algorithm and of some typical existing scheduling algorithms with various traffic and access patterns using computer simulation.

The rest of the paper is organized as follows. In Section 2, we describe the system model of our proposed multimedia content distribution service. We provide the scheduling algorithms for system in Section 3 and the metric for the system evaluation in Section 4. In Section 5, we provide results of the evaluation. In Section 6, we report on related work. Section 7 concludes this paper.

2   Proposed Service System

The broadcasting service considered here is an "on-demand" type service where a user (client) at home sends a request message to a target site (server) by using ordinary communication lines, as in existing Web accesses systems. Then, the response message with the requested multimedia content is sent back to the user via a satellite channel (See Figure 1). The satellite channel allocated for the service is supposed to broadcast the requested contents all day long. All contents are broadcast to the user.

One of the key points of our proposed service is that the distribution (broadcasting) scheduling is determined fully automatically and based completely on popularity [13]. Popularity is defined as the number of requests.

The advantages obtained by the proposed system model are as follows: (1)Congestion of the Internet is alleviated because popular multimedia content is broadcast globally; therefore, there is no need of a one-to-one correspondence between senders and receivers; (2) One may easily obtain multimedia contents from the content database (DB) site via a digital TV set at home, and store it, just like video recording of TV programs; (3) The broadcasting station side can increase its profit, as broadcasting contents can be requested by many users. Because the broadcasting cost is fixed, the more popular content that is broadcast, the more profit that can be made.

Now we explain the structure of a satellite-based multimedia content distribution system. The service system is based on a popularity vote system. A user at home sends a request message to a DB site that holds an enormous amount of contents. The request message is as follows:

Request(UserID,ContentID,CurrentDate,TermValidity).

Every request is accompanied by a piece of information called the "term of validity", which indicates the expiration time of the request. The system removes requests when they expire. Figure 2 shows the time chart of the scheduling cycle executed on the DB site for a user at home. The scheduling cycle is executed periodically and collectively. In the scheduling cycle, the scheduler first removes the expired requests, and then decides the schedule. Even if a requested data is not selected (elected) in the first scheduling cycle, there is another chance to be selected in the next one as long as the term is valid.

As shown in Figure 2, the schedule of the k-th period distribution of contents is calculated in the (k-1)-th period. We call this schedule the k-th *schedule*. When k-th scheduling is finished, the system distributes k-th schedule carried by EPG (Electric Program Guide) that explains when and what content will be broadcast. The EPG will be broadcast repeatedly to let every user know the k-th schedule order during the (k-1)-th period.

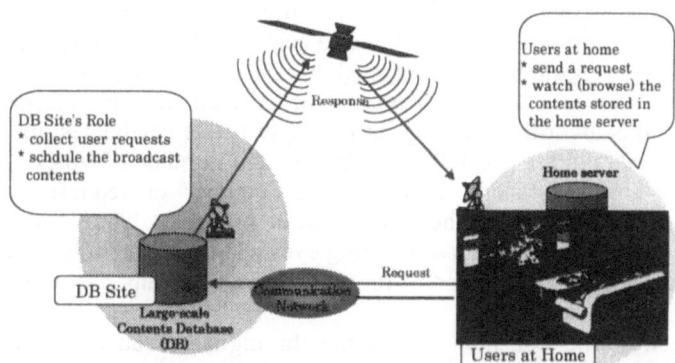

Figure 1: Service Model of the Satellite-based Multimedia Distribution System

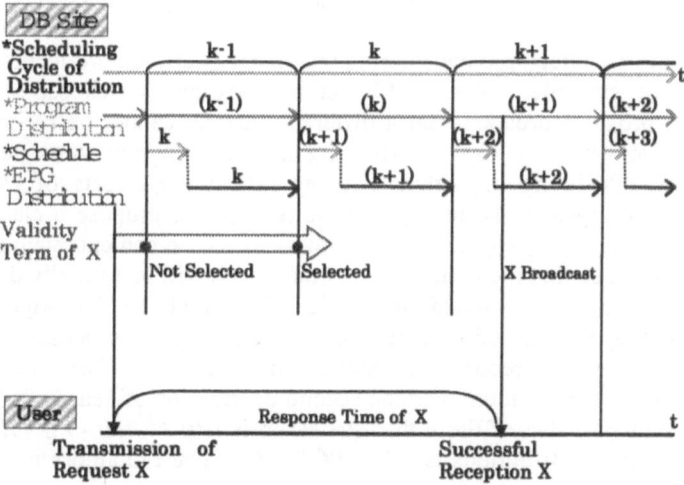

Figure 2: Scheduling Time Chart

3   Scheduling Algorithms

In this section, we review two basic relevant scheduling algorithms which can be used for digital broadcasting systems, and then describe our new algorithms in detail.

The details of two basic scheduling algorithms are as follows. We will also compare our proposed algorithms with these two existing algorithms later.

(A) High Popularity First Serve (HPFS) Algorithm: The most popular contents are selected in the order of popularity and broadcast just one time in one scheduling process. Since the HPFS algorithm is similar to the First In First Serve algorithm and is so simple, it is suitable as a comparative algorithm.

(B) Ratio Equilibrium (RE) Algorithm: This algorithm is also called *the proportional representation algorithm*, and is used for the election of Diet members. In this algorithm, relying on the party list of candidates, members with the highest rankings are elected according to the number of votes [4]. For our broadcasting service system, based on the number of requests, that is, on popularity, the system selects the contents to be broadcast. The same content may be selected several times in one scheduling cycle. This algorithm is widely used for resource allocation problems; for example, stream allocation on a Video-On-Demand system.

Now we describe our new algorithms. In digital broadcasting systems, the receiving error rate at home denoted by Pf ($0 \leq Pf \leq 1$) is considered to be one of the most important parameters that affect the system performance. The reasons for receiving errors are as follows: (a) Lack of receiving and recording functions in the TV set top box installed ; (b) Incidence of the power off state of the TV set top box ; and (c) Weather conditions such as a heavy rain and snow.

Note that the value of Pf may vary widely in a real system. The main reason is that the value of Pf depends on many of the TV set top box specifications that are decided by the manufactured considering the balance between production costs and functions. For example, unless a TV set top box has a rich set of recording functions, a program broadcast on a different channel cannot be recorded in the same time-slot when the user is watching another program. It is necessary to provide new scheduling algorithm that can reflect the effects of Pf for our proposed service system. To meet this requirement, we propose a class of Local Optimization (LO) Algorithms. The algorithms select the contents with the highest ranking using Pf, so that the total sales amount which will be formally defined later will be highest in any one scheduling cycle. Like the above "RE Algorithm," the same content may be selected several times in one scheduling process.

Denote the number of requests for content i by X. The first distribution of i earns $(1 - Pf) * X$ as the sales amount, and the second distribution of i earns $Pf * (1 - Pf) * X$, etc. The estimated value of the n-th distribution is $(Pf)^{n-1} * (1 - Pf) * X$. The total sales amount of n distributions is $(1 - (Pf)^n) * X$. The LO algorithm determines whether the system should select the same content one more time or a new other one with lower popularity should be selected, by estimating the sales amounts.

We call the above algorithm the basic LO algorithm. In a real system, it is too difficult to determine the real value of Pf accurately, since it changes dynamically.

We have to use an estimated value of *Pf* for the LO algorithms, instead of the real value of *Pf*. The estimated *Pf* value may always be somewhat different from the real value. Taking this fact into account, furthermore, we propose three varieties of the basic LO algorithm.

- Ideal LO algorithm: Use an estimated value of *Pf* that is the same as the real value. This is represented as "LO".
- Approximated LO algorithm: Monitor the real value of *Pf* periodically and use the average value within a definite period of time as the estimated value that is thought to be closely approximated to the real value. To estimate the algorithm in our simulations, we made five intervals at 20 % degree when we changed the real value of *Pf* from 0 % through 100%. At each interval, we used the center *Pf* value as the estimated *Pf* value. It is represented as "LO-".
- LO algorithm with a fixed value of "x" % as the estimated *Pf* value: Use a fixed value (*x* %) as the estimated value of *Pf*, regardless of the change of the real *Pf* value. This is represented as "LO(E=x)", whose "E" means the Estimated value of *Pf*.

We will also estimate the HPFS or RE sensitivity against the real value of *Pf*. Then we will represent the algorithms under the condition the real value of *Pf*=x%, HPFS(R=x) or RE(R=x) whose "R" means the Real value of *Pf*. Generally speaking, HPFS can distribute more variety of content, compared with RE and LO, in what is called a *small profits and wide range of content spread*. On the other hand, RE and LO tend to distribute only the most popular contents repeatedly. Furthermore, when we compare scheduling policies, we can say that RE distributes content following the percentage of request numbers exactly; on the other hand, LO follows the estimated sales amount values.

Table 1: The Default Parameter Values of the Simulations

Number of users	One million
Average number of requests	2 per week and per user
Number of content items	One million
Number of broadcast slots	2160 per a day
Scheduling cycle	One day
Term of validity	One day
Content charge	Uniformly one unit
Simulation batch size	2 weeks

4   Metrics for System Evaluation

Traditionally, the response time of a request has been used as a performance measure. In digital broadcasting systems, the receiving error rate at home is considered to be one of the most important parameters for evaluating system performance. However, the response time does not take account of the receiving error rate. Therefore, we consider other metrics that can reflect the changes of the receiving error rate are required for our service system. In this section, we propose two alternative metrics –the *total sales amount* and the *successful reception ratio*.

In order to define the *successful reception ratio,* we first describe the definition of *successful reception* of a request as follows.

Successful Reception (SR) of a request: When both the following conditions are met and only when they are met, is a request called the *successful reception*: (1) The requested content must have been selected and broadcast; and (2) The broadcast content must be received successfully at home.

The *Successful Reception Ratio*(SRR) is defined as *[the number of requests at SR] / [the number of requests from users]* for a given period. In digital broadcasting systems, the contents are all billed, but the charges will not be collected unless a user obtains the content successfully at home. Therefore, the SRR is proportional to the *Total Sales Amount* (TSA) as long as the number of users is constant. The sales amount counts as the SRR, not a real currency unit such as a dollar. If one data item is successfully received at home, then the counter is incremented by one. In addition, because SRR expresses the ratio of users who have successfully obtained the requested contents, we can say that SRR also expresses the satisfaction of both users and the broadcasting station. The traditional metric *Mean Response Time* (MRT) is also used: if the SRR/TSA values of the two algorithms are the same, we would decide which algorithm outperforms the other with MRT. These two performance metrics along with the traditional metric, MRT, provide better performance evaluation of digital satellite broadcasting systems as we can see below.

5   Performance Evaluation

In this section, we evaluate the various algorithms presented above, assuming the typical parameter settings shown in Table 1. We consider that the main application content items are video clips or music catalogs which consist of video and music information. Consider that the necessary time for viewing one content item is three to four minutes. In the full video data case in MPEG2, the compressed data size is about 150MB[1], and in the full music data case in MPEG2, AAC format, about 1.7MB[2]. We assume that the compressed data size is 50 MB per content item, and the broadcast bandwidth is 10Mbps. Then the number of broadcast slots per one day becomes 2160 as shown in the table. As the request arrival rate, we use a *Poisson distribution* because it is widely used in scheduling simulations. In this section, we describe the effects of the three important parameters: concentration level of popularity of contents, the receiving error rate, *Pf*, the validity term and the scheduling cycle ratio obtained by computer simulation. The computer simulation allows us to study the performance of scheduling algorithms in more detail than does an analytical model. When one simulation result is computed, we have taken

---

[1] The size of standard density television data items in NTSC is 3 to 8Mbps[19]. Suppose that one data item takes 3.5 minutes to watch and that the mean compressed data size is 6 Mbps. Then 3.5 min $\times$ 60sec/min $\times$ 6 Mbps $=$ 157.5MB.

[2] MPEG2 Audio AAC format has been adopted by BS digital broadcasting. In the format, using bandwidth 64 kbps,we can get the same musical quality as the original one. By the format, 3.5min$\times$60sec/min$\times$64kb/sec $=$ 1.68MB.

two weeks as a warm-up term every time. For each simulation result, relative half-widths of 10% about the mean value were calculated using a <u>batch means algorithm</u> [11] at a 90% confidence level. Each batch takes about 2 to 3 minutes using a PentiumII, 400 MHz personal computer.

5.1 Popularity Probability Distribution

We assume that popularity probability distribution follows the *normal distribution*. The normal distribution is the most important and widely used probability distribution in statistics. According to the *Central Limit Theorem* [14], the larger the sample size, the closer the distributions of the sums and averages will be to a normal distribution. Since our target service system has a large number of users and distributed contents, we consider the normal distribution is appropriate for our popularity probability distribution. Consider that the content ID that a user randomly requests is a random variable of which the density function is expressed approximately as a normal distribution. Figure 3 shows the bell-shaped curve of the normal distribution. That expresses a probability distribution function for the content ID randomly selected by a large group of users. The content ID (the horizontal axis) is sorted, according to the popularity (probability). In the field of simulation research, the **Zipf** distribution function [20] is also widely used as a popularity distribution function [1,3,7,16]. Here we adopt the normal distribution because it is the most often used distribution function and because it is easy to handle and analyze.

5.2 Effects of Concentration of the Level of Popularity

First, we study the effect of the concentration level of the popularity on the total sales amount as determined by simulations. In general, if the popularity is sharply concentrated to a few popular content items, then popular content broadcasting will earn more sales revenue than the case whose the popularity density is spreading out. We wanted to know how the total sales amount decreases as the popularity peak becomes spread out.

Figures 4 (a) and (b) show the simulation results of the relationships between the metrics and the square root of variance, σ. In these figures, we plotted three groups of data with different real values of *Pf* of 10%, 50%, and 90% to see the sensitivity. We made our simulations at 100 intervals from 300 to 2500. Figure 4 (a) shows that all the values of SRR gradually decrease when the popularity peak becomes spread out. From Figure 4 (a), we can say that LO outperforms others when the real value of *Pf* is less than 10%. However, in the range of real *Pf*>50%, there is no large difference between RE and LO where HPFS is bad and out of question. There is also no remarkable difference in <u>MRT</u> between RE and LO (See Figure 4 (b)). At which level of real *Pf* does RE become similar to LO? For this question, we need to perform the next simulation, which designed to look at the receiving error rate effects.

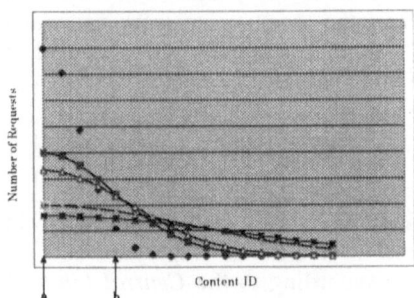

Figure 3: Normal Distribution of Requested Content IDs

Figure3:Normal Distribution of Requested Content IDs

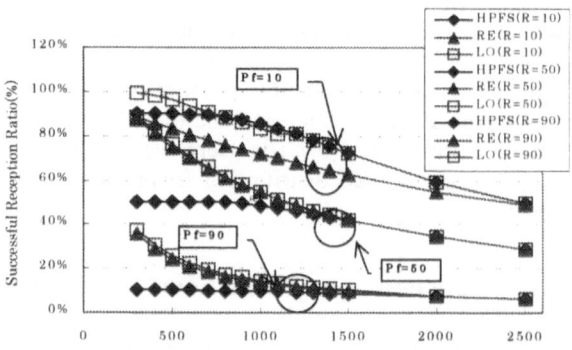

(a) Successful Reception Ratio with Standard Deviation

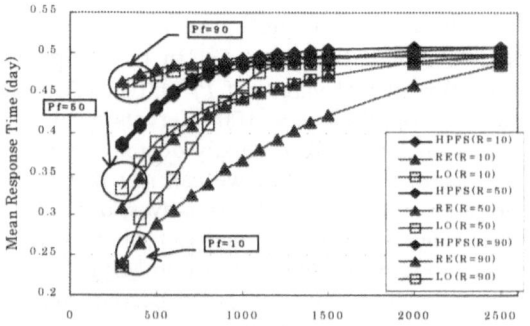

(b) Mean Response Time with Standard Deviation

Figure 4: Effect of Concentration of the Level of Popularity

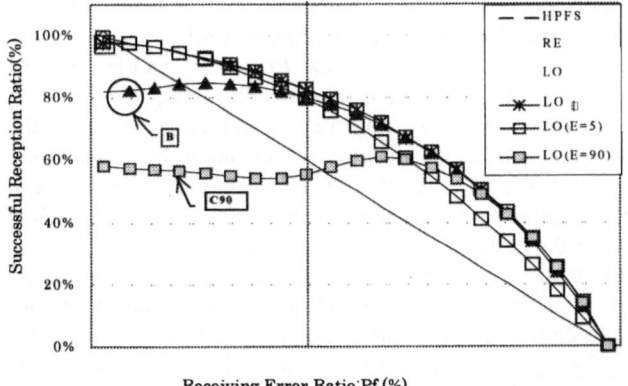

(a) Successful Reception Ratio with Receiving Error Ratio.

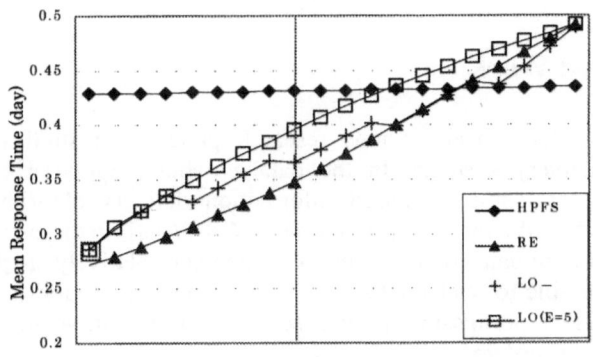

(b) Mean Response Time with Receiving Error Ratio.

Figure 5: Effect of Receiving Error Ratio at Home

5.3   Effects of Receiving Error Ratio

Next, we change Pf (the receiving error rate at home) from 0 % to 100 %. Figures
5 (a) and (b) show the simulation results which were obtained under the condition
where $\sigma = 500$. From Figure 5 (a), we can see the following: (1)The SRR values
obtainedusing the HPFS algorithm linearly decrease as the real value of Pf
increases; (2) The LO, LO-, LO(E=3), LO(E=5), and LO(E=10) algorithms always
outperform   the HPFS algorithm; and (3) When Pf is greater than 40%, the RE

algorithm outperforms the LO(E=10), LO(E=5), and LO(E=3) algorithms. The inversion occurs around the real value of Pf set at 40%.

We summarize that in the range of real Pf < 40%, LO(E=x)[x is about 5] is the best algorithm and that in the range of real Pf > 40%, RE or LO- outperform the others. Considering that LO- requires monitoring the actual situation, the implementation and maintenance cost of RE may be lower than one of LO-. Therefore, in the range of real Pf > 40%, we can say RE is the best algorithm. From the MRT comparison shown in Figure 5 (b), we cannot find any simulation data to contradict the results.

We have simulated system performance in various cases such as increasing bandwidth or increasing the number of users, in addition to the above-mentioned simulations. We can summarize the conclusions of all the simulations as follows: (1) For real Pf < 40%, LO(E=x)[x is about 5] is the best algorithm. The ratio *[scheduling cycle / validity term]* should be one used; and (2) For real Pf > 40%, RE is the best algorithm, where both SRR and MRT increase as the value of validity term increases.

6   Related Work

Recently, there have been various research papers and studies for broadcast information delivery systems. In the database field, applying broadcasting to database accesses, some broadcast information delivery algorithms have been proposed to reduce the mean response time [2,6,8,17,18]. In these existing systems, since the number of data content items is limited and relatively small, the users are supposed to be able to wait for the response. In our target environment, we have introduced a user's permissible period, so that a user request may expire and be removed from the system.

There is another group of related work, scheduling research about video on demand (VOD) and near video on demand systems(NVOD) [12]. In this research, popularity-based scheduling algorithms have been studied. However, there are the following differences between both approaches. At first, our target data item size is much smaller than that of VOD systems. The main target of VOD systems is a set of movies.

On the other hand, our target data is supposed to be a much smaller data item for example, digital music with multimedia information, Secondly, there exist differences of the viewing styles. In the VOD system, the user is supposed to view the content as a stream data on real time. In our service system, the viewed object is cache data stored in the home server; there is no interactivity on real time. However the users can watch the contents at any time. The third differences exist in scheduled resources. In the VOD system, the scheduled resources are streams (at most 100) and the video servers [5,9,10,15]. In our service system, scheduled resources consist of broadcast bandwidth. Because the data size is small, the number of broadcast slots   is large. Since there are many slots to be scheduled, the behavior of the system would be more complicated that of VOD systems.

7   Concluding Remarks

In this paper, we proposed a new satellite service system using digital broadcasting to provide the global distribution of multimedia contents. One of the key points of the service is that the distribution (broadcasting) scheduling is determined fully automatically and fully based on popularity. New scheduling algorithms and new metrics were also proposed for digital broadcasting. We have studied the performance of various scheduling algorithms by detailed computer simulation under various types of traffic and access patterns. The proposed algorithms were found to consistently do well.

References

1.   Acharya, M. Franklin, and S. Zdonik: "Dissemination-based data delivery using broadcast disks," IEEE Personal Communication, pp. 50-60, Dec. 1995.
2.   S. Acharya, R. Alonso, M. Franklin, and S. Zdonik: "Broadcast Disks: Data Management for Asymmetric Communication Environments," Proc. of ACM SIGMOD Conference, pp. 199-210, 1995.
3.   M. H. Ammar and J. W. Wong: "On the optimality cyclic transmission in teletext systems," IEEE Transactions on Communications, pp. 68-73, Jan. 1987.
4.   D. Black: A Mathematical Approach to Proportional Representation: Duncan Black on Lewis Carroll, Kluwer Academic Pub., Dec. 1995.
5.   C. K. Chang, T. T. Nguyen, and P. Mongkolwat: "A Popularity-based Data Allocation Scheme for a VOD Server," Proc. Annual International Computer Software & Application Conference., pp. 62-67 (1996).
6.   S. Hameed, and N. H. Vaidya: "Log-time Algorithms for Scheduling Single and Multiple Channel Data Broadcast," Proc. of MOBICOM 97, pp. 90-99, 1997.
7.   F. Hisham, and M. Kitsuregawa: "The simulation Evaluation of Heat Balancing Strategies for Btree Index over Parallel Shared Nothing Machines," IEICE Technical Report, DE99-83, pp. 7-12, Oct. 1999.
8.   T. Imielinski, S. Viswanathan, and B. R. Badrinath: "Energy Efficient Indexing On Air," Proc. of ACM SIGMOD Conference, pp. 25-36, 1994.
9.   T. Konishi: "Fundamental Technologies of Video Server and Settop for VOD," The Journal of the Institute of Television Engineers of Japan, Vol. 49, No. 5, pp. 605-608, 1995.
10.   T. Little, and D. Venkatesh: "Popularity-based assignment of movies to storage devices in a video-on-demand system," IEEE Multimedia, Vol. 2, pp. 280-287, Spring 1995.
11.   M. H. MacDougall: Simulating Computer Systems Techniques and Tools, The MIT Press, 1987.
12.   K. Nagasawa: "Cable TV and NVOD," The Journal of the Institute of Television Engineers of Japan, Vol. 49, No. 5, pp. 618-624, 1995.
13.   Y. Shirota, A. Iizawa, H. Mano, and J. Li: "Simulation Studies on TV Program Scheduling by Broadcasting Stations," Proc. of ITE (Institute of Television Engineers of Japan) Winter Annual Conference 1988, p. 67, Dec. 1998.

14. F. Siegel and L. J. Morgan: Statistics and Data Analysis, An Introduction, John Wiley & Sons, Inc. New York, 1996.
15. Y. Tanaka, and S. Kato: "Forecast on the Price of VOD Service and Its Traffic," IEICE Technical Report, Vol. 95, No. 397 (SSE95 116-124), pp. 43-48, Dec. 1995.
16. J. W. Wong: "Broadcast delivery," Proc. of IEEE, pp. 1566-1577, Dec. 1988.
17. E. Yajima, T. Hara, M. Tsukamoto, and S. Nishio: "On a Broadcast Data Interval of Correlative Data," Transactions of Information Processing Society of Japan, Vol. 40, No. 1, pp. 188-196, Jan. 1999.
18. E. Yajima, T. Hara, M. Tsukamoto, and S. Nishio: "Scheduling and Caching Methods for Broadcast Data Considering the Correlation among Data," Transactions of Information Processing Society of Japan, Vol. 40, No. 9, pp. 3577-3585, Sept. 1999.
19. Y. Yasuda: "Digital Broadcasting and Information Processing," IPSJ Magazine, Vol. 40,No. 4, pp. 409-413,   April 1999.
20. G. K. Zipf: Human Behavior and the Principle of Least Effort, Reading, MA, Addison-Wesley, 1949

Incremental Document Clustering for Web Page Classification

Wai-chiu Wong and Ada Wai-chee Fu

Department of Computer Science and Engineering, The Chinese University of
Hong Kong, Shatin, Hong Kong
E-mail: adafu@cse.cuhk.edu.hk

Abstract. Motivated by the benefits in organizing the documents in Web search
engines, we consider the problem of automatic Web page classification. We employ
the clustering techniques. Each document is represented by a feature vector. By
analyzing the clusters formed by these vectors, we can assign the documents within
the same cluster to the same class automatically. Our contributions are the following: (1) We propose a feature extraction mechanism which is more suitable to Web
page classification. (2) We introduce a tree structure called the DC-tree to make the
clustering process incremental and less sensitive to the document insertion order.
(3) We show with experiments on a set of Internet documents from *Yahoo!* that the
proposed clustering algorithm can classify Web pages effectively.

1 Introduction

We consider document clustering for Web pages. Traditionally, the document
classification task is carried out manually. In order to assign a document to
an appropriate class, people would analyze the contents of the document first.
Therefore a large amount of human effort would be required. There has been
some research work conducted on automatic text classification. One approach
is to learn the text classifiers by using the machine learning techniques. However, these algorithms are based on a set of positive and negative training
examples for learning the text classifiers. The quality of the resulting classifiers highly depends on the fitness of the training examples. There are many
terms and classes in the World Wide Web (or just the Web), and many new
terms and concepts are created everyday. It is quite impossible to have domain experts to identify training examples to learn a classifier for each text
class in the above manner.

In order to make the document classification process automatic, clustering techniques have been employed. The attractiveness of cluster analysis is
that it can find clusters directly from the given data, without relying on any
pre-determined information such as training examples provided by domain
experts. A document is commonly represented by a feature vector. Typically,
each feature corresponds to a key word or phrase appearing in the set of
documents. Each entry of the vector stores a numeric weight for the corresponding feature of the document. After extracting the feature vectors of

the documents, we can apply the clustering algorithm on this set of the vectors as in conventional high dimensional data clustering. The resulting document clusters together with the representative features (i.e., the key words or phrases with enough *document support* within the cluster) are thus reported to the user.

In this paper, we introduce a tree structure called the **DC-tree** (Document-Clustering Tree) which can cluster documents without any training set. With the DC-tree, an incoming data object is not forced to be inserted into the lower level when there does not exist a child node that is similar enough to this data object. This prevents some dissimilar data from being put together. As a result, the DC-tree-based clustering algorithm is less sensitive to the document insertion order and is more tolerant towards noise documents.

We believe that our method can be useful in a number of ways: (1) For preprocessing on Web page classification so that users can choose a suitable class before searching, this helps the search to be more focused and efficient. (2) For online classification, so that when a large number of results are returned from a search, the technique can classify the results and provide better guidance to user for further searching. (3) For incremental Web page classifications after updating on the repository.

2   Related Work

BIRCH [6] is a dynamical and incremental method to cluster the incoming points. An important idea of BIRCH is to summarize a cluster of points into a clustering feature vector. This summary uses much less storage than storing all data points in the cluster. A CF-tree is built which splits dynamically. Clusters are stored in the leaf nodes. In this way, the memory requirement problem of K-Means is resolved and thus the method is suitable for large data sets.

In one method presented in [5], a B^+-tree-based structure is used to index the document feature vectors. For the purpose of clustering, each leaf node is a document and each nonleaf node n is the representative of the cluster containing the documents in the leaf nodes of the subtree rooted at n. Similar to the CF-tree and the B^+-tree based method, this is a balanced tree, and has the problem of possibly forcing non-similar items into the same node or cluster.

3   Feature Extraction and Document Clustering

Our first task is to identify a good feature extracting method suitable for the Web environment. In this section, we propose such a method. The document and document cluster representation will also be described. Finally, the clustering quality evaluation method will be presented.

3.1   Document Feature Extraction

We propose a feature extracting method for the Web document clustering algorithm which does not depend on the term frequency. This method balances the trade-off between the coverage and the number of features used for document representation. In our problem domain the clustering aims to aid in information retrieval in Web searching by narrowing down the search scope. In such a scenario, the user may not want too many clusters in the result. Also, very large clusters or very small clusters are not desirable. Very large clusters cannot help to narrow the search scope. Very small clusters can increase the total number of clusters, and it may actually be caused by noise. The parameter k is used to set an *approximate* number on the cluster size. Hence the number of clusters is approximately N/k, where N is the total number of documents. The proposed method involves the following steps:

1. Randomly select a subset of documents with size m from the corpus.
2. Extract the set of words that appear at least once in the documents. Remove stop words and combine the words with the same root by using the stemming technique.
3. Count the document frequency of the words which are extracted in Step 2.
4. Set *lower* $= k$ and *upper* $= k$
5. Select all words with document frequency in the range from *lower* to *upper*
6. Check if the *coverage* of these words is larger the pre-defined threshold. If so, stop. If no, set *lower* $=$ *lower* $- 1$ and *upper* $=$ *upper* $+ 1$, and then goto Step 5.

In order to extract the representative features from the documents, we randomly select a set of sample documents for feature extraction in Step 1. We have carried out some experiments (see [4]) which show that this feature extraction method can extract a set of good features for Web document clustering. A stop-word list is used to remove the meaningless words. Stemming technique is used to combine those words in similar form.

Since shorter feature vectors lead to shorter clustering time, Steps 4 to 6 try to minimize the number of features and obtain reasonable coverage for the features. Assume the user wants the resulting cluster to contain about k documents. In the ideal case, a feature for a cluster will appear only in the cluster and hence the document frequency of the feature is k. Therefore, we first select the features with document frequency equal to k, by setting *lower* and *upper* to k in Step 4. The range { *lower, upper* } is enlarged repeatedly in Step 6 to ensure sufficient coverage for the resulting feature set. We see that N/k is only a rough guideline, the actual number of clusters of the clustering result may not be the same as N/k. The method also makes use of a **coverage threshold** to ensure that the features selected has sufficient coverage. In our experiments (see [4]), we find that 0.8 is a good coverage threshold value.

3.2   Document Representation

In our algorithm, a document (D_i) is represented in the following form: $D_i = (W_i, ID_i)$, where ID_i is the document identifier which can be used to retrieve document (D_i) and W_i is the feature vector of the document: $W_i = (w_{i1}, w_{i2}, \ldots, w_{in})$. Here n is the number of extracted features, and w_{ij} is the weight of the j-th feature, where $j \in \{1, 2, ..., n\}$. In our algorithm, a binary weighting scheme has been used. That is, w_{ij} is equal to 1 if D_i contains the j-th feature. Otherwise, w_{ij} is equal to 0. As mentioned in Section 3.1, a Web page typically does not contain many words so that the term frequency of a word cannot indicate the actual importance of this word. Therefore, the binary weighting scheme is more suitable to our problem domain.

3.3   Document Cluster (DC)

A **Document Cluster** value (DC) is a triple storing the information that we maintain about a set of documents within the same cluster: (1) the number of documents, (2) the set of document identifiers, and (3) the feature vector of the cluster.

Definition 1. (DC) Given N documents in a cluster: $\{D_i, D_2, \ldots, D_N\}$, the Document Cluster (DC) entry of a node is defined as a triple: DC $= (N, ID, W)$, where N is the number of documents in the cluster, ID is the set of the document identifiers of the documents in the cluster, i.e. $ID = \{ID_1, ID_2, \ldots, D_N\}$, and W is the feature vector of the document cluster, i.e. $W = (w_1, w_2, \ldots, w_n)$, where $w_j = \sum_{i=1}^{N} w_{ij}$, and n is the number of extracted features.

This triple not only summarizes the document frequency inside the cluster, but also can be used to measure the closeness between two clusters. The following lemma gives us the flexibility to combine two clusters into one and gives a DC value for the combined cluster.

Lemma 1. *(Additivity) Let $DC_1 = (N_1, ID_1, W_1)$, and $DC_2 = (N_2, ID_2, W_2)$ be the DC entries of two disjoint document clusters, where disjoint means a document does not belong to more than one cluster at the same time. Then the new DC entry, DC_{new}, of the cluster that is formed by merging the two disjoint clusters, is: $DC_{new} = (N_1 + N_2, ID_1 \cup ID_2, W_1 + W_2)$, where $W_1 + W_2 = (w_{11} + w_{21}, w_{12} + w_{22}, \ldots, w_{1n} + w_{2n})$, and n is the number of extracted features.*

3.4   Evaluation Techniques

In order to evaluate the quality of the clustering result, we adopt the *F-Measure* evaluation technique which was first introduced in [3]. The details of this evaluation methodology is described below.

For each hand-labeled topic T in the document set, suppose that a cluster X corresponding to that topic is formed.

N_1 = no. of documents of topic T in cluster X

N_2 = no. of documents in cluster X

N_3 = total no. of documents of topic T

P = Precision(X, T) = $\frac{N_1}{N_2}$

R = Recall(X, T) = $\frac{N_1}{N_3}$

The F-measure [3] for the topic T is defined as below:

$$F(T) = \frac{2PR}{P + R}$$

With respect to a topic T, we consider the cluster with the highest F-Measure to be the cluster C for T, and that F-Measure becomes the score for topic T. The overall F-Measure [2] for the tree clustering result is the weighted average of the F-Measure for each topic T:

$$Overall\_F\_Measure = \frac{\sum_{T \in M} (|T| \times F(T))}{\sum_{T \in M} |T|}$$

where M is the set of topics, $|T|$ is the number of documents of topic T, and $F(T)$ is the F-Measure for topic T.

4   DC-tree

In this section we propose a Web document clustering algorithm by means of a Document Cluster tree (DC-tree). In the DC-tree, each node can be considered as a document cluster. The tree structure is used to guide the incoming document object to an appropriate Document Cluster (DC) at the leaf nodes. It is similar to the B^+-tree [5] in that the index records in its leaf nodes contain pointers to data objects, but it is not a height-balanced tree. This structure is designed so that assigning a document into a cluster requires visiting only a small number of nodes.

A **DC-tree** is a tree with four parameters: branching factor (B), two similarity thresholds (S_1 and S_2, where $0 \leq S_1, S_2 \leq 1$) and the minimum number of children of a node (M). A non-leaf node contains at most B entries of the form ($DC_i, Child_i$), where $i = 1, 2, \ldots, B$, "$Child_i$" is a pointer to its i-th child node or a document, and DC_i is the DC entry of the sub-cluster represented by its i-th child or a document. So, a non-leaf node represents a cluster that is made up of all the sub-clusters represented by its entries. A DC leaf node contains at most B entries, each is an entry of the form (DC_i, Doc_i), where $i \in \{1, 2, \ldots, B\}$, "$Doc_i$" is a pointer to a document or a set of documents, and DC_i is the DC entry of the corresponding sub-cluster. We call the set of documents under such a pointer a **document leaf node**, to distinguish it from the tree leaf node or **DC leaf node** (see Figure 1). A DC leaf node also represents a cluster made up of all the sub-clusters represented by its DC entries. The DC-tree allows an incoming document entry to be inserted in a new document leaf node at different levels of the tree. So, the DC-tree is not a height balanced tree. Figure 1 shows a sample DC-tree with a height of 2, $B = 3$, $M = 2$. Note that the tree is not balanced. In the tree construction, two thresholds are used:

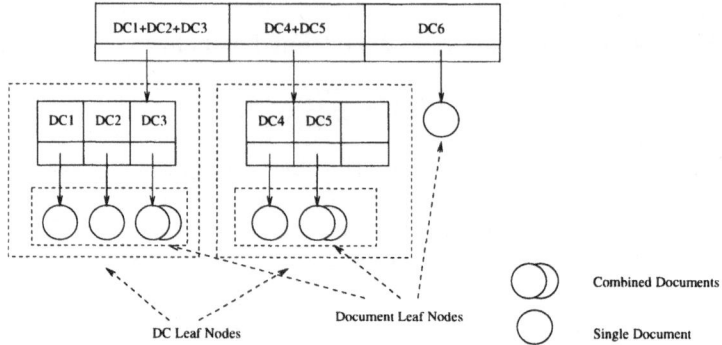

Fig. 1. Example of a DC-tree

1. **Threshold S_1**: In order to prevent poor document clustering result (i.e. documents in different classes are assigned to the same subtree or cluster) caused by document insertion order, S_1 is used to determine whether the incoming document entry E can be passed into the next level during the insertion process. If there exists an child entry of the current node such that the similarity value between this entry and the incoming entry is higher than the S_1, the incoming entry can be passed to the corresponding child node. Otherwise, the incoming entry will be added to the current node as a new document leaf node.

2. **Threshold S_2**: Since the DC-tree is used for document clustering but not indexing, it is not necessary to force each leaf entry to point to a single document. In order to reduce the insertion time, the incoming document entry can be **combined** with a leaf entry, if their similarity value is higher than S_2. This entry combination makes use of the merging as described in Lemma 1, it can save on node insertion and splitting operations so that the insertion time can be reduced.

The DC-tree is a compact representation of the dataset because each entry in a leaf node is not a single data point but a cluster of data points (the leaf node absorbs as many data points as the threshold S_2 allows). With the above DC-tree definition, the tree size will be a function of the threshold values S_1 and S_2. In general, the tree height increases with S_1 and the tree size increases with S_2. If we set S_1 to zero and S_2 to any number larger than one, the DC-tree will be similar to a balanced tree like a B^+-tree or an R-tree. The data deletion and merging algorithm is similar to that of the B^+-tree.

4.1 Identifying the Interesting Clusters

The cluster identifying process starts from the root of the tree. A breath-first-search algorithm is applied to discover the interesting clusters. An interesting cluster is defined as a cluster that contains representative features and whose size is in a predetermined range. We can make use of the *lower* and *upper* values found in our proposed feature extracting method to determine the cluster size range. Let l and u be the lower bound and upper bound of the cluster size range, then l and u can be determined by the following equations: (1) $l = lower \times \frac{N}{m}$, (2) $u = upper \times \frac{N}{m}$, where N is the data set size and m is the size of the sample data set used in the feature extraction. Also, the range can be adjusted manually to obtain a good clustering result. Once we have identified an interesting cluster, the sub-clusters in its descendent nodes will not be scanned. A **representative feature** is defined as a feature that has enough support in the cluster. That is, the document frequency of the representative features must be greater than some user-defined threshold. We call this threshold the **representative threshold**. These features will then be used to represent the cluster.

5 Experimental Results

In this section, we list some experimental results for the proposed feature extracting method and the Web document clustering algorithm. We have applied the algorithm on both synthetic data and real data for studying the performance and the relationship among the parameters of the proposed algorithms. We find that the behaviour of the algorihtms are similar for the real data and synthetic data. For interest of space, we shall report on either data set in each performance analysis. All experiments are run on the *Sun Ultra 5/270* with 512 MB of RAM. The programs are compiled using *GNU* C++ and executed on the *Solaris 2.6* operating system.

The synthetic datasets are generated by a generator that we have developed. The data generation is controlled by four parameters: (1) the number of document feature vectors, (2) the number of features, (3) the number of clusters, and (4) the **similarity level** L which is ranged from 0 to 1. Given x feature vectors and y clusters, for each cluster C, we set x/y features F randomly to represent the cluster. For each document generated for C, the features in F will have a chance of L being set to 1 and $1 - L$ being set to 0. The features not in F will have a chance of $1 - L$ being set to 1. Hence the higher the similarity level, the more similar the documents will be within the same cluster.

We have collected two sets of Web pages from the *Yahoo!* search engine. One contains ten non-correlated topics while another contains ten correlated topics. The Web pages indexed by *Yahoo!* search engine have already been classified.

To construct the non-correlated document set, we have selected ten sub-topics, namely, author, credit bank, internet game, wine, film, disease organization, job opportunity, soccer, astronomy organization, psychology department. For each topics, we collected 2000 Web pages. So, there are totally 20000 Web pages in this dataset.

For the correlated topic Web document set, we have selected ten sub-topics from the following location:
`http://dir.yahoo.com/Computers_and_Internet/Programming_Languages/`
from *Yahoo!* search engine, namely, COBOL, Fortran, Java, JavaSript, Lisp, Pascal, Perl, Python, Smalltalk and Visual Basic. For each topics, we collected 2000 Web pages. So, there are also totally 20000 Web pages in this dataset.

We use the two real data sets of 20000 web documents each for both the correlated topics and non-correlated topics.

Table 1. Real data clustering results

	non-correlated topics	correlated topics
No. of clusters found	10	10
Cluster size range	1000-3000	1000-3000
Representative threshold	0.45	0.4
Clustering time	94.21 seconds	72.27 seconds
F-Measure Value	0.6753	0.6453

The representative thresholds for the DC-tree method in the two cases are shown in Table 5, and are chosen by trial and error.

5.1   Precision

For each cluster found, we calculate the document support of each known topic, which is the number of documents containing the same topic. Then we choose the topic with the highest document support as the topic of the cluster. Tables 2 (a) and (b) show the precision values of the clusters found by these two algorithms. They show that the DC-tree always gives a better clustering result than B^+-tree in terms of the precision of the resulting clusters.

Table 5.1 also lists the representative features of each cluster. Since the classification is automatic, we do not have a simple title for each topic of the clusters found, but we can guess the topic of the clusters by their representative features. The representative features (words) are used to indicate to the users what each cluster is about.

Table 2. Precision of the clusters (a) non-correlated topics (b) correlated topic

Cluster Topic	Precision	
	DC-tree	B^+-tree
author	0.61	0.59
internet game	0.73	0.55
wine	0.63	0.65
credit bank	0.66	0.57
soccer	0.73	0.47
astronomy organization	0.88	0.77
psychology department	0.85	0.63
job opportunity	0.91	0.72
film	0.72	0.73
disease organization	0.64	0.65
Average	**0.736**	**0.633**

(a)

Cluster Topic	Precision	
	DC-tree	B^+-tree
Cobol	0.64	0.54
Fortran	0.72	0.72
Java	0.73	0.62
JavaScript	0.64	0.67
Lisp	0.73	0.63
Pascal	0.81	0.67
Perl	0.78	0.72
Python	0.82	0.55
Smalltalk	0.61	0.57
VisualBasic	0.77	0.65
Average	**0.725**	**0.634**

(b)

Table 3. The clusters found for non-correlated data

Cluster Topic	No. of Documents	Features
author	2157	book, story, year
internet game	1988	best, free, game, review
wine	2461	wine
credit bank	2302	credit, service, union
soccer	1312	report, soccer, team
astronomy organization	1712	astronomy,union
psychology department	1892	psychology, university
job opportunity	1939	career, experience, job, location
film	1664	film, star
disease organization	2245	disease, health, medical, organization

5.2 Incremental updates on Real Data Set

In order to study the impact of the incremental updating the clustering result of the non-correlated topic document set, we insert 5000 additional documents into the existing DC-tree and observe the change of clustering quality. 433.22 seconds are used to convert the 5000 documents into feature vectors. Table 5.2 shows the changes of clustering quality for each 1000 additional documents added to the existing clustering result. From the table, we notice that the F-Measure value decreases from 0.6753 to 0.6010. The clustering quality only decreases about 11% in terms of F-Measure value when 25% more documents are added to the existing document set. Note also that each update in the document set will only involve a very small amount of computation in the clustering. Therefore, our document clustering algorithm is suitable for incremental updating in Web pages.

Table 4. Incremental Update Results

No. of documents	F-Measure value
21000	0.6555
22000	0.6475
23000	0.6249
24000	0.6062
25000	0.6010

6   Conclusion

In this paper, we introduce a tree structure called DC-tree for the incremental and hierarchical Web document clustering. We propose a feature extracting method for document clustering in the Web domain. This method takes into account the special characteristics of Web pages, and the special requirements of the problem domain. We show by experiment that the features of the DC-tree give good results in terms of accuracy and efficiency.

References

1. A. Guttman. R-tree: A dynamic index structure for spatial searching. In Proceedings of ACM SIGMOD, pages 47-56, 1984.
2. Bjornar Larsen and Chinatsu Aone. Fast and effective text mining using linear-time document clustering. In Proceedings of the ACM SIGKDD International Conference on Knowledge Discovery and Data Mining, pages 16-22, San Diego, CA, USA, August 1999.
3. C. J. van Rijsbergen. Information Retrieval. Butterworth & Co (Publishers) Ltd, 1979.
4. Wai-chiu Wong and Ada Fu, Incremental Document Clustering for Web Page Classification, IEEE 2000 Int. Conf. on Info. Society in the 21st century: emerging technologies and new challenges (IS2000), Nov 5-8, 2000, Japan
5. Clement T. Yu and Weiyi Meng. Principles of Database Query Processing for Advanced Applications, chapter 10, pages 359-385. Morgan Kaufmann Publisher, Inc., 1998.
6. Tian Zhang, Raghu Ramakrishnan, and Miron Livny. BIRCH: An efficient data clustering method for very large databases. In Proceedings of the ACM SIGMOD Conference on Management of Data, pages 103-114, Montreal, Canada, June 1996.

Integration of Multiple Tailoring Interfaces in Compositional Web Applications

Igor Mejuev, Masahiro Higashida, Tohru Shimanaka and Noriyuki Makino

PFU Ltd., Solid Square East Tower, 580
Horikawa-cho, Saiwa-ku, Kawasaki-city
Kanagawa 212-8563, Japan.
E-mail: mejuev@post.kek.jp

Abstract. A tailorable software system is defined as a system that can continue its evolution after deployment in order to adapt to particular work situation and meet the diverse needs of its users. The initial cost of developing easily tailorable systems is the main reason why the majority of currently deployed software products lack this feature. In this paper, we will outline a method of declaring independence from a set of fixed tailoring interfaces as a way to deal with the problem. The approach introduced below allows multiple tailoring interfaces to be integrated within an application instance. We will show how the multiplicity of tailoring interfaces, based on compositional markup specifications can be used to reduce development costs related to easily tailorable WWW systems. Our approach will be discussed in the context of the VEDICI implementation framework as applied to the development of interactive multimedia courseware for the Web.

1   Introduction

A computer system is considered to be tailorable if it allows users to adapt the system to their particular situation and their particular needs. Two early and well- known examples of applications incorporating a degree of tailorability are the EMACS editor and Macintosh HyperCard system [1]. From the HCI perspective, tailoring can be considered the ongoing evolution of an application during use that is aimed at adapting it to handle requirements that were not anticipated in the original design [2]. Accordingly, tailorability is a natural way of dealing with user flexibility requirements and has a direct impact on application maintenance costs - which is a crucial property of software products with enterprise deployment. An evaluation [3] shows that each dollar spent in the IT industry on new development will yield 60 cents of maintenance per year during the lifecycle of the application. However, the increased initial cost of the development of tailorable systems may be the reason why current products incorporate so little tailorability [4].

This paper examines tailorable systems from software engineering perspectives, the problematic of software development process and the ways of increasing reusability in the implementation of component-based tailorable systems. Additionally, we shall propose an application independent framework for delivering of tailorable Web-based systems with high degree of cross-platform portability. The contributions of this work are as follows:

Our proposal envisions the horizontal integration of multiple tailoring interfaces as a way to deal with the problem of increased development cost of tailorable applications. The framework introduced in this paper allows the integration of multiple interfaces within a single application instance.

We will show that compositional markup specifications are useful for reducing the development cost of easily tailorable WWW systems and that a multiplicity of tailoring interfaces can be implemented practically by representing tailorable application fragments with compositional markup.

We will also consider the specific problems related to usability inspections for Web-based tailorable applications and propose a solution that can be used to perform automatic usability evaluations for Web-based systems.

2   State of the Art

User interface *tailorability* has been extensively researched from HCI perspectives. The research efforts have established tailorability function categories, classified users that would use tailorability tools and produced a number of research prototypes. Research prototypes targeting tailorability in a particular application domain range from desktop applications [5] to a collaborative Web workspace [4]. There also exists an increasing amount of interest in integrating tailorability into CSCW (Computer Supported Cooperative Work) applications [2], including the ongoing development of the generic tailoring platform for CSCW [6].

Compositional markup languages use markup syntax, such as XML to represent the composition and links among components of an application. The construction of compositional applications from reusable components, integrated by means of scripting, can resolve some deficiencies in applying object-oriented languages to component-based development [7]. The most highly developed (and freely available for commercial use) instance of compositional markup languages is BML, (Bean Markup Language), which directly represents the Java Beans' component model. BML includes a language grammar specification, represented by XML Document Type Definition (DTD) as well as API (BML player) that is used to process XML documents composed in accordance with BML DTD [8]. While representing a compositional language for beans scripting, BML "as it is" does not allow delivery of a controllable degree of granularity (nesting) and support for visualization tools. These are essential requirements for specifying the composition of tailorable applications.

3 Developing Tailorable Applications for the Web

We consider development process of tailorable Web-based applications in accordance with evolutionary and participative software process model [9] and we assume that the increment of the process consists of the following steps:

- identifying the required degree of tailorability by summarizing assumptions about the needs of the intended users' community (1)
- identifying the architectural solution or the method of implementing the necessary degree of tailorability (2)
- performing a usability inspection of deployed system (3)

The careful selection of test users involved into design process is considered to be the key issue in capturing the diversity and evolution of requirements and in identifying the required degree of tailorability [10].

This paper addresses the issues of architectural solutions (2) and problems related to usability inspections that are specific for the Web-based systems (3). We will focus on component-based systems and we identified the problems faced by a designer of a tailorable Web system as follows:

- the selection of building blocks and visualization techniques can not be fixed at the design phase without imposing limitations on the usability of the final product
- usability inspection of the application with Web deployment is problematic

In general, the proper choice of components and visualization techniques is domain dependent and user requirements and preferences regarding those continue evolving throughout the project lifecycle. Thus, building from a "minimal" set of components may be sufficient for developers, but might be rejected by end-users. In addition, the nature of the Web makes it close to impossible to precisely identify the user's community, especially at the initial stage of software project. Accordingly, the usability inspection phase normally faces difficulties due to the absence of direct communication with the users.

4 Integrating Multiple Tailoring Interfaces

In order to address the issue of reducing development costs for tailorable Web applications we propose an approach and implementation framework that can be reused as a foundation for developing a variety of component-based tailorable applications.

The basic tailorable unit in our approach is a *player* - which consists of a wrapper for a composite component with an associated *visualizer*. A player compiles a composite component in accordance with a given Compositional Markup Specification (CMS) that is also retained by the player. A visualizer defines the tailoring interface for a specific class of composite components. The functionality of a player in the context of runtime tailoring is to retain a CMS and spawn an associated visualizer parameterized with the CMS in response to an event generated by framework or GUI component. The visualizer provides a user interface for CMS authoring and asynchronously returns the updated CMS back to the player. Having received a new CMS, the player compiles a new composite component and fires an object change event in the parent application that can cause further application-dependent actions, such as repainting of GUI components. The primary intent of this technique is to decouple tailoring interfaces and runtime components. A player can be included in a composite component wrapped by another player, so that a running application represents a nested hierarchy or players. Association with a visualizer at the level of individual player allows multiple visualization schemes per application to be supported (Fig. 1). The integration of multiple tailoring interfaces can be implemented *horizontally* - on the same level of complexity, without system-wide or plane-wide switching.

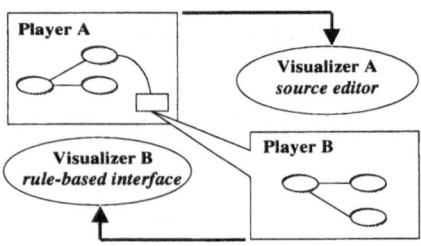

Fig. 1. Nesting

We use Java and as an implementation language and Java Beans as primitive components, integrated by an instance of player. Our beans usage in a player is defined by an XML-based bean wiring language - the current implementation uses BML 2.2 DTD and API, extended with support for visualization, player nesting, asynchronous data exchange among players and other APIs essential for Web-based applications that support applet deployment. Now, we would like to underline the usability of compositional, XML-based specifications in the architecture represented above. In general, the XML allows the creation of new specification.languages while preserving a uniform way to access and manipulate documents that conform to the new specifications. The corresponding standards on the language and APIs, used to access and manipulate documents (DOM, SAX) are well established. The use of XML documents to represent tailorable application fragments allows us to apply existing standard APIs to modify the structure of a document, correspondingly tailoring the component-based application fragment, represented by the document. The markup-based representation would allow conducting automatic usability inspection [13] of the prototype-testing phase of a software product. The inspection can be performed using the history of modifications resulting from tailoring activity of real users evaluating the prototype. The analysis of modification history can reveal the severity of the usability problems in the initial design and point out ways for improving the usability of a product. Obviously, the use of compositional XML specifications is not a silver bullet. An implementation framework for delivering of tailorable Web applications based on the compositional markup needs to provide the following infrastructure:

- integrating *runtime* with explicit support for nesting and data exchange among nested players
- persistence of customized applications in a Web-based system requires *applications repository* with authorization and access control
- application-specific or reusable *components* representing primitive application building blocks
- application-specific or reusable *visualizers*, reflecting the users' cognitive views of the task

Since first two modules, runtime and repository are application independent; they can be used to form a generic framework for the development of tailorable Web-based applications.

5   VEDICI

VEDICI is an implementation of generic tailoring platform based on the principles described above. In order to increase the usability of this platform we identified additional requirements on the implementation, such as support for zero-install clients, seamless integration with browser and support for integration of external active content into a tailorable application. Fig. 2 provides a simplified overview of VEDICI modules and their interactions.

Java Applet *Runtime* loads applications from a server and executes them on client computer. Applications are loaded from a remote repository with authorization by username and password. It is possible to use standalone HTML pages to run a particular application or use a remote repository browser. There is also a standalone player for application mode, which executes applications loaded from a client's local file system. The runtime system uses a BML API that has been extended to add support for applications nesting, asynchronous data exchange among applications running in parallel, or nested and support for application lifecycle. VEDICI application components can access APIs, provided by the environment to use functionality of Web-browser, a well as communicate with browser plug-ins and repository services in order to save or load personalized information, such as configuration

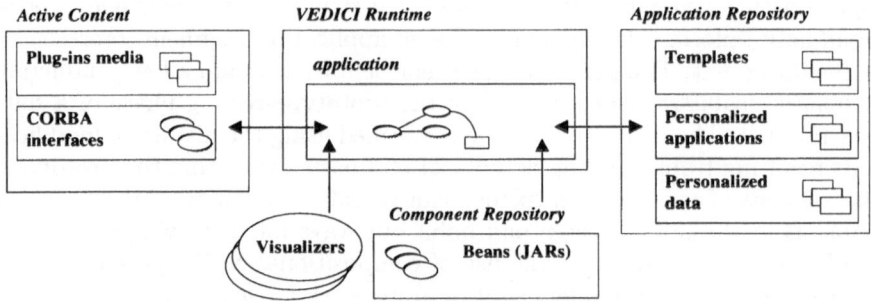

Fig. 2. Composition of VEDICI

data, for the current user. The primary function of the *Application Repository* is to provide persistent storage for personalized applications created by users when tailoring templates. The templates are basic versions of tailorable applications, provided by system developers. The repository service is also available for primitive application components. *Component Repository* holds a collection of primitive components for VEDICI applications. The repository contains a set of archive files in JAR format.

6   Applications

6.1   Sample Application

A sample application is an instance of the architecture represented in the Fig. 1. This application is a simple text editor with customizable toolbar. The application composition is represented in Fig. 3.

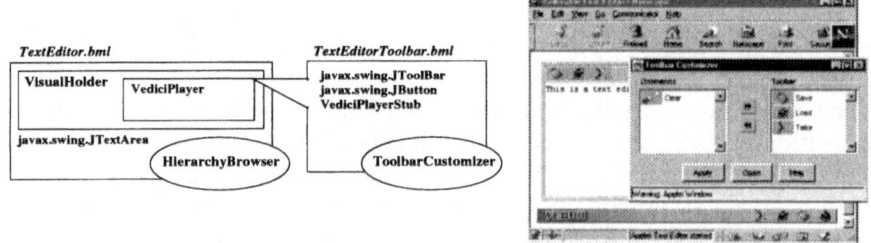

Fig. 3. Composition of a sample application

The application integrates two visualizers (Toolbar Customizer, Hierarchy Browser) and a number of reusable components. Toolbar application is nested within the application Text Editor and assigned an application-specific visualizer (Toolbar Customizer). The parent application (Text Editor) is assigned a reusable visualizer (Hierarchy Browser), which allows browsing the structure of an application and calling nested visualizers for tailoring particular aspects of the application. The Text Editor application itself does not include any facilities for toolbar customization; instead it relies on a reusable framework, which can potentially provide the tailoring possibilities needed for arbitrary component-based applications and support persistence of changes made by each user. The application is modified at the compositional level, so that each user can in fact have a personal version of a WWW-based application, customizable at runtime.

6.2   Application to the Development of Interactive Multimedia Courseware

We consider interactivity and tailorability to be required features for adding real value to traditional distance learning [14,15]. Typically, students study in different environments and use a variety of browsers with different capabilities. To facilitate an active education process, the developers of multimedia courseware for the Internet need to provide students with the ability to interact directly with the educational process, rather than simply browse. We can interpret interactivity of courseware as a functionality implementation similar to a lecturer posing questions directly to a student and tailorability as the activity by which a student is able to receive personalized representation of educational content. The VEDICI runtime system has being applied as a framework for the integration of heterogeneous educational materials into interactive presentations accessible through the Internet. The usability of our approach for reducing development cost of applications in this domain can be shown by the composition of a typical slide-show application - the source code consists of approximately 15% of application-specific integrating BML scripts and 85% of potentially reusable Java Beans, implementing sequencing, presentation and simulation components. In addition, full support for Java Bean's component model allowed us to use third-party tools and components to integrate OHP images stored in a server-side database into a Web-based distance learning application (Fig. 4). In the final stage, the visualization techniques available for tailoring evolved from a generic script source editor into a combination featuring an application hierarchy browser, component property editor and source editor. These changes required no significant modifications to the existing applications, components or runtime, thus offering a significant reduction in system development costs.

However, as it is commonly acknowledged, in order to improve the effectiveness of a distance learning application we must consider the entire system as a socio-technical framework. In this context, the practical application of end-user tailoring technology toward the delivery of pedagogically

Fig. 4. Multimedia courseware

sound courseware requires the building of a conceptual knowledge base covering the pedagogical aspects of distant education. This knowledge base should include interaction models simulating those that occur in traditional lectures and seminars or an investigation of new forms, specific for distance learning. In the case of end-user tailorable applications the expected result of this consideration is the ability to identify the required degree of tailorability in the distance learning domain, which is beyond the scope of this paper defined in the Section 3. The challenging part of efficiency consideration, in this sense, is that evolving trends of distance learning related technology appears to be causing a shift in the structure of academic teaching from that of a supervisor with personal responsibility for a group of students to that of a knowledge facilitator tasked with providing expert input to a software production team [15]. Regarding the social aspects of distance learning, the application of runtime tailoring and personalization technology can help to reduce or eliminate the extremely high dropout rates typical of early Web-based distance learning programs [16].

7   Related Work

For comparison purposes, we examined three systems that represented (in our opinion) three typical classes of currently existing platforms and which allow end-user tailoring.

OVAL [11] is a radically tailorable tool for cooperative work. OVAL applications are composed from objects, views, agents and links. The appearance and functionality of OVAL is similar to that of Lotus Notes, where documents are represented as semi-structured templates with user-definable views. However, in comparison with Lotus Notes, OVAL is more generic and customizations in OVAL can be performed by end-users with minimal required skills. OVAL was implemented with Macintosh Common Lisp for the Macintosh operating platform and thus does not provide the same degree of cross-platform portability as VEDICI. Secondly, the building blocks and tailoring interfaces are fixed in OVAL making it difficult to adapt this system for use as a generic tailoring platform beyond the scope of its intended applications - support for cooperative work.

ICE [12] is a system for end-user development of collaborative environments on the WWW. ICE is accessible via Web browsers, so no installation is required on the client side. Using ICE the Internet users can compose groupware applications from information, collaboration and interface objects. ICE uses a HTML-based user interface and in this sense VEDICI runtime can provide better GUI that is defined by Java Beans. VEDICI facilitates integration with Web browsers and can be used to emulate some functionality of ICE. Similar to OVAL, the building blocks and tailoring interface in ICE are predefined thus restricting the reusability of the entire system.

EVOLVE [6] is a generic platform for developing tailorable groupware applications, that is currently under development. EVOLVE is implemented by Java and is designed to run on any system equipped with Java Virtual Machine (JVM). The model of primitive components in EVOLVE is FLEX-IBEANS, which is a modification of Java Beans component model. The primitive components can be composed, yielding a composite component. The structure of a composite component is specified by a set of configuration files. The latest available information indicates that future versions of EVOLVE will allow users to plug-in customized tailoring interface. However the architecture of EVOLVE does not allow for the possibility for integrating multiple tailoring interfaces on the same level of complexity, as does the architecture of VEDICI. Since EVOLVE redefines the Java Beans component model, the integration of third party beans would also require their adaptation, which is not necessary in the case of VEDICI.

8   Conclusions and Future Work

In this paper we examined a process for developing tailorable Web applications and identified the problems relating to this development. We proposed the use of compositional markup specifications and the integration of multiple tailoring interfaces as measures for dealing with these problems. We then introduced the composition and modules of a generic reusable platform for tailoring and outlined the application of this platform in the development of active multimedia courseware for the Internet.

In our future work we would like to clarify the practical implications of assumptions made in this paper and verify the usability of the proposed approach in the field of developing socio-technical frameworks for distance learning. We are also in the process researching and designing a high-level XML-based specification language optimized for the supporting the end-user tailorability of distributed component-based applications.

Acknowledgements

This work was sponsored by Telecommunication Advancement Organization of Japan (TAO). We thank Professor Ochimizu and other members of Ochimizu lab at JAIST for providing a superb research environment and educational content for this work.

References

1. Williams, G., HyperCard: HyperCard extends the Macintosh user interface and makes everybody a programmer, Byte, 12: 109–117, Dec. 1987.
2. Morch, A., Stiemerlieng, O., Wulf, V., Tailorable Groupware, ACM SIGCHI Bulletin, Vol. 30, No. 2, April 1998.
3. Peter G. W. Keen, Shaping the Future: Business Design Through Information Technology, Boston: Harvard Business School Press, 1991.
4. Appelt, W., Hinrichs, E., Woetzel, G., Effectiveness and efficiency: the need for tailorable user interfaces on the Web, in: Proceedings of Seventh International World Wide Web Conference, Brisbane, Australia, 1998.
5. MacLean, A., Carter, C., Lovstrand, L., Moran, T., User-tailorable systems: Pressing the issues with buttons, in J. C. Chew, J. Whiteside (eds.), in: Proceedings of CHI '90, ACM, New York NY, 1990, pp. 175–182.
6. Stiemerling, O., Hinken, R., Cremers, Armin B., Distributed Component-Based Tailorability for CSCW Applications, in: Proceedings of the ISADS '99, IEEE Press, Tokyo, Mar. 20–23, 1999, pp. 345–352.
7. Nierstrasz, O., Tsichritzis, D., de Mey, V., Stadelmann, M., Objects+Scripts=Applications, In proceedings, Esprit 1991 Conference, Kluwer Academic Publishers, 1991, pp. 534–552.
8. Johnson, M., Bean Markup Language, JavaWorld, August 1999.
9. Floyd, C., Reisen, F.-M., and Schmidt, G., STEPS to Software Development with Users, in: Lecture Notes in Computer Science, Vol 387: ESEC'89, ed. C. Ghezzi and J. A. McDermid, Springer-Verlag, 1989, pp. 48–64.
10. Stiemerling, O., Kahler, H., Wulf, V., How to Make Software Softer - Designing Tailorable Applications, in: Proceedings of DIS'97, Amsterdam, August 18–20, 1997, pp. 365–376.
11. Malone, Th., Fry, Ch., Lai, K.-Y., Experiments with OVAL: A Radically Tailorable Tool for Cooperative Work, in: Proceedings of the Conference on Computer-Supported Cooperative Work, New York, 1992, pp. 289–297.
12. Farshchian, B. A. and Divitini, M., ICE: A Highly Tailorable System for Building Collaboration Spaces on the WWW, Tailorable Groupware, ACM SIGCHI Bulletin, Vol. 30, No. 2, April 1998.
13. Nielsen, J., Usability Inspection Methods, in: Proceedings of CHI'94 Conference Companion on Human factors in computing systems, 1994, pp. 413–414.
14. Benyon, D., Stone, D., Woodroffe, M., Experience with developing multimedia courseware for the World Wide Web: the need for better tools and clear pedagogy, International Journal of Human-Computer Studies, 47 (1), Academic Press Inc., 1997, pp. 197–218.

15. Laurillard, D., Preece, J., Shneiderman, B., Neal, L., Waern, Y., Distance Learning: Is it the End of Education as Most of Us Know It? in: Proceedings of the CHI 98 summary conference on CHI 98 summary: human factors in computing systems, 1998, pp. 86–87.
16. Wright, S. W. Y., Eleonor Lee, Distance Learning, Community College Week 11(22), 1999, pp. 6–9.

A Petri Nets Approach to Behavior Testing of SET Payment

Chun-Chia Wang[1], Jason C. Hung[2] and Lun-Ping Hung[2]

[1] Department of Information Management, Kuang Wu Institute of Technology,
PeiTou, Taipei, Taiwan 112
E-mail: ccwang@mis.kwit.edu.tw

[2] Department of Computer Science and Information Engineering, Tamkang
University, Tamsui, Taipei, Taiwan 251
E-mail: jhung@cs.tku.edu.tw

Abstract. By secure electronic transaction (SET) protocol, business and customers can construct different electronic commerce models on the Internet. In this paper, we propose a method based on Petri net models and techniques of software engineering to detect unusual electronic commerce transactions. Users can construct all electronic commerce transactions of business and customers by SET. Because of features and functions of SET, users can get security and verification on the network transactions. Using our proposed technique, electronic commerce designers can detect potential security flaws in transaction behavior on the Internet and find any electronic transaction problems that need to solve.

Keywords: Petri Nets, Reachability Tree, Secure Electronic Transaction (SET).

1 Introduction

Recently, electronic commerce has great development in theory and practice [1,2]. However, most research and practical experience focus on transaction behaviors and benefits gaining, little work being carried out to examine the completeness and accuracy of transaction status. Although many commercial applications testing techniques have been proposed, these conventional methods [10], despite their efficiency, cannot be applied without adaptation to electronic commerce systems due to new transaction models such as business to business (B2B), business to customer (B2C) and customer to customer (C2C) [3,4]. In order to analyze new transaction behavior, there is a need for developing testing techniques of electronic commerce.

In this paper, we illustrate the application of Petri nets (PNs) for all paths testing of transaction status designs. A major feature of transaction behavior is the interaction between transaction states. This interaction can be properly modeled with state transition diagrams (STDs) [9]. The STD model represents all possible states of the electronic commerce, the transaction events that can cause state transitions, and the actions that result from the state change. Therefore, STD is often used as a specification of model system in most analysis and design methods. We propose *Petri net machine* (PNM) for electronic commerce detecting. The basic features of PNM are based on PNs used in Murata's methods [8].

In our technique, we specify the behavior of transaction state in terms of PNM and generate test cases based on *reachability tree* resulted from PNM. First, we transform STD corresponding to the method sequence specification of a transaction status into a Petri net in which we restrict that each transition has exactly *one* input and *one* output arc. Then we construct a corresponding reachability tree to the Petri net and apply coverage criteria testing techniques upon the tree. This generates test cases that cover the correct sequence usage for all the transaction states of the transaction status. We can determine whether or not the causal relationships in PNM are correctly implemented in the transaction diagram with transaction behaviors.

This paper is organized as follows. Section 2 discusses definitions and basic properties of Petri nets. Section 3 introduces specifications of transaction diagrams based on STDs, and then transforms the STD into an equivalent PNM. Section 4 describes our testing technique based on the PNM. Section 5 compares our work with related works. Conclusion and future works are given in section 6.

2   Definitions and Basic Properties of Petri Nets

Petri nets (PNs) [7,8] is a graphical and mathematical modeling tool applicable to many systems. As a graphical tool, Petri nets can be used as a visual communication aid similar to flow charts, block diagrams, and networks. This section gives a formal definition of PNs, and introduces a notation of state in order to discuss behavioral analysis problems for PNs.

Definition 2.1. A *Petri Net* (PN) is a bipartite graph, i.e., a graph whose set of nodes is partitioned into two subsets, called the set of *places* $V=\{P_1...P_n\}$ and the set of *transitions* $T=\{t_1...t_m\}$, each arc connecting only nodes of different types. It is shown in Figure 1

Definition 2.2. A *marking* (or *state*) of a PN is a mapping $M:V \rightarrow N$ (numerical numbers); numerically it is represented by a vector with |V| nonnegative components and graphically by $M(P_i)$ *tokens* in the place P_i.

Definition 2.3. A transition t_i is *firable* f a given marking M if, for every place P_i, $M(P_i) \geq$ (Number of arcs connecting P_i to t_i). A marking M' is reached from M by firing t_i if t_i is firable for M and, for every P_j,
$M'(P_j) = M(P_j)$ - (Number of arcs connecting P_j to t_i) + (Number of arcs connecting t_i to P_j).

Definition 2.4. A marking M' is said to be *immediately reachable* from M if M' can be obtained by firing a transition enabled in M. The PN execution allows a sequence of markings $\{M_0, M_1, M_2,...\}$ and a sequence of transitions $\{t_1, t_2,...\}$ to be defined. The firing of t_1, enabled in M_0, changes the PN state from M_0 to M_1 and so on. A marking M'' is said to be *reachable* from M if there exists a sequence of transition firings that moves the PN state from M to M''.

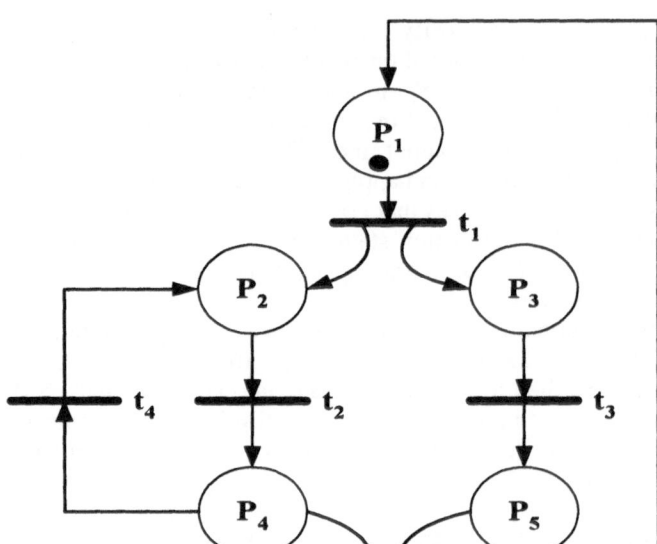

Figure 1. Example of a marked PN.

Definition 2.5. A *reachability set R(M_0)* of a PN as the set of all markings that are reachable from M_0. The reachability set of a PN can be represented by a tree. It can be shown that the tree in Figure 2 represents the reachability set of the PN in figure 1.

To represent a finite reachability tree, we stop to expand the tree when we reach an already considered marking. We shall call such markings duplicate nodes. During the construction of the reachability tree, we can also find dead markings, i.e., marking in which no transition is enabled. Dead and duplicate markings constitute the frontier markings (leaves) of the tree.

3   Petri Net Machine

3.1   A State Transition Diagram for Transaction Specification

Many system analysis and design techniques propose STDs for modeling the dynamic behavior of transaction. STDs can be used to model both inter-state and intra-state dynamic behavior. For deriving the transaction state specification, we use its intra-state STD. The STD model represents all possible states of the transaction status, the events that can cause state transitions, and the actions that result from the state change.

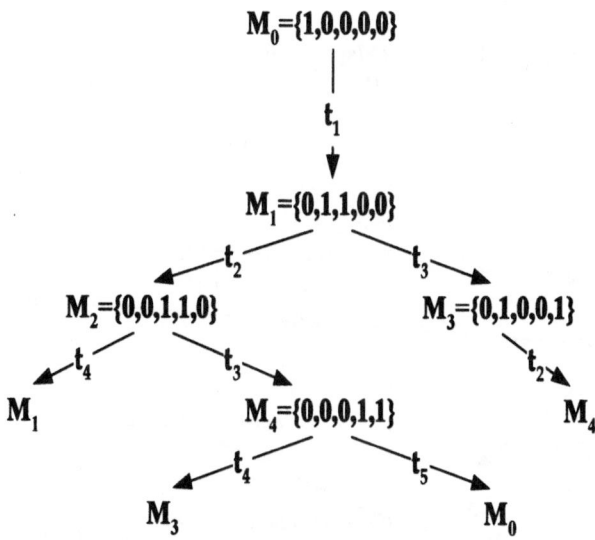

Figure 2. The reachbility tree of the PN in Figure 1

Different transaction states have their special functions and attributes. The states are linked to one another through state transitions. State transitions are caused by events, which are the stimulus received from the environment. At each state, all the events are unique and events can be received in any state. The state transition depends on the current state and the message received. Thus, the transaction state specification can be derived automatically from the STD specification of the transaction status. For the sake of deriving state specification, we use only the events. We do not consider the states and actions associated with state transitions. STDs (similar to finite automata) can be modeled as 5-tuple $M = (Q, \Sigma, \delta, s, f)$, where Q is a finite set of states, Σ is the set of methods accessible from the outside environment, δ is the transition function mapping $Q \times \Sigma$ to Q, $s \in Q$ is an initial state corresponding to the state after a class receives a *constructor* message, and $f \in Q$ is a final state corresponding to a class receiving a *delete* message.

Example: *The Set Payment Status.* The STD corresponding to the dynamic behavior of *Set Payment Status* is given in Figure 3 [5,6]. The STD consists of seven states with different types of events, each corresponding to messages.

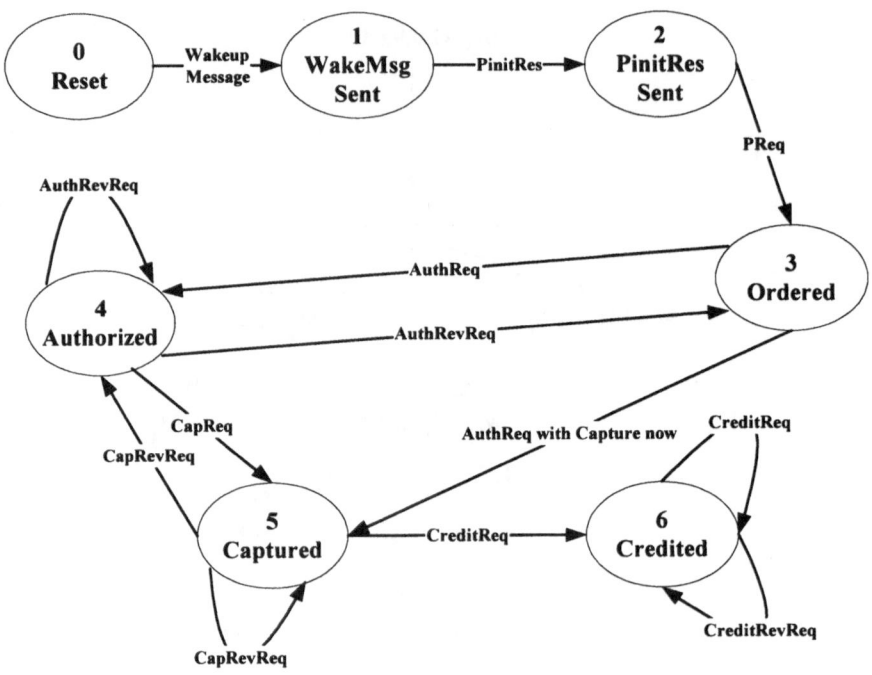

Figure 3. A STD model of SET

3.2   Transforming STD into PNM

In the analysis of Petri nets, there are two subclasses of Petri nets commonly considered, state machines (SMs) and marked graphs (MGs) [7,8]. SMs are Petri nets which are restricted so that each transition has exactly *one* input and *one* output arc. These nets are obviously finite-state. In fact, they are exactly the state machines of electronic commerce. This is clearly shown by considering the state graph of a finite-state machine, as in Figure 3. The nodes of this graph represent the states of the finite-state machine. An arc from state *i* to state *j* labeled *x* indicates that there is a transition from state *i* to state *j* with input *x*. The graph of Figure 3 can be converted to an equivalent Petri net by simply making each state a place, and making each arc between two places a transition. This is illustrated in Figure 4. Note that this Petri net is *conservative*.

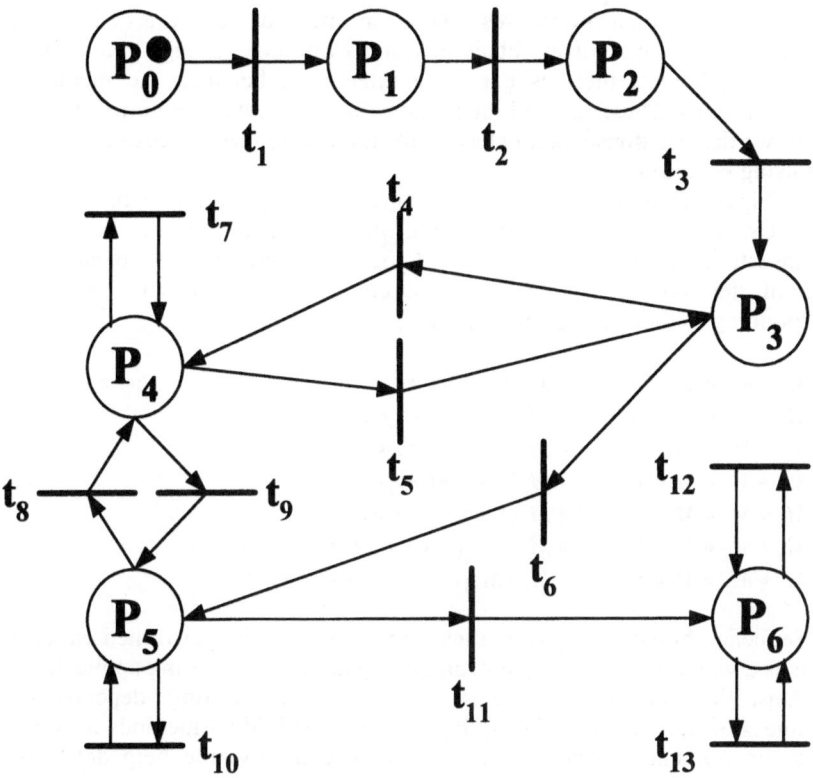

Figure 4. A PNM model corresponding to Figure 3

4   Electronic Transaction Behavior Testing from PNMs

The testing of electronic transaction behavior is used for ensuring the correctness of a transaction status against its specification by executing a transaction on a transaction status and detecting all transaction paths. The steps involved in testing are as follows:

STDs transformed to PNMs,
a reachability tree resulting from PNMs, and
evaluation of all-edge

In our technique, we focus on all transaction paths from the reachability tree of the PNM of a transaction status.

In the electronic commerce, testing a transaction behavior corresponds to testing the methods supported by the transaction status. Individual methods are similar to conventional procedures. Therefore, methods can be tested similarly to conventional procedures using black-box and white-box testing. In a paradigm of transaction behavior, there is extensive interaction between the methods of a transaction status. These method interactions must be tested for correctness. In this section, we discuss transaction behavior for the method sequences of a transaction status using *coverage criteria*.

In Figure 5, a reachability tree diagram corresponding to the Figure 4 is shown. Using different coverage criteria, different sequences can be constructed for transaction status. To satisfy the *all-edge* coverage criteria, seven sequences (paths of the tree, i.e., $R(M_0)$) can be constructed as follows and detecting corresponding to them can be generated.

$$M_0 \bullet M_1 \bullet M_2 \bullet M_3 \bullet M_4 \bullet M_3 (t_1 \bullet t_2 \bullet t_3 \bullet t_4 \bullet t_5)$$
$$M_0 \bullet M_1 \bullet M_2 \bullet M_3 \bullet M_4 \bullet M_4 (t_1 \bullet t_2 \bullet t_3 \bullet t_4 \bullet t_7)$$
$$M_0 \bullet M_1 \bullet M_2 \bullet M_3 \bullet M_4 \bullet M_5 (t_1 \bullet t_2 \bullet t_3 \bullet t_4 \bullet t_9)$$
$$M_0 \bullet M_1 \bullet M_2 \bullet M_3 \bullet M_5 \bullet M_4 (t_1 \bullet t_2 \bullet t_3 \bullet t_6 \bullet t_8)$$
$$M_0 \bullet M_1 \bullet M_2 \bullet M_3 \bullet M_5 \bullet M_5 (t_1 \bullet t_2 \bullet t_3 \bullet t_6 \bullet t_{10})$$
$$M_0 \bullet M_1 \bullet M_2 \bullet M_3 \bullet M_5 \bullet M_6 \bullet M_6 (t_1 \bullet t_2 \bullet t_3 \bullet t_6 \bullet t_{11} \bullet t_{12})$$
$$M_0 \bullet M_1 \bullet M_2 \bullet M_3 \bullet M_5 \bullet M_6 \bullet M_6 (t_1 \bullet t_2 \bullet t_3 \bullet t_6 \bullet t_{11} \bullet t_{13})$$

Sequence-based testing of a transaction status can be performed either during design as a walkthrough or implementation by actually executing applications with the transaction behavior. Because sequence-based testing depends on the correctness of individual methods, the testing of individual methods must precede testing the sequences. Those paths of the reachability tree help determine the interactions between methods of transaction status.

5 Related Works

In general, Petri Nets models are applied to many areas, such as network protocol, software complexity measure, system detecting, etc. In electronic commerce literature, several techniques have been proposed for system testing. Most of them are conventional methods including system performance, data security and verification, customer behavior. In addition to these, the detecting of transaction model is also an important issue. In an accurate and complete environment, designers can detect their electronic transaction model and provide better services for customers or business.

Our technique is specification-based, i.e., we specify the behavior of transaction behavior using PNs and a reachability tree is constructed from PNs. There exist some of feasible paths are determined by PNs. Therefore, the works in [7,8] and our work complement each other.

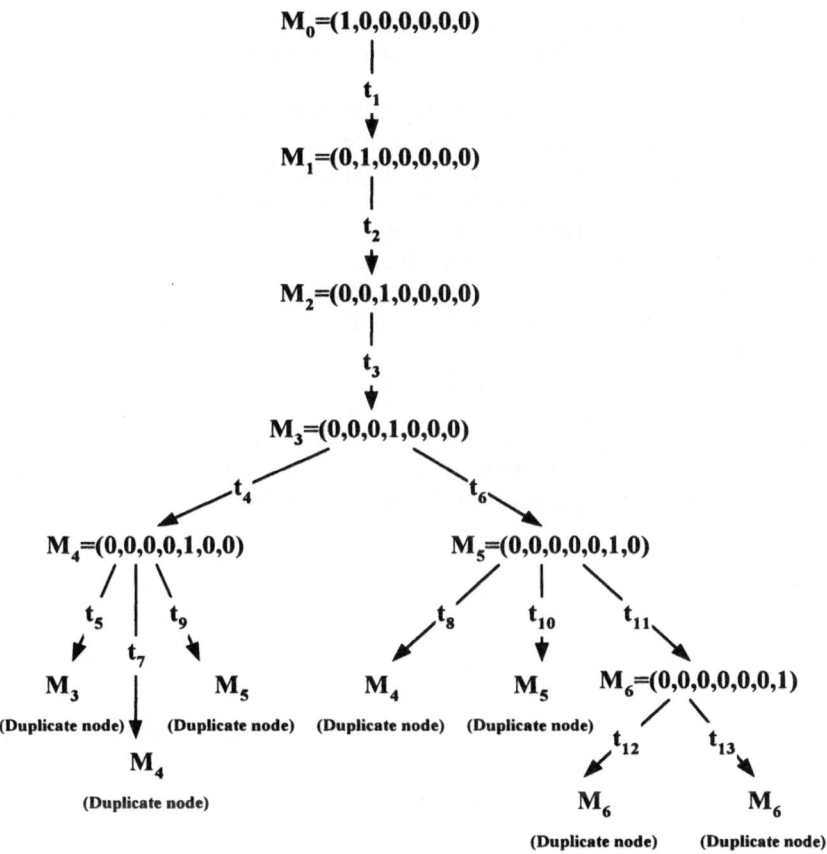

Figure 5. The reachability tree diagram corresponding to Figure 4.

6 Conclusion

In this paper, we have proposed a testing technique for specifying the causal relationship that exists between behavior of transaction designs. In our technique, we illustrated a state transition diagram of electronic commerce transactions, then transformed the STD into an equivalent Petri net machine (PNM) with restriction. In order to test the behavior of the transactions effectively, we have generated a model by converting PNM to a complete reachability tree and applying all-edge testing technique upon the different paths of the tree. We are currently working on integrating transaction specification with an assistant tool. We are also working on verifying the transaction behavior testing application and usefulness.

References

1. Visa International and MasterCard International, Secure Electronic Transaction specification (SET), Version 1.0, May 1997.
2. R. Kalakota and A. Whinston, *Electronic Commerce: A Manager's Guide*, Addison-Wesley, 1997.
3. R.F. Morgan, "An Internet Marketing Framework for the World Wide Web (WWW)", Journal of Marketing Management, Vol. 12, pp. 757-775, 1996,.
4. C. Schlueter and M.J. Shaw, "A strategic framework for developing electronic commerce", IEEE Internet Computing, pp. 20-28, Nov/Dec, 1997.
5. C.E. Landwehr and D.M. Goldschlag, "Security Issues in Networks with Internet Access", Proceedings of the IEEE, Vol. 85, No. 12, December 1997.
6. W. Mougayar, *Opening Digital Markets*, McGraw-Hill, 1998.
7. J.L. Peterson, *Petri Net Theory and The Modeling of Systems*, Prentice-Hall, Englewood Cliffs, NJ, 1981.
8. Tadao Murata, "Petri Nets: Properties, Analysis, and Applications," *Proceedings of the IEEE*, Vol. 77, No. 4, pp. 541-580, April 1989.
9. B. Bosik and M.Ú. Uyar, "Finite State Machine Based Formal Methods in Protocol Conformance Testing: from Theory to Implementation," *Computer Networks and ISDN Systems*, Vol. 22, pp. 7-33, 1991.

Electronic Commerce Transactions in a Mobile Computing Environment

Jari Veijalainen[1] and Aphrodite Tsalgatidou[2]

[1] GMD-FIT, Germany
[2] University of Jyväskylä, Finland
  E-mail: jari.veijalainen@gmd.de

Abstract. Internet E-commerce has been flourishing for the last few years, especially with the advent of World Wide Web. Mobile Electronic Commerce (MEC) has started recently to appear in the scene. It exploits the advantages of Internet, mobile computing and mobile communications in order to provide a large number of advanced services to mobile users. The potentials of MEC are enormous while related technical, business and legal issues become more complicated. The goal of this chapter is to present and discuss problems and identify requirements associated with the trading and billing of tangible and intangible goods in a mobile environment where mobile handheld devices are used for conducting the transactions.

Keywords: Transaction Processing, Mobile Electronic Commerce, Mobile Computing, Wireless Application Protocol, Wireless Networks

1 Introduction

Electronic Commerce (EC or E-Commerce) concerns the digitization of markets and the emergence of a new industry to sustain these electronic markets. The last few years, with the advent of World Wide Web (WWW) there has been a remarkable growth in the Business to Consumer (B2C) EC which to a great extent is synonymous with electronic retailing. A large number of shopping opportunities all over the Internet appeared the last few years offering every kind of goods from digital audio and video (mp3, real-audio etc.) to physical books and CDs, and lately even to cars and houses (see e.g. Amazon's site [18]).

Mobile Electronic Commerce (MEC) has started recently to appear in the scene as a result of the continuously increasing number of hand-held devices as they are an ideal channel for offering a large number of advanced services to mobile users by exploiting the advantages of Internet, mobile computing and mobile communications. As MEC we define any type of economic activity that is considered as EC by legislation of some country or by a business community *and* is performed with a mobile wireless terminal by at least one party (usually the customer) over wireless telecommunications network, although any other wireless network, such as wireless IP network could be used, too.

We are aware that the definition of MEC above is still vague and raises many questions. One reason is that the very concept of EC is currently not very precisely and uniquely laid down. Second, the concept of mobile computing is also still evolving; some people have coined the term ubiquitous computing to address the possibilities of anywhere, anytime computing. Mobility does not preclude mobile devices, but in our view the new possibilities and challenges for the EC are brought up via wireless portable terminals that are typically personal and hand-held. These provide also security mechanisms and advanced application and are called Personal Trusted Devices (PTD).

Our view is thus that MEC is a special case of EC, i.e. MEC has all the opportunities and problems that EC has, and, in addition, it offers some novel and exciting possibilities - as well as new threats and challenges. Technical, business and legal issues become more complicated in MEC than in EC performed using stationary workstations and similar devices.

A number of MEC-specific novel applications and services, especially localised and personalised services have started to appear. We consider the location-based services now emerging in 2G+ and 3G telecommunication networks to fall under MEC in this context. At the same time, applications and services already offered in Internet for PC-level fixed terminals are becoming available for mobile users. Thus, users can now order and buy goods, services, etc. using their mobile hand-held terminals instead of PCs. Although there are still differences between the quality and variety of services for different terminal types, these are becoming smaller, even vanishing in some cases.

The Wireless Application Protocol (WAP) [13] plays an important role in especially GSM-based MEC as it bridges the gap between the mobile world and the Internet world (TCP/IP networks) by optimizing standards for the unique constraints of the wireless environment. It also offers complicated enough security mechanisms and application platform for mobile electronic commerce applications to be developed. A parallel development has taken place in Japan where especially i-Mode technology introduced by NTT DoCoMo is being used by over twenty million subscribers [25].

The goal of this chapter is to present and discuss problems associated with the trading and billing of tangible and intangible goods in a mobile computing environment and to identify their transactional and other requirements. It is organized as follows: section 2 describes the steps and activities of the trading and billing process and the problems and critical issues associated with it. The issue of mobility and its effect in the e-commerce processes and transactions is examined in section 3, while section 4 discusses transactional requirements for a mobile e-commerce environment and finally section 5 concludes the chapter.

2   The trading and pricing process in b2c E-commerce and mobile E-commerce and related legal issues

2.1   The trading process and related legal and technical issues

The main phases of the trading process derived from a set of studies (e.g. [7] and from the EC Directive [3] are: Information Acquisition, Negotiation, Execution phase and After-sales phase. If everything runs smoothly, the process is terminated after a successful completion of the first three phases. However, in many cases, disputes may arise: the delivery may not correspond to the order, the product may be defect upon reception or becomes soon defect, the payment could not be settled, the ordering process might not conform to the regulations, the ordering transaction could not be made legitimate or it may be repudiated.

In order to deal with such problems and in order to support Europe's transition to a knowledge-based economy and boosting competitiveness, the European Union (EU) has published a number of directives. The main EC directive [3] defines clearly that merchants should have a place of establishment and show all their identification and contact information on the site. As place of establishment is defined the place where the merchant actually pursues an economic activity through a fixed establishment, irrespective of where the web-sites or servers are situated or where the merchant may have a mail box. This removes legal uncertainty and ensures that merchants cannot evade supervision, as they will be subject to supervision in the country where they are established.

The EC directive [3] does not deal with the law to be applied in contracts and disputes as these are handled by the Brussels and Rome Conventions [14], [15]. It has to be mentioned that the location of the customer at the time of putting the order doesn't count, as it is the customer's permanent domicile that counts.

Out-of-court dispute settlements are encouraged in [3]. This type of mechanism may appear particularly useful for some disputes on the Internet because of its low transactional cost, which is bearable for small businesses and individual customers, who might otherwise be deterred from using legal procedures because of their cost. The EC directive suggests that the legal framework of these dispute-settlement mechanisms in the various countries should not be such that it limits the use of these mechanisms or makes them unduly complicated.

2.2   Pricing, payments, intellectual property rights and taxation

Pricing of digital goods and services is affected by the fact that perfect copies, or replicates, can be reproduced and distributed almost without any cost [9]. Furthermore, new opportunities for repackaging content through bundling, site licensing, subscriptions, rentals, differential pricing, per use fees and various other mechanisms have emerged with the use of Internet [1].

Issues related with the tracking and recording revenues and especially, of literal and artistic works: who collects the payments, how the revenue is calculated and so on, are resolved in the EU's directive proposal [4], which follows the globally accepted Berne convention, its amendments, and WIPO (World Intellectual Property rights Organisation) recommendations. Most often Intellectual Property Rights (IPR)-owners transfer their rights to representatives. In digital economy this means that customers pay on a packaged product to the producer, and on browsing, when having a look upon the material on a web-site. In the first case the IPR-owner can definitely gain while in the second case, the profit depends on the agreement with the seller and whether or not the customer is allowed to browse free of charge. It seems that in some cases the operator is willing to provide copyright protection mechanisms, packaging, delivery, and charging for the packaged product as value-added services to the representatives of the copyright owners (e.g. [5]).

Regarding charges such as customs, the joint EU-USA declaration on EC (see [19] and the EC directive [3]) states that when goods are ordered electronically and delivered physically, there will be no additional import duties applied. In all other cases relating to EC, the absence of duties on imports should remain.

Concerning Value Added Taxation (VAT) the situation is changing. The problems associated with VAT together with proposed remedies can be found in [16]. The main goal is to collect VAT for Information Society Services (ISS) that also cover trading of electronic goods provided that they are consumed within the EU, no matter where the order is placed and how the goods are delivered to the customer. The directive proposal requires larger service providers based outside the EU to register themselves in one member country and to collect and remit VAT for the EU resident private consumers purchasing physical or digital goods using EC facilities. On the other hand, the proposal allows EU based service providers to sell goods without collecting VAT, provided that the goods are consumed outside the EU. This rectifies the double unfair situation for EU merchants where merchants outside the EU have been able to sell goods for customers within the EU without collecting VAT, while EU resident merchants have been obliged to collect VAT for goods electronically ordered and exported also for consumption outside EU. Notice that the rules for businesses will not be changed, i.e. the reverse mechanism is further applied as before in collecting VAT.

Another matter with taxation has to do with who is liable for paying VAT, the customer or the merchant? The latest directive proposal on taxation matters [16] tries to clarify the place of taxation as follows:

- services supplied by a non-EU merchant to an EU customer are subject to VAT, while services supplied by an EU merchant to a non-EU customer are not,
- services supplied by an EU-merchant to another EU business are subject to VAT at customer's establishment while services supplied by an EU merchant to an EU private individual or to another business in the same EU country are subject to VAT at the merchants location.

Although intuitively appealing, the rules described raise some questions. Possible criteria for determining the place of consumption, definitions for place of supply, taxable person and related issues can be found in [17]. The place of consumption in [16] is determined through the domicile of the private consumer. In future, when there will be more mobile devices at the disposal of the customers and more products like digital maps usable in them, this principle can lead to a considerable VAT avoidance by non-EU citizens who come to the territory of EU for longer periods of time, but have their domicile outside EU.

A further issue that arises is how it can be checked if the VAT has been paid properly. If both merchant and customer are businesses in the EU this is easy. But in case of individuals or non EU-merchants things are not so simple. In order to deal with such issues, in the same proposal [16] it is suggested that non-EU merchants don't have to register for tax purposes if they supply products to EU businesses EU, as the latter are responsible for the VAT. Regarding supplies to individuals, they have to register only if their annual level of sales within the EU is above 100.000 Euro. We think that, overall, this measure puts EU and non-EU merchants on an equal basis when they supply to EU customers.

3 Current mobile technologies

3.1 General Definitions

The term mobility refers to the ability of a user to change location. We view the issue of mobility from the point of view of a customer changing physical location (city, country, continent) together with his/her mobile hand-held terminal, as this will possibly cause complications for conducting trade. We view the current situation according to the following picture. The backbone network is an IP network (Internet) and the servers are attached to it. Mobile hand-held terminals, as facilitated by Mobile IP technologies, connect directly within the IP network [10] or by access technologies, like 2nd generation (2G) GSM networks or 3rd generation (3G) mobile networks.

One of the main differences between these different network generations is the bandwidth. In the current 2G networks the bandwidth ranges from 9.6 kbps to 14.4 kbps. 2G+ HSCSD (High Speed Circuit Switched Data) will offer in practice 57.6 kbps and GPRS (General Packet Radio Service) ca. 112 kbps transmission rates. The EDGE (Enhanced Data rates for Global Evolution) promises 384 kbps maximum, but in practice the transfer rates are below that. 3G networks should provide 2 Mbps in good circumstances. In worse circumstances (e.g., weak signal, or in the move) the bandwidth will be only a few hundred kbps or even less than hundred kbps.

Another dimension of the access networks is the service capability. In the basic 2G network the services are voice, circuit switched data (CSD), and short messages (SMS). Especially short messages have been used to support financial services like banking and stock services. CSD can be used as the carrier in a TCP/IP network and it is possible now to do Internet banking using e.g., hand-held Communicators over CSD.

In 2G+ networks the new standard Wireless Application Protocol (WAP) [13] provides a novel way to support MEC. It brings Internet and GSM technologies together so that contents in WWW servers can be automatically reformatted and moved to handsets. e.g. basic banking services are already made possible through WAP phones [8]. It is expected that the WAP technology will be adopted in the 3G systems, too. The major technical difference to 2G+ systems is the considerably better bandwidth, close to the present LAN-connections. The lately introduced Japanese I-mode technology serves similar purpose as WAP [25].

Bluetooth [2] is a new emerging technology that will evidently have impact on MEC. Using this technology it would be possible to conduct EC transactions without a heavy network infrastructure. Thus, handheld devices could talk directly e.g. with cash registers. Integration of Bluetooth and WAP are under way [13].

3.2 Mobility In B2C E-Commerce and its ramifications

The mobile hand-held terminals together with WAP are a new access technology to Internet-based E-commerce world. As such, E-commerce based on WAP services does not change the structures at the Internet side. Technically, mobile hand-held terminals are much smaller in size than PCs and bandwidth is still scarce. This makes the conduct of the whole transaction from Information Acquisition to Execution phases expensive, especially if there is lot of data to transmit. Additionally, AV marketing information consumes a lot bandwidth. Thus, there is a need to adapt the E-commerce services into the WAP world, and mobile world in general.

Considering security and identification of the terminals, the latter is at about the same level as in stationary PCs over a public telephone network. Actually, the phone number on the SIM card is more persistent than the IP-identity of PCs that can be easily changed. On the other hand, authentication of a person should not be based on SIM card identity or the device identity, because both can be stolen. Although the access is protected by PIN, these are at least currently rather short (4 digits) and besides this, if the terminal is stolen while it is on, the PIN is not at all asked. In practice, this would call for improved identification and security.

From the legal point of view, customers' mobility poses new challenges. The question is according to which legislation the business is conducted. The natural candidates are the legislation of the residence country of the service provider, legislation of the residence country of the customer, and legislation of the country of the customer's residence. USA seems to favor the first alternative (the merchant sites announce that the applicable law is that of their residence). In EU the current legislation is based on Rome and Brussels Conventions [14], [15] and the new EU directive on E-Commerce [3] (see section 2 above).

However, since the geographical location of a mobile user with a hand-held terminal can be easily identified, there emerge a lot of services in MEC that can utilize the location information (or that of the terminal, to be exact). The evident ones are answers to questions like "Where am I now?", "Where is the nearest X?", or "Where is Y now". Another group of location-related questions are of type "Where is the cheapest X nearest to Y/me?". To facilitate these services, new solutions are required. One question is, how the location information is provided in the case of the questions of the first type. Maps are an answer, but there might be others, too, like global coordinates. The latter are basis for the location services in any case. If maps are used, the interesting question is, how the costs and the economic yield of the service are divided among the players. Clearly, the digitized maps and other location-based services are digital goods and thus regulated by [14].

Technically it would be possible in the near future to track the location of the terminal precisely enough in order to determine the place of consumption of electronic goods. This would alleviate some of the problems discussed above with respect to taxation. To really use this kind of mechanism would require changes in regulations and also a lot of technology development.

4   Transactional requirements for Mobile E-commerce: Issues and Definitions

Traditional transactions are used to ehcapsulate database operations so as to provide Atomicity, Consistency, Isolation, and Durability (ACID). They provide clean semantics to concurrent executions and a powerful abstraction for an application developer. Since the beginning of.1980's new transaction models have been developed to support new application areas, like computer supported cooperative work, workflows, computer integrated manufacturing, international banking, etc. There is a rather comprehensive overview on the earlier work in [6] and some later developments are discussed e.g. in [21], [22].

From transactional point of view, what differentiates MEC from the earlier environments studied, is a number of issues which are analyzed in the following. The first issue is the possible hostility of the open environment. This means that the parties engaged in an E-commerce transaction might be more easily disguised or be forged ones. For instance, the merchants server might not be the one the client thinks it is, or during the E-commerce transaction another entity "hijacks" the transaction and disguises as the client changing e.g. the ordering address of the delivery or changing the amount paid.

Another issue that is related with the previous one is the vulnerability of the mobile hand-held devices. They can easily be stolen and misused. Thus, from transactional point of view, the transactional mechanism should not rely on the device identity (such as phone number or IP number) and it should not deduce user's identity based on the device identity. Thus, even if an E-commerce transaction was started by the user really possessing the device, the device might have been stolen in the meantime and the fraudulent person might change some parameters of the ongoing E-commerce transaction later in his/her benefit. The main issue is, however, that new E-commerce transactions might be started by the stolen device such that the real owner would be charged for them.

There are, on the other hand, great opportunities for useful applications that are based on the device = user identity assumption or anonymous payments based on E-cash carried within the device; consider e.g. being in a bus with a hand-held device in the pocket and accepting the payment by one touch of a button. Or paying gasoline at a gasoline station using a hand-held device (e.g. a WAP phone). Therefore, the transactional mechanisms should not be 'either or' but rather 'both and'. The user could specify the security level he or she wants in a particular case.

Third issue that is closely related with the mobility concept is the communication autonomy (C-autonomy, see e.g. [11], [12]) of the devices. It means that the devices are not always reachable through the network and that it is natural that they are rather often disconnected. This can happen for many reasons, for instance because simply the user shuts off the connection or the device runs out of battery or because the device is outside the coverage area.

From transactional point of view this means that transactional mechanisms should not assume continuous capability of the terminals to communicate, nor should they expect that there would be periods during which the terminal is able and willing to communicate with other components with (nearly) 100 per cent certainty.

The previous considerations suggest that transactional mechanisms must be tied closer with security mechanisms. How this is done, depends partially on the encryption technologies applied in PTDs. In many current applications there is the requirement for end-to-end encryption through which one can reach authentication, authorisation, and concealing of the transferred data. It seems that the weakest link is PIN-based identification and authorisation at the terminal. The reader is urged to consult [23] for further results on this.

Second, the terminal must be able to recover from failures and either recover forward or backward the interrupted transactions. For a more detailed treatment of the transactional aspects the reader is urged to consult [24] that presents the results of the Multimeetmobile project. The practical work is continuing within the project, and implement of a transactional mechanism at the terminal is under way.

5   Conclusions

Business to Consumer E-Commerce of almost every type of good or service is thriving the last few years. At the same time, there is a remarkable increase in the number of Internet-capable mobile hand-held devices (cf. WAP phones) that is expected to overtake very soon the number of PCs and other workstations. Therefore the investigation of the effect of this situation on E-Commerce seems important. In this paper we examined issues related with the B2C E-Commerce in an environment where a mobile customer initiates and concludes E-commerce transactions using his/her mobile hand-held terminal. This type of E-commerce is interesting from many points of view. The small displays and the scarce and expensive limited bandwidth may discourage the user to visit many sites and negotiate with different merchants; however, the use of mobile hand-held terminals opens a new business area in E-Commerce, the location based services, and new E-commerce scenarios seem to emerge.

We consider mobile hand-held terminals as access technology to Internet. As such, some of their characteristics like their embedded payment facilities, the secure identification mechanism guaranteed by the operator (phone numbers) and protected by PIN, facilitate respective issues in E-commerce transactions. However, others characteristics, like their limited graphics capabilities, limited bandwidth, C-autonomy and their vulnerability result in a number of interesting implications from legislative, security, application and transactional point of view.

Furthermore, when a transaction is initiated by a mobile hand-held terminal, its part that is related with the execution of the business processes at the various sites, i.e. at the merchant's site or at the bank's site, remains the same. What is affected by the customer's mobility is the part of the transaction related with customer identification, as mobile hand-held terminals can be easily stolen and appropriate end-to-end mechanisms are needed to guarantee customer identification.

Therefore, the pervasive orthogonal aspect in MEC is security and privacy as well as distribution aspects that deal with the global coherence of processes. Business processes might be different in different regulatory frameworks (EU, USA, Japan) and this may have certain impact on the transactional mechanism in a mobile hand-held device that should recognize the process type at the merchant's site.

These are some of the issues and they need further investigation. The work presented here depicts the results of our on going research in the area of mobile computing and electronic commerce.

Acknowledgements

The authors would like to thank Prof. Jukka Heikkilä from the University of Jyväskylä and Dr. Juha Laine from Helsinki School of Economics for their comments and contribution in earlier drafts of this paper.

References

1.   Bakos, Y., Brynjolfsson, E. (1997). Aggregation and Disaggregration of Information Goods: Implications for Bundling, Site Licensing and Micropayment Systems, Working paper, MIT, June, 1997. http://www.gsm.uci.edu/~bakos
2.   Bluetooth forum. www.bluetooth.com, data accessed June 30, 2000.
3.   Directive on electronic commerce. Official Journal of E.C.,Vol. 43, L178 (17.7.2000).
4.   Proposal for a European Parliament and Council Directive on the harmonization of certain aspects of copyright and related rights in the Information Society (final). http://158.169.50.70/eur-lex/en/com/reg/en_register_1720.html
5.   Amended proposal for a Community action plan on promoting safer use of Internet by combating illegal & harmful content on global networks.E.C. Proposa – COM(98)784 final.
     http://158.169.50.70/eurlex/en/com/reg/en_register_132060.html
6.   Ahmed Elmagarmid (ed.): Database Transaction Models for Advanced Database Applications. Morgan-Kaufmann Publishers, San Mateo, USA 1992.
7.   Kambil, A., van Heck E., (1998). Re-engineering the Dutch Flower Auctions: A Framework for Analyzing Exchange Organizations, Information Systems Research, Vol. 9, No. 1 (March 1998), pp. 1-19.
8.   www.merita.fi, data accessed June 30, 2000.
9.   Shapiro, C., Varian, H.R., (1999). Information Rules: A strategic guide to network economy, Harvard Business School Press, MA., USA, 352 pages.
10. Tanenbaum, A.S., Computer Networks (3rd edition). Prentice Hall, Inc. USA 1996.
11. Jari Veijalainen, Frank Eliassen, Bernhard Holtkamp: The S-transaction Model. Chapter 12 in [6].
12. Jari Veijalainen, Transaction Concepts in Autonomous Database Environments. (Ph.D. thesis). GMD-Bericht Nr. 183, ISBN 3-486-21596-5. R. Oldenbourg Verlag, Munich, Germany, April 1990
13. http://www.wapforum.com/
14. Brussels Convention on Jurisdiction and the enforcement of judgements in civil and commercial matters. Official Journal C027 of 26/01/98 (498Y0126(01)).
15. Rome Convention on the law applicable to contractual obligations (consolidated version) Official Journal C027 of 26/01/98 (498Y0126(03)). Available at http://www.ispo.cec.be/ecommerce/legal/favorite.htm
16. Proposal for a Regulation of the European Parliament and of the Council on administrative cooperation in the field of indirect taxation (VAT) and Proposal for a Council Directive for VAT arrangements applicable to certain

services supplied by electronic means. COM(2000) 349 final. Brussels, 7.6.2000

17. Working Paper of the Commission on Harmonisation of turnover taxes. XX/98/0359, 3.4.1998
18. See www.amazon.com
19. www1.freeweb.ne.jp/~cross/i/index.htm
20. DeBy, R. Klas, W., Veijalainen, J. (eds.). Transaction Support for Cooperative Applications. Kluwer, 1997
21. Elmagarmid, A., Rusinkiewics, M. Sheth, A. (eds.) Heterogeneous and Autonomous Database Management Systems. Morgan-Kaufmann 1998.
22. Tang, J., Veijalainen, J. Using Agents to Improve Security and to Assist in Negotiations for E-Commerce Transactions. Paper at HICSS-34, Minitrack on Mobile E-Commerce. Hawaii, USA, January 3-6, 2001.
23. Veijalainen, J. Transactions in Mobile Electronic Commerce. In: Gunter Saake, Kerstin Schwarz, Can Turker (eds.). Transactions and Database Dynamics. Lecture Notes in Computer Science, Nr. 1773, Springer Verlag, Berlin, December 1999, pp. 208-229.
24. Multimeetmobile site at www.cs.jyu.fi/~mmm
25. Japaninc - electronic journal. Available at http://japaninc.net/_Accessed 13.6.01.

Part III

Intelligent Robots and Auditory Interfaces

Control of Golf Swing Robot by Learning
- Generation of Optimal Trajectory for Real System -

Aiguo Ming[1], Nan Luan[2] and Makoto Kajitani[1]

[1] The University of Electro-Communications, Japan
[2] Shanhai Jiao Tong University, China
E-mail: ming@mce.uec.ac.jp

Abstract. A golf swing robot consisting of an actuated joint and a passive joint with stopper has been developed to simulate the motion control skill in human swing. This paper describes a topic of control by learning, that is, how to achieve an optimal trajectory for the real system though learning. To realize the purpose, a method by repeating swing, model improvement by learning and optimal motion generation is proposed. Method, implementation and experimental results of the control are described in this paper.

Keywords: learning control, trajectory generation, neural network, non-holonomic constraint, under-actuated system.

1 Introduction

A new type of golf swing robot consisting of an actuated joint and a passive joint with mechanical stopper has been developed by authors [1][2], as shown in Fig.1. In our previous works, a method to improve the accuracy to a given swing motion by learning has been proposed and implemented to the robot [3]. And another work has been done about the generation of optimal swing motion based on reference model of the robot [4].

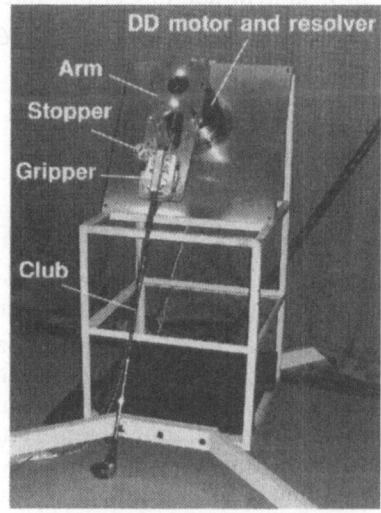

Fig.1 Prototype of golf swing robot

The purpose of this research is to generate optimal motion for the real system of the robot, that is, to achieve an optimal trajectory for the real system though learning. Usually, a golfer tries a lot of swings, according to the result of each swing, adjusts the initial positions, driving force and timing to achieve a good and stable swing, and finally remembers it as a pattern. Afterwards, the golfer playbacks swing according to the remembered pattern. A control method similar to the human swing is proposed for the golf swing robot. Real system model of golf swing robot is composed of a simple model and a compensation model. The compensation model is represented by neural network and is to be derived by learning according to the result of each swing. Then, according to the improved model of real system, optimal trajectory is generated to satisfy boundary conditions, non-holonomic constraint due to passive joint, and target of optimization. In such a way, swing, model improvement and optimal motion generation are repeated until the error of boundary condition at impact position is less than a specified tolerance.

An outline of our system, representation and improvement of real system model, generation of optimal trajectory, implementation of the control to our robot and experimental results by the robot are described in following sections.

2   Description Of The System

Golf swing robot consists of an actuated joint acting as equivalent shoulder, and a passive joint with mechanical stopper acting as wrist, as shown in Fig.2.

For simplicity, a dynamics model shown in Eq.(1) is used to express the basic characteristics of the robot [5].

$$M(\theta)\theta + h(\theta,\dot\theta) + g(\theta) = \tau \tag{1}$$

Here, M is inertia item, h is item due to Coriolis force and centrifugal force, g is gravity item, $\tau = [\tau_1,\tau_2]^T$ is torque item, and $\theta = [\theta_1,\theta_2]^T$ is angle item of joints.

Due to the passive joint with mechanical stopper, there exists a non-holonomic constraint shown by Eq.(2).

$$\tau_2 = \begin{cases} M_{21}\ddot\theta_1 + h_{211}\dot\theta_1 + g_2 & if \ |\theta_2| \geq \theta_{2t} \\ 0 & if \ |\theta_2| < \theta_{2t} \end{cases} \tag{2}$$

Here, θ_{2t} is the angle limitation of passive joint by stopper.

Because our system is an under-actuated system and passive joint is driven by dynamical coupling torque, the method for trajectory generation is different to that of conventional manipulator. That is, trajectory of manipulator can't be generated from kinematics only. A method of generating optimal trajectory for such kind of robot has been proposed in our previous work [4]. This method is based on a simple model of golf swing robot, without detailed consideration about flexibility. Besides, it is impossible to estimate dynamic parameters of real robot accurately.

For those reasons, the generated optimal motion can't be realized in real system. Therefore, it is necessary to establish a method for generate an optimal trajectory for the real system.

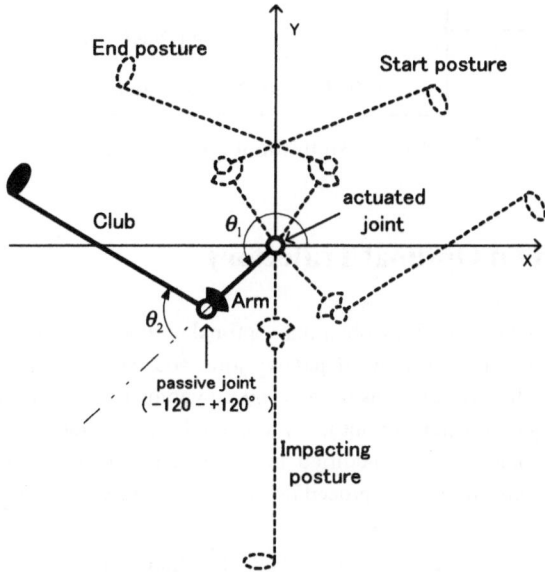

Fig.2 Simplified mechanism of golf swing robot

Our basic idea for the generation of an optimal trajectory for the real system is to build an accurate dynamics model for the real system of robot by learning, then generate optimal trajectory based on it. Those will be described in details in following chapters.

3   Amendment Of System Model

As a model for real system, a compensation model is added to the simple model discussed in Sect.2, as shown in Fig.3. The compensation model is represented by a BP (Back Propagation) neural network and is to be obtained by learning-by-error [6] through swing experiments. It is used to compensate the model errors caused by characteristics such as flexibility, friction etc, and also the errors in estimation of parameters.

Here, the torque reference series of actuated joint in swing experiment is input to the model. And the output series (angle and angular velocity) of real system are used as teacher signals for the model. The aim of learning is to make the output of this model similar to that of real system. Then, a model approximating to real system can be obtained by the learning.

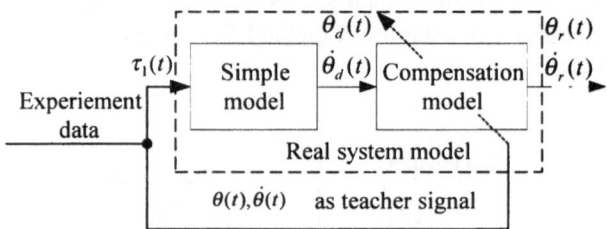

Fig.3 Real system model and learning

4   Generation Of Optimal Trajectory

Optimal trajectory is derived from obtaining optimal torque pattern to satisfy boundary conditions, non-holonomic constraint of passive joint and target of optimization [4]. And this trajectory should be expressed, as usually, by polynomial, or function of Fourier series etc. In our case, torque of actuated joint is represented by a function of Fourier series up to 6th order. And parameters to be modified in optimizing calculation are coefficients of Fourier series and swing time. The procedure for generating optimal motion is shown in Fig.4.

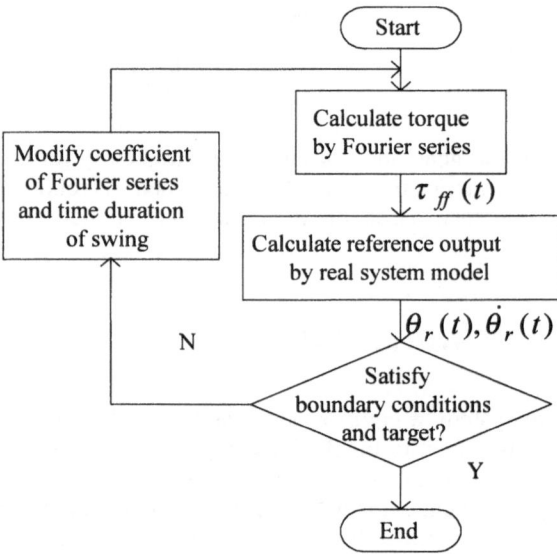

Fig.4 Procedure for optimization of trajectory

5   Implementation To Golf Swing Robot

It should be pointed out that this optimization is based on a amended system model described in Sect.3. The system model is amended repeatedly by learning to approximate to the real system according to experimental results. Therefore, the optimal trajectory for system model can be regarded as the optimal trajectory for the real system.

With the new system model obtained in Sect.3 and optimal trajectory obtained in Sect.4, a method for generation of optimal trajectory of golf swing robot by learning control shown in Fig.5 is proposed.

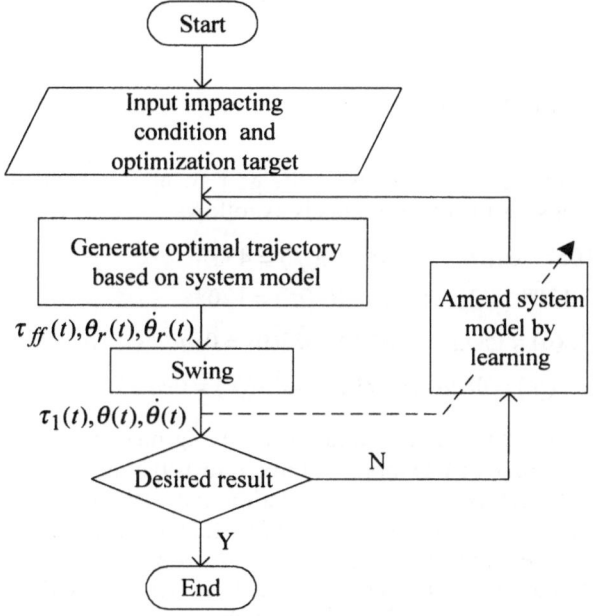

Fig.5 Flowchart for implementation

First, impacting conditions and target of optimization are input. Then optimal trajectory is generated according to the conditions and the target. Simple model is used at first time and the system model amended by learning is used afterwards in the generation of optimal trajectory. According to the generated optimal trajectory, swing experiment is done by robot. The system model is then amended according to results of swing experiment. Again, an optimal trajectory is generated based on the amended system model and swing is done. This procedure is repeated until a satisfied result is obtained. Finally, an optimal trajectory for the real system can be obtained.

Control configuration of the swing motion is shown in Fig.6. Torque trajectory is feedforwarded to DD motor of the actuated joint. A PID controller is used to assure stability of the system at beginning. The motion trajectory obtained in optimization is used as reference input of the PID controller. After several times of learning, the PID can be cut off and system runs only by feedforward control.

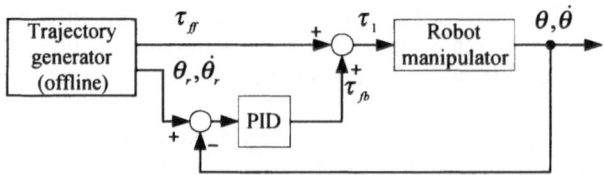

Fig.6 Configuration of control

6   Experimental Results

Some experiments have been done using the golf swing robot shown in Fig.1. The boundary conditions for the experiments is as follows:

$$\theta 1(0) = 105° \quad \theta 1(tm) = 270° \quad \theta 1(tf) = 435°$$
$$\theta 2(0) = -120° \quad \theta 2(tm) = 0° \quad \theta 2(tf) = 120°$$
$$\dot{\theta} 1(0) = \dot{\theta} 2(0) = 0 rad / s \quad \ddot{\theta} 1(0) = \ddot{\theta} 2(0) = 0 rad / s^2 \quad a(tm) = 0 m / s^2$$
$$\dot{\theta} 1(tf) = \dot{\theta} 2(tf) = 0 rad / s \quad \ddot{\theta} 1(tf) = \ddot{\theta} 2(tf) = 0 rad / s^2$$

tm is impacting time and   is the duration of swing motion. Also in our system, maximum driving torque of DD motor is limited to 100 Nm.

The results of trajectories by both simulation and experiment using a target of minimizing maximum of drive torque are shown in figures 7-15. In this experiment, the desired impacting velocity is set to 20 m/s.

In Fig.7, optimal torque trajectories based on simple model and based on amended system model 3 times of learning are shown.

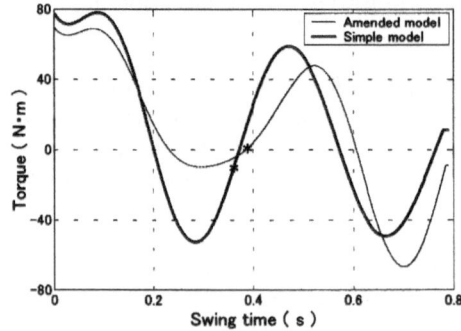

Fig.7 Comparison of optimal toque trajectory
(impacting time is marked by '*', same in other figures)

In figures 8-11, the reference motion trajectories corresponding to the two models are shown. From those figures, we can know that there is an obvious difference on trajectories of torque, angle and velocity between simple model and amended model. And by noticing at angular velocity trajectory of joint 2 in Fig.11, we can find that the influence of the club's flexibility is represented in the amended system model.

Motion trajectories of reference and experimental result before learning are shown in Fig.12 and Fig.13. And trajectories of those after learning 3 times are shown in Fig.14 and Fig.15.

After learning, errors of position and velocity during swing reduce greatly. The errors at impacting moment are shown in Table 1.

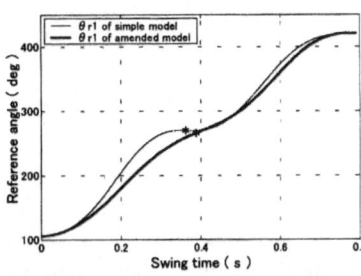

Fig.8 Angle trajectory of joint 1

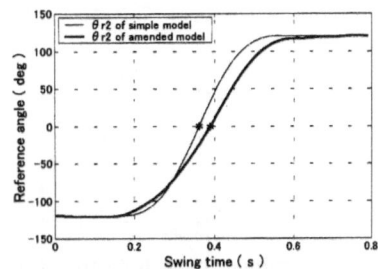

Fig.9 Angle trajectory of joint 2

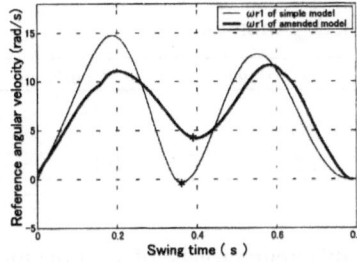

Fig.10 Angular velocity trajectory of joint 1

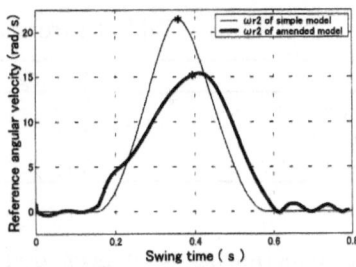

Fig.11 Angular velocity trajectory of joint 2

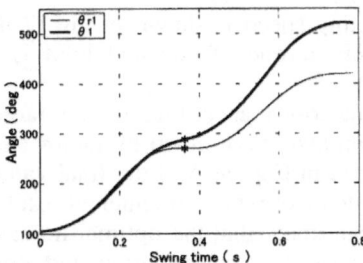

Fig.12 Angle trajectory of joint 1

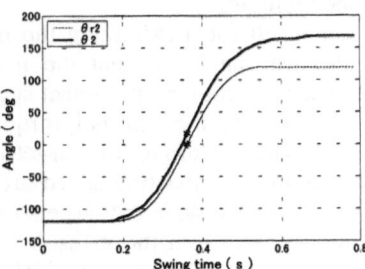

Fig.13 Angle trajectory of joint 2

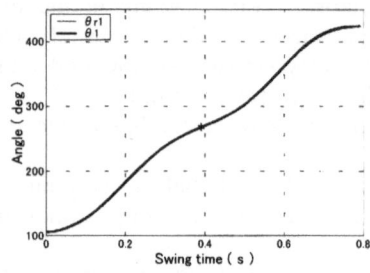

Fig.14 Angle trajectory of joint 1

Fig.15 Angle trajectory of joint 2

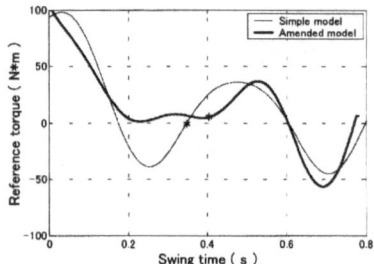 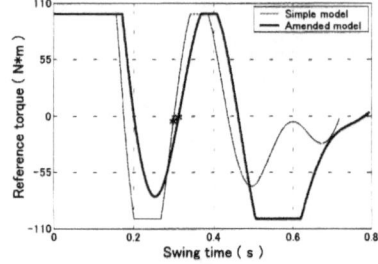

Fig.16 Optimal toque trajectory for
minimizing the work done by motor

Fig.17 Optimal toque trajectory for
maximizing impacting speed

Table 1 Errors at impacting moment

	θ_1 (deg)	θ_2 (deg)	υ (m/s)
Before learning	11.7	15.3	6.12
After one time	5.22	6.24	1.99
After three times	0.15	1.23	0.12

Other experiments have been done for different targets of optimization. In Fig.16, optimal torque trajectories based on simple model and amended system model after 4 times of learning are shown, with using a target of minimizing the work done by motor.

Another result for maximizing the impacting speed is shown in Fig.17. From this figure, we can know that the maximum torque of actuated joint is fully utilized to achieve maximum impact speed.

For comparison, the optimal torque trajectories according to the target to minimize maximum torque, the target to minimize work down by motor and the target to maximize impacting speed are shown in Fig.18. And the final values of cost-functions of the different targets calculated from the experimental results are shown in Table 2. From those results, we can know that the optimal trajectories are much different according to different targets of optimization and optimal trajectories satisfied to different targets are obtained by our method.

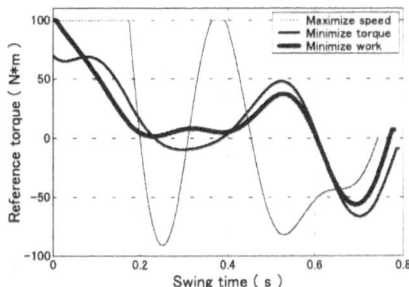

Fig.18 Optimal trajectories for different targets

Table 2 Values of cost functions

Target	Work(J)	Torque(N*m)	Speed(m/s)
Maximize speed	410.35	100.0	27.18
Minimize torque	168.01	69.45	20.12
Minimize work	125.21	100.0	19.65

7   Conclusion

A method for generating an optimal trajectory for real system of golf swing robot based on learning control is proposed and has been applied to golf swing robot successfully. With the control method, golf swing robot can realize real optimal swing motion accurately by feedforward control only.

Acknowledgement

Part of this work was supported by the Scientific Research Fund of the Ministry of Education, Science, sport and Culture, Japan (#11750202).

References

1. A. Ming, Z. Jin, M. Tujiwara and M. Kajitani: Study on golf swing robot -basic concept-, Proceedings of RSJ Annual Meeting '95, pp1139-1140 (1995).(in Japanese)
2. A. Ming and M. Kajitani: Study on golf swing robot -control method-, Proceedings of JSME Annual Conference on Robotics and Mechatronics '96, pp674-677 (1996).(in Japanese)
3. A.Ming, T.Kawano, B.Xu and M.Kajitani: A golf swing robot to simulate human skill -the introduction of learning control-, The Engineering of Sport - Design and Development-, Blackwell Science, pp.283-290 (1998).
4. A.Ming, B.Xu and M.Kajitani: Study on golf swing robot -Optimal motion planning-, The Proceedings of RSJ Meeting 1999,pp1-2 (in Japanese)(1999).
5. Carlos Canudas de Wit, Bruno Siciliano and Georges Bastin(Eds): Theory of Robot Control, Springer-Verlag, Berlin, New York(1996).

6. Kawato Y: Calculation theory of brain (in Japanese), Sangyou Tosho(1995). (in Japanese)

A Novel Obstacle Avoidance Control Scheme for Hyper-Redundant Manipulators

Shugen Ma

Ibaraki University, 4-12-1 Nakanarusawa-Cho, Hitachi 316-8511, JAPAN
E-mail: shugen@dse.ibaraki.ac.jp

Abstract. Hyper-redundant manipulators have large number of kinematic degrees of freedom (*DOFs*), thus possessing some unconventional features such as the ability to enter a narrow space while avoiding obstacles. In this article, we proposed a new obstacle avoidance control scheme for the hyper-redundant manipulator to avoid the existing static obstacles in environment while performing a pick-and-place task. Based on the analysis in the defined posture space where three parameters were used to determine the manipulator's configuration, the obstacle collision-free path has been well generated. To guarantee that the manipulator in motion has no collision with obstacles, the path-tracking control for the manipulator to trace the path in the posture space was also discussed. The joint torques were formulated in the parameter of the posture space path and the posture space path-tracking feedforward controller was introduced on the basis of the parameterized joint torque formulation.

1 Introduction

Hyper-redundant manipulators have very large kinematic DOFs. These robots, which are analogous in design and operation to the "Trunk of an Elephant", have some unconventional features such as the ability to enter a narrow space while avoiding obstacles. However, the realization of such a hyper-redundant manipulator is difficult because there are serious engineering problems involved. One is weight, another is control of their large degrees of redundancy. A novel tendon-driven manipulator mechanism was proposed [1] and a hyper-redundant manipulator called "CT-Arm" has also been developed [2] to solve the weight problem. The hyper-redundancy of the CT-Arm only exists in the vertical plane. The discussion of this study is thus limited to 2-dimension.

To solve the control problem of hyper redundant DOFs, an algorithm for the planar hyper-redundant manipulators where the hyper degrees of redundancy exists only in a plane, was introduced to resolve their kinematic redundancy in real-time [2-5]. In this article, we propose a novel obstacle avoidance control scheme for hyper-redundant manipulators to perform a pick-and-place task where the static obstacles exist in the environment. The scheme is based on analysis in the defined posture space and has the advantage over other possible ones, that this scheme can be used for the real-time control of hyper-redundant manipulators while they are utilized in a static environment. Moreover, to guarantee the manipulator in motion has no collision with obstacles, the path-tracking control for the hyper-redundant manipulator to trace the path in the posture space is also discussed. The joint torques are formulated in the parameterized parameter of the posture space path and the posture space path-tracking feedforward controller is introduced based on the parameterized joint torque formulation.

2   Control Scheme of Hyper-Redundant Manipulators

Curvilinear theory was used to represent the posture of kinematically hyper-redundant manipulators [2–5]. Therein, the arm posture of the hyper-redundant manipulator is modeled by a continuous curve with the curvature function $\kappa(s)$ and the torsion function $\tau(s)$, where s is the distance along the curve measured from the base. For controlling the planar hyper-redundant manipulators like the CT-Arm, we consider a curve only with the curvature function $\kappa(s)$ to model the arm posture of the planar hyper-redundant manipulator. As we explored, the serpenoid curve [6] is better utilized to define the arm posture of hyper-redundant manipulators, because the solution from the given boundary position and the length of curve to the form of curve is easily-obtained.

Consider a serpeniod curve, whose curvature is defined by

$$\kappa(s) = \frac{2\pi}{\ell}a_1 \cos(\frac{2\pi}{\ell}s) + \frac{2\pi}{\ell}a_2 \sin(\frac{2\pi}{\ell}s) \tag{1}$$

where a_1 and a_2 are the coefficients to define the curvature function, and ℓ is the curve length which is equal to the length of the manipulator arm that is to be configured. The angle $\alpha(s)$ that represents the inclination angle of the vector w.r.t. x-axis on the curvilinear length s, and the end-point position (x_ℓ, y_ℓ) can be derived through integration w.r.t. the curve length:

$$\alpha(s) = \alpha_0 + \int_0^s \kappa(u)du = \alpha_0 + a_1 \sin\frac{2\pi}{\ell}s - a_2 \cos\frac{2\pi}{\ell}s + a_2, \tag{2}$$

$$x(\ell) = \int_0^\ell \cos(\alpha(s))ds = \cos(a_2 + \alpha_0)J_0\left(\sqrt{a_1^2 + a_2^2}\right)\ell = x_\ell, \tag{3}$$

$$y(\ell) = \int_0^\ell \sin(\alpha(s))ds = \sin(a_2 + \alpha_0)J_0\left(\sqrt{a_1^2 + a_2^2}\right)\ell = y_\ell \tag{4}$$

where α_0 is the initial inclination angle of the vector w.r.t. x-axis at the arm base, and J_0 is the zero-order Bessel function [7].

While the end position of the curve is given, its form (*or posture*) given by the curvature $\kappa(s)$ corresponding to the given initial inclination angle α_0 can be defined by the coefficients a_1 and a_2. The coefficients a_1 and a_2 are derived by solving Eqs. (3) and (4), and given by

$$a_2 = \tan^{-1}\left(\frac{y_\ell}{x_\ell}\right) - \alpha_0, \quad a_1 = \left(\left[J_0^{-1}\left(\frac{(x_\ell^2 + y_\ell^2)^{\frac{1}{2}}}{\ell}\right)\right]^2 - a_2^2\right)^{\frac{1}{2}} \tag{5}$$

where J_0^{-1} is the restricted inverse zero-order Bessel function [7]. The inverse solution of the curve (*the from of the curve*) is thus derived and defined by the coefficients a_1 and a_2. If we change the initial inclination angle α_0, the form of the curve is changed too, as seen from Eq.(2). Thus, the form of the serpenoid curve is determined by three variables a_1, a_2, and α_0.

The arm posture of the hyper-redundant manipulator can be configured by restricting the arm on the defined serpenoid curve. In the case, the joint angles of the manipulator are derived from the grade of the tangent line, and can be expressed as

$$q_1 = \alpha(\frac{L}{2}) = a_1 \sin(\frac{\pi}{n}) + a_2 \left(1 - \cos(\frac{\pi}{n})\right) + \alpha_0,$$

$$q_i = \alpha\left((i - 1 + \frac{1}{2})L\right) - \alpha\left((i - 1 - \frac{1}{2})L\right)$$

$$= a_1 \left[\sin\left(\frac{\pi}{n}(2i - 1)\right) - \sin\left(\frac{\pi}{n}(2i - 3)\right)\right] \tag{6}$$

$$-a_2 \left[\cos\left(\frac{\pi}{n}(2i - 1)\right) - \cos\left(\frac{\pi}{n}(2i - 3)\right)\right],$$

where $i = 2, 3, \cdots, n$ (*n: number of the manipulator's joints*), and L is the length of each link, equal to ℓ/n.

As a result, we know that the inverse kinematic solution, in which the joint angles of the hyper-redundant manipulator are calculated from the given end position (x_ℓ, y_ℓ), has been simply derived by Eqs.(5) and (6). It should be understandable that the scheme is advanced in computational cost, and makes the real-time position-coordination control of hyper-redundant manipulators possible.

3 Obstacle Collision-free Path Planning through the Posture Space Analysis

Obstacle avoidance control schemes for non-redundant manipulators have widely discussed [8–10], and the algorithms to generate obstacle collision-free paths for traditional redundant manipulators were also proposed from analysis in the work space [11–13]. However, no more obstacle avoidance control schemes for hyper-redundant manipulators have been discussed, except ones that are based on the work space analysis [2,3]. Here, we propose an obstacle avoidance control scheme, which is based on the analysis in the posture space that is defined in this section.

As stated in section 2, we know that the arm posture of the hyper-redundant manipulator can be determined through the variables a_1, a_2, and α_0 while the manipulator arm is restricted onto the serpenoid curve. The posture space of the hyper-redundant manipulator is thus defined as follows.

Definition: A posture λ (a_1, a_2, α_0) of a hyper-redundant manipulator is a specification of the configuration (*or form*) of the hyper-redundant manipulator. The **posture space** of the hyper-redundant manipulator is the space

Æ of all possible postures λ of the hyper-redundant manipulator. An unique posture of Æ is arbitrarily selected ($a_1 = 0$, $a_2 = 0$, $\alpha_0 = 0$ *are generally selected, in the case that the arm posture is a straight line and the arm is on x-axis*) and is called as the **reference posture** of the hyper-redundant manipulator. It is denoted by ∅.

The proposed algorithm for the hyper-redundant manipulator to avoid the static obstacles can be briefly described as

- Map the work space of the manipulator onto its posture space;
- Create the obstacle collision-free paths in the posture space and find out the optimal one from all possible obstacle collision-free paths;
- Perform the task in the work space where the static obstacles exist.

Obstacle map in the posture space

The variables a_1, a_2, and α_0, which configure the manipulator posture, generate the posture space Æ of the hyper-redundant manipulator. Through changing **arbitrarily** the values of a_1, a_2, and α_0 between their boundary and finding out the collision data with obstacles, obstacle map in the posture space can be generated. At the same time, the unreachable area is also generated by finding out the impossible motion area of the manipulator: the area out of the manipulator's range, the area where the links of the manipulator are crossover. Fig.1 (b) shows one example of the obstacle map in the pos-

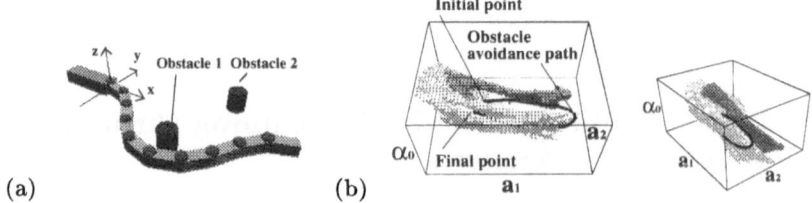

(a)   (b)

Fig. 1. Obstacles and the obtained obstacle collision-free path in the posture space. (a) Work space, (b) Posture space

ture space corresponding to that in the work space shown in Fig.1 (a). It can be seen that a simple obstacle in the work space must be not a simple one in the posture space. Note that the obstacle data shown in Fig.1 (b) is one after cell decomposition [14]. Through the cell decomposition of the original continuous data, the operation to generate the obstacle collision-free paths would become easier.

Obstacle collision-free path generation algorithms

To generate an obstacle collision-free path in the 3-dimensional (3D) space generally is extremely complicated. Here, we first discuss an obstacle avoidance problem in the 2D posture space, then extend it to the 3D posture space.

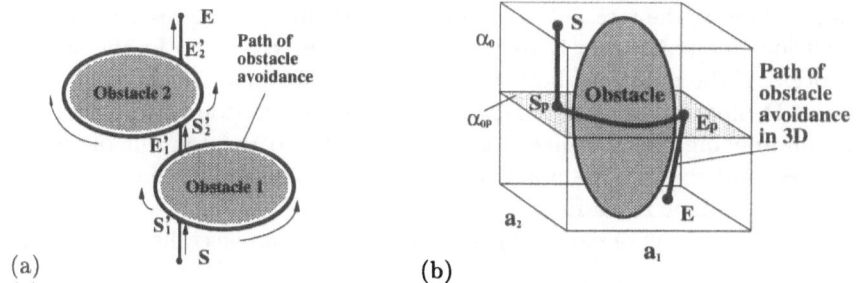

Fig. 2. Generation of obstacle collision-free paths in the posture space. (a) 2D obstacle collision-free paths, (b) 3D obstacle collision-free paths

2D obstacle collision-free path In the case of 2D posture space, shown in Fig.2 (a), the obstacle collision-free path is generated by the algorithm:

1) Draw a straight line from initial point $\mathbf{S}$ to end point $\mathbf{E}$, and find out all intersection points $\mathbf{S}'_i$ and $\mathbf{E}'_i$ with the border of obstacle i ($i = 1, \cdots, K$; K: *number of obstacles*);

2) Calculate two paths along the obstacle's contour connected the points $\mathbf{S}'_i$ and $\mathbf{E}'_i$, and choose the shorter of the two;

3) Connect each part of paths (*the straight line from* $\mathbf{S}$ *to* $\mathbf{S}'_1$, *the shorter one of two contours of each obstacle from* $\mathbf{S}'_i$ *to* $\mathbf{E}'_i$, *the straight line from* $\mathbf{E}'_{i-1}$ *to* $\mathbf{S}'_i$, *and the straight line from* $\mathbf{E}'_K$ *to* $\mathbf{E}$) to generate the obstacle collision-free path.

3D obstacle collision-free path First we define some terms used in the algorithm. The coordinate of the initial point $\mathbf{S}$ as shown in Fig.2 (b) is defined by $(a_1^s, a_2^s, \alpha_0^s)$, the coordinate of the end point $\mathbf{E}$ by $(a_1^e, a_2^e, \alpha_0^e)$, and the coordinates of the initial & end points $\mathbf{S}_p, \mathbf{E}_p$ projected onto the α_{0p} plane by $(a_{1p}^s, a_{2p}^s, \alpha_{0p}^s)$ & $(a_{1p}^e, a_{2p}^e, \alpha_{0p}^e)$. The algorithm to generate the 3D obstacle collision-free path is:

1) Project the initial point $\mathbf{S}$: $(a_1^s, a_2^s, \alpha_0^s)$ and the end point $\mathbf{E}$: $(a_1^e, a_2^e, \alpha_0^e)$ onto an arbitrarily plane $\alpha_0 = \alpha_{0p}$, to generate the projected initial point $\mathbf{S}_p$: $(a_{1p}^s, a_{2p}^s, \alpha_{0p}^s)$ and end point $\mathbf{E}_p$: $(a_{1p}^e, a_{2p}^e, \alpha_{0p}^e)$ on the plane, by setting $a_{1p}^s = a_1^s, a_{2p}^s = a_2^s, \& \alpha_{0p}^s = \alpha_{0p}$ and $a_{1p}^e = a_1^e, a_{2p}^e = a_2^e, \& \alpha_{0p}^e = \alpha_{0p}$; If the points $\mathbf{S}_p$ or $\mathbf{E}_p$ exist inside the obstacles, then find out the point $\bar{\mathbf{S}}_p$ or $\bar{\mathbf{E}}_p$ nearest to the original point on the contour of the obstacles, that minimizes $\|\mathbf{S}_p - \bar{\mathbf{S}}_p\|$ or $\|\mathbf{E}_p - \bar{\mathbf{E}}_p\|$;

2) Generate the obstacle collision-free path in the plane $\alpha_0 = \alpha_{0p}$ by the 2D obstacle collision-free path generation algorithm mentioned-above;

3) Shift the point from the initial point $\mathbf{S}$ to $\mathbf{S}_p$ and from $\mathbf{E}_p$ to the end point $\mathbf{E}$ along the straight lines connected them, to generate the obstacle collision-free path from $\mathbf{S}$ to $\mathbf{S}_p$ and that from $\mathbf{E}_p$ to $\mathbf{E}$; In the shifting process, if the point on the line goes into the obstacles, then find out the point $\mathbf{P}_i$ nearest to it (*the original point*) on the contour of the obstacles by minimizing the distance from the point $\mathbf{P}_i$ to the contour of the obstacles, and re-shift the point from $\mathbf{P}_i$ along the straight line connected $\mathbf{P}_i$ & $\mathbf{S}_p$ and/or $\mathbf{P}_i$ & $\mathbf{E}$;

4) Connect each part of paths to generate the 3D obstacle collision-free path.

It should be pointed out here that, the 3D obstacle collision-free path generation algorithm proposed only works in the case that the 2D obstacle collision-free path must exist in the plane $\alpha_0 = \alpha_{0p}$. If the 2D obstacle collision-free path does not exist in one plane $\alpha_0 = \alpha_{0p}$, we must change the plane to another one between two limit planes $\alpha_0 = \alpha_0^{min}$ and $\alpha_0 = \alpha_0^{max}$, where the 2D obstacle collision-free path exists. In the case where no 2D obstacle collision-free path exists for all planes, the 3D obstacle collision-free path could not be generated. The 3D obstacle collision-free path generation algorithm is failed to generate the obstacle collision-free path.

Note that the obstacle collision-free path in the posture space generated by above-stated algorithms is along the contour of the obstacles. It must not be the shortest one in global meaning. We derive the shortest obstacle collision-free path by finding the points on the obstacles' contour that could be connected by lines tangent to the contour. While the obstacle collision-free path in the posture space is obtained, the obstacle collision-free path in the joint space (*or configuration space*) is easily generated from Eq.(6) and that in the work space from Eqs. (3) and (4).

Computer simulation

A 10-DOF hyper-redundant manipulator is used to verify the proposed algorithm. The length of each link of the arm is 0.08 [m], and the obstacles are simply given by two circles with radius 0.05 [m] centered at (0.3 [m], -0.1 [m]) and (0.4 [m], 0.2 [m]), as shown in Fig.1 (a). Fig.1 (b) shows the obstacles and the obstacle collision-free path derived by the proposed algorithm in the posture space, where the cells were decomposed with the range $-2.0 < a_1, a_2 < 2.0$, -1.571 [rad] $< \alpha_0 < 1.571$ [rad] by the interval $\delta a_1 = \delta a_2 = 0.04$ and $\delta \alpha_0 = 0.087$ [rad]. The manipulator postures in the work space, resulted from the path shown in Fig.1 (b), are shown in Fig.3 (b). For comparison, the manipulator postures without the obstacle avoidance control algorithm are shown in Fig.3 (a). From the result, we clearly know that our algorithm generates the obstacle collision-free path which makes the obstacles existed in static state be avoided globally.

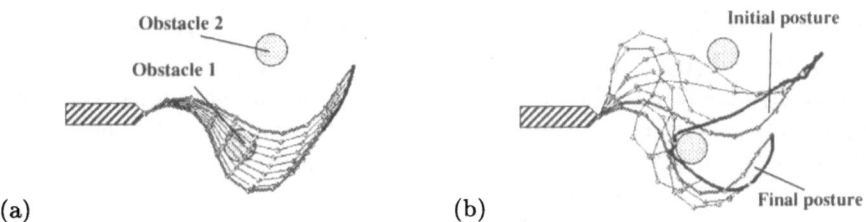

Fig. 3. Manipulator postures in the work space. (a) Without obstacle avoidance control, (b) With obstacle avoidance control

4   Posture Space Path-tracking Control Scheme

To guarantee the manipulator do not collide the obstacles, the manipulator must track accurately the posture space obstacle collision-free path. In this section, the path-tracking control scheme for hyper-redundant manipulators to track the path in the posture posture is thus presented.

Formulation of the parameterized path-tracking dynamics

Rewriting Eq.(6) in vector form, we have $q(\lambda) = \zeta(\lambda)$, where $\zeta \in \Re^n$ is the n-dimensional vector linear-function of the 3-dimensional vector λ. Differentiating it w.r.t. time, we have

$$\dot{q}(\lambda, \dot{\lambda}) = \mathbf{J}_\lambda \dot{\lambda}, \qquad \ddot{q}(\lambda, \dot{\lambda}, \ddot{\lambda}) = \mathbf{J}_\lambda \ddot{\lambda} + \dot{\mathbf{J}}_\lambda \dot{\lambda} \qquad (7)$$

where $\mathbf{J}_\lambda \in \Re^{n \times 3}$ is the Jacobian matrix, with elements given by $J_\lambda(i,j) = \partial \zeta_i / \partial \lambda_j$. The elements of the Jacobian matrix $\mathbf{J}_\lambda$ given by

$$J_\lambda(i,1) = \begin{cases} \sin(\frac{\pi}{n}), & i = 1 \\ \sin\left(\frac{\pi}{n}(2i-1)\right) - \sin\left(\frac{\pi}{n}(2i-3)\right), & i = 2,..,n \end{cases}$$

$$J_\lambda(i,2) = \begin{cases} \left(1 - \cos(\frac{\pi}{n})\right), & i = 1 \\ \cos\left(\frac{\pi}{n}(2i-3)\right) - \cos\left(\frac{\pi}{n}(2i-1)\right), & i = 2,..,n \end{cases}$$

$$J_\lambda(i,3) = \begin{cases} 1, & i = 1 \\ 0, & i = 2, \cdots, n \end{cases}$$

are constant and time-independent. Its time-derivative $\dot{\mathbf{J}}_\lambda \in \Re^{n \times 3}$ is thus the zero matrix, and the joint accelerations become into $\ddot{q}(\lambda, \ddot{\lambda}) = \mathbf{J}_\lambda \ddot{\lambda}$ and are velocity-independent or not the function of $\dot{\lambda}$.

Assume that the geometric path in the posture space is given in the parameterized form by a vector function $\eta(z) \in \Re^3$ of the scalar path parameter $z \in \Re$, $z_0 \leq z \leq z_T$, where $\eta(z_0)$ is the start point and $\eta(z_T)$ is the end point of the path. Thus, we have

$$q(z) = \zeta(\eta(z)) = \hat{\zeta}(z), \quad \dot{q}(z, \dot{z}) = \mathbf{J}_\lambda \eta' \dot{z} = \hat{\mathbf{J}}_z \dot{z} \qquad (8)$$

$$\ddot{q}(z, \dot{z}, \ddot{z}) = \mathbf{J}_\lambda \left(\eta' \ddot{z} + \eta'' \dot{z}^2\right) = \hat{\mathbf{J}}_z \ddot{z} + \dot{\hat{\mathbf{J}}}_z \dot{z}$$

where $\boldsymbol{\eta}'(z) = d\boldsymbol{\eta}(z)/dz \in \Re^3$, $\boldsymbol{\eta}''(z) = d^2\boldsymbol{\eta}(z)/dz^2 \in \Re^3$, $\hat{\boldsymbol{\zeta}}(z) = \boldsymbol{\zeta}(\boldsymbol{\eta}(z)) \in \Re^n$, $\hat{\boldsymbol{J}}_z(z) = \mathbf{J}_{\boldsymbol{\lambda}}(\boldsymbol{\eta}(z))\boldsymbol{\eta}'(z) \in \Re^n$, and $\dot{\hat{\boldsymbol{J}}}_z(z, \dot{z}) = \mathbf{J}_{\boldsymbol{\lambda}}(\boldsymbol{\eta}(z))\boldsymbol{\eta}''(z)\dot{z} \in \Re^n$, respectively. Same as joint angles, velocities, and accelerations, the joint torques can also be represented in the parameterized form. As known, the joint torques $\boldsymbol{\tau} \in \Re^n$ of the manipulator can be expressed by

$$\boldsymbol{\tau} = \mathbf{M}_{(\boldsymbol{q})}\ddot{\boldsymbol{q}} + \boldsymbol{c}_{(\boldsymbol{q},\dot{\boldsymbol{q}})} + \boldsymbol{g}_{(\boldsymbol{q})} \tag{9}$$

where $\mathbf{M} \in \Re^{n \times n}$ is the inertia matrix, $\boldsymbol{c} \in \Re^n$ is the torque vector of Coriolis and centrifugal forces, and $\boldsymbol{g} \in \Re^n$ is the torque vector of gravity force, respectively. Substituting Eq.(8) for Eq.(9), we have

$$\boldsymbol{\tau}(z, \dot{z}, \ddot{z}) = \boldsymbol{\mu}(z)\ddot{z} + \boldsymbol{\nu}(z, \dot{z}) \tag{10}$$

where $\boldsymbol{\mu}(z) = \mathbf{M}_{(\boldsymbol{q}(z))}\hat{\boldsymbol{J}}_z = \hat{\mathbf{M}}_{(z)}\hat{\boldsymbol{J}}_z \in \Re^n$, $\boldsymbol{\nu}(z, \dot{z}) = \hat{\mathbf{M}}_{(z)}\dot{\hat{\boldsymbol{J}}}_z\dot{z} + \hat{\boldsymbol{c}} + \hat{\boldsymbol{g}} \in \Re^n$, $\hat{\boldsymbol{c}}_{(z,\dot{z})} = \boldsymbol{c}_{(\boldsymbol{q}(z),\dot{\boldsymbol{q}}(z,\dot{z}))} \in \Re^n$, and $\hat{\boldsymbol{g}}_{(z)} = \boldsymbol{g}_{(\boldsymbol{q}(z))} \in \Re^n$. Eq.(10) shows the joint torques for the hyper-redundant manipulator to track the geometric path $\boldsymbol{\eta}(z)$ in the posture space.

Feedforward path-tracking controller

The parameterized path-tracking dynamics in the posture space, given in Eq.(10), can provide a feedforward path-tracking controller design strategy. The feedforward controller augments the basic PD controller by providing a set of nominal torques $\boldsymbol{\tau}_{ff}$:

$$\boldsymbol{\tau}_{ff}(z_d, \dot{z}_d, \ddot{z}_d) = \boldsymbol{\mu}(z_d)\ddot{z}_d + \boldsymbol{\nu}(z_d, \dot{z}_d) \tag{11}$$

and then the feedforward controller for the hyper-redundant manipulator to track the posture space path can be given by

$$\boldsymbol{\tau} = \boldsymbol{\tau}_{ff}(z_d, \dot{z}_d, \ddot{z}_d) + \boldsymbol{K}_v\left(\hat{\boldsymbol{J}}_z(z_d)\dot{z}_d - \dot{\boldsymbol{q}}\right) + \boldsymbol{K}_p\left(\hat{\boldsymbol{\zeta}}(z_d) - \boldsymbol{q}\right) \tag{12}$$

where $\boldsymbol{K}_v$ and $\boldsymbol{K}_p$ are $n \times n$ diagonal matrices of velocity and position gains, and $z_d, \dot{z}_d, \ddot{z}_d$ are the commanded path-tracking inputs that are given by user.

Computer simulation

Same manipulator model as that in section 3 was used to evaluate the proposed posture space path-tracking controller. The mass of each link is set as $m = 0.3[kg]$ and the inertia parameter is derived by seeing the link as an uniform beam. The posture space path generated by the proposed obstacle collision-free generation algorithm is tracked by the constant *bang-bang* acceleration in the motion time $T = 8\ [s]$. The manipulator dynamics is integrated by Euler integration at the time interval of 5 $[ms]$, where gravity is neglected. The position and velocity error feedback-gains of the PD control term are set as 4.0 and 0.02, respectively.

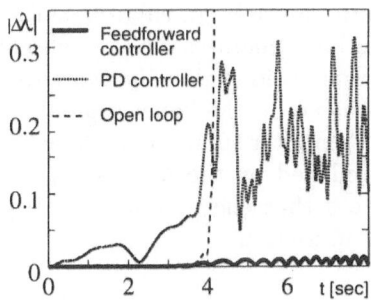

Fig. 4. Path-tracking errors of the feedforward controller (12), the PD controller $K_v \left(\hat{J}_z(z_d)\dot{z}_d - \dot{q} \right) + K_p \left(\hat{\zeta}(z_d) - q \right)$, and the open-loop controller where only the nominal torques τ_{ff} are the input of system

Fig.4 shows the path-tracking errors of the feedforward controller (12), the PD controller $K_v \left(\hat{J}_z(z_d)\dot{z}_d - \dot{q} \right) + K_p \left(\hat{\zeta}(z_d) - q \right)$, and the open-loop controller where only the nominal torques τ_{ff} are the input of system, while the hyper-redundant manipulator to track the posture space path shown in Fig.1 (b). The path-tracking errors for the open-loop controller are extremely larger, the PD controller reduced the errors, but still has large errors. The path-tracking errors are significantly reduced by the feedforward controller. The proposed feedforward controller showed good path-tracking performance. As a result, we knew that the hyper-redundant manipulator could well avoid the obstacles, while the manipulator tracks the posture space obstacle collision-free path by the proposed the feedforward controller.

At the last of this section, we make an issue of the computation time. In case of a PC (*Pentum-333MHz, 128M Memory*), the mapping of the obstacles and the possible motion area from the work space to the posture space totally takes 32.7 seconds (*including the 5 seconds' cell decomposition*), however, the generation of one obstacle collision-free path and the path-tracking control only takes 2.45 seconds (*0.26 seconds for path-generation and 2.19 seconds for path-tracking control*). The process of mapping the obstacles and the possible motion area from the work space to the posture space, moreover, can be generated in advance. After we have the obstacles' map and the possible motion area in the posture space, the path generation and the path-tracking control of the manipulator can be executed in real-time. Thus, the real-time obstacle avoidance control should be possible. This was also proven by the experiment of the developed Hyper-R Arm [4].

5   Conclusions

In this article, we proposed a novel obstacle avoidance control scheme for the hyper-redundant manipulator to perform a pick-and-place task while avoiding the existing static obstacles in environment. The computer simulations showed that our method generates the obstacle collision-free path which makes the obstacles are well avoided globally. Moreover, a path-tracking control scheme was also discussed for the hyper-redundant manipulator to trace the posture space path. Computer simulations showed that the path-tracking errors are significantly reduced by the proposed path-tracking feedforward controller. This guarantees that the manipulator does avoid the obstacles while the manipulator is in motion.

References

1. Hirose, S. and Ma, S. (1991) Coupled tendon-driven multijoint manipulator, Proc. IEEE Int. Conf. on Robotics and Automation, 1268—1275
2. Ma, S., Hirose, S., and Yoshinada, H. (1995) Development of a hyper-redundant manipulator for maintenance of nuclear reactors, Int. J. of Advanced Robotics **9-3**, 281—300
3. Chirikjian, G. S. and Burdick, J. W. (1990) An obstacle avoidance algorithm for hyper-redundant manipulators, Proc. IEEE Int. Conf. on Robotics and Automation, 625—631
4. Ma, S. and Konno, M. (1997) An obstacle avoidance scheme for hyper-redundant manipulators — Global motion planning in posture space, Proc. IEEE Int. Conf. on Robotics and Automation, 161-167
5. Chirikjian, G. S. and Burdick, J. W. (1994) A modal approach to hyper-redundant manipulator kinematics, IEEE Trans. on Robotics and Automation **10-3**, 343-354
6. Hirose, S. (1993) Biologically Inspired Robots, Oxford University Press, Oxford
7. Sneddon, I. N. (1961) Special Functions of Mathematical — Physics and Chemistry —, Oliver & Boyd, London
8. Latpmbe, J. C. (1991) Robot Motion Planning, Kluwer Academic Publishers
9. Khatib, O. (1986) Real-time obstacle avoidance for manipulators and mobile robots, Int. J. of Robotics Research **5-1**, 90—98
10. Lozano-Perez, T. (1987) A simple motion-planning algorithm for general robot manipulators, IEEE Trans. on Robotics and Automation **3-3**, 224—238
11. Kircanski, M. and Vukobratovic, M. (1986) Contribution to control of redundant robotic manipulators in an environment with obstacles, Int. J. of Robotics Research **5-4**, 112—123
12. Nakamura, Y., Hanafusa, H., and Yoshikawa, T. (1987) Task-priority based on redundancy control of robot manipulators, Int. J. of Robotics Research **6-2**, 3—15
13. Mayorga, R. V., Janabi-Sharifi, F., and Wong, A. K. C. (1995) A fast approach for the robust trajectory planning of redundant manipulators, J. of Robotic Systems **12-2**, 147—161
14. Marolo, C., and Pagello, E. (1995) A cell decomposition approach to motion planning based on collision detection, Proc. Int. Conf. on Advanced Robotics, 481—488

Estimation of Mass and Center of Mass of Unknown Curved-Surface Object Using Passing-C.M. Lines

Yong Yu, Takashi Kiyokawa and Showzow Tsujio

Kagoshima University, Kagoshima 890-0065, Japan
E-mail: yu@mech.kagoshima-u.ac.jp

Abstract. In many cases of manipulating an object stably and accurately by robot, it is required to know the mass and center of mass of the object. For the case when the weight or shape of an object is over the grasp capacity of a robot hand, this paper proposes a technique that can estimate the mass and center of mass of a graspless unknown object, which has curved surfaces and a base plane. A line called *Passing-C.M. Line* which contains the center of mass, are defined. For estimating the passing-C.M. line, *Tip Operation* by robot finger, which tips the object slowly and repeatedly in a parallel motion with a vertical operation plane, is proposed. Using the fingertip position and force information measured from tip operations, an algorithm to estimate the passing-C.M. line are described. Then an algorithm to estimate the mass and center of mass of the object is given by estimating the intersect point of several orientation-different passing-C.M. lines.

1 Introduction

In many cases for manipulating an object stably and accurately by robot, it is required to know the mass and center of mass of the object. About the estimation of the mass and center of mass of an unknown object, some researches have been carried on by firmly grasping and operating an object in robot hand [1], and by holding up and handling an object with a space robot hand [2]. When a heavy and/or big object is hard to be firmly grasped and wholly held up, the object will be operated by *Graspless Manipulation* where the object will move in contact with its environment [3]. For performing these graspless operations, it is also necessary to know the mass and the center of mass of the unknown objects.

To this end, authors gave a method that can estimate the mass and center of mass of an object by using gravity equi-effect planes [4]. This method is suitable for a polyhedral object, however, not for an object with curved surfaces such as cylinder, cone, frustum and so on. Namely, when an object is leaned on a plane environment, for a polyhedral object the contact form can be a stable contact line, wihile for a curved-surface object it is a contact point which may move uncertainly. Therefore, the gravity equi-effect planes is difficult to be obtained.

For an unknown object which is graspless and has curved surface like cylinder, cone or frustum, this paper proposes a technique that can estimate the mass and center of mass of the object. A line called *Passing-C.M. Line* is first defined, which is passing through the center of mass form a contact point where the object is in point-contact with an environment. If two or more than two orientation-different passing-C.M. lines of an object are obtained, the center of mass of the object can be estimated by the intersect point of the lines. For estimating the toward-C.M. line, *Tip Operation* by robot finger, which tips the object repeatedly in a parallel motion with a vertical plane, is available. Using the fingertip position and force information from tip operations, an algorithm to estimate the passing-C.M. line, and an algorithm to represent the estimated lines, which may displace with the uncertain contact points on environment, with respect to the same object frame are addressed. Then, an algorithm to estimate the mass and center of mass of the object is given by several independent passing-C.M. lines. Lastly, experimental verification on the proposed approach is performed and its results are outlined.

2   Passing-C.M. Line and Tip Operation

2.1   Problem

The discussion of this paper is on the bases that:

- The object is a shape-unknown rigid which has curved surface with not-large curvature (like cylinder, cone or frustum) and a plane base. The mass and center of mass of the object are also unknown. And the environment is a plane whose position and normal are unknown.
- A robot hand will touch the object with frictional point contact (touching point hereafter), where a little slipping between fingertip and object surface may occur during an object manipulation.
- The object is graspless because its weight and/or shape are over the grasping capacity of robot hand.
- When the object is tipped and leaned, the object will be in one point contact with the environment stably (contact point hereafter). The object is heavy enough and there is sufficient friction between the object and environment, so that the object can only roll without slipping on the environment.

2.2   Passing-C.M. Line

Consider leaning and tipping an object, which is in plane-contact with an environment plane, by a fingertip force acting on the object (see Fig.1). When the object is leaned, it will contact the environment plane at a point because of the curved edge of the object base plane. At the beginning of leaning, the fingertip force on the object, the object gravity and the reaction force from the contact point are unbalancing one another, so that the contact point will move uncertainly. With that the

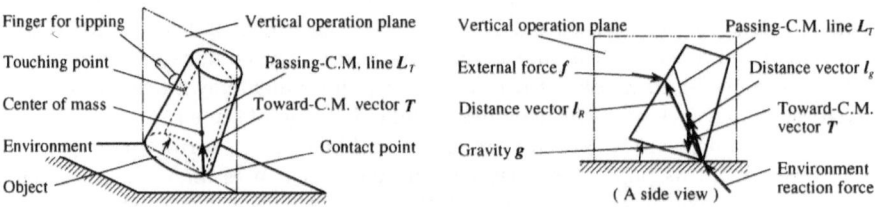

Fig. 1. Passing-C.M. line and vertical operation plane

object rolls without slipping on the environment, until the contact point, the center of mass and the fingertip touching point are all in a vertical plane. In the plane, the three forces can balance one another and the fingertip force can momentally balance the gravity of the object around the contact point. If the fingertip position and the fingertip force are kept in the vertical plane while slowly operating the object, the position of the contact point can be kept not to change. In this paper, the vertical plane containing the contact point, the touching point and the center of mass is referred to as *Vertical Operation Plane*.

In a vertical operation plane, there is a vector that is from the contact point and points toward the center of mass, which is referred to *Toward-C.M. Vector*. A toward-C.M. vector may pass through the center of mass or not, but there exists a straight line which contains the toward-C.M. vector and passes through the center of mass. In this paper, this straight line will be referred to *Passing-C.M. Line*. The different contact points at the edge of the object base correspond to different passing-C.M. lines. Two or more than two orientation-different passing-C.M. lines intersect at one point, i.e., the center of mass of the object. Hence, the center of mass of object can be estimated by estimating two or more than two orientation-different passing-C.M. lines in an object.

2.3   Parameters of Passing-C.M. Line

When an object is leaned at rest in point-contact with an environment (see Fig.1), the equilibrium condition of the moment about the contact point can be expressed as

$$l_R \times f + T \times g = 0, \tag{1}$$

$$T \triangleq ml_g, \tag{2}$$

where l_R is a distance vector from the contact point to the fingertip which keeps in touch with the object, f is the contact force at the fingertip measured by finger force sensor, g is the gravity. T is the toward-C.M. vector, m is the mass of object, l_g is a distance vector from the contact point to the center of mass. According to eq.(2), vectors T and l_g have the same direction but their magnitudes are different. In this paper, l_g and l_R are called respectively as *C.M.-Position Vector* from a contact point and *Fingertip-Position Vector* from a contact point. Note that the above vectors all exist in the same vertical operation plane.

2.4   Tip Operation by Robot

For estimating a passing-C.M. line, therefore, several independent fingertip displacements and fingertip forces in a vertical operation plane should be obtained firstly. To obtain the necessary information, we consider using robot finger to tip the object repeatedly at different fingertip positions, under the condition that the fingertip forces and fingertip displacements are in the same vertical operation plane so that the contact point between the object and environment is kept not changing. This object operation is referred to as *Tip Operation* in this paper.

In a tip operation, an object will be leaned from an initial posture where the object is in plane-contact with the environment, then stilled in a leaned posture and subsequently returned to an un-leaned posture (see Fig.2). The object position or orientation after returned to an un-leaned posture may be different from those before leaned, because the contact point will move to a vertical operation plane when the object is on leaning. Accordingly, after performed the different tip operations for obtaining several passing-C.M. lines, the object positions or orientations in un-leaned posture may be changed, so that the positions or orientations of the obtained passing-C.M. lines may also be changed with respect to a base frame.

The procedure of tip operations can be set as:

Step 1 Set the object in plane-contact with the environment. From the initial posture, use a robot finger to slowly tip and lean the object, under the condition that the fingertip is displaced along the inverse direction of the sensed fingertip force if possible.

Step 2 Measure the force and position of fingertip when the object is kept in a leaned and still posture (leaned posture hereafter), where the object is in contact with the environment at one point (contact point). Decide the vertical operation plane according to the contact point position, the directions of the fingertip force and the gravity.

Step 3 With keeping the current contact point not displacing, move the fingertip slowly in the vertical operation plane to return the object to a posture in plane-contact with the environment (un-leaned posture hereafter). Then measure the fingertip position (touching point) on the object which was touched and measured by the fingertip at Step 2.

Step 4 With changing the touching point position of the fingertip and keeping the fingertip in the vertical operation plane, repeat Step 1 to Step 3 $n(\geq 2)$ times around the same contact point.

Step 5 Under the un-leaned posture after nth operation, measure a different touched point from nth touched point by putting a fingertip on the object surface, where the two points are on the same horizontal plane and $\Delta E^T (g \times f) \geq 0$ (ΔE denotes the distance vector from nth point to the different point).

Step 6 Repeat Step 1 to Step 5 $h(\geq 2)$ times with h contact points between the object base and the environment. Then, under the un-leaned posture about contact

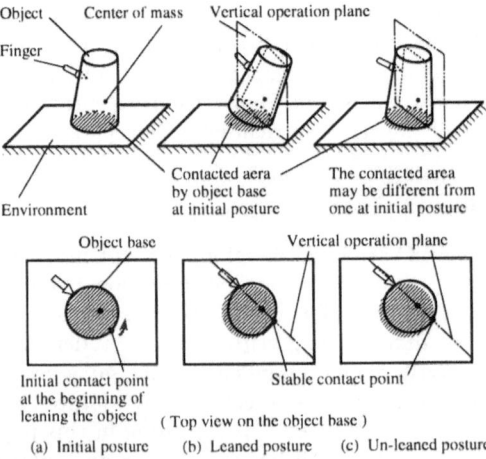

Fig. 2. Object postures in tip operation

point h, perform Step 5 again for all nth touched point and their different touched point.

On performing these steps, the force values of finger sensor will also be checked to avoid tumbling down the object. For example, if the value is less than the half of the value when a finger just starts to tip an object, a judgement can be given to stop tipping the object.

3   Estimation of Passing-C.M. Line

3.1   Estimation of Fingertip-Position Vector

As mentioned in subsection 2.3, at first, let us consider estimating the fingertip-position vector which is from the contact point to a touching point of fingertip. As shown in Fig.4, let $O - XYZ$ denote the base frame on the environment. About a contact point j, let $\boldsymbol{L}_{Rij} \in \boldsymbol{R}^3$, $\boldsymbol{l}_{Rij} \in \boldsymbol{R}^3$ denote two fingertip-position vectors respectively for an un-leaned object posture and a leaned object posture of ith tip operation, $\Delta \boldsymbol{l}_{Rij} \in \boldsymbol{R}^3$ denote ith fingertip displacement from the un-leaned object posture to ith leaned object posture. Let $\Delta \boldsymbol{l}_{ij} \in \boldsymbol{R}^3$ denote the distance vector of fingertip positions from ith leaned object posture to $(i + 1)$th leaned object posture (see Fig.5). Note that the angle between $\Delta \boldsymbol{l}_{Rij}$ and $\Delta \boldsymbol{l}_{R(i+1)j}$, the magnitude difference between the two vectors, the distance of touching points in an un-leaned posture corresponding to the two vectors are better made larger for making estimated errors as small as possible.

Since vectors $\boldsymbol{L}_{Rij}$, $\boldsymbol{l}_{Rij}$, $\Delta \boldsymbol{l}_{Rij}$ and $\Delta \boldsymbol{l}_{ij}$ are all on a vertical operation plane (see Fig.4 and 5), let us analyze the position relations among the vectors on the plane. For ith and $(i + 1)$th tip operations, we have

$$\boldsymbol{l}_{Rij} - \boldsymbol{L}_{Rij} = \Delta \boldsymbol{l}_{Rij}, \tag{3}$$

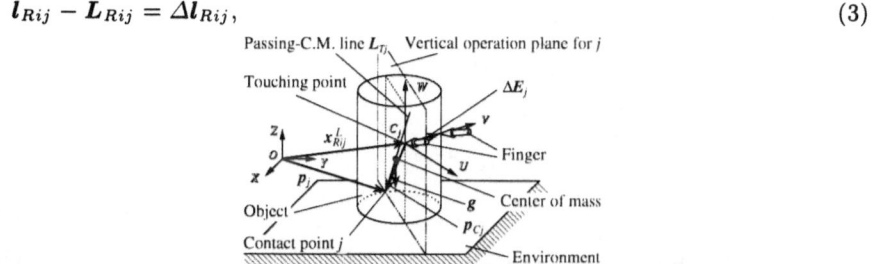

Fig. 3. Un-leaned posture about contact point j

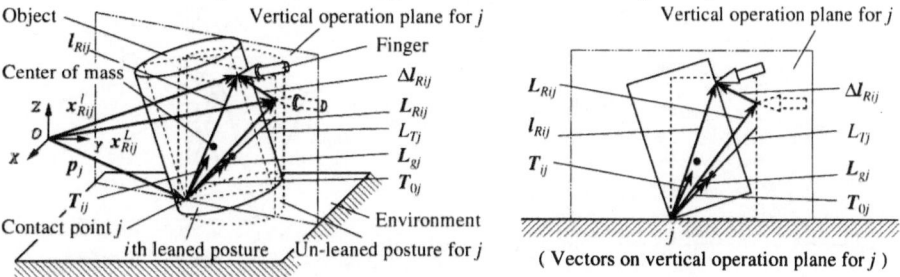

Fig. 4. ith tip operation about contact point j

$$l_{R(i+1)j} - l_{Rij} = \Delta l_{ij}, \tag{4}$$

Also, since fingertip-position vectors l_{Rij}, L_{Rij} have the same magnitude, we can get

$$[\Delta l_{Rij} \times \Delta l_{R(i+1)j}]^T l_{Rij} = 0, \tag{5}$$

$$[\Delta l_{Rij} \times \Delta l_{R(i+1)j}]^T L_{Rij} = 0, \tag{6}$$

$$l_{Rij}^T l_{Rij} - L_{Rij}^T L_{Rij} = 0. \tag{7}$$

By using eq.(3), eq.(7) can be rewritten as

$$-2\Delta l_{Rij}^T L_{Rij} = \Delta l_{Rij}^T \Delta l_{Rij}. \tag{8}$$

To conveniently use the above relation equations for the fingertip-position vector estimation, we define the following matrices when the tip operation is repeated $n(\geq 2)$ times about contact point j:

$$C_{1j} \triangleq [\; I_{3n} \quad -I_{3n} \;] \in R^{3n \times 6n}, \tag{9}$$

$$C_{2j} \triangleq [A_{2j} \quad O_{3(n-1) \times 3n}] \in R^{3(n-1) \times 6n}, \tag{10}$$

$$A_{2j} \triangleq \mathrm{diag}\,[\; [-I_3 \quad I_3], \cdots, [-I_3 \quad I_3]\;] \in R^{3(n-1) \times 3n}, \tag{11}$$

$$C_{3j} \triangleq \mathrm{diag}\,[A_{3\{1j\}}^T, A_{3\{2j\}}^T, \cdots, A_{3\{(n-1)j\}}^T, A_{3\{(n-1)j\}}^T,$$
$$A_{3\{1j\}}^T, A_{3\{2j\}}^T, \cdots, A_{3\{(n-1)j\}}^T, A_{3\{(n-1)j\}}^T] \in R^{2n \times 6n}, \tag{12}$$

$$A_{3\{ij\}} \triangleq [\Delta l_{Rij} \times \Delta l_{R(i+1)j}] \in R^3, \tag{13}$$

$$C_{4j} \triangleq [O_{n \times 3n} \quad -2A_{4j}] \in R^{n \times 6n}, \tag{14}$$

$$A_{4j} \triangleq \mathrm{diag}\,[\Delta l_{R1j}^T, \cdots, \Delta l_{Rnj}^T] \in R^{n \times 3n}, \tag{15}$$

$$c_{1j} \triangleq [\Delta l_{R1j}^T \quad \cdots \quad \Delta l_{Rnj}^T]^T \in R^{3n}, \tag{16}$$

$$c_{2j} \triangleq [\Delta l_{1j} \quad \cdots \quad \Delta l_{(n-1)j}]^T \in R^{3(n-1)}, \tag{17}$$

$$c_{3j} \triangleq O_{2n \times 1} \in R^{2n}, \tag{18}$$

$$c_{4j} \triangleq [\; \Delta l_{R1j}^T \Delta l_{R1j} \quad \cdots \quad \Delta l_{Rnj}^T \Delta l_{Rnj} \;]^T \in R^n. \tag{19}$$

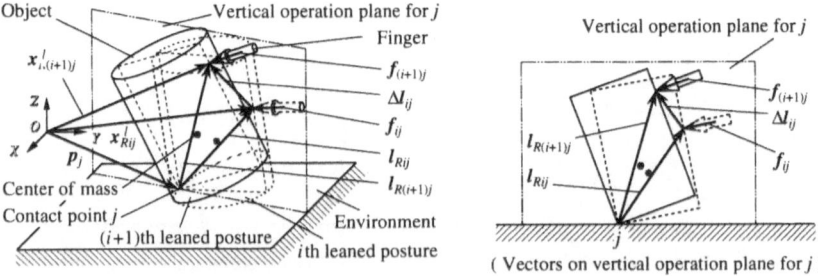

Fig. 5. ith and $(i+1)$th leaned postures

By eqs.(3) (4) (5) (6) (8) and the above defined matrices, we can get

$$C_j l_j = c_j \in R^{3(3n-1)}, \tag{20}$$

$$C_j \overset{\triangle}{=} \begin{bmatrix} C_{1j}^T & C_{2j}^T & C_{3j}^T & C_{4j}^T \end{bmatrix}^T \in R^{3(3n-1)\times 6n}, \tag{21}$$

$$l_j \overset{\triangle}{=} \begin{bmatrix} l_{R1j}^T & \cdots & l_{Rnj}^T & L_{R1j}^T & \cdots & L_{Rnj}^T \end{bmatrix}^T \in R^{6n}, \tag{22}$$

$$c_j \overset{\triangle}{=} \begin{bmatrix} c_{1j}^T & c_{2j}^T & c_{3j}^T & c_{4j}^T \end{bmatrix}^T \in R^{3(3n-1)}, \tag{23}$$

where I_* denotes a $*$-dimensional identity matrix and $O_{*_1 \times *_2}$ denotes a $(*_1 \times *_2)$ zero matrix. When $n \geq 2$ and rank$C_j = 6n$, the unique solution (if no measured error) or the optimal approximate solution (if measured errors exist) to l_j can be obtained from eq.(20) since $3(3n - 1) > 6n$. Therefore, considering that some measured errors may exist in Δl_{Rij} and Δl_{ij}, the vectors l_{Rij}, L_{Rij} $(i = 1, 2, \cdots, n, n \geq 2)$ for contact point j can be estimated by

$$l_j = C_j^+ c_j, \tag{24}$$

where $C_j^+ \in R^{6n \times 3(3n-1)}$ is the pseudoinverse of C_j.

3.2   Estimation of Toward-C.M. Vector

This subsection gives the method for estimating the toward-C.M. vector according to the estimated l_j, and the fingertip forces f_{ij} $(i = 1, 2, \cdots, n, n \geq 2)$ which are measured when the object is on leaned postures [4].

By repeating the tip operation $n(\geq 2)$ times, the following matrices can be derived from eq.(1),

$$G_{1j} T_j = b_{1j} \in R^n, \tag{25}$$

$$G_{1j} \overset{\triangle}{=} \begin{bmatrix} O_{3n\times 3} & B_{1j} \end{bmatrix} \in R^{3n\times 3n}, \tag{26}$$

$$B_{1j} \overset{\triangle}{=} \text{diag} \begin{bmatrix} -[g\times], \cdots, -[g\times] \end{bmatrix} \in R^{3n\times 3(n-1)}, \tag{27}$$

$$T_j \overset{\triangle}{=} \begin{bmatrix} T_{0j}^T & T_{1j}^T & \cdots & T_{nj}^T \end{bmatrix}^T \in R^{3(n+1)}, \tag{28}$$

$$b_{1j} \overset{\triangle}{=} \begin{bmatrix} [l_{R1j} \times f_{1j}]^T & \cdots & [l_{Rnj} \times f_{nj}]^T \end{bmatrix}^T \in R^{3n}, \tag{29}$$

where $[g\times]$ represents a skew symmetry matrix defined by $[g\times]l_{Rij} \overset{\triangle}{=} g \times l_{Rij}$, T_{0j} and T_{ij} correspond to the un-leaned or ith leaned object posture respectively.

When the object is leaned and turned about contact point j with ith tip operation on a vertical operation plane, the angle between toward-C.M. vectors T_{ij} and T_{0j} is the same as the angle between vectors l_{Rij} and L_{Rij}, and the magnitudes of T_{ij} and T_{0j} are the same. Accordingly, there are

$$T_{0j} - R_{Rij} T_{ij} = O_{3\times 1} \in R^3, \tag{30}$$

$$R_{Rij} \overset{\triangle}{=} r_{ij} R_{ij} r_{ij}^T \in R^{3\times 3}, \tag{31}$$

$$r_{ij} \overset{\triangle}{=} \begin{bmatrix} \dfrac{L_{Rij} \times [L_{Rij} \times l_{Rij}]}{\|L_{Rij} \times [L_{Rij} \times l_{Rij}]\|} & \dfrac{L_{Rij}}{\|L_{Rij}\|} & \dfrac{L_{Rij} \times l_{Rij}}{\|L_{Rij} \times l_{Rij}\|} \end{bmatrix} \in R^{3\times 3}, \tag{32}$$

$$R_{ij} \triangleq \begin{bmatrix} \dfrac{L_{Rij}^T l_{Rij}}{\|L_{Rij}\|\|l_{Rij}\|} & -\dfrac{\|L_{Rij} \times l_{Rij}\|}{\|L_{Rij}\|\|l_{Rij}\|} & 0 \\[2ex] \dfrac{\|L_{Rij} \times l_{Rij}\|}{\|L_{Rij}\|\|l_{Rij}\|} & \dfrac{L_{Rij}^T l_{Rij}}{\|L_{Rij}\|\|l_{Rij}\|} & 0 \\[2ex] 0 & 0 & 1 \end{bmatrix} \in R^{3 \times 3}, \tag{33}$$

where $\|*\|$ denotes the norm of vector $*$. Repeating the tip operation $n(\geq 2)$ times, we have

$$G_{2j} T_j = O_{3n \times 1} \in R^{3n}, \tag{34}$$

$$G_{2j} \triangleq [\; E_{2j} \;\; -B_{2j} \;] \in R^{3n \times 3(n+1)}, \tag{35}$$

$$B_{2j} \triangleq \mathrm{diag} \left[\; R_{R1j}^T, \cdots, R_{Rnj}^T \;\right] \in R^{3n \times 3n}, \tag{36}$$

$$E_{2j} \triangleq [\; I_3 \;\; \cdots \;\; I_3 \;]^T \in R^{3n \times 3}. \tag{37}$$

By eqs.(25) and (34), we can get

$$G_j T_j = b_j \in R^{6n}, \tag{38}$$

$$G_j \triangleq \left[\; G_{1j}^T \;\; G_{2j}^T \;\right]^T \in R^{6n \times 3(n+1)}, \tag{39}$$

$$b_j \triangleq \left[\; b_{1j}^T \;\; O_{3n \times 1}^T \;\right] \in R^{6n}. \tag{40}$$

Same as the solution to l_j, when $n \geq 2$ and $\mathrm{rank} G_j = 3(n+1)$, the optimal approximate solution of T_j can be obtained from eq.(38) since $6n > 3(n+1)$. Accordingly, considering that some measured errors may exist, the toward-C.M. vectors T_j can be estimated by

$$T_j = G_j^+ b_j, \tag{41}$$

where $G_j^+ \in R^{3(n+1) \times 6n}$ is the pseudoinverse of G_j.

3.3   Estimation of Passing-C.M. Line

Now let us consider estimating the position of contact point j and giving the equation of the passing-C.M. line, based on the estimated vectors l_{Rij}, L_{Rij}, T_{0j}, $T_{ij}(i = 1, 2, \cdots, n, \; n \geq 2)$.

On the base frame $O - XYZ$, the contact point position p_j can be obtained by

$$p_j \triangleq \frac{1}{2n} \left\{ \sum_{i=1}^{n} \left(x_{Rij}^l - l_{Rij} \right) + \sum_{i=1}^{n} \left(x_{Rij}^L - L_{Rij} \right) \right\}, \tag{42}$$

where x_{Rij}^l, x_{Rij}^L denote ith touching point positions from the origin of $O - XYZ$ with a leaned object posture or un-leaned object posture respectively (see Fig.4).

After nth tip operation about contact point j has been performed, let us set an object frame $C_j - UVW$ under the un-leaned posture about j, whose origin is set at nth touching point. By the Step 5 of operation procedure, we can obtain a horizontal distance vector $\Delta E_j \in R^3$ from the nth touching point (see Fig.3). According to the horizontal ΔE_j and the vertical gravity g, the orientation of

$C_j - UVW$ can be settled and the position $\boldsymbol{p}_{Cj}$ of contact point j with respect of $C_j - UVW$ will be

$$\boldsymbol{p}_{Cj} = {}^{O}\!\boldsymbol{R}_{Cj}^{T}(\boldsymbol{p}_j - \boldsymbol{x}_{Rnj}^L), \tag{43}$$

$$ {}^{O}\!\boldsymbol{R}_{Cj} = \left[\frac{\Delta\boldsymbol{E}_j \times (-\boldsymbol{g})}{\|\Delta\boldsymbol{E}_j \times (-\boldsymbol{g})\|} \quad \frac{\Delta\boldsymbol{E}_j}{\|\Delta\boldsymbol{E}_j\|} \quad \frac{-\boldsymbol{g}}{\|\boldsymbol{g}\|} \right] \in \boldsymbol{R}^{3\times 3}. \tag{44}$$

Notice that $\boldsymbol{p}_{Cj}$ can also be gotten by $\boldsymbol{p}_{Cj} = -{}^{O}\!\boldsymbol{R}_{Cj}^{T}\boldsymbol{L}_{Rnj}$, but it may contain a larger margin of error.

Therefore, with respect to the frame $C_j - UVW$ under the un-leaned posture about j, the equation of passing-C.M. line $\boldsymbol{L}_{Tj}$, which contains point $\boldsymbol{p}_{Cj}$ and the center of mass, can be estimated as

$$\boldsymbol{x}_{Cj} = \boldsymbol{p}_{Cj} + k_j {}^{O}\!\boldsymbol{R}_{Cj}^{T}\boldsymbol{T}_{0j}, \tag{45}$$

where k_j denotes the coefficient related to the distance along the line form point $\boldsymbol{p}_{Cj}$ to point $\boldsymbol{x}_{Cj}$.

Under the un-leaned posture about the last contact point h, let us consider representing the line $\boldsymbol{L}_{Tj}$ with respect to $O - XYZ$. Since the positions or orientations of the un-leaned posture about contact point h may different from those about contact point j, the touching point position $\boldsymbol{x}_{Rnj}^L$ will change to $\boldsymbol{x}_{Rnj}^{Lh}$ with respect to the base frame $O - XYZ$. In general, the change is uncertainty for an unknown object. To know the changes, we will get a new distance vector $\Delta\boldsymbol{E}_{hj}$ with performing the Step 6 of operation procedure to the un-leaned posture about contact point h. Then, a new frame $C_{hj} - UVW$ from $C_j - UVW$ can be set on the fingertip touching point $\boldsymbol{x}_{Rnj}^{Lh}$ (see Fig.6). The transform matrix ${}^{O}\!\boldsymbol{R}_{Chj}$ form $C_{hj} - UVW$ to $O - XYZ$ is

$$ {}^{O}\!\boldsymbol{R}_{Chj} = \left[\frac{\Delta\boldsymbol{E}_{hj} \times (-\boldsymbol{g})}{\|\Delta\boldsymbol{E}_{hj} \times (-\boldsymbol{g})\|} \quad \frac{\Delta\boldsymbol{E}_{hj}}{\|\Delta\boldsymbol{E}_{hj}\|} \quad \frac{-\boldsymbol{g}}{\|\boldsymbol{g}\|} \right] \in \boldsymbol{R}^{3\times 3}. \tag{46}$$

Accordingly, in the un-leaned posture about contact point h, the passing-C.M. line $\boldsymbol{L}_{Tj}$ is represented with respect to $O - XYZ$ by

$$\boldsymbol{x}_{Oj} = \boldsymbol{p}_{hj} + k_j \boldsymbol{T}_{h0j}, \tag{47}$$

$$\boldsymbol{p}_{hj} = \boldsymbol{x}_{Rnj}^{Lh} + {}^{O}\!\boldsymbol{R}_{Chj}\boldsymbol{p}_{Cj}, \tag{48}$$

$$\boldsymbol{T}_{h0j} = {}^{O}\!\boldsymbol{R}_{Chj}{}^{O}\!\boldsymbol{R}_{Cj}^{T}\boldsymbol{T}_{0j}. \tag{49}$$

By computing the intersection point of the different lines $\boldsymbol{L}_{Tj}(j = 1, 2, \cdots, h)$, the center of mass can be estimated.

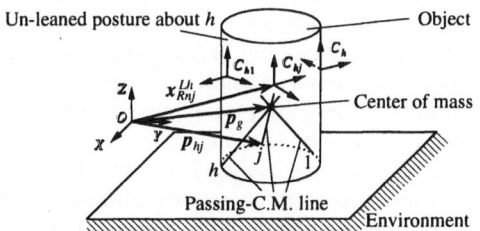

Fig. 6. Un-leaned posture about contact point h

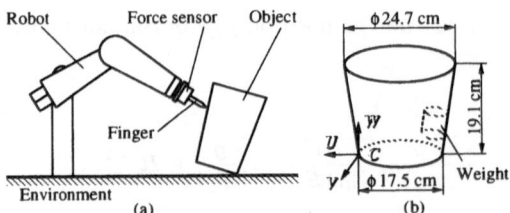

Fig. 7. Experimental setup and object

4   Estimation of Mass and Center of Mass

Under the un-leaned posture about contact point j, let us consider estimating the center of mass with the plural ($j = 1, 2, \cdots, h$, $h \geq 2$) passing-C.M. lines with respect to base frame $O - XYZ$.

Let P_g denote the position of center of mass. Since a passing-C.M. line contains the center of mass as mentioned previously, we have $P_g = p_{hj} + k_g T_{h0j}$ from eqs.(47) and (2) with respect to $O - XYZ$, where $k_g = 1/m$. For the obtained passing-C.M. lines L_{Tj} ($j = 1, 2, \cdots, h$, $h \geq 2$), there are

$$Qu = s \in R^{3h}, \quad h \geq 2, \tag{50}$$

$$Q = \left[[-T_{h01} \ \ I_3]^T \ \cdots \ [-T_{h0h} \ \ I_3]^T \right]^T \in R^{3h \times 4}, \tag{51}$$

$$u = \left[k_g \ \ P_g^T \right]^T \in R^{4 \times 1}, \tag{52}$$

$$s = \left[p_{h1}^T \ \cdots \ p_{hh}^T \right]^T \in R^{3j \times 1}. \tag{53}$$

When $h \geq 2$ and rank$Q = 4$, the optimal approximate solution of u, $u = Q^+ s$, which contains the object mass and the position of center of mass, can be obtained from eq.(50) since $3h > 4$, where $Q^+ \in R^{4 \times 3h}$ is the pseudoinverse of Q. From the obtained u, we can obtain the center position P_g of mass with respect to frame $O - XYZ$, and the object mass m, $m = 1/k_g$.

5   Verification by Experiment

The experiments were performed using a robot arm PUMA260 shown in outline by Fig.7(a). The unknown object is a plastic frustum of a cone shown in Fig.7(b), where a weight is added in the frustum. The experimental environment is an unknown plane and there is sufficient friction to prevent object slipping.

In the experiment, when the object is slowly being turned to an un-leaned posture with keeping the fingertip moving in a vertical operation plane, the contact points between the objects and environment plane are kept not to slip because of the sufficient friction, while the touching point positions between the fingertip and objects are allowed to slip a few. After an object was leaned and the touching point position and the fingertip force are measured, the touching point position will be marked on the object. Then, after the object was slowly returned to its un-leaned posture, the marked point will be positionally measured again by fingertip so that fingertip displacements Δl_{Rij} can be obtained.

Table 1. Result of experiment

	p_{qu}[cm]	p_{qv}[cm]	p_{qw}[cm]	m[kg]
Estimated value	−10.46	−0.28	8.21	0.746
Reference value	−10.38	0.00	7.85	0.728
Error	0.08	0.28	0.36	0.018

The estimated results and the reference values about the masses and centers of mass of the objects are shown in Table 1. For convenience, the centers of mass are given with respect to an object frame $C - UVW$, whose origin is at the curved edge of the object base. The reference values are obtained by human skill for the center of mass and by a dial scale for mass. Comparing the estimated and reference values, the position errors for the center of mass are less than 4mm, and the error about mass is 18g.

References

1. C. G. Atkeson, C. H. An and J. M. Hollerbach, "Rigid Body Load Identification for Manipulators," *Proc. of IEEE Int. Conf. on Decision and Control*, Vol.2, pp.996-1002, 1985.
2. Y. Murotsu, K. Senda, M. Ozaki and S. Tsujio, "Parameter Identification of Unknown Object Handled by Free-Flying Space Robot," *AIAA Jour. of Guidance, Control, and Dynamics*, Vol.17,No.3, pp.488-494,1994.
3. Y. Aiyama, M. Inaba and H. Inoue, "Proviting: A New Method of Graspless Manipulation of Object by Robot Fingers," *Proc. of IEEE Int. Conf. on Intelligent Robots and Systems*, Vol.1, pp.136-143, 1993.
4. Y. Yu, K. Fukuda and S. Tsujio, "Estimation of Mass and Center of Mass of Graspless and Shape-Unknown Object," *Proc. of IEEE Int. Conf. on Robotics and Automation*, Vol.4, pp.2893-2898, 1999.

Sound and Visual Tracking by Active Audition

Hiroshi G. Okuno[1,2], Kazuhiro Nakadai[1], Tino Lourens[1,3] and
Hiroaki Kitano[1,4]

[1] Kitano Symbiotic Systems Project, ERATO, Japan Science and Technolog
   Corp, Mansion 31 Suite 6A, 6-31-15 Jingumae, Shibuya, Tokyo 150-0001 Japan
[2] Graduate School of Informatics, Kyoto University, Sakyo, Kyoto 606-8501,
   Japan
[3] Starlab DF-1, B-1180 Brussels, Belgium
[4] Sony Computer Science Laboratories, Inc., Shinagawa, Tokyo 141-0022
   E-mail: {okuno, nakadai, tino, kitano}@symbio.jst.go.jp

Abstract. Active perception in vision and audition is essential in robot-human
interaction. The audition system of the intelligent humanoid requires localization
of sound sources and identification of meanings of the sound in the auditory scene.
However, the performance of these processing may be deteriorated because coupling
of perception and behavior causes mechanical noises. The active audition system reported in this paper adaptively cancels motor noises by using heuristics with motor
control signal, and localizes multiple sound sources. The sound and visual tracking
system implemented on the *SIGthe humanoid.* demonstrates the effectiveness and
robustness of sound and visual tracking in multiple sound source environments.

1   Introduction

Active perception is common in human perception. For example, when we see
something strange, we may approach it to examine the details. When we hear
a sudden sound, we may turn the head to see what happened. We may listen
with a hand cupped to our ear to hear better, or move closer to a speaker
to make better communication. The essential of active perception resides in
multi-modality, in other words, integration of multiple sensory information.

Human audition is always active, since people hear a mixture of sounds
and focus on some parts of input. Usually, people with normal hearing can
separate sounds from a mixture of sounds and focus on a particular voice
or sound even in a noisy environment. This capability is known as the *cocktail party effect*. While traditionally, auditory research has been focusing on
human speech understanding, understanding auditory scene in general is receiving increasing attention.

Active perception is important in robotics or mechanical perception, because it signifies coupling of perception and behavior. In vision, a lot of
research has been carried out in the area of active vision, because it will provide a framework for obtaining necessary additional information by coupling
vision with behavior, such as control of optical parameters or actuating camera mount positions [1]. Such activities include moving a camera or cameras,

changing focus, zooming in or out, changing camera resolution, and widening or narrowing iris and so on. Therefore, active vision system is always coupled with servo-motor system, which means that it always induces motor noises and mechanical ones such as clattering and creaking.

Active audition, however, has not been studied yet, in particular in robotics, although it is important in human perception. This is partially because various kinds of noises caused by such movements make sound processing difficult. Therefore, mobile robots with auditory perception usually adopt "*stop-perceive-act*" principle to avoid sounds made during moving due to motor noises or a bumpy road. Although this principle reduces the complexity of the problems involved sound processing for mobile robots, it restricts their capabilities of sound processing as well as the integration of multi-modal sensory processing.

A general framework of processing and understanding a mixture of sounds is needed for active audition, since robots and we usually hear a mixture of sounds including mechanical sounds. The study of this framework is called Computational Auditory Scene Analysis (CASA) [2–5]. It requires not only understanding of meaning of specific sound, but also identification of spatial relationship of sound sources, so that sound landscapes of the environment can be understood.

As an example of active perception, in particular, active audition, sound and visual tracking of multiple sound sources is investigated in this paper. The upper-torso humanoid robot called *SIGthe humanoid* [6] is used as the platform, because multi-modality of perception and high degree-of-freedom is essential to simulate intelligent behavior. The proposed system is expected to attain robust object tracking by compensating each drawbacks of sound or visual tracking. Visual tracking may be difficult in case of occlusion, while sound tracking may be ambiguous in localization due to the nature of auditory processing.

2   Issues in Active Audition

Active audition system should cope with the "*stop-perceive-act*" strategy to in order to move even while it is listening to some sounds. However, most robots equipped with microphones developed so far process sounds without motion or obtain speech inputs directly from a microphone attached to a speaker [7–10]. *Kismet* of MIT AI Lab [7] can recognize speeches by speech-recognition system from the direct input and express various kinds of sensation. *Hadaly* of Waseda University [9] can localize the speaker, but recognize speeches by speech-recognition system from the direct input.

For a compact implementation of robot such as SONY AIBO entertainment robot, stop-perceive-act strategy won't work well, because motor noises caused by a cooling fan is too loud to hear speeches clearly. Since these in-

ternal sound sources are much closer than other external sources, even if the
absolute power of noises is much lower, input sounds are strongly influenced.

2.1 Internal Sound Suppression with Cover

Since active perception causes sounds by the movement of various movable
parts, internal sound suppression is critical to enhance external sounds. A
cover of humanoid body reduces sounds of motors emitted to the external
world by separating internal and external world of the robot. Such a cover is,
thus, expected to reduce the complexity of sound processing caused by motor
sounds.

A cover affects the spectrum of sounds like a dummy head in which a
pair of dummy headphones are embedded. This spectral effect is known as
HRTF (Head-Related Transfer Function). HRTF and actual transfer function plays an important function in localizing (calculating the position of)
a sound source. To obtain HRTF by measuring impulse response for each
spatial position is timeconsuming. In addition, actual transfer function depends on environments such as room, wall, objects and so on. Therefore, a
new localization method without using HRTF or by adjusting HRTF to a
real-world should be invented.

2.2 General Sound Understanding — Computational Auditory Scene Analysis

Since CASA research investigates a general model of sound understanding,
input sound is a mixture of sounds, not a sound of single source. One of the
main research topics of CASA is *sound stream separation*, a process that separates sound streams that have consistent acoustic attributes from a mixture
of sounds, and *sound source localization*.

In extracting acoustic attributes, some systems assume the humans auditory model of primary processing and simulate the processing of cocklear
mechanism [11]. Brown and Cooke designed and implemented a system that
builds various auditory maps for sound input and integrates them to separate
speech from input sounds [11]. Since this system needs to access all data, real-
time processing is difficult to attain. Nakatani *et al* used harmonic structures
as the clue of separation and developed a monaural-based harmonic stream
separation system, called HBSS. HBSS is modeled by a multi-agent system
and extracts harmonic structures *incrementally*. They extended HBSS to use
binaural (stereo microphone embedded in a dummy head) sounds and developed a binaural-based harmonic stream separation system, called Bi-HBSS
[12].

Bi-HBSS finds a pair of harmonic structures extracted by left and right
channels similar to stereo matching in vision where camera are aligned on a
rig, and calculates the *interaural time/phase difference* (*ITD* or *IPD*), and/or

the *interaural intensity/amplitude difference* (*IID* or *IAD*) to obtain the direction of sound source. The mapping from ITD/IPD, and/or IID/IAD to the direction of sound source and vice versa is based on the HRTF associated to binaural microphones. Finally Bi-HBSS separates sound streams by using harmonic structure and sound source direction. These systems are evaluated only in an anechoic room.

Huang *et al* [13] developed a robot that had three microphone installed on the surface of the sphere (the body of the robot), composing a triangle. HRTF has been measured in an anechoic room. Comparing the input power of microphones, two microphones that have more power than the other are selected and the sound source direction in the horizontal plane is calculated by taking into account reverberation. By selecting two microphones from three, they solved the problem that two microphones cannot determine the place of sound source in front or backward. In addition, one microphone installed on the top of the sphere is used to solve the vertical direction.

2.3   Sensor Fusion for Sound Stream Separation

Separation of sound streams from perceptive input is a nontrivial task due to ambiguities of interpretation on which elements of perceptive input belong to which stream [14]. For example, when two independent sound sources generate two sound streams that are crossing in the frequency region, there may be two possibilities in interpretation; crossing each other, or approaching and departing. The key idea of Bi-HBSS is to exploit spatial information by using a binaural input.

The error in direction determined by Bi-HBSS is about $\pm 10°$, which is similar to that of a human, i.e. $\pm 8°$ [15]. However, this is too coarse to separate sound streams from a mixture of sounds. Nakagawa *et al* [14] improved the accuracy of the sound source direction by using the direction extracted by image processing, because the direction by vision is more accurate. By using an accurate direction, each sound stream is extracted by using a *direction-pass filter*. In fact, by integrating visual and auditory information, they succeeded to separate three sound sources from a mixture of sounds by two microphones. They also reported how the accuracy of sound stream separation measured by automatic speech recognition is improved by *adding more modalities*, from monaural input, binaural input, and binaural input with visual information. However, these results are verified only in an anechoic room.

3   Active Audition System

The humanoid robot called *SIG* is used as a testbed [6]:

- 4 DOFs of body driven by 4 DC motors — Its mechanical structure is shown in Figure 1b. Each DC motor is controlled by a potentiometer.

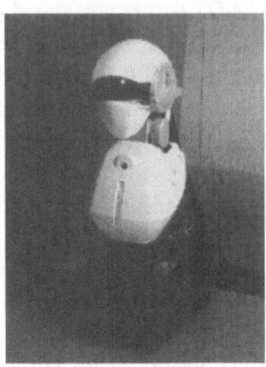

a) Cover

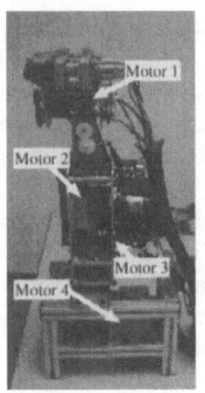

b) mechanical structure

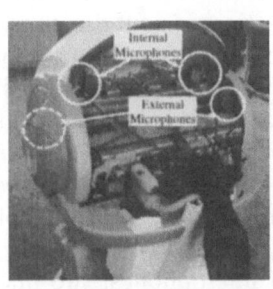

c) Inter microphones (top)
and cameras

Fig. 1. *SIG* the Humanoid

- A pair of CCD cameras of Sony EVI-G20 for visual stereo input — Each camera has 3 DOFs, that is, pan, tilt and zoom. Focus is automatically adjusted. The offset of camera position can be obtained from each camera (Figure 1b).
- Two pairs of omni-directional microphones (Sony ECM-77S) (Figure 1c). One pair installed in the ear gather sounds from the external world. The other pair installed very close to the corresponding microphone gather sounds from the internal world.
- A cover of the body (Figure 1a) reduces sounds to be emitted to external environments, which is expected to reduce the complexity of sound processing.

The active audition system consisting of two components; **internal sound suppression** and **sound stream separation** (see Figure 2). The head direction is obtained from potentiometers in the servo-motor system. Hereafter, it is referred as *the head direction by motor control*. By combining visual localization and the head direction, *SIG* can determine the position in world coordinates. The idea of sound stream separation is that the sound source direction is obtained by *visual and auditory epipolar geometry* and then each sound stream is extracted by direction-pass filter.

3.1   Internal Sound Suppression System

Internal sounds of *SIG* are caused mainly camera and body motors. Camera motor sounds of movement are quiet enough to ignore, but sounds of standby is about 3.7 dB. Body motor sounds of standby and movement are about 5.6 dB and 23 dB, respectively. Comparison of noise cancellation by adaptive filtering, ICA, case-based suppression and model-based suppression, we concluded that only adaptive filters work well. Four microphones are not enough

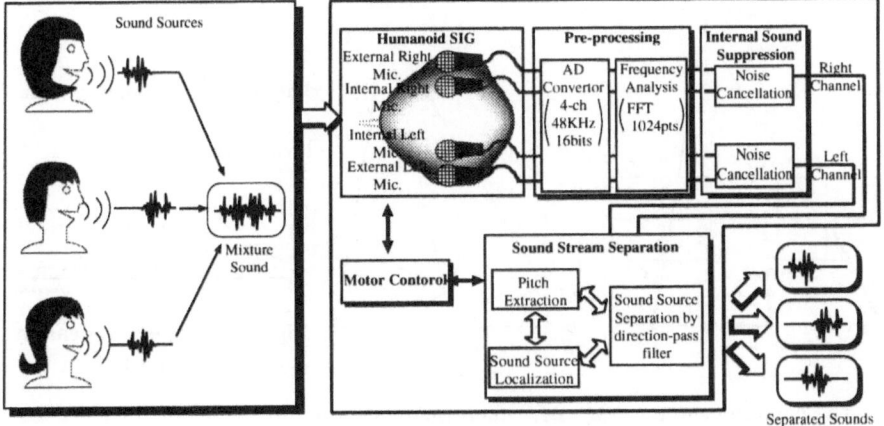

Fig. 2. Active Audition System

for ICA to separate internal sounds. Case-based and model-based suppression affect the phase of original inputs, which causes errors of IPD.

We tried to make as adaptive filter an FIR (Finite Impulse Response) filter of order 100, because this filter is a linear phase filter. This property is essential to localize the sound source by IID or IPD. The parameters of the FIR filter is calculated by least-mean-square method as adaptive algorithm. Noise cancellation by the FIR filter suppresses internal sounds but some errors occur. These errors make poor localization compared to results of localization without internal sound suppression. Case-based or model-based cancellation is not adopted, because the same movement generates a lot of different sounds and thus it is difficult to construct case or model-based cancellation.

Our adaptive filter uses *heuristics about internal microphones* to discard subbands destroyed by burst noises, which are mainly caused by stoppers, friction between cable and body, and creaks at joints of cover parts. The subband is discarded if the following conditions are satisfied:

1. Intensity difference between external and internal microphones is similar to that of motor noise intensity differences measured in advance.
2. Intensity and pattern of the spectrum are similar to that of motor noise frequency responses measured in advance.
3. A motor command is being processed.

3.2   Sound Stream Separation by Localization

Localization by Visual Epipolar Geometry: Consider a simple stereo camera setting where two cameras have the same focal length, their light axes are in parallel, and their image planes are on the same plane (see Figure 3.2a). Suppose that a space point $P(X, Y, Z)$ in the world coordinate is projected on each camera's image plane, (x_l, y_l) and (x_r, y_r). Let f be the focal length of each camera's lens and b be the baseline. Disparity d is defined as $d = x_l - x_r$. The following relations hold: $X = \frac{b(x_l + x_r)}{2d}, Y = \frac{b(y_l + y_r)}{2d}, Z = \frac{bf}{d}$

180   Hiroshi G. Okuno et al.

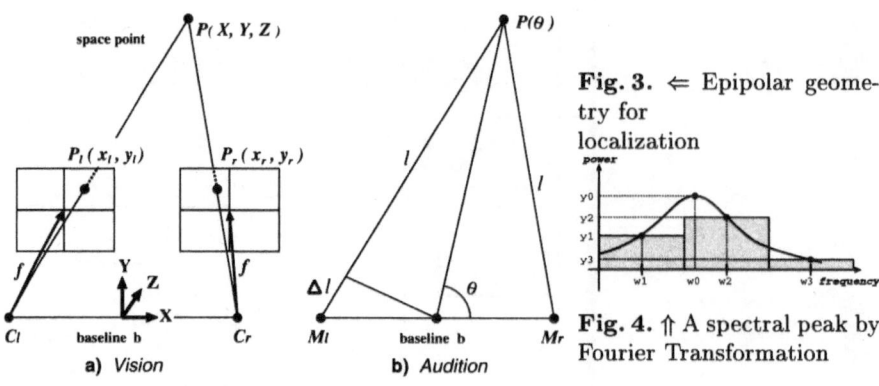

Fig. 3. ⇐ Epipolar geometry for localization

Fig. 4. ⇑ A spectral peak by Fourier Transformation

C_l, C_r: camera center, M_l, M_r: microphone center

The current implementation of common matching in *SIG* is performed by using corner detection algorithm [16]. It extracts a set of corners and edges then constructs a pair of graphs. A matching algorithm is used to find corresponding left and right image to obtain depth.

Localization by Auditory Epipolar Geometry: Auditory system calculates the direction by using epipolar geometry. First, it extract peaks by using FFT (Fast Fourier Transformation) for each subband of 47Hz, and then calculates the IPD.

Let $Sp^{(r)}$ and $Sp^{(l)}$ be the right and left channel spectrum obtained by FFT at the same time tick, respectively, and f_p be a peak frequency on the spectrum.

The IPD $\triangle\varphi$ is calculated as follows:

$$\triangle\varphi = \tan^{-1}\left(\frac{\Im[Sp^{(r)}(f_p)]}{\Re[Sp^{(r)}(f_p)]}\right) - \tan^{-1}\left(\frac{\Im[Sp^{(l)}(f_p)]}{\Re[Sp^{(l)}(f_p)]}\right)$$

where $\Re[Sp]$ and $\Im[Sp]$ are the real and imaginary part of the spectrum $Sp^{(r)}$, respectively. The angle θ is calculated by the following equation: $\cos\theta = \frac{v}{2\pi f_p b}\triangle\varphi$ where v is the velocity of sound. For the moment, the velocity of sound is fixed to 340m/sec and remains the same even if the temperature changes.

Pitch Extraction: Pitches are extracted by spectral subtraction. It uses peak approximation method based on characteristics of FFT and window function. When a peak $[\omega_2, y_2]$ is detected by FFT, usually it is not the true peak (see Figure 4). Let $[\omega_1, y_1]$ and $[\omega_3, y_3]$ be values of both neighbors. The true peak $[\omega_0, y_0]$ is estimated as follows:

$$\omega_0 = \begin{cases} \omega_2 + \dfrac{2\pi\left(2|y_1| - |y_2|\right)}{T\left(|y_1| + |y_2|\right)} & (\omega_1 < \omega_0 \leq \omega_2) \\[3mm] \omega_2 - \dfrac{2\pi\left(-|y_2| + 2|y_3|\right)}{T\left(|y_2| + |y_3|\right)} & (\omega_2 < \omega_0 < \omega_3) \end{cases} \tag{1}$$

$$Arg(y_0) = \tan^{-1}\left(\frac{\Im[y_0]}{\Re[y_0]}\right) = \tan^{-1}\left(\frac{\Im[y_2]}{\Re[y_2]}\right) + \frac{T}{2}\left(\omega_2 - \omega_0\right) \tag{2}$$

$$|y_0| = \frac{\Delta\omega\left(-T^2\Delta\omega^2 + 4\pi^2\right)}{2\pi^2 \sin\frac{T}{2}\Delta\omega}|y_2|,$$
$$\Delta\omega = \omega_2 - \omega_0 \tag{3}$$

Since the above equations require relatively small number of calculations, our method can run faster and extract more accurate pitches. For example, it takes only 1/200 of amount of calculations per a peak required by Bi-HBSS [5].

Direction-Pass Filter by Epipolar Geometry: As opposed to localization by audition, the direction-pass filter selects subbands that satisfies the IPD of the specified direction. The algorithm of the direction-pass filter is described as follows:

1. The specified direction θ is converted to $\Delta\varphi$ for each subband (47 Hz).
2. Extract peaks and calculated IPD, $\Delta\varphi'$.
3. If IPD satisfies the condition $\Delta\varphi' = \Delta\varphi$, then collect the subband.
4. Construct a wave consisting of collected subbands by inverse FFT.

By using the relative position between camera centers and microphones, it is easy to convert from epipolar plane of vision to that of audition (see Figure 3.2b), because the baselines for vision and audition are in parallel in *SIG*. Therefore, whenever a sound source is localized by visual epipolar geometry, it can be converted easily into the angle θ as described in the following equation: $\cos\theta = \frac{P \cdot M_r}{|P||M_r|} = \frac{P \cdot C_r}{|P||C_r|}$.

Sound and Visual Tracking System: The sound and visual tracking system consists of active audition, active vision, motor control, association, and foucus of attention subsystems. The association subsystem maintains the consistency between directions extracted by vision, audition, and motor control subsystems. The current implementation of association module gives the highest precedence to vision module over audition module. Focus of attention is based on the selective attention mechanism [16].

In the next section, the sound and visual tracking system is evaluated by a simple scenario.

4   Experiments of Sound and Visual Tracking

Scenario: Two load speakers are located in a room of 10 square meters. The room is a conventional Japanese residential apartment facing a road with busy traffic, and exposed to various daily life noise. One sound source A (Speaker A) plays a pure tone of 500 Hz, while the other one B (Speaker B) plays that of 600 Hz. A is located in front of SIG (5° left of the initial head direction) and B is located 69° to the left. The distance from SIG to each sound source is about 210cm (the maximum distance in the room). Since the visual field of camera is only 45° in horizontal angle, SIG cannot see B at the initial head direction, because B is located at 70° left to the head direction, thus it is outside of the visual fields of the cameras. Figure 5 shows this situation.

1. A plays a sound at 5° left of the initial head direction.
2. SIG associates the visual object with the sound, because their extracted directions are the same.
3. Then, B plays a sound about 3 seconds later. At this moment, B is outside of the visual field of the SIG. Since the direction of the sound source can be extracted only by audition, SIG cannot associate anything to the sound.
4. SIG turns toward the direction of the unseen sound source B using the direction obtained by audition.
5. SIG finds a new object B, and associates the visual object with the sound.

Results: Spectrogram of input sound is shown in Figure 6, which shows steady motor noises and burst motor noises (around 4, 6, 8 seconds). The results of tracking, without and with internal noise suppression, are shown in Figure 7 and 8, respectively. In these figures, temporal series of directions obtained by either active vision or audition are plotted with the ego-centric polar coordinate, where 0° indicates the direction in front of the head, and minus indicates the right of the head direction.

The results of the experiment are very promising. First, accurate sound source localization is attained by the proposed system. Auditory epipolar geometry without HRTF proves very effective and locates approximate direction of sound sources. The effect of adaptive noise cancellation is clearly shown. Without internal noise suppression, sound direction estimation is seriously hampered when the head is moving (around time 5 - 6 seconds) as is shown in Figure 7.

Such accurate localization by audition makes association between audition and vision possible. While SIG is moving, sound source B comes into its visual field. The association module checks the consistency of localization by vision and audition. If the discovered loud speaker does not play sounds, inconsistency occurs and the visual system would resume its search finding an object producing sound. If association succeeds, B's position in world

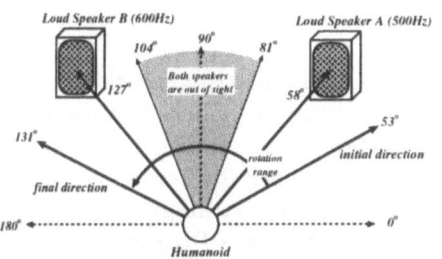

Fig. 5. Experiment: sound and visual tracking while *SIG* moves.

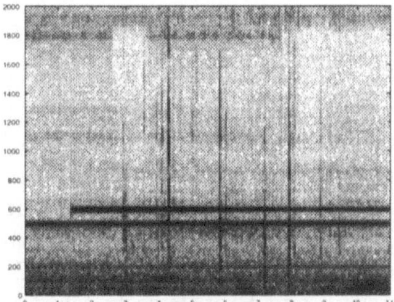

Fig. 6. Spectrogram of input sound

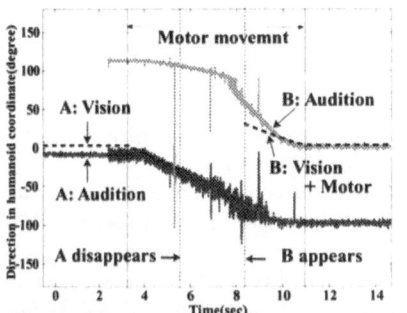

Fig. 7. Localization without internal noise suppression

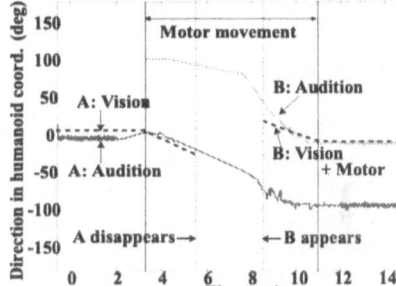

Fig. 8. Localization by internal noise suppression

coordinates is calculated by using motor information and the position in humanoid coordinates obtained by vision.

5   Discussion and Future Work

Experimental results indicate that position estimation by audition and vision is accurate enough to create consistent association even under the condition that the robot is constantly moving and generating motor noise.

When a humanoid hears sound by facing the sound source in the center of the pair of microphones, ITD and IID is almost zero if the pair of microphones are correctly calibrated. Given the multiple sound sources in the auditory scene, a humanoid actively moves its head to improve localization by aligning microphones orthogonal to the sound source and by capturing the possible sound sources by vision.

The important future work includes real-time processing, and improving sound source localization by adding more modalities. One idea of improving sound source localization is to use hierarchical integration of auditory and visual processing. Some levels of integration includes association at the signal level, at the physical location level, and at the speaker identification level. At speaker identification, face recognition and speaker identification may be used.

6   Conclusion

This paper reports the preliminary results of sound and visual tracking. We are now attacking real-time implementation by using distributed processing as well as multi-level integration [17]. We believe that multi-modality will enable robots or humanoids to behave more intelligently by recognizing environments more precisely without the *stop-perceive-act* strategy.

We thank our colleagues of Kitano Symbiotic Systems Project, Tatsuya Matsui, Yukiko Nakagawa, and Dr. Iris Fermin (currently with Aston University), and Prof. Hiroshi Ishiguruo of Wakayama University, for their discussions.

References

1. Y. Aloimonos, I. Weiss, and A. Bandyopadhyay., "Active vision," *International Journal of Computer Vision*, vol. 1, no. 4, pp. 333–356, 1987.
2. M. P. Cooke, G. J. Brown, M. Crawford, and P. Green, "Computational auditory scene analysis: Listening to several things at once," *Endeavour*, vol. 17, no. 4, pp. 186–190, 1993.
3. T. Nakatani, H. G. Okuno, and T. Kawabata, "Auditory stream segregation in auditory scene analysis with a multi-agent system," in *Proc. of AAAI-94*, pp. 100–107, AAAI, 1994.
4. D. Rosenthal and H. G. Okuno, eds., *Computational Auditory Scene Analysis*. Mahwah, New Jersey: Lawrence Erlbaum Associates, 1998.
5. K. Nakadai, T. Lourens, H. G. Okuno, and H. Kitano, "Active audition for humanoid," in *Pro. of AAAI-2000*, pp. 832–839, AAAI, 2000.
6. H. Kitano, H. G. Okuno, K. Nakadai, I. Fermin, T. Sabish, Y. Nakagawa, and T. Matsui, "Designing a humanoid head for robocup challenge," in *Proc. of Agents 2000*, ACM, 2000.
7. C. Breazeal and B. Scassellati, "A context-dependent attention system for a social robot," in *Proc. of IJCAI-99*, pp. 1146–1151, 1999.
8. R. Brooks, C. Breazeal, M. Marjanovie, B. Scassellati, and M. Williamson, "The cog project: Building a humanoid robot," in *Computation for metaphors, analogy, and agents* (C. Nehaniv, ed.), pp. 52–87, Spriver-Verlag, 1999.
9. Y. Matsusaka, T. Tojo, S. Kuota, K. Furukawa, D. Tamiya, K. Hayata, Y. Nakano, and T. Kobayashi, "Multi-person conversation via multimodal interface — a robot who communicates with multi-user," in *Proc. of EUROSPEECH-99*, pp. 1723–1726, ESCA, 1999.
10. A. Takanishi, S. Masukawa, Y. Mori, and T. Ogawa, "Development of an anthropomorphic auditory robot that localizes a sound direction (*in japanese*)," *Bulletin of the Centre for Informatics*, vol. 20, pp. 24–32, 1995.
11. G. J. Brown, *Computational auditory scene analysis: A representational approach*. University of Sheffield, 1992.
12. T. Nakatani and H. G. Okuno, "Harmonic sound stream segregation using localization and its application to speech stream segregation," *Speech Communication*, vol. 27, no. 3-4, pp. 209–222, 1999.
13. J. Huang, "Spatial sound processing for a hearing robot," in *Enabling Society with Information Technology*, LNCS, This volume, Springer-Verlag, 2001.

14. Y. Nakagawa, H. G. Okuno, and H. Kitano, "Using vision to improve sound source separation," in *Proc. of AAAI-99*, pp. 768–775, AAAI, 1999.
15. S. Cavaco and J. Hallam, "A biologically plausible acoustic azimuth estimation system," in *Proc. of IJCAI-99 Workshop on CASA (CASA'99)*, pp. 78–87, IJCAI, 1999.
16. T. Lourens, K. Nakadai, H. G. Okuno, and H. Kitano, "Selective attention by integration of vision and audition," in *Proc. of Humanoids2000*, IEEE/RSJ, 2000.
17. K. Nakadai, K. Hidai, H. Mizoguchi, H. G. Okuno, and H. Kitano, "Real-time auditory and visual multiple-object tracking for robots," in *Proc. of IJCAI-01*, pp. 1425–1432, 2001.

Speech Enhancement and Segregation Based on Human Auditory Mechanisms

Masato Akagi[1], Mitsunori Mizumachi[2], Yuichi Ishimoto[1] and Masashi Unoki[3]

[1] Japan Advanced Institute of Science and Technology, Ishikawa 923-1292, Japan
[2] ATR Spoken Language Translation Research Laboratories, Kyoto 619-0288, Japan
[3] CNBH, Physiology Department, University of Cambridge, CB2 3EG, U.K.
E-mail: akagi@jaist.ac.jp

1   Introduction

Humans can perceive specific desired sounds without difficulty, even in noisy environments. This is a useful ability that many animals possess, and is referred to as the 'Cocktail party effect'. We believe that by modeling this mechanism we will be able to produce tools for speech enhancement and segregation, or for other problems in speech recognition and analysis.

To construct models that mimic human sound perception ability, engineering know-how and knowledge of auditory physiology and/or psychoacoustics are required. This paper, first, introduces the basic concepts used to construct models such as "cancellation on the neural system" [5, 6, 7] and "auditory scene analysis" [2]. It then proposes models based on these concepts.

Specifically, this paper discusses the following;
(1) Speech enhancement: a cancellation model and speech enhancement, and
(2) Speech segregation: auditory scene analysis proposed by Bregman [3] and an auditory sound segregation model based on auditory scene analysis.

2   Speech Enhancement [1,10,11,12]

2.1   Method

This paper assumes that the noises considered are unevenly distributed with regard to time, frequency, and direction. In this situation, spatial filtering is useful to extract target signals. Thus, we will discuss this filtering method with respect to inter-aural time differences (ITDs).

Models of systems used to reduce noise have been constructed using knowledge about auditory physiology and/or psychoacoustics. We used a cancellation method to design our filters (Durlach [7], Culling & Summerfield [5] for binaural masking level difference (BMLD) modeling, and de Cheveigne [6] for fundamental frequency estimation). The original cancellation method is a subtraction method that reduces periodical target signals with period T, using the circuit in Fig. 1. We considered delay time T as to be the ITD for spatial filtering.

We modified the circuit with an engineering point of view, as shown in Fig. 2.

2.2   Algorithm

Our method uses a microphone array with three linear and equally spaced (10 cm) omni-directional microphones, which estimates the largest noise at the position of the center microphone in each time period. Then, noise is reduced by subtracting the estimated noises from the signal received by the center microphone.

2.2.1   Estimation of noise

Noises are estimated by using the signals received by the paired microphones. These microphones are located at both ends of the microphone array (main pair), or with one in the center and one at both ends of the array (sub pair). Assume that a speech signal comes from a certain direction, and that noises come from directions other than that of the speech signal. Assuming that the speech signal $s(t)$ comes from a direction such as the difference in arrival time between main paired microphones 2ζ, and the largest noise $n(t)$ comes from a direction that is 2δ, signals received at each microphone are described as follows:

left mic. : $l(t) = s(t - \zeta) + n(t - \delta)$ (1)

center mic. : $c(t) = s(t) + n(t)$ (2)

right mic. : $r(t) = s(t + \zeta) + n(t + \delta)$ (3)

For simplicity, we assume that speech signals come from the front. Then, $l(t)$ and $r(t)$ are shifted $\pm\tau$ in time, where τ is a certain constant ($\tau \neq 0$), and these make function $g_{lr}(t)$. The function $g_{lr}(t)$ is a beamformer in the time domain, and its short-term Fourier transformation (STFT) is $G_{lr}(\omega)$. The function is defined as

$$g_{lr}(t) = \frac{\{l(t+\tau) - l(t-\tau)\} - \{r(t+\tau) - r(t-\tau)\}}{4} \equiv g(l,r,\tau,t), \quad (4)$$

$$G_{lr}(\omega) = \text{STFT}[g(l,r,\tau,t)] = N(\omega)\sin\omega\delta\sin\omega\tau, \quad (5)$$

where $N(\omega)$ is the STFT of the largest noise $n(t)$. Note that $G_{lr}(\omega)$ does not have the component of $S(\omega)$, the STFT of the speech signal $s(t)$, that is, $S(\omega)$ was cancelled.

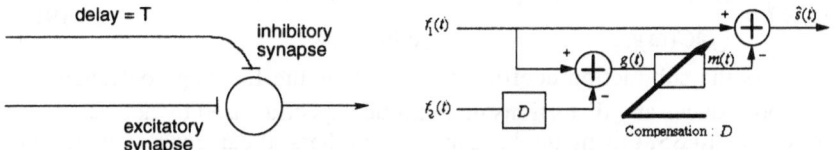

Fig. 1. Basic cancellation model.   Fig. 2. A cancellation model circuit.

The item δ in Eq. (5) represents the direction from which the largest noise comes, so it is determined by estimating where the noise comes from in each frame (this is described later). The spectrum of the noise can be calculated by setting a certain value τ at the estimation of δ and dividing Eq. (5) by $\sin^2 \omega\delta$. However, it is not accurately calculated in the case of $\omega\delta = n\pi$, n: integer. In that frequency band, $G_{cr}(\omega)$ can be expressed form the other beamformer $g(c, r, \tau_2, t)$ as follows:

$$G_{cr}(\omega) = \text{STFT}[g(c, r, \tau_2, t)] = N(\omega)\exp\left(j\omega\frac{\delta}{2}\right)\sin\omega\frac{\delta}{2}\sin\omega\tau_2 . \quad (6)$$

Then, the spectrum of the largest noise $n(t)$ is estimated over the entire frequency range as

$$\hat{N}(\omega) = \begin{cases} G_{lr}(\omega)/\sin^2 \omega\delta, & \sin^2 \omega\delta > \varepsilon_1 \\ G_{cr}(\omega)/\sin^2 \omega(\delta/2), & \sin^2 \omega\delta \le \varepsilon_1 \text{ and } \sin^2 \omega(\delta/2) > \varepsilon_2, \\ G_{lr}(\omega)/\varepsilon_2^2, & \sin^2 \omega(\delta/2) \le \varepsilon_2 \end{cases} \quad (7)$$

where ε_1 and ε_2 are threshold values.

2.2.2   Estimation of noise direction

The arrival directions of noises are automatically estimated frame by frame. In this paper, two signals, in which the speech signal is perfectly eliminated, provide these noise directions, and they are calculated by using Eq. (6) and $G_{lc}(\omega) = \text{STFT}[g(l, c, \tau_2, t)]$. Here, the speech signal has no effect on the estimation of noise directions, as $G_{cr}(\omega)$ and $G_{lc}(\omega)$ do not include speech signals at all. Setting τ_2 arbitrary, the following is calculated,

$$d(t) = \text{IFFT}\left[\frac{G_{lc}(\omega)G_{cr}^*(\omega)}{|G_{lc}(\omega)||G_{cr}(\omega)|}\right] \quad \text{and} \quad \delta = \arg\max[d(t)] \quad (8)$$

The value δ, half of the difference in the arrival time between the main paired microphones is given by Eq. (8).

2.2.3   Signal enhancement

After estimating the spectrum of noise $\hat{N}(\omega)$, it must be subtracted from that of the noisy-speech signal received by the center microphone $c(t)$. This method employs a non-linear spectral subtraction (SS), expressed as

$$|\hat{S}(\omega)| = \begin{cases} |C(\omega)| - \alpha \cdot |\hat{N}(\omega)|, & |C(\omega)| \ge \alpha \cdot |\hat{N}(\omega)| \\ \beta|C(\omega)|, & \text{otherwise} \end{cases}, \quad (9)$$

where α is the subtraction coefficient, and β is the flooring coefficient. Thus, this method reduces any distortions in amplitude spectra cased by acoustic noises.

In regards to SS, this method is superior to others; it can cope with all types of acoustic noise by estimating the spectra of each noise in frames. Other methods, however, are poor at eliminating non-stationary, like sudden, noise. This is because they substitute signals received in the past in greater or lesser degree.

This method can also employ wave subtraction (WS) [1].

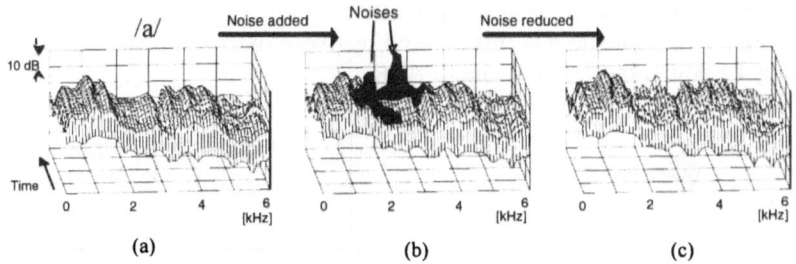

Fig. 3. Simulated results using sound data A. (a) original noise-free speech wave (vowel /a/),
(b) noise-added speech wave, (c) noise-reduced speech wave.

2.3   Evaluation

2.3.1   Sound data simulation conditions

Two types of noise-added speech waves were evaluated. Both sound data were sampled at 48 kHz with 16-bit accuracy.

Sound data A, shown in Fig. 3, is a vowel /a/ in the ATR speech database. Two sudden narrow-band noises with center frequencies of 1500 Hz and 2500 Hz, bandwidth of 200 Hz, and duration of 50 ms are included. They were mixed on a computer with the speech signal coming from the front, and both of noises coming from about 30 degrees to the right. The noises are marked in black.

Sound data B is real sound waveform presented by two speakers in a soundproof room (reverberation time: about 50 ms at 500 Hz). The speech and noise come from 0 and 30 degrees to the right, both 3 meters from the microphones. The noise is wide-band white noise between 125 Hz to 6 kHz. Three SNRs (-10, 0, and 10 dB) were used. The speech waves without noise, and the speech wave with an SNR of 0 dB, are illustrated in Fig. 4.

2.3.2   Simulation conditions

The noise reduction experiments were done under the following conditions. The frame length was 5.3 ms, the frame shift was 2.7 ms, and the window function is Hamming. The threshold values ε_1 and ε_2 were 0.6 and 0.2, and the coefficients α and β in Eq. (9) were 1 and 0.001, respectively. Here, the frame length was set to be as short as possible to decrease the distortions caused by the SS. The other parameters were set experimentally.

2.3.3   Results

For sudden noise in the sound data A, the noise-reduced speech signal for the simulation using the proposed method is shown in Fig. 3(c). By comparing Figs. 3(a), (b) and (c), we see that sudden noises are greatly reduced.

For sound data B, Fig. 4(c) shows the noise-reduced sound from the 0-dB SNR. The amplitude of the noise was reduced, and was almost the same as that of the 10-dB SNR speech wave (Fig. 4(d)). This demonstrates that our method reduces noise in all segments. Figure 5 shows the log-spectra of the vowel /u/ at about 16000 points. Large peaks and dips are evident. The spectra of noise-added speech, by contrast, are flattened, especially in the higher-frequency region. Our results (Fig. 5(c)) indicate that this method recovers spectrum peaks and dips, and thus, may be helpful at the front end of ASR.

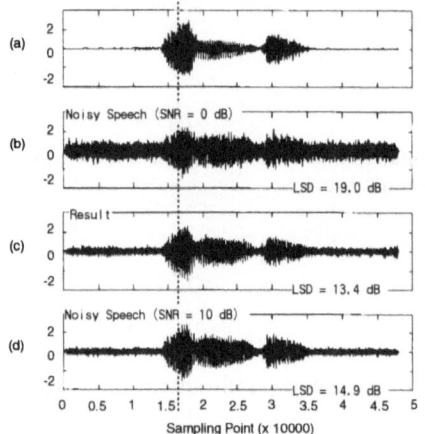

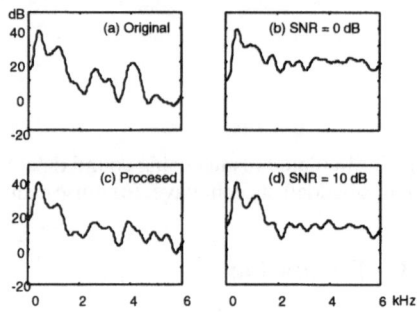

Fig. 4. Simulated results for Sound data B, (a) noise-free speech wave presented by speaker (ATR, mht14348 /bunri/),(b) noise-added speech wave: SNR = 0 dB, (c) noise-reduced speech wave, and (d) noise-added speech signal (SNR = 10 dB).

Fig. 5. Log-spectra of sound of vowel /u/ at about 16000 points, (a) original sound, (b) noise-added speech wave (SNR = 0 dB), (c) noise-reduced speech wave, and (d) noise-added speech signal (SNR = 10 dB).

2.3.4   Front-end of automatic speech recognition [13]

We studied the decline in ASR performance under additive noise conditions and the subsequent improvement offered by noise reduction. We used speaker-dependent HMM with 12th order MFCCs, as a baseline ASR. The phoneme recognition tests were conducted using 1048 words from the ATR Japanese speech database for training. Experiments were conducted using open data. A total of 216 phoneme-balanced words were used for testing, uttered by the same speaker in the same database. Some test sets were prepared by adding random noise (125-6000 Hz) to several SNRs, and then reducing them. The speech signal came from the front, and the noise signal came from 30 degrees to the right. For comparison, a conventional delay-and-sum beamformer [9], was used as a typical algorithm for noise reduction. We assume that the signal directions are known for the delay-and-sum beamformer. On the other hand, the proposed method estimates them automatically.

The results of the phoneme recognition tests are shown in Fig. 6. There are three bars in each SNR. They correspond to the phoneme error rates of the noise-added speech, the speech noise-reduced by the optimized delay-and-sum beamformer, and that reduced by our proposed method. Our proposed method clearly decreased phoneme error rates.

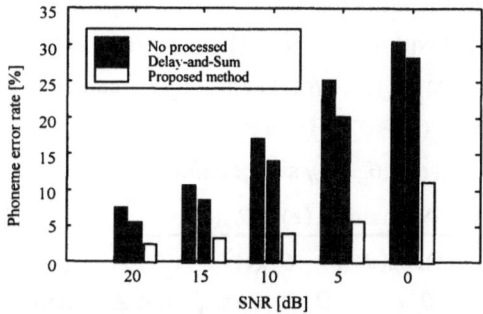

Fig. 6. Phoneme error rates. Three bars correspond to phoneme error rates of noise-added speech (black bar), noise-reduced speech obtained by optimized delay-and-sum beamformer (gray bar), and noise-reduced speech obtained by the proposed method (white bar).

3   Speech Segregation [15,16,17,18]

3.1   Method

Bregman reported that the human auditory system uses four psychoacoustically heuristic regularities related to acoustic events to solve the problem of auditory scene analysis (ASA) [2, 3]. A number of ASA-based segregation models have been proposed to computationally solve this problem [4, 8, 14]. All models use a subset of the four regularities, and the amplitude (or power) spectrum as the acoustic feature. As a result, they do not completely segregate the desired signal from the noisy one, when the signal and noise are in the same frequency region.

We have addressed the necessity of using both the amplitude and the phase spectrum to completely extract the desired signal from a noisy one, thus solving the problems associated with segregating two acoustic sources [16]. This problem is defined as follows [16, 17, 18]. First, only the mixed signal $f(t)$, where $f(t) = f_1(t) + f_2(t)$, can be observed. Next, the observed signal $f(t)$ is decomposed into its frequency components by using a filterbank (K channels).

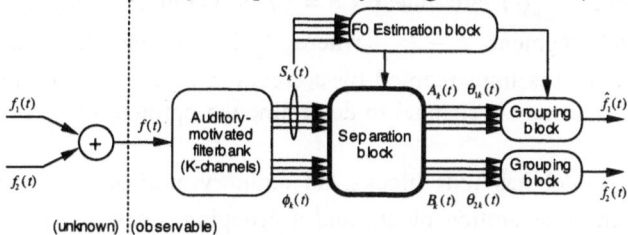

Fig. 7. Auditory sound segregation model.

The output of the k-th channel $X_k(t)$ is represented by

$$X_k(t) = S_k(t) \exp\left(j\omega_k t + j\phi_k(t)\right).$$ (10)

Here, if the outputs of the k-th channel, which correspond to $f_1(t)$ and $f_2(t)$, are assumed to be $A_k(t)\exp\!\big(j\omega_k t + j\theta_{1k}(t)\big)$ and $B_k(t)\exp\!\big(j\omega_k t + j\theta_{2k}(t)\big)$, then instantaneous amplitudes $A_k(t)$, $B_k(t)$, and $\theta_k(t)$ can be determined by

$$A_k(t) = S_k(t)\sin\!\big(\theta_{2k}(t) - \phi_k(t)\big)\big/\sin\theta_k t, \tag{11}$$

$$B_k(t) = S_k(t)\sin\!\big(\phi_k(t) - \theta_{1k}(t)\big)\big/\sin\theta_k t, \text{ and} \tag{12}$$

$$\theta_k(t) = \arctan\!\left(\frac{S_k(t)\sin\!\big(\phi_k(t) - \theta_{1k}(t)\big)}{S_k(t)\cos\!\big(\phi_k(t) - \theta_{1k}(t)\big) + A_k(t)}\right), \tag{13}$$

where $\theta_k(t) = \theta_{2k}(t) - \theta_{1k}(t)$, $\theta_k(t) \neq n\pi$, $n \in \mathbf{Z}$, and ω_k is the center frequency of the k-th channel [18]. However, the solution of this problem, $A_k(t)$, $B_k(t)$, $\theta_{1k}(t)$, and $\theta_{2k}(t)$, cannot be uniquely determined without some constraints. The problem, therefore, is an ill-inverse problem.

This paper proposes an auditory sound segregation model to solve this problem by using constraints related to the heuristic regularities.

3.2   Algorithm

This paper assumes that the desired signal $f_1(t)$ is a harmonic complex tone, where $F_0(t)$ is the fundamental frequency. The constraints used in this model are shown in Table 1.

Constraint (i) is implemented by comparing the onset/offset ($T_{k,\mathrm{on}}$, $T_{k,\mathrm{off}}$) of $X_k(t)$ with the onset/offset (T_S, T_E) of $X_i(t)$ corresponding to $F_0(t)$, where $\Delta T_\mathrm{S} = 25$ ms and $\Delta T_\mathrm{E} = 50$ ms [17]. Constraint (iii) is implemented by determining the channel number corresponding to the integer multiples of $F_0(t)$ [17]. Constraints (i) and (iii) are used to determine the concurrent time-frequency region of the desired signal in background noise.

To segregate the desired signal from the mixed one by constraining the temporal differentiation of $A_k(t)$, $\theta_{1k}(t)$, and $F_0(t)$, constraint (ii) is implemented such that $C_{k,R}(t)$ and $D_{k,R}(t)$ are linear ($R = 1$) polynomials, and $E_{0,R}(t)$ is zero (R=0) in a small segment $T_h - T_{h-1}$, where T_h is the continuous point of $F_0(t)$ [18]. Constraint (iv) is implemented by correlation function of the instantaneous amplitudes with the across-channel to determine the optimal $C_{k,R}(t)$ and $D_{k,R}(t)$ [17][18].

The proposed model has four blocks: an auditory-motivated filterbank, an F_0 estimation block, a separation block, and a grouping block, as shown in Fig. 7.

The auditory-motivated filterbank (a constant Q gammatone filterbank) decomposes the observed signal $f(t)$ into $S_k(t)$ and $\phi_k(t)$ [16].

The F_0 estimation block determines the fundamental frequency of $f_1(t)$ using the Comb filtering on an amplitude spectrogram $S_k(t)$s [15].

Table 1. Constrains corresponding to Bregman's psychoacoustical heuristic regularities.

Regularity [3]	Constraint [17,18]	
(i) common onset/offset	synchronous onset/offset	of $\left\|T_s - T_{k,on}\right\| \le \Delta T_s$, $\left\|T_E - T_{k,off}\right\| \le \Delta T_E$
(ii) gradualness change (smoothness)	of piecewise-differentiable polynomial approximation (spline interpolation)	$dA_k(t)\big/dt = C_{k,R}(t),\ d\theta_k(t)\big/dt = D_{k,R}(t)$ $dF_0(t)\big/dt = E_{0,R}(t)$ $\sigma_A = \int_{t_l}^{t_h}\left[A_k^{(R+1)}(t)\right]^2 dt \Rightarrow \min$ $\sigma_\theta = \int_{t_l}^{t_h}\left[\theta_k^{(R+1)}(t)\right]^2 dt \Rightarrow \min$
(iii) harmonicity	multiples of the fundamental frequency	$n \times F_0(t),\ n = 1, 2,\ ...,\ N_F$
(iv) changes occurring in the acoustic event	correlation between the instantaneous amplitudes	$\dfrac{A_k(t)}{\left\|A_k(t)\right\|} \approx \dfrac{A_l(t)}{\left\|A_l(t)\right\|},\ k \neq l$

The separation block determines the optimal $C_{k,1}(t)$ and $D_{k,1}(t)$ in every small segment using constraints (iv), and then determines $A_k(t)$, $B_k(t)$, $\theta_{1k}(t)$, and $\theta_{2k}(t)$ from $S_k(t)$, $\phi_k(t)$, $C_{k,1}(t)$, and $D_{k,1}(t)$ using Eqs. (11) - (13), in the concurrent time-frequency region. This concurrent region is determined by using constraints (i) and (iii), and the small segments are determined from the length of $T_h - T_{h-1}$ on the discontinuity of $F_0(t)$. $C_{k,1}(t)$ and $D_{k,1}(t)$ are determined as optimal arguments when the correlation between the instantaneous amplitudes with the across-channel, obtained from the candidates of the smoothed (the spline-interpolated) $C_{k,1}(t)$ and $D_{k,1}(t)$, is to be a maximum, in which the estimated region for $C_{k,1}(t)$ and $D_{k,1}(t)$ are determined by using the Kalman filtering.

The grouping block reconstructs the segregated instantaneous amplitude and phase using the inverse wavelet transformation [17].

3.2   Evaluation

3.2.1   Sound and simulation conditions

To show that our proposed method segregates the desired signal $f_1(t)$ from a noisy signal $f(t)$ that has precisely even waveforms, we ran two simulations using the following signals: (a) a noisy real vowel (/a/, /e/, /i/, /o/, /u/); and (b) a noisy real continuous vowel (/aoi/), where the noise was pink, and the SNRs of the noisy signals were between 5 and 20 dB, in 5-dB increments. These vowels were in the ATR database uttered by four speakers (two males and two females).

We used segregation accuracy, that is, the SNR in which S is an original signal and N is a difference between original and the extracted signals, to evaluate the segregation performance of the proposed method. Next, to show the advantages of the constraints in Table 1, we compared the performance of our method, when (1) extract without the smoothness of constraint (ii); (2) extract without constrains (ii) and (iv); and (3) extract with no constrains.

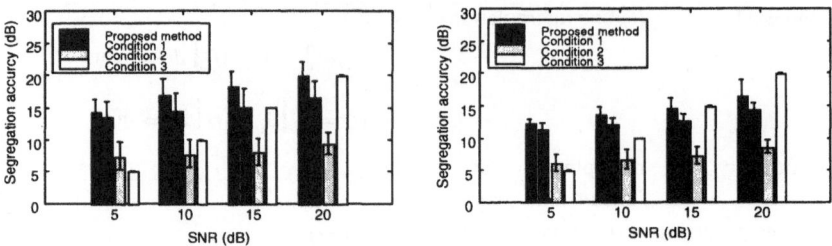

Fig. 8. Segregation accuracies for simulations. (a) vowel and (b) continuous vowel.

3.2.2   Results and discussion

The segregation accuracy in the two simulations and the four comparisons is shown in Fig. 8. In this figure, the bars show the mean of segregation accuracy and the error bar shows the standard deviation of segregation accuracy. The results show that the segregation accuracy of the proposed model was better than that of the others. These results also prove that, even in waveforms, the proposed model is capable of precisely segregating a desired vowel sound from a noisy one. In addition, by comparing the proposed model and (2), we see that simultaneous signals can be precisely segregated using the instantaneous amplitude and phase. Finally, when compared with (3), the proposed method improved segregation accuracy at an SNR of 5 dB in both simulations by about 8 dB.

4   Conclusion

This paper introduced some models associated with the 'Cocktail party effect'. Specially, it described;
 - speech enhancement done by spatial filtering, and
 - an auditory sound segregation model based on auditory scene analysis.
Simulated results showed that spatial filtering is useful in speech enhancement, and thus can be effectively used at the front-end of automatic speech recognition. Even in waveforms, the sound segregation model is capable of precisely extracting a desired signal from a noisy one.

Acknowledgments

This work was supported by CREST, JST, and by Grant-in-Aid for Science research from the Ministry of Education, Japan (No. 10680374 and Research Fellowship of the Japan Society for the promotion of science for Young Scientists).

References

1. Akagi, M, Mizumachi, M. (1997): Noise reduction by paired microphones. Proc. EUROSPEECH97, Rodes, 335-338
2. Bregman, A.S. (1990): Auditory Scene Analysis. Academic Press.
3. Bregman, A.S. (1993): Auditory Scene Analysis: hearing in complex environments. In: Thinking in Sounds. Oxford University Press, New York, pp. 10-36
4. Cooke, M. P., Brown, G.J. (1993): Computational auditory scene analysis : Exploiting principles of perceived continuity. Speech Communication 13, 391-399
5. Culling, J. F., Summerfield, Q. (1995): Perceptual separation of concurrent speech sounds: Absence of across-frequency grouping by common interaural delay. J. Acoust. Soc. Am. 98(2), 785-797
6. de Cheveigne, A. (1993): Separation of concurrent harmonic sounds: Fundamental frequency estimation and a time-domain cancellation model of auditory processing. J. Acoust. Soc. Am. 93(6), 3271-3290
7. Durlach, N. L. (1963): Equalization and Cancellation Theory of Binaural Masking-Level Difference. J. Acoust. Soc. Am. 35(8), 1206-1218
8. Ellis, D. P. W. (1996): Prediction-driven computational auditory scene analysis. Ph.D. thesis, MIT Media Lab
9. Flanagan, J. L, et al. (1991): Autodirective microphone systems. Acoustica 73(2), 58-71
10. Mizumachi, M, Akagi, M. (1998): Noise reduction by paired-microphones using spectral subtraction. Proc. ICASSP98 II, 1001-1004
11. Mizumachi, M., Akagi, M. (1999): Noise reduction method that is equipped for robust direction finder in adverse environments. Proc. Workshop on Robust Methods for Speech Recognition in Adverse Conditions, Tampere, Finland. 179-182

12. Mizumachi, M., Akagi, M. (1999): An objective distortion estimator for hearing aids and its application to noise reduction. Proc. EUROSPEECH99, Budapest, 2619-2622
13. Mizumachi, M., et al. (2000): Design of robust subtractive beamformer for noisy speech recognition. Proc. ICSLP2000, Beijing, IV-57-60
14. Nakatani, T., et al. (1994): Unified Architecture for Auditory Scene Analysis and Spoken Language Processing. Proc. ICSLP '94, Yokohama, 24(3)
15. Unoki, M., Akagi, M. (1998): Signal Extraction from Noisy Signal based on Auditory Scene Analysis. Proc. ICSLP'98, Sydney, 1515--1518
16. Unoki, M., Akagi, M. (1997): A method of signal extraction from noisy signal. Proc. EUROSPEECH97, Rodes, 2587-2590
17. Unoki, M., Akagi, M. (1999a): Signal Extraction from Noisy Signal based on Auditory Scene Analysis. Speech Communication 27(3), pp. 261—279
18. Unoki, M., Akagi, M. (1999b): Segregation of vowel in background noise using the method of segregating two acoustic sources based on auditory scene. Proc. EUROSPEECH99, Budapest, 2575-2578

Integration of Spatial Localization Cues
– Auditory Processing for a Hearing Robot –

Jie Huang

The University of Aizu, Aizu-Wakamatsu, 965-8580 Japan
E-mail: j-huang@u-aizu.ac.jp

Abstract. In this article, we describe the auditory system for a multimodal mobile robot. The system contains four microphones that are spatially arranged to form Cartesian coordinates to localize sound azimuths and elevations. Different pairs of microphone will provide localization cues for three orthogonal dimensions. By using the top-mounted microphone, elevations of sound sources can also be localized based on the time difference and intensity difference cues. Different methods of spatial cue integration are proposed and compared. By incorporate the model of the precedence effect, the influence of echoes and reverberations are inhibited. Other auditory functions such as sound source separation, sound understanding, and 3D sound reproduction are expected to be developed in the future.

1   Introduction

Mobile robot technology is an emerging field with wide applications. For example, a mobile robot can serve as a guard robot that can detect suspicious objects by audition and vision. The robot can also be used as an Internet-connected agent robot by which the user can explore a new place without being there. The robot can even attend a meeting instead of its users so that the users can get the remote auditory and visual scenes of the meeting room

For the above purposes, the robot must be capable of treating multimedia resources, especially sound media, to complement vision [1]. Visual sensors are the most popular sensors used today for mobile robots. Since a robot generally looks at the external world from a camera, difficulties occur when a object does not exist in the visual field of the camera or when the lighting is poor. A robot cannot detect a non-visual event that in many cases may, however, be accompanied by sound emissions. In these situations, the most useful information is provided by audition. Audition is one of the most important senses used by humans and animals to recognize their environments. Although the spatial resolution of audition is relatively low compared with that of vision, the auditory system can complement and cooperate with vision systems. For example, sound localization can enable the robot to direct its camera to a sound source. The auditory system of a mobile robot and can also be used for a teleconference system to guide its camera to pick up the faces of speakers automatically [2,3]. In such practical applications, sound localization is usually performed in reverberant environments. In the latter sections of this paper, we will focus on the techniques of spatial sound processing and echo avoidance in reverberation environments [4–6].

The auditory system used in our multimodal robot has some properties similar to those of the human auditory system. The microphones are arranged on the surface of a sphere "head" and with an interval of 30 cm about 1.5 times that of humans. Spatial cues including the time difference and intensity difference cues are used for the multimodal mobile robot. However, the multimodal mobile robot is not designed to simulate the human auditory system. It has some appropriate features based on the engineering needs of efficiency and accuracy. The sphere shaped head can simplify the formulation of time difference calculation. We use four microphones to form the Cartesian coordinates with the origin at the top of the sphere head. Different pairs of microphone will provide localization cues for three orthogonal dimensions. By using the top-mounted microphone, we can localize the elevation of sound sources based on the time difference and intensity difference cues without using the relatively uncertain spectral difference cue.

2   Other Expected Auditory Functions

3D Sound Conversion Since the microphone head of the robot is not the same as the human head, we have to convert the sound received by the robot to binaural 3D sound that can be perceived by humans. The pinna cues of the human auditory systems are also need to be created by all four of the spatially arranged microphones [7].

Blind Source Separation As a mathematic model, the task of separating multiple sources is often described as solving a multiple input and multiple output system by knowing only the output but not the input and the system itself [8]. The principle of those methods is that the signals of different sources are usually mutually independent. One weakness of this method is the need of intensive computation power, especially when the positions of sound sources or the positions of receivers are time variant. This weakness, however, can be overcome by incorporating a sound localization method to initially inform the system of the real source positions.

Computational Auditory Scene Analysis The computational auditory scene analysis methods are based on the human auditory model of sound stream organization [9–12]. Although those methods have achieved some effects for automatic sound organization and separation, they are still not as flexible as the human auditory system. This is partially because the discovered psychological rules are much more qualitative than quantitative. In future developments, we will try to construct a quantitative computational model for the primary and middle sound organization stage of the auditory system [13].

Sound Recognition Sound recognition or understanding will enable the robot to act in response to what is happening, e.g. sound of human voice, phone bell, door knocking, door opening, walking steps, siren, crash, and so on. Existing technologies of speech recognition and neural networks will be used. Here, sound recognition does not include speech recognition, which refers to the understanding of the meaning from a spoken language.

Auditory Navigation Compared to vision, audition is all-directional. By audition, it it easier to locate any urgent or emergency situation. Audition requires no illumination and enables a robot to work in darkness or low-light conditions. Audition also is less effected by obstacles. A robot can then perceive auditory information from sources behind obstacles [2]. One example is to localize a sound source outside of a room or around a corner. The robot will first localize the sound source in the area of the door or corner, travel to that point, and listen again to locate the sound source. The ability to localize sound sources can also be used to cancel positioning errors, instead of visual landmarks.

3   Spatial Localization in the Human Auditory System

3.1   Interaural spatial localization cues

The interaural arrival time differences and interaural intensity differences play particularly important roles in sound localization [14]. The spectral cues are also important. For example, sound sources in the median plane is mainly due to the spectral cues. However, compared to the interaural cues, the spectral cues are weaker and easily confused.

When a sound source is far from the head ($r \gg D/2$), the time difference can be approximated as

$$\Delta t = \frac{D}{2}(\theta + sin\theta) \tag{1}$$

where D is the diameter of the head and θ is the azimuth of the sound source. For sound sources in 3D space, the locus of all possible source positions will be approximately a conical shell known as the cone of confusion.

In the human auditory system, interaural time differences are coded by a phase-lock mechanism, i.e., auditory neurons fire at a particular phase angle of a tonal stimulus up to about 5 kHz. There is a problem when the neural circuits recovers the time difference from a phase difference, i.e., the time difference cannot be uniquely determined from a phase difference. Suppose the measured phase difference of frequency component f is $\Delta\omega_f$ ($0 < \Delta\omega_f < 2\pi$), the possible real phase difference $\Delta\hat{\omega}_f$ can be

$$\Delta\hat{\omega}_f(n) = \Delta\omega_f + 2\pi n_f \tag{2}$$

with a 2π period, where n_f is an integer differing for different frequency.

Biological studies about owls' auditory systems revealed that the redundancy is reduced through the characteristic delay (CD), the common time difference among many different frequency components [15]. Thus, the task becomes to find an integer n_f for every frequency component, so that the time difference t_{CD} is the same.

$$\Delta t_{CD} = \frac{1}{2\pi C f}(\Delta \hat{\omega}_f) = \frac{1}{2\pi C f}(\Delta \omega_f + 2\pi n_f) \tag{3}$$

While the time difference cue is used for low frequency components (up to about 5 kHz due to the phase-lock mechanism), the intensity difference cue is available for high frequency components. It is more complex to formulate the intensity difference than the time difference. The sound intensity depends not only on the azimuth θ and the elevation ϕ, but is also effected by its frequency. Represent the head-related transfer function (HRTF) as $H_l(\theta, \phi, f)$ and $H_r(\theta, \phi, f)$ for left and right ears. The cross interaural transfer function can be calculated as

$$H_x(\theta, \phi, f) = \frac{H_l(\theta, \phi, f)}{H_r(\theta, \phi, f)} = \frac{|H_l(\theta, \phi, f)|}{|H_r(\theta, \phi, f)|} e^{jp(\theta, \phi, f)} \tag{4}$$

or the opposite ($H_x = H_r/H_l$), where p is the phase difference. The amplitude part of H_x provides the interaural intensity difference. The intensity difference mainly depends on the shape of the head and the pinnas. It is large when the sound comes from the left (or right) side and small when the sound from front and back.

3.2   The precedence effect and echo avoidance

When a sound is presented in a reverberant environment, listeners usually can localize it correctly without being aware or influenced by the surrounding reflections. This phenomenon is referred to as the "precedence effect" [14]. We believe that there should be a mechanism that can estimate the level of reflected sounds in the human auditory system. By the Echo-Avoidance (EA) model, this mechanism can generate an inhibition signal, so that the neural pathway from low to high level of localization processing can be controlled to avoid the influence of reflections [4].

As shown in Fig. 1, the Echo-Avoidance Model consists of two paths, one for localization cue processing and one for inhibition signal generation. We assume that the echo estimation and inhibition mechanism is independent for each frequency. The path of inhibition generation will take a monaural signal, possibly the mixed signal of left and right channels. In the integration process, the first stage will be time averaging for each localization cue in each frequency subband. Integration over different frequency subbands and different cues will then take place.

The echo estimation process can be approximated by the following equation,

$$a_e(f, t) = \sum \{a(f, t - t') \, h_p(t')\} \text{ for } 0 < t' < \infty. \tag{5}$$

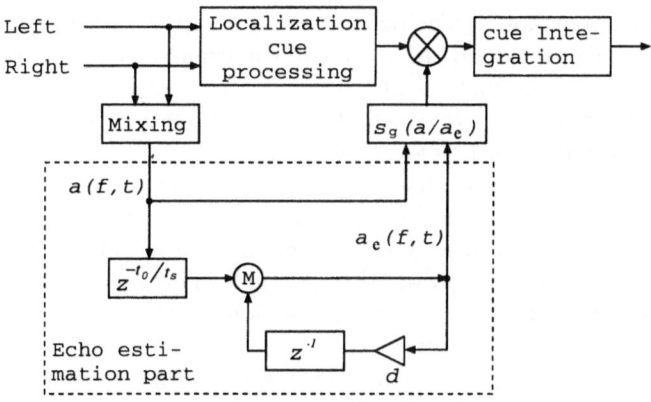

Fig. 1. The EA model of the precedence effect

Here,

$$h_p(t) = \begin{cases} 0 & , \ 0 \le t < \tau_o \\ k_p(e^{\frac{t-\tau_o}{\tau_a}} - 1)^3 \ e^{-\frac{t-\tau_o}{\tau_b}} & , \ t \ge \tau_o \end{cases} \tag{6}$$

$\tau_a = 1.50$ ms, $\tau_b = 0.31$ ms and $\tau_o = 0.3$ ms. $k_p = 12.5$ is the normalization value that sets the value at the peak position $t_p = -\tau_a \ln(1 - 3\tau_b/\tau_a)$ to about 0.5.

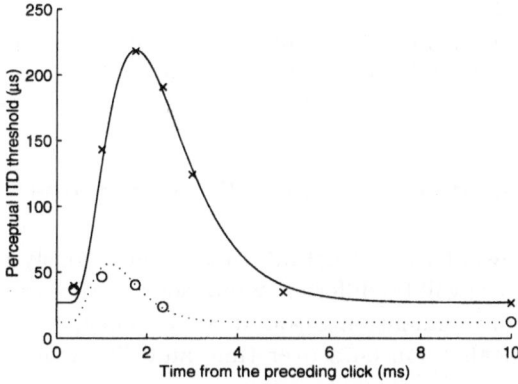

Fig. 2. This figure shows the increase in the interaural time difference perceptual threshold after a preceding impulsive sound. Saberi and Perrott's experiment results are indicated by 'x' marks (experiment I) and 'o' marks (experiment II, same subjects after several extended practice sessions) [16]. The solid line is the calculated approximation of experiment I ($a \ h_p(t) + b$, $a = 384$ μs and $b = 27$ μs.) and the dashed line for experiment II ($\tau_b = 0.22$ ms, $b = 12$ μs).

The most important psychological results about the precedence effect include the double click sound tests [16–19], the Franssen effect (constant-level pure tone) [20], and the Hass effect (speech and filtered continuous noise) [21]. Computational evaluation revealed that the EA model can exactly explain the above mentioned psychological results [4,22].

We examined the echo influence on arrival time differences around the onsets evaluated as echo-free by the EA model [4]. From the results, it is shown that the standard divergence of time differences is remarkably smaller near the echo-free onsets than in other portions. Those results demonstrated that the EA model indeed can find the portions in the time-frequency space that are less influenced by echoes.

For easy engineering treatment, the impulse response is generalized by the following formula to reflect its delay and decay features.

$$g_e = k \, e^{-(t-t_0)/\tau}. \tag{7}$$

The delay time t_0 and decay factor τ are chosen to match the most general cases in an ordinary environment. The decay factor τ, however, does not severely effect the result of echo estimation because, in the above approximation, the signal $a(f,t)$ contains not only direct sound but also the echoes. Thus, $a(f,t)$ itself has a decay feature due to the echo portions. Because of this feature, the time decay factor can be much smaller (about 2 to 5 ms) than that of real environments.

The summation in the convolution is replaced by the maximum operation 'M'. Thus,

$$a_e(f,t) = M\{a(f,t-t') \, g_e(t')\} \text{ for } 0 < t' < \infty. \tag{8}$$

By using the exponential decay feature of the generalized impulse response, we can implement the echo estimation algorithm by a very fast feedback mechanism as shown in Fig 1.

4   Integration of Spatial Localization Cues

Sound signals are usually not constant, but is continuously time variant. At a different time, there will be different sound sources that are mixed together to form a single one dimensional sound wave. Thus, a method is needed to integrate the localization cues over time and distinguish different sound sources.

4.1   Weighted cross correlation method

One traditional approach is to use cross correlation and multi-sensor array beamforming methods [23,24]. The cross correlation based methods are popularly used to calculate the time delay of two similar signals. However, those methods do not distinguish the direct sound and its reflections. To eliminate the influence of echoes, we will need a long time period of data for statistic averaging. Here, we propose an improved method, the weighted cross correlation method [25]. By this method (as shown in Fig. 3), the signals are transferred into the time-frequency space, and weighted by the estimated sound-to-echo ratio. Finally, the signals are returned to the time domain, and cross correlation is performed on the weighted signals.

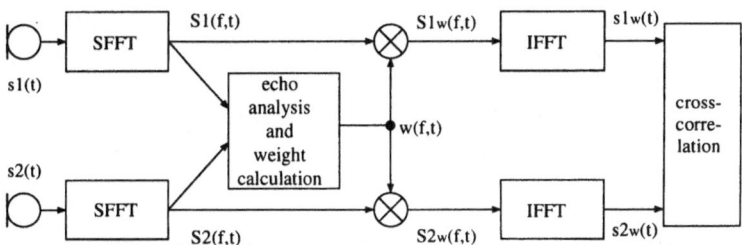

Fig. 3. Weighted cross correlation method for time delay estimation

We conducted experiments of time delay estimation in an ordinary room with walls , floor, and ceiling made of concrete. The room area was 30 m^2. The room was empty when the experiments were conducted, so that the reverberation in the room was very strong. The test sound was a radio weather forecast presented by a male announcer. Two microphones (numbers 1 and 3) were detached from the robot head, and placed at an interval of about 13.5 cm. The test sound was played from a speaker positioned about 2.9 m from the center of the two microphones and with an angle of 60 degrees to the center line. In Fig. 4, conventional and weighted cross correlations for sounds between microphones 1 and 3 are indicated by solid and dashed lines. The dotted vertical line near the time point of about 0.333 ms indicates the real arrival time delay of the test sound. It is clear that while the conventional cross correlation was strongly influenced by the echoes and reverberations, the weighted cross correlation showed the correct time delay.

The disadvantage of cross correlation based method is the low spatial resolution because of the gently sloped peaks. It is difficult to localize multiple sound sources when the interval distance between microphones is small. However, this disadvantage can be overcome by enlarging the microphone interval distance.

4.2   Time difference histogram method

Another approach is to use a time difference histogram [5]. This method is very similar to the characteristic delay calculation discovered in the owl's auditory system [15]. There may be two or more time difference candidates from

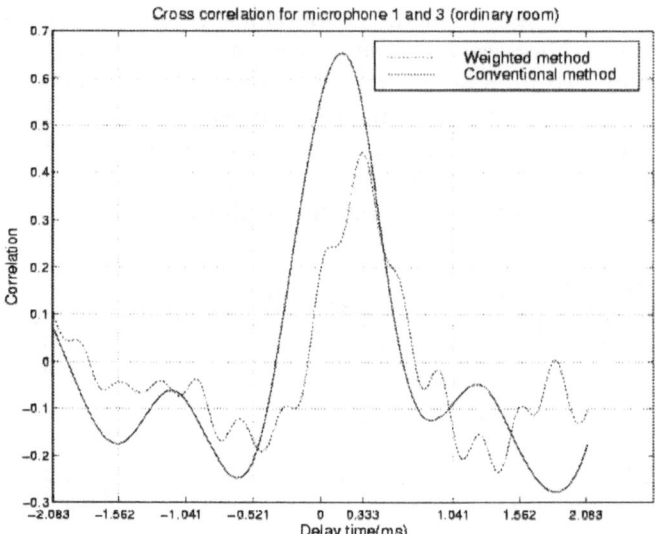

Fig. 4. Comparison for conventional cross correlation and weighted cross correlation method

a value of phase difference. To reduce the ambiguity, an azimuth histogram for the sound source direction is used. First, time difference histograms are formed for all microphone pairs by adding all of the possible candidates Δt_c of all frequency bands over a certain time segment. The time difference histograms of different microphone pairs are then mapped to the azimuth domain with a spread depending on the azimuth estimation sensitivity to the time difference $d\hat{\theta}/d(\Delta t)$. The histograms in the azimuth domain are then integrated by the arithmetical average to form a single azimuth histogram. Sound sources can be localized as the positions of peaks by the final azimuth histogram. Compared to the cross correlation based method, the histogram method has higher spatial resolution and is available for multi-source localization. Experiments showed this method could localize two simultaneous sound sources in an ordinary room with an accuracy of ±2 degrees.

In the previous version of the robot, the microphones were mounted directly in space without any kind of "head" between them. the intensity difference cue does not play any role in the above mentioned two methods Sounds can go directly to the microphones without any shadow effect. The intensity difference is only caused by the distance difference, and it is trivial to use this difference as a sound localization cue. In the new version of the robot, the microphones are arranged on the surface of a spherical "head". To analyze the intensity difference cue of the spherical head, we measured the head-related transfer functions for all azimuths and elevations of a five-degree step. Due to the shadow effect of the spherical head, the intensity difference between different microphones became significant. The intensity difference can be used to help determine the unique time difference from the phase difference in the above mentioned histogram method. Suppose the azimuth and elevation are estimated to be $\hat{\theta}$ and $\hat{\phi}$. The measured intensity difference d_i then must satisfy the following equation

$$d_i = |H_x(\hat{\theta}, \hat{\phi}, f)| \tag{9}$$

where H_x is the pre-measured interaural transfer function. This restriction is expected to reduce the redundancy and improve the localization accuracy.

5   Conclusion

In this article, we describe the auditory system for a multimodal mobile robot. The system contains four spatially arranged microphones for azimuth and elevation localization of multiple sound sources. By using different integration methods and incorporating the model of the precedence effect, the ambiguity of time difference calculation is solved and influence of echoes and reverberations are inhibited.

The important feature of this project is that we concentrate on the sound technologies as well as visual processing because interaction through sound media between robots and humans is indispensable. With the auditory functions, the robot will be aware when a person is talking and be able to understand where the speaker is. When dangerous accidents occur with a crash sound, the robot will be aware and direct the camera to the sound source.

References

1. Jie Huang. Spatial sound processing and a hearing robot. In *Proc. Int. Conf. Information Society in the 21st Century*, pages 281–287, Aizu-Wakamatsu, November 2000. U. Aizu.
2. J. Huang, T. Supaongprapa, I. Terakura, F. Wang, N. Ohnishi, and N. Sugie. A model based sound localization system and its application to robot navigation. *Robotics and Autonomous Systems*, 27(4):199–209, 1999.
3. J. Huang, N. Ohnishi, and N. Sugie. Building ears for robots: Sound localization and separation. *Artificial Life and Robotics*, 1(4):157–163, 1997.
4. J. Huang, N. Ohnishi, X. Guo, and N. Sugie. Echo avoidance in a computation model of the precedence effect. *Speech Communication*, 27(3-4):223–233, April 1999.
5. J. Huang, N. Ohnishi, and N. Sugie. Sound localization in reverberant environment based on the model of the precedence effect. *IEEE Trans. Instrum. and Meas.*, 46(4):842–846, August 1997.
6. J. Huang, N. Ohnishi, and N. Sugie. Spatial localization of sound sources: Azimuth and elevation estimation. In *Proc. Instrum. Meas. Technol. Conf.*, pages 330–333, St. Paul, May 1998. IEEE.

7. William L. Martens. Pseudophonic listening in reverberant environments: Implications for optimizing auditory display for the human user of a telerobotic listening system. In *Proc. Int. Conf. Information Society in the 21st Century*, pages 269–275, Aizu-Wakamatsu, November 2000. U. Aizu.

8. M. Kawamoto, K. Matsuoka, and N. Ohnishi. Real-would blind separation of non-stationary signals. In *Proc. Int. Conf. Information Society in the 21st Century*, Aizu-Wakamatsu, November 2000. U. Aizu.

9. A. S. Bregman. *Auditory Scene Analysis: The Perceptual Organization of Sound*. The MIT Press, London, 1990.

10. M. Cooke. *Modeling Auditory Processing and Organisation*. Cambridge University Press, Cambridge, 1993.

11. D. P. W. Ellis. A computer model of psychoacoustic grouping rules. In *Proc. 12th Int. Conf. on Pattern Recognition*, 1994.

12. T. Nakatani, H. G. Okuno, and T. Kawabata. Multi-agent based harmonic stream segregation for auditory scene analysis. *Journal Japanese Society for Artificial Intelligence*, 10(2):68–77, March 1995.

13. K. Yoshida. Interaction between different primary cues for sound integration and segregation. Graduation thesis, Univ. Aizu, 2001.

14. J. Blauert. *Spatial hearing: the psychophysics of human sound localization*. The MIT Press, London, revised edition, 1997.

15. T. Takahashi and M. Konishi. Selectivity for interaural time difference in the owl's midbrain. *J. Neuroscience*, 6(12):3413–3422, 1986.

16. K. Saberi and D. R. Perrott. Lateralization thresholds obtained under conditions in which the precedence effect is assumed to operate. *J. Acoust. Soc. Am.*, 87:1732–1737, 1990.

17. H. Wallach, E. B. Newman, and M. R. Rosenzweig. The precedence effect in sound localization. *J. Psychol. Am.*, 62(3):315–336, 1949.

18. W. A. Yost. The precedence effect: Revisited. *J. Acoust. Soc. Am.*, 76:1377–1383, 1984.

19. P. M. Zurek. The precedence effect and its possible role in the avoidance of interaural ambiguities. *J. Acoust. Soc. Am.*, 67:952–964, 1980.

20. N. V. Franssen. Eigenschaften des naturlichen Richtungshorens und ihre Anwendung auf die Stereophonie (The properties of natural directional hearing and their application to stereophony). In *Proc. 3rd Int. Congr. Acoustics*, volume 1, pages 787–790, 1959.

21. H. Haas. Uber den eingluss eines einfachechos auf die horsamkeit von sprache. *Acustica*, 1:49–58, 1951. English translation in: "The influence of a single echo on the audibility of speech", *J. Audio Eng. Soc.*, Vol. 20, pp. 146–159, (1972).

22. Y. Utsuno. Computational evaluation for the ea model of the precedence effect. Graduation thesis, Univ. Aizu, 2000.

23. R. O. Schmidt. Multiple emitter location and signal parameter estimation. *IEEE Trans. Antennas and Propagation*, AP-34(3):276–280, 1986.

24. P. Stoica and K. C. Sharman. Maximum likelihood method for direction-of-arrival estimation. *IEEE Trans. Acoust., Speech, Signal Processing*, ASSP-38(7):1131–1143, 1990.

25. T. Goto. A weighted cross correlation method for sound localization in reverberant environments. Graduation thesis, Univ. Aizu, 2000.

Part IV

New Models and Approaches for a

Knowledge Economic Society

Multicountry Modelling for the Japan Sea Rim Economic Relations

Hiroshi Ohnishi and QingZhu Yin

Graduate School of Economics, Kyoto University, Kyoto, JAPAN
E-mail: ohnishi@econ.kyoto-u.ac.jp

Abstract. This article shows a new small multicountry Econometric Model which includes Japan, Korea, Russia and the Northeast district of China. By this model, a future projection of this area and some policy simulations are done. Especially, the effects of the Japan-Korea Free Trade Area is estimated, and the result of this estimation is favorable for both countries. International trade between two countries is promoted, and in the long run, GDP of both countries are raised.

1 A Survey of the Japan Sea Rim Model

Economic relations among the Japan Sea[1] rim regions are going to be an important issue more and more and day by day, especially after a plan of the Japan-Korea free trade area was revealed. And already there is a huge scale multicountry econometric model (NAMIOS I, see Shishido et al (1999)) maintained by ERINA (Economic Research Institute for Northeast Asia)[2] and it include 7 countries (including USA) and can analyze industry by industry international relations. Furthermore, it divides Chinese sector into its Northeast region sector and the other sector. Such a division is very important because its Northeast region is the nearest and most influential for the rest of the Japan Sea rim countries. And, the size of population and its economic activity can be comparable with other countries. Its population is over 100 million. However, NAMIOS model's international trade bloc doesn't have the Chinese Northeast sector. That is, in NAMIOS model, there is the Chinese Northeast sector's macroeconomic model, but there is not its international trade bloc. Therefore, NAMIOS model cannot analyze the trade relations with this region directly.

A purpose of our model that we show in this paper is to overcome this weakpoint. Using the data of China Statistical Yearbook and these three provincial statistical yearbooks, we built the Chinese Northeast model that has both its domestic macro model and its trade bloc. Therefore, this sector is dealt like as an independent country.

To deal the Chinese regions and provinces as 'countries' has some reasons. One is their size of population. The average size of population of provinces is

---

[1] 'Japan Sea' is called as 'East Sea' in the North and South Korea.
[2] A Japanese Research Institute established by Niigata Prefecture and for the research of the Japan Sea rim economic relations.

40 million. And other reason is their independence. In Shanghai all of taxies are Santana, and in Tianjin Sharade ("Xiali" in Chinese). These cars are made in Shanghai and Tianjin respectively. Policy makers of each province want to be independent from the other provinces. In this sense, to make the Chinese regional or provincial model itself has its special value,[3] and our model is a kind of pioneer of this field.

2   Framework of Our Model

As a Japan Sea rim model, our model has some characteristics except for the above mentioned.

First, incorporated countries and regions are Japan, South Korea, Russia and the Chinese Northeast region. We could not take reliable data on North Korea. If we can divide Russia into its mainland and the Far East, it is better. However, we could not take such divided data. It also a subject for the second version model.

Second, to analyze the trade relations of the Japan Sea rim economies, each macro model is a Keynesian type demand side model.

Third, our model deals prices of trade goods in dollar terms in the trade bloc. Here, we firstly determine export prices in dollar terms by export price equations, and then determine import prices in dollar terms by using the following identities. That is;

$$PM_j = \sum_i \alpha_{ij} \times PE_i \qquad (1)$$

where, PM, PE is import prices and export prices respectively, and α_{ij} is the rate of import from economy i of the total import of economy j and $\sum_j \alpha_{ij} = 1$. Trade equations measured in each economies' currencies in the macro bloc are introduced from these dollar term trade equations by using the exchange rates.

There are the main characteristics of this model, the details of which are shown in the Home Page of our university (http:// i.econ.kyoto-u.ac.jp/ pacific/ yo_bunn_model/ index.htm).

Table 1 and 2 shows the result of the final test which was done from 1991 to 1997. Japanese and Korean sectors' results are good, but Russian sector's results are very bad. It is because of the reliability of the data and the shortage of its term. Russian data is only from 1990 to 1998. And the trade bloc's results are not good between each country and Russian and between the Chinese Northeast and Korea. This reason is same as the former. Trade relation between China and Korea is not long by a political reason. In this

---

[3] Although NAMIOS's regional macro model does not have trade bloc, it is a pioneer of the Chinese regional macro model. As a provincial model for the Chinese economy, one of us made a Xinjiang macro model (Ohnishi, 2000).

sense, our model has some problems and has to be rebuilt after gathering more reliable and longer data. However, the fitness that is shown in it is the level that can allow policy analyses.

Table 1. Absolute Mean Rate of Error of the Final Test (Macro Variables, %, at 1990 constant price)

	JAPAN	KOREA	CHINESE NORTHEAST	RUSSIA
GDP	2.3	3.7	4.7	18.6
CP^a	1.2	2.5	3.8	8.9
IF^b	2.9	4.8	8.2	16.3
IM^c	5.5	8.7	20.5	12.7
EX^d	6.8	9.8	15.6	15.0
CU^e	2.8	4.5	–	–
UR^f	12.6	15.7	20.3	–
WI^g	3.2	8.3	10.2	35.7
WPI^h	2.6	–	8.5	–
PDD^i	–	7.6	–	–
$PGDP^j$	7.5	7.1	9.1	40.5

[a] Private Consumption. [b] Private Investment. [c] Import . [d] Export.
[e] Unit Cost. [f] Unemployment Rate. [g] Wage Index. [h] Wholesale Price Index.
[i] Price Index of Domestic Demand. [j] GDP Deflator.

3 Policy Simulation

Although our model has many problems, using this model gives us many useful and beneficial information. Therefore, in this section, we simulate two kinds of policies and show the results of these simulation tests. One is the effect of Government Expenditure, and the other is the effect of the Japan-Korea Free Trade Area.

3.1 International Effects of Government Expenditure

Table 3 and 4 show the international effects in this area of an increase in each countries' government expenditure. Here, the sizes of these increases are 1 percent of each countries' GDP, and these simulation tests are done through the projection period 1999 - 2005.

Table 2. Absolute Mean Rate of Error of the Final Test (Trade Matrix, %, dollar base at current price)

exporter / importer	JAPAN	KOREA	CHINESE NORTHEAST	RUSSIA	REST OF THE WORLD
JAPAN	–	10.6	12.4	63.3	8.0
KOREA	6.3	–	39.0	32.7	7.3
CHINESE NORTHEAST	8.6	14.3	–	58.0	5.9
RUSSIA	53.0	36.6	27.1	–	11.1
REST OF THE WORLD	7.2	7.7	8.8	10.2	–

According to the result, the effects on their own country or region's GDP is 4.308-7.832 in Japan, 1.812 - 3.233 in Korea, 1.012 - 2.688 in the Chinese Northeast (These effects are not shown in the tables). Therefore, all of the Keynesian multipliers are larger than one, and we can understand that more advanced countries are, more effective such a fiscal policy is.

Such an effectiveness is also on the other countries'. The largest influence on the other three economies' GDP is made by the Japanese government expenditure, and the Korean, the Chinese Northeast's and the Russian's are following (The last two economies' effects are not also shown in the tables). In this sense, we can recognize that Japan is the most influential country in this area.

However, such an influential order is a matter of course, because (1 percent of) the sizes of these four economies are different. Therefore, the true effectiveness have to be compared by adjusting the size of their government expenditure, and Table 5 is the adjusted one for the former Table 3. In this table, the effects are multiplied by $1/15.5 = 0.0645$ which is the average ratio of the Korean GDP to the Japanese GDP through the simulation period. According to this table, the Korean expenditure is more effective on the Russian economy than the Japanese expenditure. This reason may be that the Korean economy has more strong relations with the Russian economy, especially as an absorber. However, for the other economies, scales of the Korean and the Japanese effects are almost same.

3.2   Effects of the Japan-Korea Free Trade Area

Table 6 shows the effect of the planned Japan-Korea Free Trade Area. Here, reduction of custom duties are simulated by the cut of export prices, and the ratios of this price-cut are assumed 2.2 percent in the Japanese export price, and 3.7 percent in the Korean export price. These figures of the price-cut

Table 3. Effects of 1 percent GDP increase in the Japanese Government Expenditure   (deviaiton from the standard projection, at 1990 constant price, percent)

	in 2000	in 2005
GDP of JAPAN	4.308	7.832
GDP of KOREA	2.889	7.321
GDP of CHINESE NORTHEAST	2.113	4.568
GDP of RUSSIA	2.011	3.717

Table 4. Effects of 1 percent GDP increase in the Korean Government Expenditure (deviaiton from the standard projection, at 1990 constant price, percent)

	in 2000	in 2005
GDP of JAPAN	0.211	0.776
GDP of KOREA	1.812	3.223
GDP of CHINESE NORTHEAST	0.111	0.674
GDP of RUSSIA	1.226	1.813

Table 5. Effects of 0.0645 percent GDP increase in the Japanese Government Expenditure (deviaiton from the standard projection, at 1990 constant price, percent)

	in 2000	in 2005
GDP of KOREA	0.176	0.501
GDP of CHINESE NORTHEAST	0.129	0.313
GDP of RUSSIA	0.123	0.255

are the two countries' rate of custom duties for rest of the world in the year 1998. Therefore, this simulation can be understood as the establishment of a perfect free trade area.

According to this result, both countries' amount of trade increase, and the impacts on the Korean trade activities is larger than the Japanese in the term of percentage. One more interesting point of the effects on GDP is that Korea loses in 2000, but gain a lot in 2005. The latter gain is the result of increase in its gross domestic investment and consumption. Therefore, gains from such a free trade can be checked not only by the trade surplus but also by the domestic indicators.

Table 6. Effects of the Japan-Korea Free Trade Area   (deviation from the standard projection, percent, at constant price of each currency)

	in 2000	in 2005
GDP of JAPAN	0.247	1.940
GDP of KOREA	-0.585	7.437
EXPORT of JAPAN	2.787	5.700
EXPORT of KOREA	3.628	7.208
IMPORT of JAPAN	5.008	5.875
IMPORT of KOREA	7.334	9.983

References

1. Ohnishi, H. (2000) Structure and Simulation of Xinjiang Econometric Model (in Japanese). Research and Study **20**, 1–16
2. Shishido, S. et al. (1999) A multiregional Econometric Model for Northeast Asia (NAMIOS I): Estimation and Policy Analysis, J. of Econometric Study of Northeast Asia **1**, 13-52

State-Owned Enterprises and Their Contract with Government in China: An Econometric Analysis

Go Yano[1] and Maho Shiraishi[2]

[1] Faculty of Integrated Arts and Sciences, The University of Tokushima, Tokushima, Japan
[2] Graduate School of Economics, Kyoto University, Kyoto, JAPAN
E-mail: yano@ias.tokushima-u.ac.jp

Abstract. In this paper we attempt to investigate empirically the cause of inefficiency of Chinese state-owned enterprises in 1989-95, in the contract relation between Chinese government and state-owned enterprises. It is found that several moral hazards arose, in 1989-95 Chinese state-owned enterprises, in textile industry. To put it another way, the enterprises chose less private effort and risk than the first-best levels, because of the incentive structure designed by the government. Especially, concave payoff function to the enterprises designed by the government made them institutional risk averters and choose too little risks.

1 Introduction

In this paper we attempt to empirically clarify what contract relation between Chinese government and state-owned enterprises caused what performance of the state-owned enterprises in 1989-95.

We can find many studies which analyze the contract relation between government and public enterprises, and the performance theoretically in transitional and socialist economies (e.g. Goldfeld and Quandt (1988), (1992); Qian (1994); Prell (1996); Zou and Sun (1996); Hsiao et al. (1998)). The basic idea of much of these studies depends on Kornai's famous idea; the soft budget constraints.

Theoretically, these studies describe the contract relation between government and public enterprises as a game in which principal-agent relation is typical, as an exogenous institution which is implicitly assumed to be designed by government and public enterprises behaving in the institution. Especially Qian (1994), Zou and Sun (1996) and Hsiao et al. (1998) explicitly deal with the model of Chinese transitional economy.

In this paper we adopt the basic idea of Zou and Sun (1996)'s theoretical model among theoretical studies mentioned above, because their model is not only interesting but also testable, if the form of the model is transformed appropriately.

The rest of this paper is organized as follows. Section 2 discusses a principal-agent model between Chinese government and state-owned enterprises. In Section 3, the data used is explained. Section 4 discusses the estimation procedure and results. Finally, Section 5 presents some conclusions, policy implications and suggestions for further research.

2   The Model

In this paper we attempt to investigate empirically whether any kind of moral hazard arose, avoiding the direct measurement of private efforts and risks, since they are unobservable for outsiders by assumption. For the purpose, it is a best measure to clarify what is the form of firms' behavior equations, first order conditions of firms' optimization problem. The firms' behavior equations indirectly show whether any kind of moral hazard arose. This is our strategy.

Our model depends on the basic idea of Zou and Sun (1996)'s theoretical model. To put it another way, we transform it to be testable by an econometric method.

2.1   Technology and Production

Zou and Sun (1996) express technological condition for production implicitly in revenue function, for generality and simplicity of model description. However, we express technological condition for production explicitly in production function, for empirical test afterward.

A higher level of effort increases expected yield of the firm at a cost explained below. A higher level of risk taking first increases expected yield of the firm, but increase uncertainty of yield, too. It's natural to think that taking risk, for instance, investment decision into new field, increases expected yield of the firm.

Therefore, we assume that the firm's production function is

$$Y = Y(K, L, e, r) = F(K, L, e, r) + \varepsilon (r) = f(K,L) + M(e, r) + \varepsilon (r)^1, \qquad (1)$$

where Y is output whose price is normalized to one, K is capital stock, L is labor input, e is the firm's private effort, r is the measure of risk taken by the firm,

$$M_e' > 0, M_e'' \leq 0, \qquad (2)$$

$$M_r' \geq 0 \text{ if } 0 \leq r \leq r^*, \quad M_r' < 0 \text{ if } r^* < r, \quad M_r'' < 0 \qquad (3)$$

$$\partial^2 M / \partial e \partial r = \partial^2 M / \partial r \partial e = \text{sufficiently small}, \qquad (4)$$

$\varepsilon \sim N(0, \sigma^2)$, $\sigma^2 = \sigma^2(r)$ and $\partial \sigma^2(r) / \partial r > 0$. f(K,L) is the part which can be explained by ordinary observable inputs, K and L. On the other hand, M(e, r) is

---

[1]   This production function does not have multiplicative (logarithmic linear) form but additive (linear) form about these three terms. We set this unusual form of production function in order that firms' behavior equations, first order conditions of firms' optimization problem, which are gotten using production function in the model, can be estimated by regression. If we adopted usual multiplicative form of production function, these equations would have very complicated form and can be hardly estimated for the complexity. This setting has important relation to f(K, L)'s specification, equation (9) or (10), and nonlinear estimation of production function afterward.

each firm's productivity term, which is expressed as unexplained residual in usual model but as the part explained by unobservable inputs, e and r, in our model.

The firm make a choice of effort $e \geq 0$ at a individual cost $C_i(e)$,

$$C_i' > 0 \text{ and } C_i'' > 0, \qquad (i=1 \sim n) \tag{5}$$

and a choice of risk $r \geq 0$, where i is the index of firm. What has to be noticed is that both the choices of e and r are the firm's private knowledge and they are not observable by outsiders.

Assuming that the economy on a whole is risk neutral, the first-best effort level and risk level in social viewpoint, e^* and r^*, are solved by maximizing $F(K, L, e, r)-C_i(e)$ or $M(e, r)-C_i(e)$. From (2), (3) and (5), these are characterized by the first-order conditions

$$M_e'(e^*) = C_i'(e^*) \qquad \text{and} \qquad M_r'(r^*) = 0. \tag{6}$$

The prices of output and cost are normalized in this paper.

That is all of technological condition necessary for theoretical analysis. In the following of this sub-paragraph, the setting necessary only for econometric analysis is introduced.

Each firm's private input of e and r is unobservable. Therefore, we are going to look for $M(e, r)$'s proxy directly for econometric analysis.

As a descriptive statistics indicating a kind of residual or productivity of each firm, we can find the following TE and M as the function of TE:

$$TE = 1 + (\ln Y - \ln Y_0) - 0.65(\ln K - \ln K_0) - 0.35(\ln L - \ln L_0) \text{ ,}^{2}$$

$$M = P_0 + P_1 TE + P_2 TE^2 + \exp(PP_1 TE + PP_2 TE^2) \tag{7}$$

where Y_0, K_0 and L_0 are the output, capital stock and labor input of benchmark firm and $\partial M / \partial TE > 0$. The benchmark firm is chosen randomly. This TE can be considered as a total factor productivity when Cobb-Douglas functional form is assumed in production function. The P_0, P_1, P_2, PP_1 and PP_2 are parameters to be estimated.

Therefore, the production function used in the estimation procedure is

$$Y = f(K,L) + P_0 + P_1 TE + P_2 TE^2 + \exp(PP_1 TE + PP_2 TE^2) + \varepsilon(r), \tag{8}$$

where ε is not only stochastic term of theoretical model but also error term of econometric model. We should notice that the regression of equation (8) as econometric model is set to be heteroscedastic by theoretical necessity, since choice of risk r is different by each firm because of C_i's individuality.

---

2   The weights, 0.65 and 0.35 are based on the estimated capital stock or labor elasticity of production in ordinary Cobb-Douglas production function by ordinary least squared method (OLS) and our total 1503 data of state-owned enterprises mentioned in section 3 below.

Finally f(K,L) is specified as below:

$$f(K,L) = \exp(\alpha_0)K^{\alpha_K}L^{\alpha_L} \tag{9}$$

or

$$f(K,L) = \exp(\alpha_0 + \alpha_K \ln K + \alpha_L \ln L$$

$$+ 1/2\,\beta_{KK}(\ln K)^2 + 1/2\,\beta_{LL}(\ln L)^2 + \beta_{KL}\ln K\,\ln L). \tag{10}$$

(9) is Cobb-Douglas functional form and (10) is a translog functional form.

2.2   Incentive Structure of the State-Owned Enterprises, and Their Choices of Risk, Effort, Capital and Labor

State-owned enterprises are assumed to maximize their expected net payoff to them:

$$NP(K,L,e,r) = E\,[Sv(\,\cdot\,)] + Sf - R \cdot K - W \cdot L - C_i(e), \tag{11}$$

where Sv is the variable part of payoff depending on K, L, e, r, and the realized revenue (profit), $\pi = Y(K,L,e,r) - R \cdot K - W \cdot L$, which is paid by government to the firm, Sf is the fixed part of payoff paid by government. R is rental fee of capital and W is wage rate. $C_i(e)$ is a individual effort cost at a effort level e.

The variable part of payoff depending on various variables, Sv( ), itself is what shows the incentive structure of state-owned enterprises designed by government.

Zou and Sun (1996)'s payoff function bends at several points and is convex. Based on the idea, we adopt the simplest payoff function that can express convexity or concavity of payoff function and is continuously differentiable.

Therefore, we assume the Sv($\cdot$) is the following:

$$Sv(\,\cdot\,) = (S_0 + S_\pi\,\pi\,)(\,\pi + S_{KL}\,(R \cdot K + W \cdot L)),$$

where payoff base is $\pi + S_{KL}\,(R \cdot K + W \cdot L)$ in the second parenthesis and payoff rate is $S_0 + S_\pi\,\pi$ in the first parenthesis. S_0, S_π and S_{KL} are payoff parameters designed by government, and

$$\pi = f(K,L) + M(e, r) + \varepsilon\,(r) - R \cdot K - W \cdot L.$$

If S_0 is positive and S_π is positive, the payoff function to state-owned enterprises is an increasing and *convex* function of the realized revenue (profit), π. If S_0 is positive and S_π is negative, the payoff function is an increasing and *concave* function of the realized revenue (profit). $S_{KL}(R \cdot K + W \cdot L)$ expresses existence of a subsidy to the input cost of capital stock and labor controlled by the parameter, S_{KL}.

Consequently, when the firm solves the maximizing problem:

$$\text{Max}_{K, L, e, r} \ NP(K,L,e,r)$$

its private effort and risk choices satisfy the first-order condition:

$$SS \cdot M_e' \ (e) - C_i' \ (e) = 0 \tag{12}$$

$$SS \cdot M_r' \ (r) + S_\pi (\partial \ \sigma^2 / \ \partial r) = 0. \tag{13}$$

$$SS = S_0 + S_\pi \ [\ 2(f(K,L) + M(e, r) - R \cdot K - W \cdot L) + S_{KL}(R \cdot K + W \cdot L) \ ] \tag{14}$$

Because M_e' (e) and C_i' (e) are positive as are shown in (2) and (5), SS is theoretically expected to be positive for the equality in order to hold in (12). From (2), (4) and (5), if $0 < SS < 1$, the firm's choice of effort e is lower than the first-best level e*. It's the first type of moral hazard of the two moral hazards among two types of moral hazards that will be discussed below If SS = 1, no moral hazard arise in the firm's choice of effort: e = e*[3]   From (3) and (4), if SS is positive and S_π is positive, which means a *convex* payoff function of the realized revenue (profit) if S_0 is positive, the firm's choice of risk r is higher than the first-best level r*. This is, the firm is an institutional risk-lover. On the other hand, if SS is positive and S_π is negative, which means a *concave* payoff function of the realized revenue (profit), the firm's choice of risk r is lower than the first-best level r*. This is, the firm is an institutional risk-averter. In both cases, a moral hazard arises. It's the second type of moral hazard. If S_π is zero and SS is not zero, no moral hazard arise in the firm's choice of risk: r = r*.

Let's investigate the firm's choices of capital stock, K, and labor, L. What has to be noticed is that the choices of K and L are observable in real Chinese economy's data used here. When the firm solves the maximizing problem mentioned above, its capital stock and labor choices must satisfy the first-order condition:

$$S_0 \ \{(f_K - R) + S_{KL}R\} \ + S_\pi \ \{ \ [2(F - R \cdot K - W \cdot L) + S_{KL}(R \cdot K + W \cdot L)] \ (f_K - R)$$

$$+ S_{KL}R(F - R \cdot K - W \cdot L) \ \} \ - R = 0 \tag{15}$$

$$S_0 \ \{(f_L - W) + S_{KL}W\} \ + S_\pi \ \{ \ [2(F - R \cdot K - W \cdot L) + S_{KL}(R \cdot K + W \cdot L)] \ (f_L - W)$$

$$+ S_{KL}W(F - R \cdot K - W \cdot L) \ \} \ - W \doteq 0. \tag{16}$$

In the estimation procedure, we use these equations, (15) and (16).

It should be noticed that theoretically, if $S_0 = 1$, $S_\pi = 0$ and $S_{KL} = 1$, no moral hazards arise.

---

[3]   On this point, see equation (4).

3   DATA

Data of Chinese textile state-owned enterprises comes from *Data file of Chinese state-owned enterprises, Basic Data File of Asian Firms vol.1 Chinese State-Owned Enterprises* (Nikkei Asia Kigyou Kihon File), of *NEEDS* (Nikkei Economic Electronic Databank System) compiled by Nippon Keizai shinbun-sha data bank bureau. Data of firms in Chinese textile industry were obtained for the period 1989-95.

We composed 1503 data of 626 state-owned textile enterprises in the Shanghai region and the Beijing region[4] in 1989-95. The descriptive statistics of these micro data is shown in

Table 1.   Descriptive Statistics of State-owned Entrprises Micro Data

	Mean	Minimum	Maximum	Standard deviation
Output (1000yuan)	57457.12	50.33	1270616.86	93153.04
Capital stock (1000yuan)	44910.13	22.12	3164044.7	152484.44
Labor input (workers)	1536	4	9990	1755.09
TE	0.7362271	0.0260541	2.522231879	0.59690882

Note. Number of firms is 626 and Number of Observations is 1503.

We use the average marginal productivity of foreign affiliates in China as rental fee of capital.

Almost all of the other price and wage rate data used for the estimation procedure were taken from *China Statistical Yearbook 1990-1996* and deflated by the overall retail price index in *China Statistical Yearbook 1990-1996*.

4   Estimation Procedure and Results

In the estimation procedure, we use (8), (15) and (16).   We firstly carry out the estimation of the production function (8) and secondly, using the estimation results, estimate behavior equations (15) and (16).

---

[4]   The Shanghai region includes Shanghai city, Jiangsu province and Zhejiang province, and the Beijing region includes Beijing city, Tianjin city, Hebei province and Shandong province.

4.1   Technology and Production

In the first place, let's see the estimation procedure and results of production function (8). In (8), the TE (or estimated M which is calculated by TE) measured in practice is a proxy of true productivity, and so K 's measurement error may occur.

Therefore, in the estimation of (8), we use instrumental variables and consider the heteroscedasticity as stated above.[5]

Table 2.   Estimated Parameters of Production Function (8)
Nonlinear instrumental variables estimation (virtual GMM)

f(K,L)	Cobb-douglas		Translog	
Coefficient	Estimates	t value	Estimates	t value
α_0	1.679	2.10	-103.002	-5.34
α_K	0.710	12.74	13.090	5.63
α_L	0.234	5.32	9.158	5.28
β_{KK}			-0.574	-4.54
β_{LL}			-0.028	-0.27
β_{KL}			-0.761	-5.86
			0	
P_0	-29336.2	-4.48	15.095	26.59
P_1	-32870.8	-2.81	-5.419	-13.73
P_2	28208.6	3.59	4399.4	2.20
PP_1	25.575	15.56	-1485.8	-1.63
PP_2	-14.109	-9.07		
No. of Obs.	1503		1503	
Adj. R^2	0.573		0.463	

Note. When f(K,L) is translog functional form, we estimate (8) with the restriction P_0=0. Because in the estimation result without the restriction the theoretical necessity , $\partial M / \partial TE > 0$ does not hold in the sample area.

Table 2 shows the estimation results of (8). The R-squares are approximately 0.5-0.6 and, therefore, the part which should be explained by the uncertainty is about 40-50 percent. We can find the influence of uncertainty is not so little.

4.2   Incentive Structure of the State-Owned Enterprises, and Their Choices of Risk, Effort, Capital and Labor

Now let's turn to the estimation procedure and results of behavior equations (15) and (16).   In the estimation of (15) and (16) also, the instrumental variables estimation is used.

---

[5]   Therefore, this estimation method is virtually same as GMM (Generalized Method of Moments).

Table 3. Estimated Parameters of Behavior Equations (15) and (16)
Nonlinear instrumental variables estimation (virtual GMM)

f(K,L)	Cobb-douglas		Translog	
Coefficient	Estimates	t value	Estimates	t value
S_0	$0.278*10^{-7}$	456.5	$0.202*10^{-7}$	14.85
S_{KL}	$0.360*10^8$	456.5	$0.495*10^8$	14.85
S_π	$-0.107*10^{-20}$	-4.60	$-0.807*10^{-22}$	-8.13
No. of Obs.	1503		1503	
J statistics (d.f.)	$0.106*10^{-5}$ (41)	p-value 1.00	$0.791*10^{-5}$ (43)	p-value 1.00

Note. The estimation results are gotten by using the estimation results of production function (8) as is shown in Table 2.

Also in the estimation of (15) and (16), we consider heteroscedasticity. Therefore the nonlinear instrumental variables estimation becomes virtually the same as (Generalized Method of Moments)GMM estimation.

Based on the estimated parameters shown in Table 3 and the used data of capital stock and labor input, K and L, the computed SS is positive and less than 1 in almost all of the data except for 2 of 1503 data when f(K,L) isestimated in the Cobb-Douglas functional form. It is also positive and less than 1 in all of the 1503 data when translog functional form is adopted. The average computed SS is $0.249*10^{-7}$ when f(K,L) is estimated in the Cobb-Douglas functional form, and $0.199*10^{-7}$ in translog functional form. Therefore, we find that the firsttype of moral hazard, that is moral hazard about the firm's choice of effort e, arose in almost every state-owned enterprise in 1989-95' Chinese textile industry. In other words, almost every state-owned enterprise's choice of effort was much lower than the first-best level in 1989-95' Chinese textile industry. Because SS is positive in almost all of cases as mentioned above and the estimated S_π is negative and significant as shown in Table 3, we find that the payoff function of the realized revenue (profit) to state-owned enterprises was concave and the firm's choice of risk r was lower than the firstbest level in 1989-95' Chinese textile industry. Namely we may say that the secondtype of moral hazard, which is about the firm's choice of risk r, arose and the state-owned enterprises were institutional risk averters in 1989-95' Chinese textile industry.

Finally, we mention that the second-order condition of maximization problem of the firm about K, L, e, and r is very likely to hold, based on the parameters shown in Table 2 and Table 3.

5   Concluding Remarks

This paper has shown that the contract relation between Chinese government and state-owned enterprises caused the inefficiency of the state-owned enterprises in 1989-95. Zou and Sun (1996)'s idea has been testified to be valid for explaining the cause of Chinese state-owned enterprises' inefficiency, although with some modification to their theoretical model and original idea.

Namely, two moral hazards about each firm's choices of private effort and risk were caused by the incentive structure of the contract. Almost all of firm's choice of private effort and risk were too little. In other words, the institution of contract made almost all of firm too lazy and too conservative in their behavior. It arose technical inefficiency.

Acknowledgement

We thank Hiroshi Ohnishi, Akira Kosaka, Yasukichi Yasuba, and Futoshi Yamauchi for helpful comments but views expressed and errors are strictly ours.

References

1. Goldfeld, S. and Quandt, R. E.: Budget Constraints, Bailout, and the Firm under Central Planning. Journal of Comparative Economics 12, 502-520(1988)
2. Goldfeld, S. and Quandt, R. E.: Effect of Bailouts, Taxes and Risk Aversion on the Enterprise. Journal of Comparative Economics 16, 150-167(1992)
3. Hansen, L. P.: Large Sample Properties of Generalized Method of Moments Estimators. Econometirca 50, 1029-1054(1982)
4. Hsiao, C., Nugent, J., Perrigne, I. and Qiu, J.: Share versus Residual Contracts: The Case of Chinese TVEs. Journal of Comparative Economics 26, 317-337(1998)
5. Prell,M.A.: The Two Kornai Effects. Journal of Comparative Economics 22, 267-276(1996).
6. Qian, Y.: A Theory of Shortage in Socialist Economies Based on the 'Soft Budget Constraint'. American Economic Review 84, 145-156(1994)
7. Zou, L. and Sun, L.: Interest Rate Policy and Incentive of State-Owned Enterprises in the Transitional China. Journal of Comparative Economics 23, 292-318(1996)

Evolution of Cooperation in a Situation with a Risk: a Closed Society versus an Open Society

Hideki Fujiyama

Dokkyo University, Saitama, Japan
E-mail: fujiyama@dokkyo.ac.jp

Abstract. This paper analyzes the formation of cooperation in the two-player "Prisoner's Dilemma Game" and "Trust Game." Cooperation is attained in the Long-Run Equilibrium (Kandori et al [1993]) if players form expectations about their payoffs simply based on their experiences and make a "cautious" experimentation. Using this model, the closed society (Japanese society) and the open society (the United States society) is characterized by the difference of the level of experimentation.

1 Introduction

How do individuals cooperate with each other in situations with a risk? What character induces the cooperation? In this paper, using the evolutionary model, we argue the formation of cooperation and the problems of trust that is discussed in both Japan and the United States.

The action including a risk in this paper shows that, if you take the action, the payoff depends on the other's action and so the payoff is not necessarily desirable. This kind of problem about cooperation has been argued up to now. First, we can give the study of the "Chain Store Game" (Kreps and Wilson [1982], Milgrom and Roberts [1982]). Dasgupta[1988] and Sato[1999] changed the payoff of the "Chain Store Game," and argue the formation of the trust. Second is the studies of the "Prisoner's Dilemma Game" (Fudenberg [1992] and Fudenberg and Tirole [1991, Chapter 5]).

There are some problems in the earlier works. First, in the "Chain Store Game," only the interaction between a Long-Run player and Short-Run players is dealt with. If we consider the interaction of individuals in ordinary life, we should rather focus on the interaction between Long-Run players. Secondly, in both studies, there is no discussion about how (and which) the equilibrium is realized, although there are many equilibria in general. Thirdly, there is a criticism about "Common Knowledge" assumed in both studies implicitly. This notion means not only the mutual knowledge among individuals but also that each individual knows that all other individuals know it, each individual knows that all other individuals know that all other individuals know it, and so on. This assumption is criticized when we consider ordinary social phenomena (Gambetta[1988] and Williams[1988]).

A purpose of this paper is to overcome these weak points considering an interaction between individual behaviors instead of a strategic interaction. We are not so strategic in daily life. In business life, of course, strategic actions or contracts may force a person into being trustworthy. This strategic force, however, affects one's activity or motivation negatively in daily life (Hatano and Inagaki [1981]).

2   The Model

2.1   Player, Strategy and Payoff

We consider a situation where two players are repeatedly matched to play the 2×2 strategic game in Fig. 1.a. (or .b) and adjust their strategy over time.[1] The payoffs in Fig. 1. are described by concrete numbers for convenience.[2] In Fig. 1.a., strategy C represents cooperation with the other player. strategy D represents non-cooperation with the other player. In this game, strategy C for Player 1 includes a risk, because, if Player 2 also chooses strategy C, he gets the most desirable payoff, that is 4, but otherwise, he gets the worst payoff, that is 0. If we express this strategic game as the extensive game, it is the same as the "Trust Game" defined in Sato[1999] and Dasgupta[1989] without the fact of timing. That is, strategy C for Player 1 can be interpreted as the "placing of trust" and strategy C for Player 2 as "living up to this trust." [3] We also will call this game the "Trust Game" hereafter. The game in Fig. 1.b. is the "Prisoner's Dilemma Game." In this game, both of players have a risk concerning his strategy.

2.2   Formation of Expected Payoff

Each player's expected payoff about each strategy is formulated as follows: Each player remembers n times payoffs about each strategy. That is, each

---

[1] Whether the repetition is finite or infinite does not matter in our model because each individual's memory is finite. See next subsection.

[2] The essential relationships between payoffs are as follows: A set of payoffs for two players are (a, b), (c, d), (e, f) and (g, h), if a set of strategies for two players are (C,C), (C,D), (D,C) and (D,D) respectively. The first factor in the parentheses is for Player 1's payoff or strategy and the second factor is for Player 2's. As for Fig. 1.a., the essential relationships are $e = g$, $a > g > c$ and $a - g > g - c$ for Player 1's payoff and $f = h$ and $d > b > h$ for Player 2's payoff. As for Fig. 1.b., the essential relationships are $e > a > g > c$ and $a - g > g - c$ for player 1's payoff and $d > b > h > f$ and $b - h > h - f$ for player 2's payoff.

[3] There are three streams in the study of trust: functional analysis, psychological analysis, and rational analysis (Sato[1999]). The position of this paper is in between psychological analysis and rational analysis because players in this paper are not completely rational and are assumed to have some behavioral patterns, which psychological analysis must deal with. But the players behave rationally under the constraints of behavior patterns.

Player 2

	C	D
Player 1 C	(4, 4)	(0, 5)
D	(1, 1)	(1, 1)

a

Player 2

	C	D
Player 1 C	(7, 7)	(0, 8)
D	(8, 0)	(1, 1)

b

Fig. 1. Payoff Matrix of **(a)** the "Trust Game," **(b)** the "Prisoner's Dilemma Game"

player has n memories for each strategy. The payoffs in the memory are values which is realized when the player chose the strategy in the past. Each player averages these memorized payoffs concerning each strategy and the player considers this average payoff as his expected payoff relatively. Each player chooses strategy that has higher expected payoff. If both strategies have the same expected payoff, then the player chooses one of these strategies with equal probability.[4]

2.3   Cautious Experimentation

With a small probability, p, each player chooses a strategy that is not optimal. We call this action an experimentation. This probability, p, is determined by the difference between expected payoffs about each strategy.[5] That is, although we describe this probability as ε ordinarily, our probability of experimentation is described as $p = \varepsilon^{\alpha(\cdot)}$ where $\alpha(\cdot)$ is the increase function of the difference between expected payoffs.[6] This assumption means that the more preferable the strategy that the player chooses now, the less probability he experiments with it. In other words, this assumption represents a behavior in which each player experiments cautiously.

3   Formation of Cooperation

We have the following results under the model presented in the previous section.

---

[4] If a dominant strategy exists (in Fig. 1.a., strategy C for Player 2 is the dominant strategy) and expected payoffs are equal, it might be reasonable to assume that the player chooses the dominant strategy with probability 1. Under this assumption, we can derive the same results of the next section in the same way.

[5] Even if we assume that experimentation is determined by the ratio of expected payoffs about each strategy, we can have the same result in the next section.

[6] Bergin and Lipman [1996] treat a general argument of state-dependent mutations. An aim of this paper is not to consider such a general argument, but to present a concrete model and to derive a cooperate equilibrium from the model.

Proposition 1:   In the repeated "Trust Game," when the probability of experimentation, p, becomes small enough according to the difference between expected payoffs, both of players choose strategy C in the Long-Run Equilibrium.[7]

Proof [8]   This proof is organized as follows: In Step 1, we seek limit states without experimentations. Next, we try to find a minimum cost tree in the limit states. To do this, in Step 2, we examin the limit states in detail. In Step 3, we construct an equilibrium in which the difference between expected payoffs is larger than any other equilibrium. In Step 4, we prove that the cost tree of this equilibrium has the smallest cost.

Step 1: In this step, we prove that limit states without experimentations are [C, C] or [C, CD] where the first (second) factor of this [. , .] denotes the strategy Player 1 (2) takes and "CD" denotes the situation in which a player takes either strategy C or strategy D with equal probability. In principle, we consider all possible cases one by one.

We consider the case that [D, C] continues. That is, Player 1's optimal strategy is strategy D and Player 2's optimal strategy is strategy C. In this case, the expected payoffs for Player 1 are not affected by the choice (or change) of strategy by Player 2. So Player 1 continues to use strategy D. Therefore, the expected payoff of strategy D for Player 2 is 1. On the other hand, the expected payoff of strategy D for Player 2 is equal to or larger than 1 by the structure of the payoff matrix in Fig 1.a. If the expected payoff of strategy C for Player 2 is equal to 1, the state of [C, D] shifts to the state of [D, CD] immediately. If the expected payoff of strategy C for Player 2 is larger than 1, Player 2 switches his strategy to D. After this switch, if n periods are passed, the expected payoff of strategy D also becomes 1. In the end, both of the expected payoffs for Player 2 become equal. That is, the state of [D, CD]

---

[7] The definition of Long-Run Equilibrium is as follows. Let P^ε be an aperiodic irreducible Markov chain derived from the experimentation, ε. We express a stationary distribution as μ^ε. That is, it is satisfied that $\mu^\varepsilon P^\varepsilon = \mu^\varepsilon$. To the end, we consider the concept of the limit distribution: $\mu^* = \lim_{\varepsilon \to 0} \mu^\varepsilon$. If the limit distribution places positive probability on a state, for example "h", this "h" is called a Long-Run equilibrium. See also Kandori et al [1993] and Young [1993].

[8] Since states in this game are determined by strategies that players choose and finite histories that players have, the number of states is also finite. Both optimal strategy and experimentation for the players depends only on his history. So, the transition of state in this game is a Markov chain. Since experimentation exists, any state can be reached after n periods with positive probability. So, this Markov chain satisfies irreducibility and aperiodicity. Since the probability of experimentation is described as $p = \varepsilon^\alpha$, we employ a cost adjusted by α here. Given these conditions, we can apply the same argument in Young [1993] and Vega-Redondo [1993, Chapter 5 and Chapter 6] to our model. In the proof, we use the concrete number in Fig. 1.a. for simplicity of argument. Of course, this proof applies to any payoff satisfying the conditions presented in the previous section.

is realized. As there is no factor to change any expected payoff in [D, CD], the state of [D, CD] continues forever without experiments.

In any other case, we can also prove that any such state shifts to [C, C] or [D, CD] by the same but tedious argument as the one above. Therefore, we omit other cases here.

Step 2: In this step, we examine the limit states as an equilibrium in detail.

In the equilibrium of [D, CD], the expected payoff of strategy C for Player 1 is different from that of strategy D for Player 1. This difference depends on his history. Taking account of the facts that the expected payoff of strategy D for Player 1 is always 1 and that the optimal strategy for Player 1 is strategy D in this case, the expected payoff of strategy C is higher than 0 and strictly lower than 1. On the other hand, for Player 2, the expected payoff of strategy C is equal to that of strategy D. Consequently, for both players, the experimentation is determined by the payoff difference that is above 0 and below 1 in this equilibrium.

In the equilibrium of [C, C], for Player 1, the expected payoff of strategy C is 4 and that of strategy D is 1. For Player 2, the expected payoff of strategy C is 4 and that of strategy D is above 0 and strictly below 4, which depends on his history. Consequently, for Player 1, the experimentation is determined by the payoff difference of 3 and, for Player 2, the experimentation is determined by the payoff difference that is strictly above 0 and below 3.

Step 3: In this step, we construct an equilibrium in which the difference between expected payoffs is the largest.

We consider the path through which the equilibrium of [D, CD] shifts to the equilibrium of [C, C]. Suppose that Player 1 makes an experimentation and Player 2 uses strategy C in the equilibrium [D, CD]. This occurrence makes strategy C optimal for Player 2. Suppose that sequentially Player 1 makes experimentations until strategy C becomes optimal for Player 1. As the expected payoff is determined by the history that includes n times past occurrence, finite consequent experimentations make strategy C optimal for Player 1. After these consequent experimentations, the equilibrium of [C, C] is realized. In this equilibrium of [C, C], for each player, the expected payoff of strategy C is 4 and that of strategy D is 1. We call this equilibrium Equilibrium A.

By the argument of Step 2, in Equilibrium A, the difference of the expected payoffs is maximal for each player. The rate of experimentation depends on the difference of the expected payoffs. That is, the more difference of the expected payoffs there are, the less probability he experiments with it. Under this assumption, the cost of a path from Equilibrium A to another state is strictly larger than that of any other path.

Step 4: In this step, we prove that the top of the minimum cost tree is Equilibrium A.

Consider the following cost tree: The root of this cost tree is an equilibrium which is other than Equilibrium A and suppose that this cost tree has minimum cost. Here, consider the following operations. First, cut the path from Equilibrium A to the state that is closer to the root than Equilibrium A. Second, make a new path linking the root of the original cost tree to Equilibrium A. These operations make a new cost tree of which the root is Equilibrium A. By Step 3, the paths from Equilibrium A to any other state have the largest cost in all paths. Therefore the decreasing cost by cutting the path is larger than the increasing cost by adding the path. That is, the cost of the new tree is less than that of the original one. This is a contradiction. Consequently, both players take strategy C in the Long-Run Equilibrium.

The same proposition is derived in the case of the "Prisoner's Dilemma Game," of which the payoff matrix is denoted in Fig 1.b. The proof in the "Prisoner's Dilemma Game" is so similar to the argument above, we omit it and give the result only.

Proposition 2:   In the repeated "Prisoner's Dilemma Game," when the probability of experimentation, p, becomes small enough according to the difference between expected payoffs, both of players choose strategy C in the Long-Run Equilibrium.

In the remainder of this section, we use a computer simulation in order to understand the Long-Run Equilibrium more concretely. the payoff matrix in Fig. 1.a. (or b.) is used in the computer simulation. Each player has five memories for each strategy. The probability of experimentation is described as $p = \varepsilon^{-x}/6$ where x is the difference between expected payoffs. A repetition of the game is 2,000.[9] A simulation result of the "Trust Game" (the "Prisoner's Dilemma Game") is showed in Fig. 2.a. (Fig. 2.b.). The vertical axis indicates the situation of the game, where "4" represents that both players use strategy C, "3" represents that Player 1 uses strategy D and Player 2 uses strategy C, "2" represents that Player 1 uses strategy C and Player 2 uses strategy D, and, "1" represents that both players use strategy D. The horizontal axis indicates the number of repetitions. The initial history at the beginning of the game is assumed that payoff 0 was realized in all prior tries and past all strategies. That is, there is no information about each strategy initially. In both Fig. 2.a. and b., we can points out that even though there is a transition of the equilibria, the most frequent equilibrium is the Long-Run Equilibrium in which both players use strategy C. In the "Trust Game" (the "Prisoner's Dilemma Game"), Pareto-efficient payoff (4, 4) ((7, 7)) is realized in the Long-Run Equilibrium.

---

[9] This simulation is made on Mathematica.

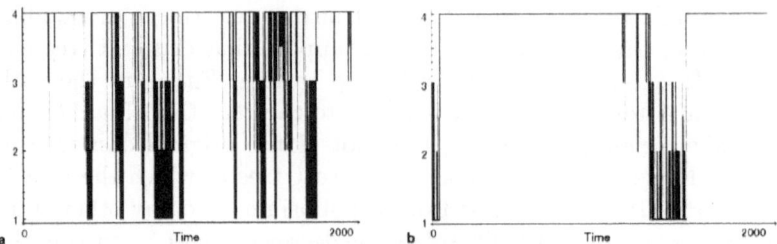

Fig. 2. Result of the simulation **(a)** in the "Trust Game," **(b)** in the "Prisoner's Dilemma Game"

4   Application to the social problems about cooperation in Japanese society and United States society

In the definition of the Long-Run Equilibrium, the rate of experimentation converges on zero. The transition of equilibria is not discussed. This transition of equilibria, however, is also important in real life. Taking account of this point, in this section, we consider a problem about cooperation in two societies that have a different culture from each other.

First, consider the two societies. One is a closed society and the other is an open society. We describe this difference of the cultures as a difference in the rate of experimentation. In the closed society, an opportunistic behavior is avoided and members in the closed society act in the same way. Therefore, different actions from ordinary ones are restricted. On the other hand, in the open society, the different actions from ordinary ones are accepted as an action to take a chance. We consider Japanese society as a representation of the closed society and Unites States society as a representation of the open society. This assumption is supported by Yamagishi[1998] in which it is shown that the "Trust" in unknown others is higher in the United States than in Japan and that an outside chance is made use of more frequently in the United States.[10]

The same social problem of cooperation is discussed in both countries. On the one hand, corruption of the Japanese system is discussed. It is said that, in the past, it was relatively easy to form social cooperation which was advantageous for Japanese society. However, today, forming a social cooperation is becoming more and more difficult with the collapse of the Japanese system (Arai [1997]). On the other hand, it is said that the level of social trust

---

[10] The "Trust" in our model is different from the "Trust" in Yamagishi [1998]. The "Trust" in Yamagishi [1998] corresponds to the "rate of experimentation" in our model. The "Trust" or "Cooperation" in our model corresponds to the "commitment" in Yamagishi [1998]. Yamagishi [1998] also emphasizes the social intellect by which one can perceive the other's credibility. In our model, we ignore this element and focus on the possibility of taking a risky action with no information.

is decreasing in the United States and that this causes social inefficiency (Fukuyama [1995]).[11]

Using our model, we will interpret these two social phenomena. Based on the simulation of the "Trust Game" in Fig. 2.a., we only change the rate of experimentation. In Fig. 3.a., the rate of experimentation is lower than the based simulation model: $p = \varepsilon^{-x}/32$ where x is the difference between expected payoffs. In Figure 3.b., the rate of experimentation is higher than the based simulation model: $p = \varepsilon^{-x}/2$. With the low rate of experimentation ("Japanese society"), a transition to the other equilibrium does not occur frequently. On the other hand, with the high rate of experimentation ("United States society"), a transition to the other equilibrium occurs frequently.

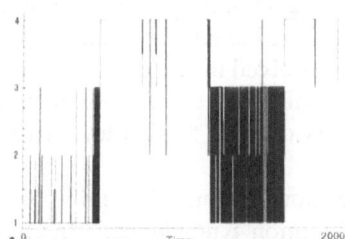 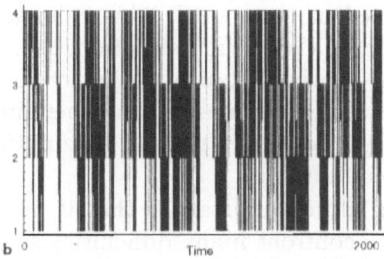

Fig. 3. Result of the simulation in the "Trust Game " **(a)**with a low rate of experimentation (Japanese type society), **(b)**with a high rate of experimentation the United States type society)

We can interpret the difficulty of cooperation in Japan as follows: in Fig. 3.a., a transition to the other equilibrium does not occur frequently. This means that it is difficult to discover another equilibrium, which possibly might be a desirable one. That is, even if another equilibrium is a desirable one, it is difficult to discover that equilibrium. This difficulty is a disadvantage to the present society that changes rapidly. On the contrary, of course, this difficulty has an advantage if a desirable equilibrium has already been realized and the society is rigid. This difficulty induces the stability of the desirable equilibrium. Therefore it is possible to say that the same behavior pattern which was desirable before is getting to be undesirable now.

We can interpret the difficulty of cooperation in the United States as follows: experimentation itself is desirable in the sense that it enables the discovery of the more desirable equilibrium. The high rate of experimentation causes the instability of equilibrium as in Fig. 3.b. Therefore, this instability brings losses to the society. That is, this demerit of instability overcomes the merit of the discovery of other possibly desirable equilibrium. This expresses the situation in the United States as a low-trust society in Fukuyama [1995].

---

[11] The "Trust" in Fukuyama [1995] corresponds to the "Trust" in our model and the "commitment" in Yamagishi [1998]. See also a previous footnote.

5 Concluding Remarks

We summarize some features of this model. First, the "Cooperation Equilibrium" is discovered by the experimentations of players. This discovery does not depend on the initial situation. In addition, the transition of the equilibria is also described in the simulation model. Secondly, the realized payoff in the Long-Run Equilibrium is unique and the Pareto-efficient. The main implication is summarized as follows: under a certain environment, it is not so important to know (or infer) the opponent's strategy for the formation of cooperation. It is important to behave cautiously based on one's experience (or realized payoffs).

We make some comments on the validity of the behavior pattern that is assumed in our model. This behavior pattern is so simple that it is not restricted in a particular situation. In addition, this simplicity does not imply that players who follow this behavior pattern are deceived in the game forever. Furthermore, experimentation depending on the difference between expected payoffs is a relatively natural assumption, as it is used in the notion of the proper equilibrium.[12]

Even more important is that if we consider more rational behavior patterns, we confront many difficulties such as "Common Knowledge," "multiplicity of equilibrium" and so on. If we consider the private information, the "Cooperation Equilibrium" is not attained under a rational behavior model (Matsushima [1994]). Therefore, it is also important to considere how simple behavior patterns lead the "Cooperation Equilibrium."

Finally, using our model, we can express the problems of cooperation, which is discussed both in Japan and the United States, in the same dimension. A suggestion derived from our model analysis is that, in Japanese society, it is needed to accelerate experimentations using certain social institutions, on the other hand, in the United States society, it is needed to restrain experimentations.

References

1. Arai, Kazuhiro, *Shushin Koyousei to Nihon Bunnka: Game Rironteki Approach*, Chuko Shinsyo, 1997. (In Japanese)
2. Bergin, James and Barton L. Lipman, "Evolution with State-Dependent Mutation," *Econometrica* 64, 1996, pp.943-956.
3. Dasgupta, Partha, "Trust as a Commodity," in *Trust: Making and Breaking Cooperative Relations*, ed. by Diego Gambetta. New York: Basil Blackwell, 1988, pp.49-72.

---

[12] Of course, as there are many facts derived from experimental economics and psychology, it is necessary that we learn these facts and refine our model in the future.

4. Fudengerg, Drew, "Explaining cooporation and commitment in repeated games," *Advances in Economic Theory*, Vol. I., ed. by Laffont, J,-J., Cambridge: Cambridge University Press, 1992.
5. Fudenberg, Drew. and Jean Tirole, 1991, *Game Theory* MIT Press.
6. Fukuyama, Francis, *Trust: The social virtues and the creation of presperity*, New York, Free Press, 1995.
7. Gambetta, Diego, "Can We Trust Trust," in *Trust: Making and Breaking Cooperative Relations*, ed. by Diego Gambetta, New York: Basil Blackwell, 1988, pp.213-237.
8. Hatano Gyoo and Kayko Inagaki, *Mukiryokuno Shinrigaku*, Chuko Shinsyo, 1981. (In Japanese)
9. Kandori, Michihiro, Mailath, George, and Rob, Rafael, "Learning, Mutation, and Long Run Equilibria in Games," *Econometrica* 61, 1993 , pp.29-56.
10. Kreps, David M. and Robert Wilson, "Reputation and Imperfect Informatioon," *Journal of Economic Theory* 27, 1982, pp.253-279.
11. Matsushima Hitoshi, "Kako, Genzai, Mirai: Kurikaeshi Game to Keizaigaku," in *Gendai no Keizai Riron*, ed. by Iwai Katsuhito and Itoh Motoshige, Tokyo University Press, 1994. (In Japanese)
12. Milgrom, Paul and John Roberts, "Predation, Reputation, and Entry Deterrence," *Journal of Economic Theory* 27, 1982, pp.280-312.
13. Sato Yoshimichi, "Trust and Communication," *Riron to Houhou* (In Japanese) 24(2), 1999, pp.155-168.
14. Vega-Redond, Fernando, *Evolution, Games, and Economic Behavior*, Oxford, Oxford University Press, 1996.
15. Williams, Bernard, "Formal Structure and Social Reality," in *Trust: Making and Breaking Cooperative Relations*, ed. by Diego Gambetta, New York: Basil Blackwell, 1988, pp.3-13.
16. Yamagishi Toshio, *Shinrai no Kouzou: Kokoro to Syakai no Shinka Game*, Tokyo University Press, 1998. (In Japanese)
17. Young, H. Payton, "The Evolution of Conventions," *Econometrica* 61, 1993 , pp.57-84.

Effect on Spectral Properties by the Splitting Correction Preconditioning for Linear Systems that Arise from Periodic Boundary Problems

Shoji Itoh[1], Yoshio Oyanagi[2], Shao-Liang Zhang[3] and Makoto Natori[4]

[1] Science Information Processing Center, Inst. of Info. Sci. and Elec., University of Tsukuba, Tsukuba, Ibaraki, Japan
[2] Department of Computer Science, University of Tokyo, Bunkyo, Tokyo, Japan
[3] Department of Applied Physics, University of Tokyo, Bunkyo, Tokyo, Japan
[4] Institute of Information Sciences and Electronics, University of Tsukuba, Tsukuba, Ibaraki, Japan
E-mail: itosho@nalab.is.tsukuba.ac.jp

Abstract. In this paper, the spectral properties of the preconditioned systems by the "Splitting Correction (SC)", proposed by the present authors, are studied and it is conjectured that the degeneracy not the clustering of the eiganvalues plays an important role in the convergence. The SC preconditioner is one of new preconditioners based on block factorization for solving linear systems that arise from periodic boundary problems. From the viewpoint of the convergence of residual norm, the behaviors of the residual norm of the conjugate gradient (CG) method preconditioned by the SC and the block incomplete Cholesky (block IC) are very peculiar. Generally, the convergence of the CG method depends on spectral properties, such as the clustering and the degeneracy of the eigenvalues, of the coefficient matrix. Some numerical results suggest that the fast convergence of the SC is due not to the clustering but to the degeneracy of the eigenvalues of the preconditioned coefficient matrix.

1 Introduction

The discretization of partial differential equations (briefly PDEs) by finite difference method leads to large and sparse linear systems

$$Ax = b. \tag{1}$$

Especially, under the periodic boundary conditions, the coefficient matrix A has periodic boundary matrix elements (in this research, we call so, briefly PBEs). The PBEs means the matrix elements corresponding to the periodic boundary conditions under discreted system. To solve these systems, various preconditioned iterative methods are applied to. For example, the preconditioned conjugate gradient (PCG) method [8][11] is used for symmetric positive definite systems. Here, preconditioners should be chosen to attain fast convergence. The "preconditioning" means the transformation of a linear system to an equivalent system which is easier to solve than the given one

[3][6]. When deciding on which preconditioner K to use, several issues must be considered, of which the most important are (i) resemblance between K^{-1} and A^{-1}, (ii) cost of construction K and (iii) cost of computing $r' = K^{-1}r$ [3]. Here, the decided preconditioner $K = K_L K_R$ is applied to (1), such that the preconditioned system

$$(K_L^{-1} A K_R^{-1})(K_R x) = (K_L^{-1} b) \tag{2}$$

is converged faster than the given system (1).

In this research, "Splitting Correction (SC)" preconditioner for linear systems that arise from PDEs with periodic boundary conditions was proposed [9]. This preconditioner is based on block preconditioning [1][4]. The convergence of the iterative methods with this preconditioner is improved much more than the block incomplete factorization. Nevertheless, its calculating cost increases only a little for the incomplete one.

About the numerical results in [9], the converging behavior is distinctive between the SC and the block incomplete factorization..

The convergence rate of the CG method depends on spectral properties of the given matrix, such as the eigenvalue distribution and the condition number, and on the given right-hand side [3][4][11][12]. In this paper, the spectral properties by using the SC and block incomplete Cholesky factorization are evaluated.

In section 2, physical model, the linear system and typical solver for this system is presented.

In section 3, the overview of the SC preconditioner is explained, and the effect of the SC and the convergence behavior of the PCG are presented.

In section 4, the evaluation by the clustering of the eigenvalues of preconditioned coefficient matrices is shown, in section 5, the evaluation by the condition number of preconditioned coefficient matrices is shown, and in section 6, the evaluation by the clustering of the eigenvalues of preconditioned coefficient matrices is shown. These numerical results suggest that the fast convergence of the SC is due not to the clustering but to the degeneracy of the eigenvalues of the preconditioned coefficient matrix.

2   Model Problem and Numerical Solution

In this research, the poisson equation (3) in two-dimensional unit square domain $\Omega = [0, 1] \times [0, 1]$

$$-\Delta u = f, \quad (x, y) \in [0, 1] \times (0, 1), \tag{3}$$

$$u(0, y) = u(1, y), \quad \text{(periodic boundary conditions)}, \tag{4}$$

$$u(x, 0) = g_0, \quad \text{(Dirichlet conditions)}, \tag{5}$$

$$u(x, 1) = g_1, \quad \text{(Dirichlet conditions)} \tag{6}$$

is discussed.

2.1   Coefficient Matrix

Eq.(3) is discreted by 5-points central differences, with stepsize $h = 1/(n+1)$ in each direction. Then, the coefficient matrix A is a sparse symmetric positive define matrix of size $n(n+1) \times n(n+1)$ with PBEs, because the grid size of x-direction is $n+1$ and y-direction is n.

$$
A = \begin{bmatrix}
P_1 & B_1 & & & & \mathbf{0} \\
B_1 & P_2 & B_2 & & & \\
& \ddots & \ddots & \ddots & & \\
& & B_{n-2} & P_{n-1} & B_{n-1} \\
\mathbf{0} & & & B_{n-1} & P_n
\end{bmatrix}, \tag{7}
$$

where P_l, B_l $(l = 1, 2, \cdots, n)$ are block matrices whose size is $(n+1) \times (n+1)$. B_l is diagonal matrix. The block diagonal matrix is

$$
P_l = \begin{bmatrix}
d_1^{(l)} & b_1^{(l)} & & & \mathbf{0} & p_1^{(l)} \\
b_1^{(l)} & d_2^{(l)} & b_2^{(l)} & & & \\
& \ddots & \ddots & \ddots & & \\
& & b_{m-2}^{(l)} & d_{m-1}^{(l)} & b_{m-1}^{(l)} \\
p_1^{(l)} & \mathbf{0} & & b_{m-1}^{(l)} & d_m^{(l)}
\end{bmatrix}, \tag{8}
$$

which is tridiagonal matrix with PBEs. Here, $p_1^{(l)}$ is PBEs of the l-th block, and $m = n + 1$.

2.2   Iterative Methods

To this system, the iterative methods with preconditioning are often used. When the coefficient matrix is symmetric positive definite, usually the PCG method is adapted [8][11]. In this algorithm, the preconditioning operation is calculated as solving the system, $r' = K^{-1}r$ in each iteration step.

   This preconditioned system (2) is solved repeatedly (with appropriately chosen right-hand side vectors b) in such a way that the solution to the original system can be obtained in the limit.

   The details of the preconditioner are explained in the next section.

3   Block Preconditioning for the Linear Systems with PBEs

The block preconditioner K is defined as follows:

$$
K = \begin{bmatrix}
K_1 & & & & \mathbf{0} \\
& K_2 & & & \\
& & \ddots & & \\
& & & K_{n-1} & \\
\mathbf{0} & & & & K_n
\end{bmatrix}, \tag{9}
$$

where K_l's are block matrices with size $(n + 1) \times (n + 1)$.

3.1   Block incomplete Cholesky Preconditioner

By block preconditioning for (7), K_l is assigned for diagonal block (8) [4]. Usually K_l is generated with block incomplete Cholesky (block IC) factorization, in order to decrease its calculating costs [5]. In other words, the incomplete factorization without *fill-in* is done. Fill-in is the behavior that the zero elements of original matrix change into non-zero by an exact factorization. That is to say,

$$K_l^{-1} \approx P_l^{-1}. \tag{10}$$

3.2   Splitting Correction Preconditioner

On the other hand, from a convergence point of view, it is expected that

$$K_l^{-1} = P_l^{-1} \tag{11}$$

brings better convergence than using (10) [4]. Namely this is algebraically equivalent to the complete factorization to diagonal blocks. However, this arithmetic operation costs more flops. A new preconditioner SC was proposed [9]. This preconditioner satisfies eq.(11), but the cost of this new preconditioner adds only a little to one of the incomplete factorizations. In this section, the SC is discussed in detail.

First, PBEs are split from the original K_l. Here, the first and the last elements of the diagonal are corrected. Then

$$K_l = \begin{bmatrix} d_1^{(l)} - p_1^{(l)} & b_1^{(l)} & & & \\ b_1^{(l)} & d_2^{(l)} & b_2^{(l)} & & \LARGE 0 \\ & \ddots & \ddots & \ddots & \\ & & b_{m-2}^{(l)} & d_{m-1}^{(l)} & b_{m-1}^{(l)} \\ \LARGE 0 & & & b_{m-1}^{(l)} & d_m^{(l)} - p_1^{(l)} \end{bmatrix} + \begin{bmatrix} p_1^{(l)} & 0 \dots 0 & p_1^{(l)} \\ 0 & 0 \dots 0 & 0 \\ \vdots & \vdots \quad \vdots & \vdots \\ 0 & 0 \dots 0 & 0 \\ p_1^{(l)} & 0 \dots 0 & p_1^{(l)} \end{bmatrix}$$

$$= T_l + \left[p_1^{(l)} \, 0 \cdots 0 \, p_1^{(l)} \right]^T \left[1 \, 0 \cdots 0 \, 1 \right] = T_l + u_l v_l^T. \tag{12}$$

Consequently, K_l is split into two matrices, the tridiagonal matrix and the rank-1 matrix made up with PBEs. The latter is represented as the correcting term by outer product of two vectors.

By using eq.(12), the residual vector r_l updated by preconditioning is represented as r_l'. That is

$$r_l' = K_l^{-1} r_l = (T_l + u_l v_l^T)^{-1} r_l. \tag{13}$$

In order to solve eq.(13), the Sherman-Morrison formula [7]

$$(T + uv^T)^{-1} = T^{-1} - T^{-1} u (1 + v^T T^{-1} u)^{-1} v^T T^{-1}, \tag{14}$$

$$T \in R^{m \times m}, \quad u, v \in R^m$$

is applied to. Then, eq.(13) is changed into another equations with fewer arithmetic operation.

3.3   Numerical Experiment

In numerical examination, some linear systems based on physical problem (3) was examined and the analytic solution was $u(x, y) = \sin(2\pi(x + y))$ in all cases.

Experiments were carried out in double precision and executed on IBM RS/6000 SP 1PE RISC processor. Compiler is xlf based on Fortran77. The iterations were started with $x_0 = 0$, and stopped when $\|r_k\|_2/\|r_0\|_2 \leq 10^{-12}$. Since this coefficient matrix (7) was symmetric, the CG method[8] could be

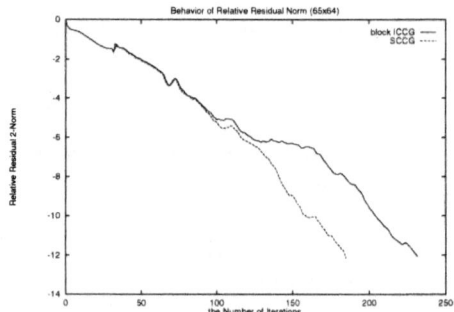

Fig. 1. Behavior of Convergence between block ICCG and SCCG (65 × 64).

adapted as solver and the effect of block preconditioning by the conventional block IC (briefly block ICCG) and the SC (SCCG) was compared.

3.4   Discussion

Fig.1 shows the behavior of the *log* scaled relative residual 2-norm of the grid size 65 × 64.

This behavior of the residual norms is almost the same about half way through the convergence, but from there, they are branching off. In other sizes, the character of the converging behavior is almost the same as Fig.1, too [9]. Furthermore, this converging tendency for nonsymmetric cases is the same as the tendency for the symmetric cases[9].

Through all results, this phenomenon is very interesting. It is known that the converging speed of the CG method depends on spectral properties of the given matrix, such as the eigenvalue distribution and the condition number, and on the given right-hand side [3][4][11][12]. Here, the given matrix means preconditioned coefficient matrix.

In this paper, the spectral properties of preconditioned matrices by the SC and the block IC are evaluated. The details are explained in the sections that follow.

4   Evaluation by the Eigenvalue Distribution

To the symmetric system, the converging property of the CG is related to the eigenvalue distribution of the coefficient matrix [10].

4.1   Convergence of the CG method and the Eigenvalues

The residual vector r_k and the search direction vector p_k at the k-th iteration is as follows:

$$r_{k+1} = r_k - \alpha_k A p_k, \tag{15}$$

$$p_{k+1} = r_{k+1} + \beta_k p_k. \tag{16}$$

Here, $r_0 = b - A x_0$, $p_0 = r_0$ and x_0 is an arbitrary initial approximation to x. From eq.(15) and (16),

$$r_k = r_0 + \sum_{l=1}^{k} a_l^{(k)} A^l r_0 \equiv R_k(A) r_0. \tag{17}$$

$R_k(A)$ is residual polinomial which is the k-th degree polinomial by A.

For the coeffcient matrix $A \in R^{N \times N}$, λ_i's are the eigenvalues and v_i's are the eigenvectors. Here, let

$$r_0 = \sum_{i=1}^{N} c_i v_i. \tag{18}$$

Namely, r_0 is expanded by v_i [12]. This equation is applied to eq.(17), such that,

$$r_k = R_k(A) r_0 = \sum_{i=1}^{N} c_i R_k(\lambda_i) v_i. \tag{19}$$

If $\lambda_p, \lambda_{p+1}, ..., \lambda_{p+q}$ are degenerate, there is a relation

$$R_k(\lambda_p) = R_k(\lambda_{p+1}) = ... = R_k(\lambda_{p+q}). \tag{20}$$

Further, from eq.(19), the constituent ratio on $v_p, v_{p+1}, ..., v_{p+q}$ included in r_k, $c_p R_k(\lambda_p) : c_{p+1} R_k(\lambda_{p+1}) : ... : c_{p+q} R_k(\lambda_{p+q})$, is equivalent to the constituent ratio of $c_p : c_{p+1} : ... : c_{p+q}$ included in r_0 (eq.(18)). Therefore, the dimension of subspace of r_k is $N-q$. After all, the residual norm converges at most the $N-q$ times. If the eigenvalues are not completely degenerate, the clustering of the eigenvalues may give fast convergence [10][12], because this is approximately equivalent to the fact mentioned above.

4.2   Numerical Result

The clustering of the eigenvalues was evaluated. To the coefficient matrix (8), the eigenvalues were calculated by three ways, (*i*) with no preconditioning (ASIS), (*ii*) with preconditioning by the block incomplete Cholesky factorization (block IC) and (*iii*) with preconditioning by the block complete Cholesky factorization (block CC). Here, the SC preconditioning is algebraically equivalent to the block complete Cholesky factorization and these converging behavior are equivalent.

Two cases with grid sizes 17×16 (Left of Fig. 2) and 33×32 (Right of Fig. 2) were calculated. The abscissa indicates the rank of the eigenvalues in the increasing order, and the ordinate indicates the log_{10} scaled eigenvalue.

From these figures, the distribution of the eigenvalues is noticeable different between ASIS case and the block IC, the block CC(SC) cases, further the clustering of the eigenvalues are certified to the both preconditioned matrices. However, the distribution of the eigenvalues between the block IC and the block CC(SC) is almost the same. From the fact mentioned above, it

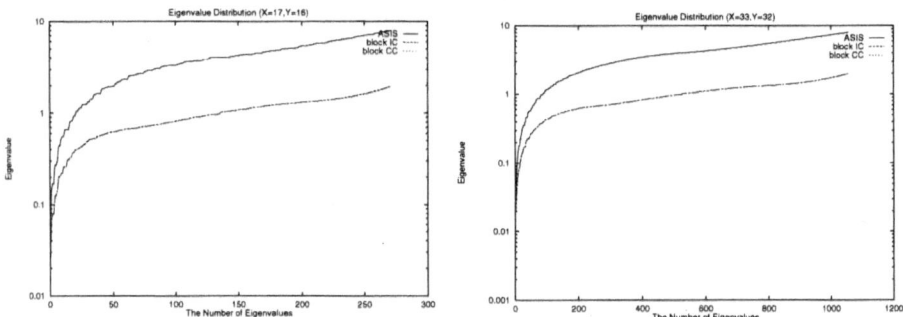

Fig. 2. Eigenvalue Distribution (17×16 : Left, 33×32 : Right).

is difficult to say that the effect of both preconditioning is depend on the clustering of the eigenvalues.

5   Evaluation by the Condition Number

The number of iterations to reach a relative reduction in the error is proportional to the condition number[2].

5.1   Convergence of the CG method and the Condition Number

The coefficient matrix $A \in \boldsymbol{R}^{N \times N}$ is symmetric positive define and $\boldsymbol{b} \in \boldsymbol{R}^{N}$. If the CG method produces iterates $\boldsymbol{x}_k$ at the k-th iteration, then

$$\|\boldsymbol{x} - \boldsymbol{x}_k\|_A \leq 2\|\boldsymbol{x} - \boldsymbol{x}_0\|_A \left(\frac{\sqrt{\kappa} - 1}{\sqrt{\kappa} + 1}\right)^k \tag{21}$$

where κ is the "condition number" of A, $\kappa = \kappa_2(A) = |\lambda_{max}|/|\lambda_{min}|$, and $x = A^{-1}b$ [7][10][11].

5.2   Numerical Result

In the same way of the section 4, the condition number of each case, ASIS, block IC and block CC(SC), were calculated. The result is Table 1. The condition number of the matrix preconditioned by the block CC(SC) is almost equal to that by the block IC. From the results of section 4 and Table 1, the

Table 1. The Condition Number of Each Size.

grid size	ASIS	block IC	block CC(SC)
17×16	232.92	117.40	116.46
33×32	881.39	443.14	440.70

effect of the preconditioning between the block IC and the block CC is almost the same. It can be considered that these results show the reason why the behavior of the residual norms is almost the same about half way through the convergence in Fig. 1.

6   Degeneracy of the Eigenvalues

In this section, it is discussed why the residual norms are branching off from the half way through the convergence in Fig. 1. It was observed in the previous section that the outlines of the eigenvalue distributions are almost the same for the two preconditionings. However, to the detailed structures of the spectra, it was found that most eigenvalues for the block CC preconditioning are doubly degenerate.

Figs. 3 - 6 show the degeneracy of the eigenvalues for two different grid sizes, 17×16 (Figs. 3 , 4) and 33×32 (Figs. 5 , 6). The critria of the degeneracy is the agreement of the eigenvalues to 10 digits to the right of the decimal place. Figs. 3 and 5 show the eigenvalue distributions of the matrix preconditioned by the block IC, while Figs. 4 and 6 show those by the block CC. The abscissa indicates the eigenvalue, and the ordinate indicates the degrees of the degeneracy. About the ordinate, easy to see, the unique eigenvalues are shown as the bars at "1", the degenerate eigenvalues are shown at "2". Here, the maximum degree of the degeneracy is 2 (namely, "duplicate") about all of the degenerate eigenvalues.

These figures point out that the systems preconditioned by the block CC have the degenerate eigenvalues on both sizes, but the systems by the block IC don't have the degenerate eigenvalues on both sizes.

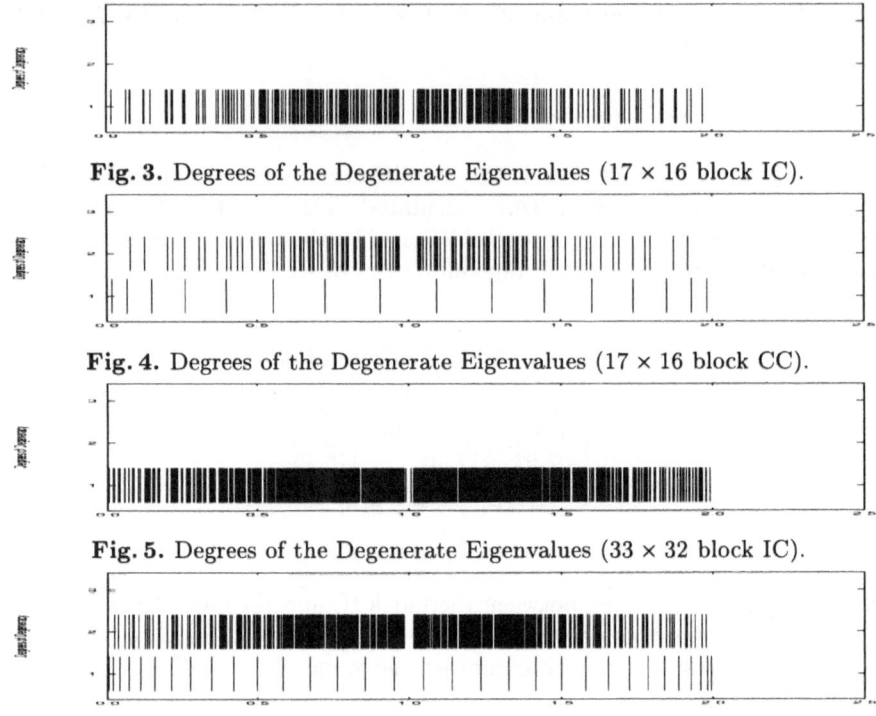

Fig. 3. Degrees of the Degenerate Eigenvalues (17 × 16 block IC).

Fig. 4. Degrees of the Degenerate Eigenvalues (17 × 16 block CC).

Fig. 5. Degrees of the Degenerate Eigenvalues (33 × 32 block IC).

Fig. 6. Degrees of the Degenerate Eigenvalues (33 × 32 block CC).

It can be considered that the degenerate eigenvalues cause the branching off from half way through the convergence in Fig. 1. Because the degenerate eigenvalues give fast convergence by eq.(19) and (20), (Section 4).

7   Concluding Remarks

In this paper, we have evaluated the spectral properties by block preconditioning from a viewpoint of the coefficient matrix improvement between the block IC and the SC preconditioner. In the section 4, we have evaluated the clustering of the eigenvalues of the preconditioned coefficient matrices. In the section 5, we have calculated the condition number of the preconditioned coefficient matrices. These numerical results show that the differences of the eigenvalue clustering and the condition number between the block IC and the SC are not remarkable. We consider that these results show the reason why the behavior of the residual norms is almost the same about half way from the begin through the convergence in Fig. 1.

On the other hand, the difference of the converging behavior is certified by several numerical results (Fig. 1, [9]). In order to consider this phenomenon by the preconditionings, in the section 6, we have focused attention on the degeneracy of the eigenvalues of the preconditioned coefficient matrices.

From these results, we consider that the difference of converging behavior in Fig. 1 and the fast convergence of the SC is due not to the clustering but to the degeneracy of the eigenvalues of the preconditioned coefficient matrix.

Acknowledgements

The authors wish to thank the anonymous reviewers for their comments on this paper. One of the authors (S.I.) wish to acknowledge valuable discussions with professor Henk A. van der Vorst (University of Utrecht, The Netherlands) at the international conference on numerical analysis on the 40th Anniversary of the journal BIT held at Lund (Sweden) in August, 2000. This work is partially supported by Center for Computational Science and Energy of JAERI (Japan Atomic Energy Research Institute) in 1997 – 1999.

References

1. Axelsson O., Incomplete Block Matrix Factorization Preconditioning Methods. The Ultimate Answer?, *J. Comp. Appl. Math.*, 12&13, pp. 3–18, 1985.
2. Barrett R., et al., *Templates for the Solution of Linear Systems: Building Blocks for Iterative Methods* , SIAM, Philadelphia, USA, 1994.
3. Bruaset A. M., *A Survey of Preconditioned Iterative Methods*, Longman Scientific & Technical, 1995.
4. Concus P., Golub G. H. and Meurant G., Block Preconditioning for the Conjugate Gradient Method, *SIAM J. Sci. Stat. Comput.*, 6, pp. 220–252, 1985.
5. Eisenstat S. C., Efficient Implementation of a Class of Preconditioned Conjugate Gradient Methods, *SIAM J. Sci. Stat. Comput.*, 2, pp. 1–4, 1981.
6. Golub G. H. and O'Leary D. P., Some History of the Conjugate Gradient and Lanczos Algorithms: 1948–1976,*SIAM Review*, 31, pp. 50–102, 1989.
7. Golub G. H. and van Loan C. F., *Matrix Computations*, Johns Hopkins University Press, 1996.
8. Hestenes M. R. and Stiefel E., Methods of Conjugate Gradients for Solving Linear Systems, *J. Res. Nat. Bur. Standards* , 49, pp. 409–435, 1952.
9. Itoh S., Zhang S. -L., Oyanagi Y. and Natori M., Splitting Correction Preconditioner for Linear Systems that Arise from Periodic Boundary Problems, *ISE-Technical Report* , ISE-TR-00-170, University of Tsukuba, June, 2000.
10. Kelley C. T., *Iterative Methods for Linear and Nonlinear Equations* , SIAM, Philadelphia, 1995.
11. Meijerink J. A. and van der Vorst H. A., An Iterative Solution Method for Linear Systems of Which the Coefficient Matrix is a Symmetric M-Matrix, *Math. Comput.*, 31, pp. 148–162, 1977.
12. Natori M., Numerical Analysis and its Applications, *Corona Publishing*, Tokyo, 1990 (in Japanese).

Statistical Disclosure Control Based on Random Uncertainty Intervals

Jinfang Wang

The Institute of Statistical Mathematics, 4-6-7 Minami-Azabu, Minato-ku, Tokyo
106—8569, Japan
E-mail: wang@ism.ac.jp

Abstract. In this paper we propose a statistical framework for controlling the risk
in disclosing public micro-data. The idea is to replace the micro-data by controllable quasi-data represented as uncertainty intervals. An uncertainty interval is an
interval covering a genuine datum with specified probability. We also discuss statistical inferences based on random intervals. Problems discussed include point and
interval estimation of the mean, two-sample tests and density estimations.

1   Introduction

"Each [government] agency, in accordance with published rules, shall make
available for public inspection and copying copies of all records, regardless of
form or format, ..." (*The Freedom of Information Act*, 5 U.S.C. §552)

"No [government] agency shall disclose any record which is contained in
a system of records by any means of communication to any person, or to
another agency, ..."(*The Privacy Act*, 5 U.S.C. §552a)

The purpose of *statistical disclosure control* is to study methods for releasing to public availability micro-data or tables for ordinary statistical inspections while keep individual information not being identified or predicted
too accurately.

The purpose of this paper is to propose a statistical framework within
which the balance between the two seemingly conflicting ends of the same
spectrum may be attained. Section 2 proposes an approach based on the idea
of random intervals. These intervals depend on an uncertainty level ϵ, which
is determined by the data publisher. The uncertainty level $\epsilon \in [0, 1]$ controls
the information contained in the published data. A larger value of ϵ is chosen
if the micro-data is considered highly sensitive.

Section 3 proposes an alternative approach for constructing uncertainty
intervals. These random intervals are based on regression prediction intervals
when covariates are present. One advantage of this approach is that it may
be easily generalized to high dimensional data.

Statistical inferences based on random intervals are considered in Section
4. Problems discussed there include point and interval estimations for the
mean, testing the equality of two means and density estimations. The last
section contains a short discussion for future problems.

2   Random Uncertainty Intervals

2.1 ϵ-uncertainty intervals

Let x be a univariate random variable with distribution function $F(x)$. Assume that the support of $F(x)$, $s(F)$, is an interval. The interior of $s(F)$ is denoted by $s^\circ(F)$

Definition 1. Let $0 \leq \epsilon \leq 1$. That $i_\epsilon(x)$ is an ϵ-uncertainty interval of x, if $i_\epsilon(x)$ is an interval containing x and

$$\int_{y \in i_\epsilon(x)} dF(y) = \epsilon.$$

If $\epsilon = 0$, then $i_\epsilon(x) = \{x\}$ for every x. So a zero-uncertainty interval of x is x itself. No information loss occurs at uncertainty level zero. On the other hand, if $\epsilon = 100\%$, then $i_{100\%}(x) = s(F)$. So a 100%-uncertainty interval of any x is the support of F generating the data x. This interval therefore contains no information about the magnitude of x.

In our application x will be a datum or an observation. Publishing an uncertainty interval $i_\epsilon(x)$ instead of the datum x provides a systematic way of controlling disclosure risk. The higher the level of uncertainty ϵ we choose, the more blurred information we shall get by receiving the interval.

Definition 2. An ϵ-uncertainty interval of x is not unique. The collection of all ϵ-uncertainty intervals

$$I_\epsilon(x) = \{i_\epsilon(x) \,|\, i_\epsilon(x) : \epsilon\text{-uncertainty interval of } x\}$$

form the ϵ-uncertainty interval space of x.

Given each datum x and uncertainty level ϵ we have an ϵ-uncertainty interval space $I_\epsilon(x)$. The next step in our disclosure control process is to systematically choose an interval $i_\epsilon(x)$ from $I_\epsilon(x)$. To this end we shall introduce a probability measure in $I_\epsilon(x)$. Let $\text{vol}\{i_\epsilon(x)\}$ be the length of $i_\epsilon(x)$. For any $0 \leq \epsilon < 1$ and $x \in s^\circ(F)$, there exists an $i_\epsilon(x) \in I_\epsilon(x)$ such that $\text{vol}\{i_\epsilon(x)\} < +\infty$. In other words, among the intervals in the space $I_\epsilon(x)$, there is at least one interval that is finite.

Definition 3. An interval $i_\epsilon^*(x) \in I_\epsilon(x)$ is a most informative ϵ-uncertainty interval if

$$\text{vol}\{i_\epsilon^*(x)\} \leq \text{vol}\{i_\epsilon(x)\}, \quad \forall\, i_\epsilon(x) \in I_\epsilon(x).$$

A most informative interval is in general not unique as may be easily seen by considering the case when $F(x)$ is the uniform distribution. If, however, the density is not flat at x then uniqueness will be guaranteed. The following results play an important role in the construction of random intervals.

Proposition 1. *Let $0 \le \epsilon < 1$ and $x \in s^\circ(F)$. Let $F(x)$ be the distribution function of X. Then there exists a 1-1 correspondence between the uncertainty interval space $I_\epsilon(x)$ and the interval $[\ell_\epsilon(x), u_\epsilon(x)]$, which is defined by*

$$\ell_\epsilon(x) = \begin{cases} F^{-1}\{F(x) - \epsilon\}, & \text{if } F(x) > \epsilon \\ F^{-1}(\epsilon), & \text{if } F(x) \le \epsilon \end{cases}$$

$$u_\epsilon(x) = \begin{cases} min\{x, F^{-1}(1 - \epsilon)\}, & \text{if } F(x) > \epsilon \\ F^{-1}\{min[1 - \epsilon, F(x)] + \epsilon\}, & \text{if } F(x) \le \epsilon \end{cases}$$

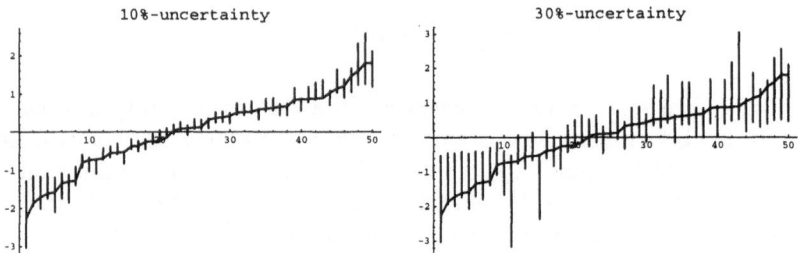

Fig. 1. Uncertainty random intervals for 50 artificial data.

2.2 Disclosure control based on random uncertainty intervals

By Proposition 1, to assign a probability measure on the space $I_\epsilon(x)$ we need only to consider the issue of choosing a distribution on $[\ell_\epsilon(x), u_\epsilon(x)]$, which is called the *representative interval* of the space $I_\epsilon(x)$. Each point in this interval is called a representative point. Note that if $F(x) > \epsilon$ then any $a \in [\ell_\epsilon(x), u_\epsilon(x)]$ is mapped to $[a, b] \in I_\epsilon(x)$; if $F(x) \le \epsilon$ then any $b \in [\ell_\epsilon(x), u_\epsilon(x)]$ is mapped to $[a, b] \in I_\epsilon(x)$, and vice versa. When $F(x) > \epsilon$, the representative interval consists of the lower ends of $i_\epsilon(x)$; when $F(x) < \epsilon$ the representative interval consists of the upper ends.

Definition 4. *Let $x \in s^\circ(F)$ and $0 \le \epsilon < 1$. Let $[\ell_\epsilon(x), u_\epsilon(x)]$ be the ϵ-uncertainty representative interval of x. Let $P_\epsilon(x)$ be a random variable on $[\ell_\epsilon(x), u_\epsilon(x)]$ having distribution η. The interval corresponding to $P_\epsilon(x)$ is called an ϵ-uncertainty random interval having distribution η.*

The framework for statistical disclosure control based on ϵ-uncertainty random intervals consists of the following components.

1. Let $x_1, \cdots, x_n$ be i.i.d. from a known distribution $F(x)$.
2. Let $\epsilon \in (0, 1)$. Compute the representative intervals, $[\ell_\epsilon(x_j), u_\epsilon(x_j)]$, from the ϵ-uncertainty space, $I_\epsilon(x_j)$, $j = 1, \cdots, n$.

3. Choose a sampling scheme η_j for $[\ell_\epsilon(x_j), u_\epsilon(x_j)]$ and generate a random number $P_\epsilon(x_j)$ according to η_j, $j = 1, \cdots, n$.

4. Publish $i_\epsilon(x_j)$, $j = 1, \cdots, n$, where each $i_\epsilon(x_j)$ is the ϵ-uncertainty interval corresponding to the random points $P_\epsilon(x_j)$ obtained in step 3.

There are two factors affecting the level of information contained in the published intervals. The first is the choice of the uncertainty level ϵ. The closer is ϵ to unity, the less is the usable information. The second factor is the choice of a sampling scheme for each representative interval. One may choose the uniform distribution for each interval. The uncertainty level is the more important one in controlling disclosure risk as well as the statistical usefulness of the publish data. A choice of ϵ depends on the sensitivity of the micro-data. Figure 1 shows random uncertainty intervals for artificial data, $x_j \sim N(0,1)$, $j = 1, \cdots, 50$. The data, arranged in ascending order, are shown with their respective random intervals.

The procedure above has been described in a static fashion. An on-line version is also possible. In the latter case a user (or an attacker) is allowed to repeatedly obtain the intervals for a given ϵ. Mote Carlo studies based on these intervals are thus possible. If the user can specify ϵ within a given range, then an ϵ-sensitivity analysis is also possible.

The theory of ϵ-uncertainty random intervals implicitly assumes that we know, or can estimate with good accuracy, the distribution function $F(x)$ of the random samples $x = \{x_1, \cdots, x_n\}$, which form the micro-data. In practice, we may assume a parametric model $F(x|\theta)$ and estimate $F(x)$ by $F(x|\hat{\theta})$, where $\hat{\theta}$ is the maximum likelihood estimate of θ.

3   Predictive Random Uncertainty Intervals

3.1   Micro-data arising from linear models

In practice the data or responses, x, are often related to other variables or covariates, z say. Now we consider a situation where releasing the covariates z causes no risk but disclosure of x needs control. More formally, suppose that the x's in the micro-data $x = \{x_1, \cdots, x_n\}$ are i.i.d. normal variables: $x_j \sim N(\mu_j, \sigma^2)$. The mean μ_j relates to z_j by the linear relation $\mu_j = z_j'\beta$, where β is a p-dimensional parameter. In matrix form, we then have

$$x = Z\beta + \epsilon, \tag{1}$$

which is known as the *linear model*, where Z is an $n \times p$ matrix having z_j as its j-th row. The error is also assumed to be normal: $\epsilon \sim N(0, \sigma^2 I)$, where σ^2 is an unknown scalar and I is the $n \times n$ identity matrix.

Under these assumptions the least squares estimator for β is written as

$$\hat{\beta} = (Z'Z)^{-1}Z'x. \tag{2}$$

And the mean of x, using (1) and (2), can then be estimated by the fitted values, $\hat{x} = Z\hat{\beta} = Z(Z'Z)^{-1}Z'x$.

3.2   Prediction intervals

Consider a known covariate z_+ and an unknown response x_+, related by

$$x_+ = z'_+ \beta + \epsilon_j . \tag{3}$$

Using (3) we may estimate the mean of x_+ given x, $\hat{\mu}_+ = E(x_+|x)$, by the quantity $\hat{\mu}_+ = z'_+ \hat{\beta}$, where $\hat{\beta}$ is defined by (2).

We can also construct a *confidence interval* for μ_+ given x and the relation (3). The $100(1 - \alpha)\%$ symmetric confidence interval is given by

$$\hat{\mu}_+ \pm t_{1-\alpha/2} \sqrt{\hat{\sigma}^2 z'_+ (Z'Z)^{-1} z_+} \tag{4}$$

where $\hat{\sigma}^2 = (x - \hat{x})'(x - \hat{x})/(n - p)$ and t_α is the α-th quantile of the t-distribution with $n - p$ degrees of freedom.

3.3   Predictive random uncertainty intervals

Consider a data base $D = \{(x_1, z_1) \cdots, (x_N, z_N)\}$, where the x's and z's are related by the linear model (1). The statistical bureau, who has full control of D, select a sub-set $d = \{(x_1, z_1) \cdots, (x_n, z_n)\}$ from D. Given d the bureau can use $\hat{\beta}$ of (2) to estimate β, ans so on. Now we describe a disclosure procedure that systematically controls the risk and the amount of information cotained in the released data. The following operations are carried out before data publication.

1. Randomly select a sub data-set d of size n from D. Let x and Z be the response vector and the covariate matrix, respectively.
2. Assume the linear model (1). Estimate the error size, $\sigma^2 = \text{var}(x_j)$, by

$$\hat{\sigma}^2 = (x - \hat{x})'(x - \hat{x})/(n - p) \tag{5}$$

   where $\hat{x} = Z\hat{\beta}$ is the estimate of the mean of x and $\hat{\beta}$ is given by (2).
3. Choose an appropriate uncertainty level, $0 < \epsilon < 1$. An ϵ-sensitivity analysis may be useful in assisting such a choice.
4. Randomly select a point $d_+ = (x_+, z_+)$ from D and compute the interval

$$i_+ = x_+ \pm t_{(1+\epsilon)/2} \sqrt{\hat{\sigma}^2 z_+ (Z'Z)^{-1} z'_+} . \tag{6}$$

5. Generate a uniform number U_+ on i_+ and compute the interval

$$I_+ = U_+ \pm t_{(1+\epsilon)/2} \sqrt{\hat{\sigma}^2 z_+ (Z'Z)^{-1} z'_+} . \tag{7}$$

Now the statistical bureau, upon each request, can disclose the following set of information.

- The linear model (1) and the uncertainty level ϵ.
- The response/covariate pair, (I_+, z_+), where I_+ is defined by (7).

To aid statistical analyses based on the released data, the covariate matrix $\boldsymbol{Z}$ in (7) and the estimated error size, $\hat{\sigma}^2$, may also be published optionally.

Note that as ϵ goes to zero $t_{(1+\epsilon)/2} \to t_{0.5} = 0$ since the t-distribution is symmetric about zero. It follows by (7) that in the limit $I_+ = U_+$. But U_+ is uniformly distributed on i_+. By (6) we conclude that random uncertainty interval I_+ must tend to the genuine datum x_+ as ϵ goes to zero.

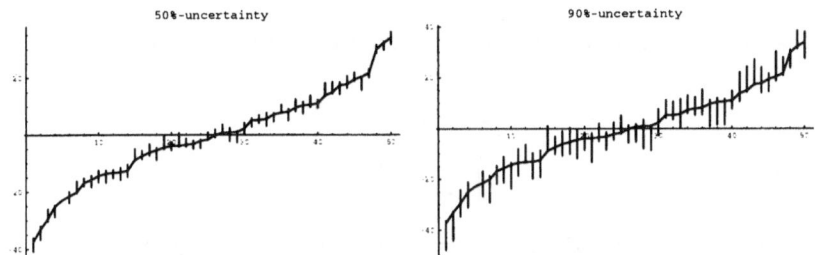

Fig. 2. Predictive uncertainty random intervals for 50 artificial data at uncertainty levels $\epsilon = 0.5, 0.9$. The data, arranged in ascending order, are also shown.

Figure 2 shows the predictive uncertainty random intervals for 50 artificial data, $x_j, j = 1, \cdots, 50$, at uncertainty levels $\epsilon = 0.5, 0.9$, together with the data arranged in ascending order. These data were generated by the model, $x_j = z'_j \beta + \epsilon_j$, where $\beta = (0.1, 1.0, 2.5)'$ and $\epsilon_j \sim N(0, 15^2)$. The size of $\boldsymbol{d}$ was set to $n = 100$. The covariates were chosen to be independent Bernoulli variables with success probability 0.7.

4   Statistical Inferences

Four problems are studied in this section: point and interval estimation of the mean, testing the equality of two means and estimation of density functions.

4.1   Point estimation

Let $x = \{x_1, \cdots, x_n\}$ be an i.i.d. sample from $F(x)$. The sample mean $\bar{x} = n^{-1} \sum_j x_j$ is known as the uniformly minimum variance unbiased estimator for the population mean μ. Based on the published ϵ-uncertainty intervals, $i_\epsilon(x_j), j = 1, \cdots, n$, a natural extension of $\bar{x}$ is the ϵ-mean

$$\bar{i}_\epsilon = \frac{1}{n} \sum_{j=1}^{n} U_j \tag{8}$$

where U_j is a uniformly distributed random variable on $i_\epsilon(x_j)$. As $\epsilon \to 0$, we naturally expect that such an estimator will have higher and higher an accuracy in estimating the target estimator. This property may be formally studied through the concept of ϵ-consistency.

Definition 5. Let $\theta = \theta(F)$ be a functional of F. Let F_n be the empirical distribution function. An estimator $\hat{\theta}_\epsilon$ is called ϵ-consistent for θ if

$$\lim_{\epsilon \to 0} \hat{\theta}_\epsilon = \theta(F_n). \qquad (9)$$

It can be shown that the ϵ-mean defined by (8) is ϵ-consistent.

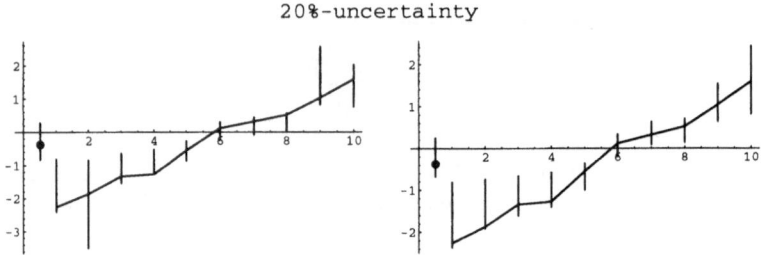

Fig. 3. Minkovski mean statistics for $\epsilon = 0.2$

4.2   Interval estimation

With data in the form of random intervals, a more natural way of estimating the mean is to construct an interval estimate. To do so we need to consider operations in the space of intervals. The idea discussed in this section is similar to that of [4] in studying the estimation of variance.

Let $i_1, \cdots, i_n$ be an independent interval sample of size n. To estimate the population mean we propose the use of the *Minkovski mean* defined by

$$i_M = \frac{1}{n} \sum_{j=1}^{n} i_j, \qquad (10)$$

where the summation is in the Minkovski sense. Asymptotically correct inference based on the Minkovski mean may be argued by making an appeal to the generalized laws of large numbers concerning random sets[1,2,5–7], random intervals being a special case.

Figure 3 displays 10 random intervals for 10 data on two occasions. The Minkovski means of the 10 intervals, together with the original data, are also shown. The black dots are the empirical mean, $\bar{x} = n^{-1} \sum_j x_j$, which is a point in the Minkovski means.

4.3   Testing the Equality of Two Means

Consider i.i.d. samples from two populations: $x_j \sim F(x), j = 1, \cdots, n$ and $y_k \sim G(y), k = 1, \cdots, m$. A formal test of the equality of means

$$H_0 : \mu_x = \mu_y \quad \text{vs.} \quad H_A : \mu_x \neq \mu_y. \tag{11}$$

is of interest in varities of situations, where $\mu_x = \int x \, dF(x)$ and $\mu_y = \int y \, dG(y)$. We now consider testing (11) based on two sets of ϵ-uncertainty random intervals, $i_\epsilon(x) = \{i_\epsilon(x_1), \cdots, i_\epsilon(x_n)\}$ and $i_\epsilon(y) = \{i_\epsilon(y_1), \cdots, i_\epsilon(y_m)\}$.

To construct a test statistic we use the *Hausdorff distance* between two non-empty sets,

$$\rho(A, B) = \max \left\{ \sup_{a \in A} \inf_{b \in B} \|a - b\|, \ \sup_{b \in B} \inf_{a \in A} \|a - b\| \right\},$$

which, when $A = (a_1, a_2)$ and $B = (b_1, b_2)$ are intervals, reduces to

$$\rho(A, B) = \max \{|a_1 - b_1|, \ |a_2 - b_2|\}. \tag{12}$$

Now let $\bar{x}_M$ and $\bar{y}_M$ be the Minkovski means of random intervals $i_\epsilon(x)$ and $i_\epsilon(y)$ respectively. In the classical case, the mean difference $\bar{x} - \bar{y}$ is often used as a test statistic. Since the Minkovski mean differs from the sample mean only by an amount controlled by the level of ϵ, a natural test statistic for the hypothesis (11) can therefore be defined by

$$T = \rho(\bar{x}_M, \bar{y}_M) \tag{13}$$

where $\rho(.)$ is the Hausdorff distance defined by (12).

4.4   Density Estimation

Estimation of probability density functions is of great importance in decision-making involving uncertainty. Now we study this problem when data are random intervals. Let $x = \{x_1, \cdots, x_n\}$ be the original micro-data, the x's being i.i.d. from a density function $f(x)$. Our aim is to estimate $f(x)$ based on the published ϵ-uncertainty random intervals $i_1, \cdots, i_n$.

Let $\chi_j(x)$ be the indicator function, i.e. $\chi_j(x) = 1$ if $x \in i_j$ and 0 otherwise. Then the density $f(x)$ must satisfy the constraints

$$E\{\chi_j(X)\} = \int_{x \in i_j} f(x) dx = \epsilon, \quad j = 1, \cdots, n \tag{14}$$

Let $g(x)$ be an unconstrained density estimate, such as a kernel estimator based on the middle points of the uncertainty intervals. A natural estimate of $f(x)$ is to minimize the *relative entropy* or the *Kullback-Leibler divergence*

$$D(f, g) = \int f(x) \log \frac{f(x)}{g(x)} dx \tag{15}$$

under the constraints (14). The solution to this problem is of the simple form

$$\hat{f}(x) = \frac{\exp < \tau, \chi(x) >}{M(\tau)} g(x) \tag{16}$$

where $M(\tau) = \int \exp < \tau, \chi(x) > g(x) dx$ is the normalizing constant and

$$< \tau, \chi(x) >= \sum_{j=1}^{n} \tau_j \chi_j(x) \quad \epsilon = \frac{\partial}{\partial \tau_j} \log M(\tau), \quad j = 1, \cdots, n$$

To have an idea of what the estimator would look like, consider the small-ϵ asymptotics. Let ϵ be small so that $i_j \cap i_k = \emptyset, j \neq k$. Let $A = \cup_{j=1}^{n} i_j, \beta_j = E_g \chi(i_j)$ and $c = E_g \chi(\bar{A})$. Then we have $\epsilon = \beta_i e^{\tau_i}/M(\tau)$. So τ must satisfy

$$B(e^{\tau_1}, \cdots, e^{\tau_n})' + (c, \cdots, c)' = 0,$$

where

$$B = \begin{pmatrix} \beta_1(1 - 1/\epsilon) & \beta_2 & \cdots & \beta_n \\ \beta_1 & \beta_2(1 - 1/\epsilon) & \cdots & \beta_n \\ \vdots & \vdots & \vdots & \vdots \\ \beta_1 & \beta_2 & \cdots & \beta_n(1 - 1/\epsilon) \end{pmatrix}$$

The final ϵ-asymptotic maximum entropy estimator is found to be

$$\hat{f}(x) = \begin{cases} \frac{\epsilon}{\beta_j} g(x), & \text{if } x \in i_j \\ 0, & \text{if } x \in \bar{A} \end{cases} \tag{17}$$

This is a reasonable estimator in a number of ways.

5   Discussions

The success of statistical disclosure control needs the cooperation of scientists from many disciplines including statistics, probability theory and computer sciences. Some case studies (e.g. [8,9]) have been reported recently. [3] gave an interesting discussion on a use of Fisher's logarithmic series model in risk assessment associated with micro-data disclosure; see also the references contained therein. Many fundamental questions along the line of the paper however remain to be solved. I now list two of them.

Statistical. Statistics concerns the logic of induction from the part to the whole. Thus, from a random sample of incomes, $x = \{x_1, \cdots, x_n\}$, of salaried men, statisticians are concerned with the income of a 'typical' salaried man, for which the mean $\bar{x} = \sum_{i=1}^{n} x_i/n$ .often makes sense. In fact, constructing such "best" summaries has been the dominant task of the traditional statistics.

On the other hand, once x is open to the public, a potential *attacker* may attempt to identify some data points in x with unique characteristics, which necessitates measures for privacy protection. In this sense, the problem of disclosure control may be viewed as an inverse problem of the traditional statistics. The central issue here is to develop methods for creating data with the amount of aggregate statistical information controllable, and in the meantime no individual data may be identified. Development of statistical methods for analyzing such data is also of first priority. The approaches based on random intervals outlined in this paper show some of the possibilities. More works, especially real applications, would be highly desirable.

Mathematical. The behaviors of the derived summaries based on the disclosed quasi-data need careful assessments. For example, will the generalized Minkovski sample mean based on random intervals obey a version of the central limit law?

Acknowledgments

This work is partially supported by Grand-in-Aid 12780181 from the Japanese Ministry of Education, Science, Sports and Culture.

References

1. Artstein, Z. and Vitale, R.A. (1975). A strong law of large numbers for random compact sets, *Ann. Prob.* **3**, 879–882.
2. Giné, E. Hahn, M.G. and Zinn, J. (1985). *Limit Theorems for Random Sets*, Lecture Notes in Mathematics **990**, 112–135, Springer, New York.
3. Hoshino, N. and Takemura, A. (1998). Relationship between logarithmic series model and other superpopulation models useful for microdata disclosure risk assessment. *J. Japan Statist. Soc.* **28**, 125–134.
4. Kruse, R. (1987). On the variance of random compact sets, *J. Math. Anal. Appl.* **122**, 469–473.
5. Puri, M.L. and Ralescu, D.A. (1983). Differentials of Fuzzy functions, *J. Math. Anal. Appl.* **91**, 552–558.
6. Taylor, R.L. and Inoue, H. (1985). A strong law of large numbers for random sets in Banach spaces, *Bull. Inst. Math. Academia Sinica* **13**, 403–409.
7. Uemura, T. (1993). A law of large numbers for random sets, *Fuzzy Sets and Systems* **59**, 181–188.
8. Willenborg, L. and Waal, T. (1996). *Statistical Disclosure Control in Practice*, Lecture Notes in Statistics **111**, Springer, New York.
9. Willenborg, L. and Waal, T. (2000). *Elements of Statistical Disclosure Control*, Springer, New York.

Part V

IT-Based Innovative Education Systems and Strategies

Knowledge Management System for Information System Design and Implementation Education

Atsuo Hazeyama

Department of Mathematics and Informatics, Tokyo Gakugei University
4-1-1 Nukui-kita-machi, Koganei-shi, Tokyo 184-8501, Japan
E-mail: hazeyama@u-gakugei.ac.jp

Abstract. Software development is knowledge intensive work. It is therefore important to store, share, and reuse knowledge (artifacts, experiences) in information system development education. The authors have been developing a system that supports group exercises for information system design and implementation education in a university. The system not only supports the development processes but also is a kind of knowledge management system in that it stores knowledge and utilizes stored knowledge. This paper describes an overview of the system, and some results which were gained from an experiment on knowledge utilization.

1 Introduction

With rapid permeation of information and communication technology like the Internet into our society and with advancement of the needs, demands for information system (IS) development increase and the complexity of such systems also increases. From such background, capable people who can design and implement information systems are required and rearing capable people becomes important. Information system development is knowledge intensive work, so it is not easy to educate it.

Several phases are done in development of an information system such as planning, analysis, design, programming, and testing. Via these phases, an information system is released for use. Development of an information system is usually performed by organizing a project which consists of plural members. So in system development project management techniques are also important that allocate members to tasks, create schedules, and manage the progress. Furthermore in information system development, it is important to analyze business processes to be systematized, to design the system architecture, data structure, to document the results, and to communicate them among members as well as to write computer programs. As such, in information system development, not only programming skills but also various types of skills are required.

On the other hand, education on informatics in universities mainly focuses on skills' acquisition of each student such as programming languages, algorithms, database, network, etc. However there is little opportunity that these skills are applied to development of a total application system which is supposed to practical settings.

I think various types of skills for information system design and implementation will be acquired more effectively by means of not only lecture by a teacher but also students tackling issues for themselves. However only a few case studies have been reported, for example, [8]. So in our department, I have been doing a class which aims at designing and implementing a practical information system whose goal is to learn and acquire total skills with respect to information system design and implementation, especially system analysis and design, project management, and group work [3].

A supporting system is strongly required in order to do such kind of class effectively and efficiently. However, only a few educational environments were reported [1, 9]. Drummond and Boldyreff constructed a group software engineering learning environment called SEGWorld on the BSCW, which mainly focused on the shared workspace [1]. However they do not clarify usage of knowledge that is stored in the system. Shoenig automated three of the most time-consuming processes associated with the course on the Lotus Notes: project registration, team assignment, and review of document [9]. However Shoenig automated only a part of the software processes and did not describe reuse of the accumulated artifacts.

In the exercises of information system design and implementation education, various aspects exist such as group organization, mutual agreement on concept creation, cooperation and coordination based on the roles and communications [7]. One promising approach to support such kind of knowledge intensive work is to provide a Knowledge Management System (KMS) [6]. We think effectiveness of a KMS in this type of education is large because stored knowledge can be shared by a lot of students: members within a group, members of other groups within the same year, and learners of the subsequent years.

We aim at developing a knowledge management system that supports group learning of information system design and implementation that possesses such various aspects. As we applied the first version of the system to an actual class, we describe overview of the system, and show an experiment on knowledge utilization stored in the system and some results.

2   Requirements to a KMS for IS design and implementation education

We describe some requirements to a knowledge management system for information system design and implementation education in a university based on our experience of its education and the results of our previous work.

(1) This is the first experience for almost all students to do all the phases of the software development processes. So it is not enough to understand a series of processes. Therefore, the system should support a series of processes from group organization till design and implementation of an information system. By this support the students can acquire the skills that are required in workplaces.

(2) The artifacts that were created during the exercises are not well utilized. We think it is effective for the students to promote information sharing on account of efficient learning. Here the scope of information sharing is mainly within the group the artifacts were created but also other groups within the same year and the groups of other years on the nature of education in universities. Therefore the system should store the artifacts created during the exercises, manage them so that the users could share and reuse them.

(3) From the viewpoint of a teacher, we would like to provide more concrete and better materials for education because information system development is knowledge intensive work in nature. The system should support to evaluate or analyze the stored artifacts to improve the contents of knowledge.

(4) The system should provide a learning environment that anyone can access from anywhere at anytime. For this purpose, the system should be constructed on the Internet, so the users can use the system via a WWW browser. Shoenig constructed the system on the Lotus Notes that is a specific environment [9].

3   The system

3.1   System architecture

We have been developing a group learning support system for information system design and implementation education that realizes the requirements mentioned in the previous section [2, 4]. The system is composed of three sub-systems, group organization, textbook creation, and development process support.

Fig. 1 shows the overall architecture of the system. These sub-systems are integrated via DBs.

The system is installed in a server machine on the Internet. Any machines which are connected to the Internet can utilize the system at any time from any place. The system can be used from the Web browser without any special application software, therefore the users can construct usage environment at low cost. This system consists of the CGI (Common Gateway Interface) programs which are developed by using Perl programming language on the SunOS. We describe details of facilities that have been implemented thus far.

3.2   Group organization

This sub-system is composed of the following two functions: group organization and group information registration (generate a group working environment). It is important for success of the group exercises to organize groups optimally. For group organization, the students enter their personal information with respect to system development, and the teacher enters some sort of evaluation data for each student. The system separates input data (personal data for group organization) and output data (result of group organization) from group organization scheme so that different group organization schemes can be introduced.

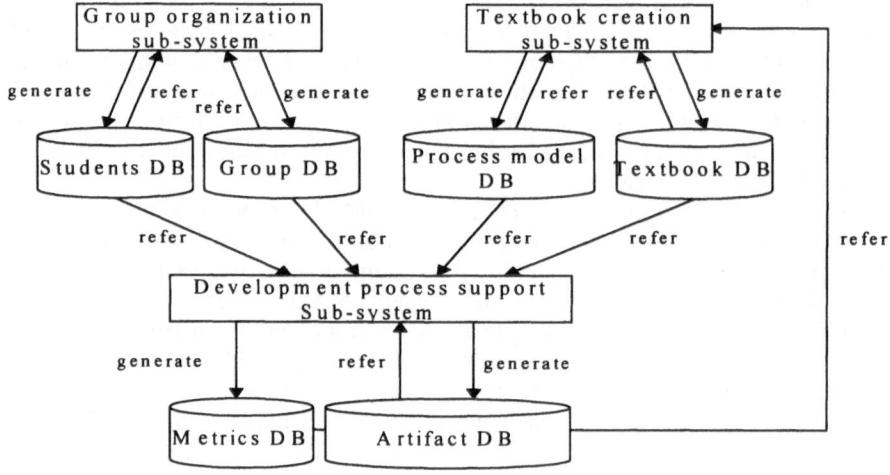

Fig. 1 The system architecture

After group organization, the students register the group information (group name, group password, etc.). These data are checked, and if no problems occur, the data are stored into the database for group administration. At the same time the work space for the group is automatically generated. The group members perform their work within the group's work space. The created artifacts are stored into the work space and they could be referred.

3.3   Textbook creation

An electronic textbook provides various information on information system development. It is written using the HTML (Hyper Text Markup Language). It is flexible and extensible because the contents of it can be appended and modified easily. An electronic textbook is continuously enhanced by the knowledge, which reflects know-how extracted from the insights gained from metrics data for the processes and products (efforts spent on learning by individuals, by groups, by phases, access log for each document), and/or FAQs (Frequently Asked Questions). The system also provides "process model DB", which is used as a textbook of software life cycle process as well as to support development work. The contents are specified as activity and task based on the SLCP (Software Life Cycle Process) [5].

3.4 Development process support

This sub-system supports software development work by group, especially various types of document creation based on template, information sharing, and communication. Fig. 2 shows the functions and the DBs each function generates and their relationships. "Process model DB", "Group DB", "Student DB" are DBs that other sub-systems generate and this sub-system only refers. Hereafter we describe the functions for development process support.

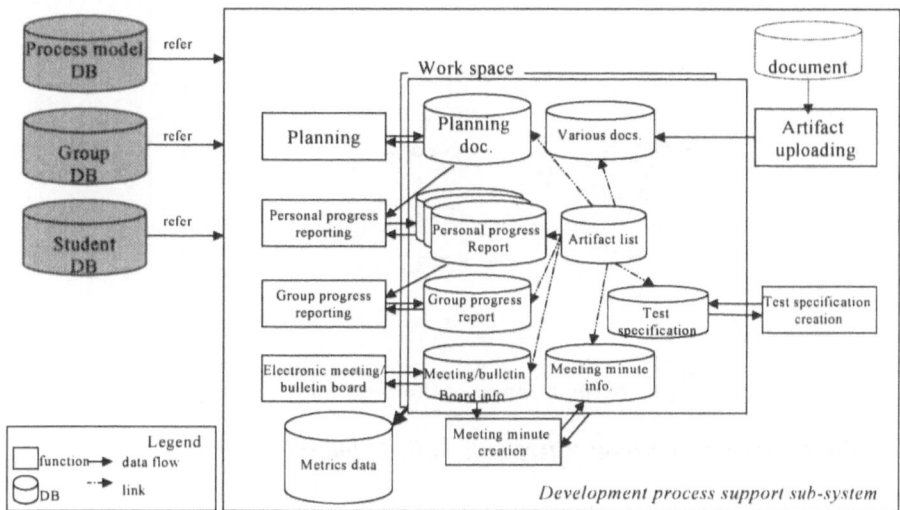

Fig. 2 Structure of the development process support sub-system

(a) Planning

A development plan is a document in which concept of a system the group develops, work items, roles of group members, and schedules are written. In planning it is important to show the work activities in the whole life cycle of software development because this is the first experience for students to do the work. The process model DB plays the role and this data is used by the system in setting work items in the planning stage. Fig. 3 shows the screen image of the planning function. The students fill in the blanks of the template.

(b) Progress reporting

Tasks that are specified in the development plan and that are to be performed by a student are shown in the form of his/her To-do list. When a student reports the progress of his/her assigned tasks from the list, it is reflected as the progress of his/her group.

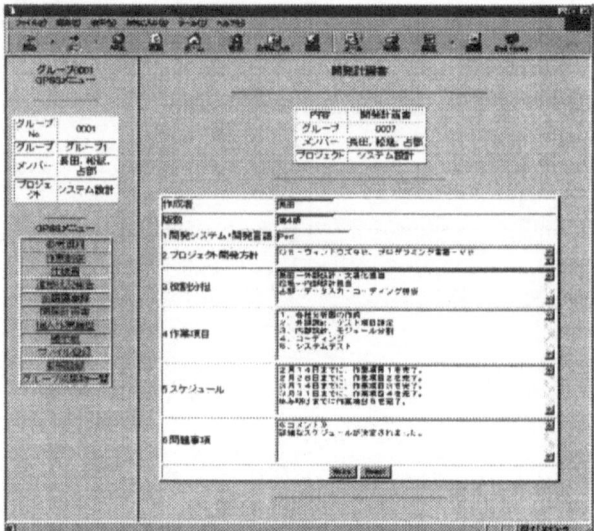

Fig. 3 Screen image of the planning function

(c) Electronic meeting room/Electronic bulletin board

We provided an electronic meeting room and an electronic bulletin board so that the group members could collaborate, communicate, coordinate, discuss, and notify in geographically dispersed settings.

(d) Meeting minutes creation

In group work (learning), it is important to keep decisions and the progress of discussions in a meeting as a record. We also found that it was important that a meeting should be goal driven. We therefore prepared a template of a meeting minute and the system supported creation of a meeting minute. The created meeting minutes are stored into a DB.

(e) Test specification creation

We provided this function to create a test specification which can be written with text media only. Items of a specification such as title, author, version No., issued date, test items can be written according to a template.

(f) Artifacts uploading

In documents such as requirements specification or design specification, the contents are often written with not only texts but also multi-media such as diagrams, figures, graphs, images, and so on. We are supposed to use word processors, and/or presentation tools in creating these kinds of documents. The system provides an uploading function of a document, which stores the files into the system.

4   A profile of the class

This section describes a profile of the class we applied the system. This class is a full year optional subject (4 units), which is assigned to the 3rd year undergraduate students of department of Educational Informatics in Tokyo Gakugei University (the number of students to be admitted each year is 40). Before the class, the students have already studied programming languages C, Visual Basic (VB), and classes of data structure and algorithms, database, operating systems, and network systems, and so on. So this class mainly focuses on studying various techniques on software development (software engineering) not programming techniques. This class has been done by the author since 1997. The organization of the class is almost same during the last four years as follows: in the first half year of the class, I at first lectured on software lifecycle models. After that, I lectured on some analysis and design methodologies, such as the structured analysis (SA), real-time SA, the entity-relationship model, the concept of object-oriented, object-oriented analysis and design. As a summary of the half year, the students were required to analyze a business process and to model it by using OMT method in the form of group exercises. At the final unit of the first half year, the teacher announced group organization as well as the problems to be tackled in the second half year. In the 2nd half year, a lot of time is spent for the exercises. According to the progress of the exercises, lectures on project management techniques such as schedule management, quality management, software metrics, etc. and lectures on verification techniques such as inspection and testing were given and they were put into practice in the exercises. The following problems were given as ones for software development: a meeting room reservation system (1997 class), a super-express seat reservation system (1998 class), a problem report management system (1998 class), a liquor stock management system (1999 class), a restaurant information management system (1999 class), and a library information management system (1999 class). I considered that the business processes of the problems are easy to understand for the students and that the system a problem is realized will be composed of several modules and the size of the system will be several hundreds of lines of code so that only one student of a group can not do all the tasks of the project. I also considered the problems had functions similar to the past years' problems so that the past years' know-how could be reused. No restrictions were given on programming language from the teacher. From understandability of user-interface, all the teams in 1997 and 1998 classes selected VB as the development programming language. In 1999 class, seven teams selected VB and one team selected Perl (CGI program).

5   An experiment on knowledge utilization

We applied the system to the 1999 class for the first time. Eight groups (31 students) were organized in the 1999 class (each group consists of around four students). The number was twice as many as that in the 1997 and 1998 class. 4 groups selected "library information management system", 3 selected "liquor stock management system", and one selected "restaurant information management system". All groups could complete their system development and they demonstrated their system at the final unit of the class.

The class was operated on the traditional style, that is, a teacher, teaching assistants, and the students meet in a classroom once a week, not a virtual classroom in the cyberspace. The teacher did not force usage of the system. Even groups that used the system did not always use the system for its all processes. But the teacher requested to create artifacts electronically and to submit them via on-line or floppy disk. As a means of on-line communication, mailing lists (MLs) for each group, for staff (teacher and teaching assistants), for all members (all students and staff) were provided.

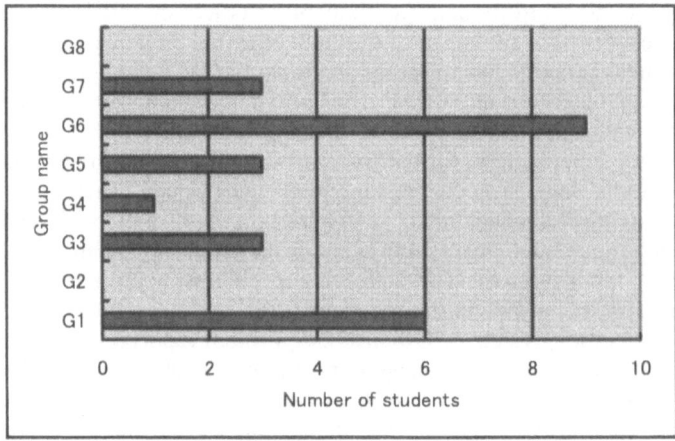

Fig. 4 Number of students who selected each group

Document types the teacher requested to create during the exercises are as follows: development plan, personal progress report, group progress report, meeting   minute,   requirement   specification,   design   document,   test specification/report, problem report, and development completion report. More than three hundreds of documents were created during the exercises of 1999 class.

I asked the students of the 2000 class to investigate the artifacts of a group in the 1999 class and to describe what they observed in the early days of the class. I asked them to report the following items: •
- which group they selected
- why they selected the group
- what they could observe

- furthermore needed information for learning

I have two objectives to this experiment:
- one is to clarify how useful the stored artifacts are at each stage of the exercises
- another is to explore requirements of a KMS

The experiment was performed at the stage before starting their exercises (May 2000). I got 25 responses. Fig. 4 shows the number of students who selected each group for observation.

The most students selected group 6 as a target of observation. The most reasons was why the task of "restaurant information system" the group selected was familiar with the students. Some students described that they selected this group because only this group selected the task. On the other hand, the second most students selected group 1 because this group was arranged at the top of the list. This means the order is one major criterion for selection.

Fig. 5 shows the result on what was observed. The most students (more than half of the respondents) pointed out "allotment of parts and importance of responsibility". "The exercises took a lot of efforts", "importance of planning" and "satisfaction after completion", "importance of documentation" followed by this order. The students pointed out matters with respect to the development process. A lot of students told that although the exercises seemed very hard, satisfaction after completion would be obtained. So this experiment gave them motivation for this class.

6 Conclusion

This paper has described a system that supports group learning of information system design and implementation. I performed one basic experiment and found some results on knowledge utilization. The experiment on knowledge utilization I reported in this paper was very limited, i.e., it was performed at the stage before starting the exercises. I am now investigating knowledge utilization during the whole exercises. We are also enhancing the system to add a function that collects data to observe students' learning behavior.

Acknowledgements

The study is supported by the Grant-in Aid for Encouragement of Young Scientists (No. A 12780120) from The Ministry of Education, Science, Sports and Culture of Japan. The author would also like to thank Mr. K. Osada for his efforts to develop the system.

266   Atsuo Hazeyama

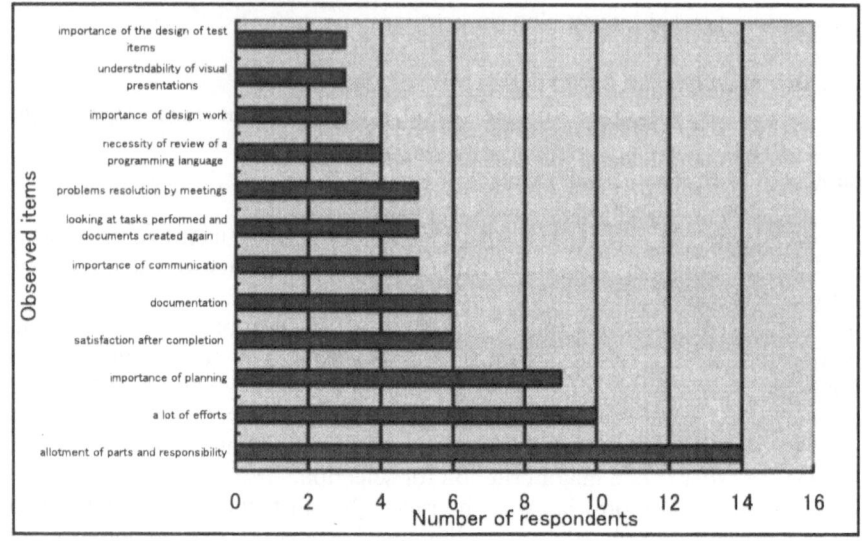

Fig. 5 The result on what was observed

References

1. Drummond S, Boldyreff C (2000) The Development and Trial of SEGWorld. Proceedings of the International Conference on Software Engineering Education and Training, IEEE CS Press
2. Hazeyama A, Miyadera Y, Xiangning L, Yokoyama S, Souma S (1999) Development of Group Programming Support System, Proceedings of the 7th International Conference on Computers in Education (ICCE99), IOS Press, Vol. 1, pp 669 - 676
3. Hazeyama A (2000) An Education Class on Design and Implementation of an Information System in a University and Its Evaluation. Proceedings of the 24th IEEE Annual International Computer Software and Applications Conference (COMPSAC2000), IEEE CS Press, pp 21-27
4. Hazeyama A, Osada K, Miyadera Y, Yokoyama S (2000) An Education Support System of Information System Design and Implementation and Lessons Learned from Its Application, Proceedings of the 7th Asia Pacific Software Engineering Conference (APSEC2000), IEEE Computer Society Press, pp 392-396
5. ISO/IEC 12207 (1995), Software Life Cycle Processes
6. Nakayama Y, Manabe T, Sasaki K, Suzuki M (1999) Knowledge Management – Development of a knowledge and information on demand system "KIDS" -. Symposium of Japanese Society for Artificial Intelligence SIG-J-9901-25, pp 137-142 (In Japanese)
7. Okada K, Matsushita A (1995), How to make a model of human interaction. SIG Groupware Technical Report of Information Processing Society of Japan 14-5, pp 25-30 (In Japanese)
8. Rein G L (1995) Teaching IS Design and Development in a Group Learning Setting. Proceedings of the Computer Supported Collaborative Learning(CSCL'95) http://www-cscl95.Indiana.edu/cscl95/rein.html

9. Shoenig S (1998) Supporting a Software Engineering Course with Lotus Notes, Proceedings of the International Conference on Software Engineering Education and Practice, IEEE CS Press

Learning Strategies for Information Systems Students

Lorna Uden and Neil Willis

School of Computing Staffordshire University, Beaconside,
Stafford, ST18 0AD. UK
E-mail: l.uden@staffs.ac.uk

Abstract. Today, students in Information Systems studies are expected to learn on their own. On top this, employers are demanding graduates with problem solving, critical thinking and independent learning skills. Students, however, find these types of demand very difficult to meet because many have no idea how to do so. To help students to become effective learners and acquire lifelong learning skills, they need to be taught higher order thinking skills such as problem solving and independent learning skills. We believe that these skills can be effectively taught to students in our Information Systems curriculum. This paper describes a case study involving the teaching of higher order-thinking skills to a group of Information Systems students at Staffordshire University in U.K. The outcomes and lessons learned are also discussed.

1 Introduction

Universities in Great Britain are expected to produce more graduates using existing resources. This can only imply larger classes. Larger classes means students have fewer opportunities for personal contact with their tutors. Students are expected to become self-directed learners. However, many students found this type of learning difficult. They often complain that we expect them to learn, yet seldom teach them how to do so. This situation is further compounded by the fact that today's students come from all sorts of backgrounds. Many of these students lack basic learning skills. Some may not even possess the necessary prerequisites for the courses they are taking. We believe that the rationale of good teaching includes teaching students how to remember, how to solve problems, how to think and how to learn and how to motivate themselves. In order to meet the above needs, a new paradigm shift in our teaching is required. This new paradigm shift requires that students be taught these higher–order thinking skills. To help our students to acquire these important skills, we have decided to incorporate them in our information systems teaching. Subsequent sections of this paper describe a case study showing how these skills can be taught to students to help them to learn better. The case study involves the teaching of these skills as part of our undergraduate modules in information systems, known as Instructional Software Design (ISD). Section two of the paper provides an overview of higher-order thinking skills. Section three is a case study showing how these skills are incorporated in our teaching. The outcomes and lessons learned are described in section four. Section five concludes the paper by urging for further research in this new paradigm.

Higher–order thinking skills

These are skills that can be applied across subject matter domains. They are often referred to as generic skills. Higher-level skills tend to be more complex and take longer to acquire than domain-specific skills. They have an *application aspect* in that one must learn to generalise the skills to various, previously unencountered sets of inputs or conditions. Usually they have an *understanding aspect* in that certain understandings are often necessary to transfer the skills to such diverse situations across subject matter domains. Sometimes they have a *recall aspect* in that it may entail remembering the sequence of several activities. Hence, to learn to do higher-level thinking (e.g. problem solving), it is helpful to be taught appropriate *procedures* (identify the goal, analyse the givens, etc.) and *understandings* (what approaches or strategies work best in different situations). Higher-order thinking skills can be categorised into two main groups: learning strategies and problem solving.

Learning strategies

Learning strategies, sometimes referred to as cognitive strategies, can be defined as behaviour and thoughts that a learner engages during learning, which are intended to influence the learner's encoding process (Weinstein & Mayer 1986). They represent complex mental operations that assist learners to perceive, store, retain and recall different forms of knowledge or performance. Unlike traditional instructional techniques, learning strategies are not intended to teach learning-specific course content. Rather they are generalisable, transferable mental skills designed to teach learners how to learn. Weinstein and Mayer (1986) listed several categories of learning strategies. These include basic and complex rehearsal strategies, basic and complex elaboration strategies, basic and complex organisational strategies and effective and motivational strategies. Some of the learning strategies that can be used across subject domains are the chunking or organising strategies, the spatial strategies, bridging strategies and general-purpose strategies.

Chunking Strategies comprise a large assortment of organising strategies. These strategies enable the rational ordering, classifying, or arranging of complex arrays. They aid learners in intellectual management of large amounts of data or very complex processes or events. The Spatial Strategies generally consist of patterns which may be visually displayed and consist of a 'big picture' displaying and organising a substantial amount of information. There are several types of spatial strategies available. These include concept mapping and networking. Bridging strategies help students to apply prior knowledge to new information in relatively systemic ways. The two bridging strategies are (i) advance organisers and (ii) metaphors and analogies. The general purpose strategies are so called because they may be used to process many kinds of material for many purposes. General-purpose strategies include rehearsal, imagery and mnemonics.

Problem solving skills

Problem-solving skills are among the most important higher order thinking skills. Problem-solving involves the use and application of skills for finding solutions, making decisions, and thinking inventively. Effective problem solving involves a number of specific skills that include: (a) problem identification/posing (including problem representation), (b) distinguishing relevant from irrelevant information and understanding the problem well enough to know what information is missing, (c) searching for appropriate information (both existing knowledge and new information), (d) identifying and evaluating alternative outcomes and solution strategies, (e) knowing when and how to try out the selected alternative and (f) the ability to use both general and domain-specific strategies.

Teaching higher order-thinking skills

There is general consensus among researchers (Weinstein & Mayer 1986; Derry & Murphy 1986) that learning strategies can be trained or taught, that is, learners may acquire, through instruction and practice, the strategies mentioned. Typically, there are two methods of teaching higher-order thinking skills: Detached training and Embedded training.

(i) Detached training

Learning strategies may be explicitly-aught study skills (detached). Most programs designed to teach problem solving and learning strategies have treated academic subject matter as incidental practice material. This approach is exemplified by the learning strategies courses developed by Dansereau (1978) and Weinstein and Underwood (1985). These programs are stand-alone curricula in which tactics and strategies acquisition, rather than subject-matter learning is the primary aim. They teach and provide practice in using general processing and self-management schemes that are 'detached' from any particular curriculum, but are applicable to a wide variety of learning situations. A potential strength of detached strategies is their generalisation for other tasks.

(ii) Embedded training

An alternative method that can supply long-term practice is embedded strategies training, which provides instruction and experience in the use of learning goals. In this approach, the learning strategies are embedded into regular instructional materials. This technique incorporates explicit instruction on text processing directly into the instructional materials. This is accomplished by adding metacognitive cues to the regular materials in the form of step by step prompts, directions on how to think, think-aloud models, or study prompts. Evaluation of this approach by researchers Campione and Armbruster (1985), showed improved performance. For best results, Derry and Murphy (1986) recommend a combined approach.

2   Case Study

We have been concerned about how we can help students to acquire more effective learning strategies.   Our research shows us that the learning of higher-order thinking skills could indeed be taught to students as demonstrated by researchers Weinstein & Underwood, (1985). We decided to apply what we have learned to our teaching for our Information Systems students.

We believe that one of the main aims of education, whether stated explicitly or implicitly, is to that students must be able to appropriately transfer knowledge and skills acquired in one setting to another (e.g. from one course to another or from courses to a job situation).   Given the central importance of transfer in our educational system, it is surprising that relatively little attention has been paid to this issue.   As a step towards remedying this neglect, we have decided to incorporate the teaching and learning of transfer skills to our Information Systems students in one of our modules, Instructional Software Design (ISD).   ISD was a final year Information Systems module offered to undergraduate students at Staffordshire University.   There are two main aims for the ISD module: (a) to apply sound software engineering principles to the design and development of instructional materials and (b) to show students how to learn effectively. The latter would help students to develop skills that can be transferable to other Information Systems subjects.

ISD Overview

The ISD module draws on a wide range of subject areas such as instructional design and learning theories, software engineering principles and methods, information systems methodologies, HCI, hypermedia and multimedia, cognitive science, collaborative working and Internet technology. Students enrolled on the module came from various backgrounds, many of the students being from the lower ability group.   In order to achieve our objectives in ISD, we needed to consider how best to teach for transfer – to teach skills that are transferable, as opposed to specific skills for each situation, which builds students' performance on a narrow range of school tasks Perkins & Salamon, 1988). To begin to address the issue of transfer and to meet employers' needs, higher-order thinking skills such as problem solving and learning strategies must be an integral part of our information system teaching. We need to provide an environment where students would be exposed to the promotion of learning of these skills.   To provide such an environment, we have adopted both an embedded and a detached approach to our ISD teaching.

Integrating learning strategies into ISD

This section briefly reviews how we integrated higher order thinking skills in our ISD teaching. We followed the recommendation of Derry and Murphy (1986) by adopting both embedded and detached approaches.

Embedded strategies in ISD

During the normal classes, students were taught the various components of the ISD module. Embedded in the teaching was the use of general purposes strategies such as rehearsal, imagery, mnemonics, and bridging strategies such as advance organisers, metaphors and analogies, and conceptual modelling.

Rehearsal is a category name for another set of miscellaneous ways of study or comprehension. Examples are reviewing material, asking questions, answering those questions, predicting possible questions, predicting material to follow, and summarising. Imagery is the mental visualisation of objects, events and arrays. A typical technique is to ask students to form a mental picture. This can be a very powerful learning aid. Mnemonics are artificial aids to memory. There are several types, one of which is *First Letter Coding*. First letter coding is the forming of some words or sentences, or some other verbal strings to aid recall. Presented prior to new material, an advance organiser is a brief, abstract passage of prose. It is a bridge, a transition statement, which is not only a summary of prior learning prerequisites to new material, but is also a brief outline of the new material. Advance organisers are unique among the strategies in that, generally, students cannot be expected to create them. This is the task of the tutor. Metaphor and Analogy strategies are used to transpose meaning from one idea, concept, procedure or event to another. They help to sensitise students to similarities across knowledge arrays. Well known analogies can, according to Halpern (1987), be used as an aid to comprehension, memory and problem solving. Analogies often make abstract concepts more concrete, usually by providing a memorable mental image. One promising instructional technique for improving students' understanding of scientific explanation is the use of a conceptual model. A conceptual model is defined as words and/or diagrams that are intended to help learners to build mental models of the systems being studied. It highlights the key concepts from the text and suggests relations among them. Students given the conceptual model instruction may be more likely to generate creative solutions to transfer problems (Mayer 1989).

Detached strategies in ISD

In the tutorial sessions, detached training was taught. During these sessions, students were exposed to problem solving strategies including both well-structured and ill-structured problem-solving methods, spatial strategies such as concept mapping and networking, and general strategies such as paraphrasing, imagery, and Vee diagramming. Throughout the lessons we tried to emphasise to students the importance of applying learning strategies that can help them improve their learning. To help our students to learn more effectively, we have included the following three learning strategies: (i) Concept Mapping, (ii) Vee Diagramming, and (iii) Networking. Concept mapping is a meta-learning strategy based on the Ausubel-Novak-Gowin theory of meaningful learning (Novak, 1990). Cognitive psychologists believe that the use of concept mapping enhances thinking and learning. It stimulates organisation and elaboration of knowledge. Concept mapping is a way of graphically displaying concepts and relationships between, or among concepts. In concept mapping, concepts are placed in a visual array.

Relationships are recorded in spaces between connected concepts. The complete map is a display of those concepts with relationships plotted and reveals a single view of patterns of interrelationships. Concept mapping is useful for the learning of concepts and principles in the knowledge domain. It is also very appropriate for concept classification, procedure application and principle application in cognitive skills learning. Vee diagrams are a heuristic tool developed by Gowin (Novak, 1990) to represent the structure of knowledge and the epistemological elements that are involved in new knowledge construction. This structure is based upon a constructivist epistemology that sees the production of new knowledge as a human construction. The Vee heuristic represents a constructivist view of knowledge that illustrates the dozen or so epistemological elements that interact in the process of new knowledge construction. Unlike the paraphrase/imagery technique that requires the student to transform text into natural language or pictures, the networking strategy requires the materials to be transformed into node-link maps, or networks. During acquisition, the student identifies important concepts or ideas (nodes). As an aid to this endeavour, students are taught a set of named links that can be used to code the relationships between ideas. The networking process emphasises the identification and representation of *hierarchies* (type/part), *chains* (lines of reasoning/temporal orderings/causal sequences) and *clusters* (characteristics/definitions/analogies). Assessments of networking (Dansereau, 1978) have shown that students using this strategy perform significantly better on text-processing tasks than do students using their own methods. The transformation of prose into a network assists the student in seeing the overall concept being presented by a lecturer. In addition, having coded the material in terms of named links gives the student the option of using these links to gain access to the material during retrieval.

The Outcomes

In order to evaluate the benefits of this learning, we decided to interview students. Most students expressed overwhelmingly that they benefited from the teaching of these skills. They agreed that many of the learning strategies were very useful. Students particularly found that conceptual modelling and concept mapping techniques very useful to help them unravel difficult concepts and principles with which they were unfamiliar. Many commented on the higher grades they had since obtained with other subjects following their being taught higher-level thinking skills. One student who has now graduated and is working in Information Systems in Singapore wrote in recently. He expressed his gratitude for having the opportunity of learning the higher-order thinking skills, which he is convinced have enabled him to be a more effective and efficient employee than his colleagues, as observed by his superiors. However, the greatest impact we believe these skills had on these students was the comment made to us that for the first time in their lives, they actually *enjoyed* learning and found it fun.

Lessons Learned

Much of the training research literature documents the problems of transfer without specific training. However, we have found effective methods of dealing with this problem in detached training during our tutorial sessions. These include (a) referring to a variety of academic content areas in information systems studies when presenting material about learning principles and strategies; (b) directly addressing the issue of transfer when providing examples; (c) providing practice exercises in a variety of content areas; (d) conducting group discussions of strategies or skills use, using a 'brainstorming' format; and (e) requiring that students document their use of learning strategies and problem-solving methods in their log books which were reviewed by ourselves.

As for us, many lessons were learned. We were very surprised to find that students really had no idea of any basic learning skills. Many had no idea how to break a problem down, how to identify the relevant information and analyse the problem. They had no idea that there are methods and techniques available that could help them to better understand the problem and to solve it. Students were amazed that they could actually help themselves to become better learners with the necessary learning strategies. Most found learning to be much easier having learned the strategies.

3   Conclusion

Students need higher-order thinking skills to equip themselves to learn better. The learning of those skills can be efficiently taught to IS students embedded in their subject domains. Our case study has shown that students benefited from the teaching of these skills. Of course, our evidence is only anecdotal evidence. However, it is rare to find students who are able to point to specific elements in their course and relate them to their assignments in other subjects. This is particularly so when they make explicit comments about certain strategies they used in their assignments. This makes their feedback more substantial as an assessment of the course's success. Even more important is the fact that the students felt able to make this assessment - that is, they clearly knew what they were learning and how they had learned.

Although feedback from our students revealed that they had improved their learning strategies and work, the result is difficult to interpret due to the lack of control data. We had problems in obtaining an appropriate control group, which included: (a) resources too limited to have another tutor taking another ISD group; (b) students are not easily comparable; and (c) it was not possible to impose on the time of other tutors for the purposes of this research. To properly assess the impact of the higher-order thinking skills would require further empirical studies.

We are aware that these higher order thinking skills were taught to ISD students and not other subjects areas such as E-Commerce or Knowledge management, however, it is our belief that no matter what domain subject we teach, students all required these skills in order to learn effectively. We therefore urge our colleagues to join with us in further research in an effort to help students become better learners.

References

1. Campione, J.C. & Armbruster, B. (1985). Acquiring Information from Texts: an analysis of four approaches. In J.W. Segal, S. Chapman & R. Glaser (eds.), Thinking and Learning Skills (Vol. 1.pp 297-317) Hillsdale, NJ: Lawrence Erlbaum Associates.
2. Dansereau, D.R. (1978). The development of a learning strategy curriculum. In H.F. O'Neil Jr. (ed.), Learning Strategies. pp.1-29. New York, Academic Press.
3. Derry, S. & Murphy, D.A. (1986) Designing Systems that Train learning ability. From Theory to Practice, Journal of Educational Research, 56, 1-39.
4. Halpern, D. F. (1987). Thoughts and knowledge: An introduction to critical thinking. Hillsdale, NJ: Lawrence Erlbaum Associates.
5. Mayer, R.E. (1989). Models for Understanding. Review of Educational Research. Spring, No. 1, 43-64.
6. Novak, J.D. (1990). Concept Maps and Vee Diagrams: Two metacognitive tools to facilitate meaningful learning: Instructional science, 19, 29-52. Kluwer Academic Publishers, Netherlands.
7. Perkins, D. & Salomon, G. (1988). Teaching for transfer. Educational Leadership, September, 22-32.
8. Turner, R. & Lowry, G. (1999). The Complete Business Information System Graduate: What students think employers want and what employers say they want in new graduates.
9. Weinstein, C.E., & Underwood, V.L. (1985). Learning Strategies: the how of learning. In J.Segal, S. Chipman & R. Glaser (eds.) Relating Instruction to Basic Research (pp. 241-258). Hillsdale, NJ: Lawrence Erlbaum Associates.
10. Weinstein, C.E., & Mayer, R. (1986). The teaching of learning strategies. In Merlin C. Whitrock (ed.), Handbook of Research on Teaching (3rd edition) Macmillan Publishing

Do-It-Yourself Electronic Lectures in Microsoft Powerpoint

Dan Diaper, Jacqui Taylor and Lee Hadaway

School of Design, Engineering and Computing, Bournemouth University, Talbot Campus, Fern Barrow, Poole, Dorset BH12 5BB, U.K.
E-mail: {ddiaper, jtaylor, lhadaway} @bournemouth.ac.uk

Abstract. Do-It-Yourself Electronic Lectures (DIYELs) are intended to allow academics to easily and effeciently convert lecture material in Microsoft Powerpoint into an e-lecture that can be delivered to students on their own computer. Our current design of DIYELs is described, and how these can be created. Example tricks when using Powerpoint are provided to illustrate how to increase the ease and efficiency of DIYEL production. The potential, global market for e-lectures is discussed.

Keywords: Do-It-Yourself Electronic Lectures, Microsoft Powerpoint, video recording, multimedia, hypertext.

1   Introduction

Traditional university lectures are only weakly interactive. Lectures are therefore a good, initial candidate for converting to an electronic format because they require less understanding of modern, socio-constructivist theories of learning [8] than more interactive teaching methods such as seminars. It has been argued that such theories are essential for developing quality distance learning materials [5, 6]. While lecturing is only a small part of most academics' job [1], because lectures are the most formal means of teaching students, generally they take longer to prepare than other teaching methods. The Do-It-Yourself Electronic Lecture (DIYEL) approach is intended to provide a means of easily and quickly converting traditionally delivered lectures into electronic ones.

Viewed by students on a computer, ideally e-lectures will include a hypertext architecture to support access to specific parts of the e-lecture and additional materials. While this chapter does call for the development of a global, e-lecture market, it primarily focuses on the production of DIYELs. Our aim is to expose the feasability of the approach.

2   Microsoft Powerpoint

Excluding word processors, Microsoft Powerpoint is almost certainly the most widely used software for lecture preparation. Many lecturers are familiar with basic Powerpoint features and our DIYEL approach uses only Powerpoint so there are no additional software purchase and learning costs. The Powerpoint reader is available free from the Microsoft web site and, as part of Microsoft Office, Powerpoint is widely available to most PC users. Our use of Powerpoint is therefore inclusive in that most lecturers around the world will be able to produce DIYELs on low specification PCs using their existing software.

Powerpoint is a multimedia, hypertext authoring tool. It is, however, highly constrained functionally. This facilitates ease of usage. Preparing Powerpoint DIYELs, however, pushes the software to its limits. For example, while it is extremely easy to insert a video clip into a Powerpoint slide, to control the automatic presentation of video and coordinated text and graphics requires a range of tricks to overcome Powerpoint's limited functionality.

3   A DIYEL Example

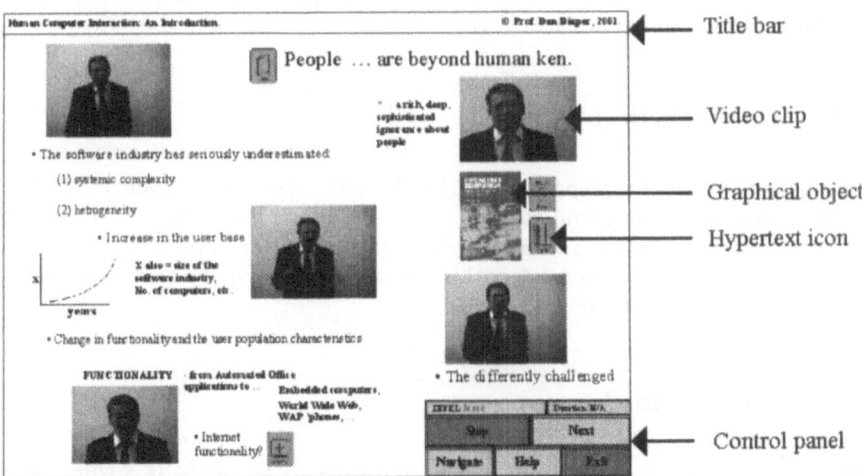

Figure 1. An Example DIYEL screen.

Figure 1 shows a typical DIYEL screen. When viewed as an e-lecture, each screen starts blank execept for the top title line and the Control Panel in the bottom right corner. Each video clip then appears in turn and the text and graphics appear during the clip. Slides in our design take around 4 minutes to run.

The first DIYEL we produced used a single video clip per slide, always located in the same place. One criticism made of this was that viewers soon ignored the clip. Our current design tries to maintain attention by using several shorter clips, in different locations and sizes and with some variety in camera shot.

A slide's animation can be halted with the control panel's [Stop] button, otherwise at its end, after eight seconds or if the [Next] button is selected, the next slide will start. To the user, the [Stop] button causes the video clip to halt and the rest of the slide to be displayed. In the software, the user has been moved by a hyperlink to a copy of the slide; a control page, which has the slide and control panel hyperlinks enabled. Hyperlinks allow the user to move to other parts of the DIYEL and to its associated documents. Video clips can be viewed directly from the control page; an automatic Powerpoint facility. The [Navigate] button moves the user to a page that shows titled icons of all the slides and additional materials and how these are connected, i.e. the hypertext semantic net. Selecting an icon moves the user to the control page version of a slide which can then be started or other hyperlinks followed. Currently the help pages provided are not context sensitive, i.e. the same help information is provided from wherever accessed.

Hypertext semantic net design can become very complicated. To ameliorate this and make errors less likely during production and subsequent maintenance, we have developed a generic, constrained semantic net design. Central to this is that all hypertext facilities are only accessed by a control page. More complex designs can be implemented in Powerpoint but this quickly becomes difficult, particularly where there are cyclical semantic net structures and hyperlinks use unnamed links, e.g. last slide viewed, previous/next slide in sequence.

4   DIYEL Production

There are five stages to preparing a DIYEL and these are introduced in the following subsections. A complete description of all the tricks involved in each stage, however, is beyond the scope of this chapter, but examples in each stage exemplify our DIYEL approach of pushing Powerpoint's capabilities to the limit while keeping things as simple as possible.

5   Slide Preparation

Usually when preparing Powerpoint slides, the text on the slide is written in a small number of text boxes. Text within these boxes is then animated so as to be progressively exposed. This works fine when manually triggered, but fails under automatic control because the temporal properties of each text box are global to it. It is virtually impossible to coordinate a video clip with Powerpoint's progressive exposure within a text box, unless both are very short. There is also a problem displaying graphics during text box animation because Powerpoint has a linear control structure to slide content exposure. This can be overcome by using a large number of text boxes, one for each bit of text that is to appear.

It is tedious to create slides using many text boxes. While heavily dependent on personal style, we commonly use more than 20 text boxes per slide. One trick that considerably reduces the burden of using many text boxes is to first prepare the slide using Powerpoint's two default text boxes and then use cut-and-paste. This is a simple example of a solution based on many hours of playing with Powerpoint's low level features and it should be noted that the trick involves both knowing what to do and how to do it, as efficiently as possible, i.e. it involves both structural and procedural knowledge.

We have produced a number of templates that consist of styles of slide which contain invariant features, such as title and copyright, and the appropriate settings of each type of slide's DIYEL Control Panel.

6   Lecture Recording

Modern Digital Video Cameras (DVCs) are now relatively cheap and record at a high quality ("broadcast"). Indeed, the problem with them is that their quality is far higher than necessary for a DIYEL and their computer files are massive. This means that a DVC recording has to be compressed before it can be sensibly used in a DIYEL. We are currently investigating using webcams as these are extraordinarily cheap (about £30 sterling) and compression is done at recording. Their disadvantage is that, while fine for 'talking-head' shots, they are harder to use than a DVC for more distant views and, of course, one is tied to one's PC.

To record a DIYEL is very simple. It is easy to just locate a DVC on a tripod in a lecture theatre and record the lecture as given to the students. Lecturing to students is a performance and our experience, admittedly using only very experienced lecturers, is that most of a live lecture can be used in a DIYEL. We've also recorded lectures in empty lecture theatres and an office, which has the advantage that one can easily address the DVC and monitor oneself on it's screen. This results in a video clip which when viewed has the lecturer making eye contact with the viewer. When shooting without an audience, we've recorded a lecture twice and, bar perhaps a couple of minutes, there's generally at least one example of each required clip that is good enough for use in a DIYEL.

There exists a view that people are extremely sophisticated viewers of television and films [4] and they therefore have very high expectations of production quality in these media. We question the relevance of this view to e-lectures because, just as student's do not apply the same production criteria to a live university lecture as they would to something performed by professional actors, so they will be prepared to have different production quality criteria for e-lectures to those of professionally produced television programmes and films. Furthermore, many students are familiar with the poor quality of current virtual reality systems, which might, in any case, be a more appropriate metaphor.

We've found that using relatively distant shots of a lecturer, somewhere between 'head-to-toe' and 'waist-up', to be successful and to have the following advantages. First, this is the view student's have of a lecturer in a lecture theatre so they can recruit their prior knowledge of lectures. Second, such shot styles provide variety and, third, they support paralingustic communication, particularly with respect to hand and arm movements. Both variety and paralinguistic advantages, we believe, make our style of distant shots better than only using 'talking-head' ones. Undoubtedly this style means that there is some loss of paralinguistic facial cues, but we are unsure as to how serious is this problem until we have conducted some experimental evaluation of it. Fourth, the camera's apparent ability to exaggerate behaviours, make people look fatter, etc. seems to us reduced by distance. Fifth, the space in which the lecturer is appropriately 'in-shot' is larger the more distant the shot, which means that all but the maddest lecturing "pacers" can be accommodated without changing their lecturing style.

7   Video Clip Insertion and Slide Animation

Once a lecture has been recorded, then it is broken up into video clips. We currently use a software video editing package which also compresses the DVC recording. Recognising that many academics will not have access to such software, we are also investigating using the DVC controls to cut the recording into clips. Our clips last about 30-120 seconds, usually with four to six per slide.

Inserting video clips into Powerpoint slides is extremely easy, but animating the text and graphics so that they appear in a coordinated fashion with the clips is a tedious process because each clip has to be repeatedly viewed and the time of each event set to the nearest second. The linear control structure of Powerpoint, where each event is triggered so many seconds after the immediately previous one, means that if N seconds are added to one event, then N seconds must be substracted from one or more later ones. One trick which makes this process much easier is to work on the clips in reverse order on each slide. This saves an enormous amount of time as only the clip being worked on needs to be repeatedly viewed while the timings are being set.

8   Hyperisation

Hyperisation is the process of converting a linear document into a hyperdocument [7]. For e-lectures to be more than simple video recordings, it is necessary that students can choose which parts they access. We advise students to watch the DIYEL first, as if attending a lecture, and then to return to parts of it for more thorough study by using the Navigate screen. Our DIYEL slides also contain hyperlinks to: additional slides not part of the main lecture sequence; associated documents for students to read; reference lists; contact information; web site addresses; and, we hope in the future, advertisements from publishers, professional organisations, and others. Powerpoint creates hyperlinks in two ways, which function identically. First, objects such as text boxes, graphics and action buttons can be made links. Second, a text string can be made a link and if done so will be underlined. An easy error to make is to make the text in a text box or on a button the link, rather than the object itself. Not only can this lead to confusion, but also to maintenance problems if both text and object have links which, in error, no longer point to the same location. Keeping things simple, we only use objects and we have created a small number of icons to indicate links that can be followed from a control page (See Figure 1).

The amount of additional material with a DIYEL will naturally depend on topic, style and so forth. In U.K. universities, students are expected to do several hours of reading with each hour of traditional lecturing and obviously it would be desirable for some of this reading to be available with a DIYEL. The major problem we foresee is that of the copyright of commercial publishers, particularly if DIYELs are sold. Our initial DIYELs are based our own publications so as to minimise this problem. How amenable publishers will be remains to be tested.

9 Delivery

To deliver Powerpoint with video clips to other people's PCs, the DIYEL must be run through Powerpoint's Pack and Go facility under the File menu. This creates a directory containing the DIYEL and the clips. It is best to then use a short-cut to the Powerpiont DIYEL in the directory to start it.

Currently we intend to use CD-ROMs as the main way of delivering DIYELs. Most of our students own their own PC and they will borrow a CD-ROM and load this on to their hard disc. We have noticed on many older PCs that running a DIYEL from the CD-ROM drive causes consistent, repeatable crashes which we attribute to a mismatch of information transmission from CD-ROM to RAM, which we've not observed from hard disc. We are obliged to provide our DIYELs on the University's intranet as PC ownership is not required of our students, but we are concerned about the volume of network traffic that might arise if more than a few students tried to access a DIYEL simultaneously. Increased bandwidth and ubiquitous compression algorithms should, however, alleviate our current problems with network transmission.

10 Electronic Lecture Markets

The primary market of e-lectures is an academic's own university. The students have a week or two to go through a DIYEL and then they attend their seminars, etc. as usual. A small benefit to the lecturer is that they do not have to physically deliver the lecture. There are larger advantages to the university. The expansion of First World universities over the last decade [2] means that lecture theatres that were once of an adequate size are not so anymore. Building lecture theatres involves major capital costs. Using e-lectures extensively on a course could reduce pressure on existing lecture theatre space, creating greater flexibility in time-tabling, for example, which is commonly a relatively expensive operating cost in universities. E-lectures may allow a university to expand in the future beyond the limitations imposed by their current physical facilities.

The development of a secondary market for e-lectures is more visionary. One concern with recently proposed e-universities is that these will impose standardisation, globally, on university education because preparing distance learning materials is expensive [3] so an economy of scale, i.e. many students, is essential. Our proposal is intended to increase the diversity of e-lecture provision be allowing many lecturers around the world to produce DIYELs easily and cheaply. With a sufficient number of specific topics and alternatives, by different people, and at different levels of difficulty, etc., then it would be possible in future to construct a university course where nearly all the lecturing was electronic. The standard of university education around the world is not uniform so, given an adequate pool of e-lectures, then their use may lead to improvements in university education globally, without enforcing standardisation. There would be considerable, non-English speaking markets for both translation operations as well as for new materials.

This view of e-lectures may provide a marketing opportunity for either existing organisations or new ones. Assuming that the secondary market is basically a form of e-commerce, then organisations such as academic publishers, professional bodies, or governments might act as repositories of e-lectures and deal with the marketing, revenue streams, etc. Furthermore, the market may develop more quickly if handled by professional, centralised management than left to the anarchy of the web and fallible search engines. Centralised repositories might standardise formats and styles, be quality assured and academics may find a new source of revenue, which for far less effort than, for example, writing a book, may actually provide better remuneration.

11   Conclusions

Our research primarily involves taking a single software package, Microsoft Powerpoint, and investigating how it can support a particular sort of task, e-lecturing. We have produced DIYELs as described. More critically, can Powerpoint DIYELs be produced easily and efficiently by academics who do not have a computing background and the time to investigate how the software works? This is a vital consideration if large numbers of DIYELs on many topics are to be produced, as we think is desirable. Illustrated in the chapter are some of the tricks we have discovered using Powerpoint to produce DIYELs. Often we have made design choices based on simplicity and many of the detailed tricks of using Powerpoint involve knowing both what to do and how to do it efficiently. We intend within the next year to produce a DIYEL about producing DIYELs.

During the next academic year we will be using DIYELs with many groups of students for evaluation purposes as we are aware that we have made numerous low level design decisions with our first DIYELs. We intend to compare student education using either DIYELs or traditional lectures. We expect to release one, free DIYEL on a general subject to universities so as to obtain feedback when used by different students, in different pedagogic contexts around the World.

We argue that there is a potential, global market for DIYELs which might become very large. If only a relatively small proportion of lecturers each produced one or two DIYELs then this should mean that an adequate critical mass of DIYELs in different academic disciplines could be achieved within a few years. Overall, to have an adequate impact it is essential that academics have an adequate range of DIYELs to choose from, i.e. just the odd one or two isn't going to change much at all. To return to one of our main goals, a pre-requisite to establishing adequate corpii of DIYELs is that they can be easily and efficiently created by academics, most of whom are already overloaded with work.

Acknowledgement

The authors thank Bournemouth University for funding the DIYEL Project.

References

1. Hales, S. and Hazemi, R. (1998) *Reinventing the Academy.* in Hazemi, R., Hailes, S. and Wilbur, S. (Eds.) *The Digital University: Reinventing the Academy.* 8-24. Springer-Verlag.
2. Jones, A., Scanlon, E., Tosunoglu, C., Morris, E., Ross, S., Butcher, P. and Greenberg, J. (1999) *Contexts for Evaluating Educational Software.* Interacting with Computers, 11, 5, 499-516.
3. Kaye, A.R. (1993) Computer Networking for Development of Distance Education Courses. in Sharples, M. (Ed.) Computer Supported Collaborative Writing. 41-67. Springer-Verlag.
4. Kent, R. (1994) Measuring Media Audiences. Routledge.
5. Matravers, J. (1999) *Educational Systems and Social Context.* in Brookes, L. and Kimble, C. (Eds.) *Proceedings of the 4th UKAIS Conference: Information Systems - The Next Generation.* 710-719. McGraw-Hill.
6. Pouloudi, A., Baldwin, L.P., Angelopoulos, C. and O'Keefe, R.M. (1999) *Internet Technology in Distance – Not Distant – Learning.* in Brookes, L. and Kimble, C. (Eds.) *Proceedings of the 4th UKAIS Conference: Information Systems - The Next Generation.* 698-709. McGraw-Hill.
7. Rada, R. and Diaper, D. (1989) *Converting Text to Hypertext and Vice Versa.* in *Proceedings of Hypermedia/Hypertext and Object Oriented Databases.* 20-37. Unicom Seminars Ltd.
8. Squires, D. (1999) Usability and Educational Software Design: Special Issue of Interacting with Computers. Interacting with Computers, 11, 5, 463-466.

An Overview of an Interactive and Personalized Multimedia Tele-Education Environment over a Gigabit Network

Z. Cheng[1], A. He[2], T. Huang[3], A. Koyama[1], S. Noguchi[4], N. Honda[5], Y. Shibata[6] and N. Shiratori[7]

[1] School of Computer Science and Engineering, University of Aizu, Japan.
[2] Core and Information Technology Center, University of Aizu, Japan.
[3] Information System and Technology Center, University of Aizu, Japan.
[4] Sendai Foundation for Applied Information Sciences, Sendai City, Japan.
[5] Fukushima Technology Center, Fukushima Prefecture, Japan.
[6] Department of Software and Information Science, Iwate Prefecture University, Japan.
[7] Research Institute of Electrical Communication, Tohoku University, Japan
E-mail: z-cheng@u-aizu.ac.jp

Abstract. With the rapid progress of information technologies in network and multimedia fields, to build an virtual educational environment over high-speed network becomes possible and is strongly requested. Many efforts have been made for development of virtual educational environments and/or virtual universities. However, there is still a lack of a practical virtual educational environment, which supports educational activities with high degree of interactive and personalized teaching and learning.

Our goal is to develop an interactive and personalized tele-education environment, by applying the state-of-the-art technologies in high-speed network, multimedia delivery, and intelligent software agent. The tele-education mainly contain four sub-environments which are Tele-Lecture Classroom, Tele-Exercise Classroom, Tele-Self-Learning Classroom, Tele-Group Learning Classroom, which are equipped with a set of toolkits developed based on existing techniques and new established techniques. Our principle is to mix real physical classrooms and virtual online classrooms, in which high degree of interactive and personalized educational activities can be performed. By interactive, we mainly mean: (1) A teacher can instruct and discuss with a learner in a tele-class, in real-time. (2) A teacher can catch the understanding states and requests of a tele-class of learners, quickly, and respond to the requests as many as possible, with the support of provided tools. By personalized, we mainly mean: (1) A learner can ask his/her own interested question, and get responses. (2) The course contents and teaching/learning methods are provided in accordance with every learner's situation as much as possible.

In this paper, we present an overview of the environment, and discuss the required tools and techniques to build such environment. The detailed design and implementation of the environment will be described in other papers.

1 Introduction

Recent years, Information Technologies (IT) are being developed rapidly, specially in network and multimedia fields. For example, Japan Gigabit Network has been established as a test environment for developing super-high speed networks and applications based on the networks. MPEG2 coding/decoding techniques for transmitting video/audio streams become mature and practical, since some codec boards are available in PCs.

To build an virtual educational environment over a high-speed network, such as the Japan Gigabit Network, becomes possible and is strongly requested. Many efforts have been made for development of virtual educational environments and/or virtual universities. However, there is still a lack of a practical virtual educational environment, which supports educational activities with high degree of interactive and personalized teaching and learning.

Our goal is to develop an interactive and personalized education environment by applying the state-of-the-art technologies in high-speed networks, multimedia delivery, and intelligent software agents.

The whole environment will mainly contain four tele-classrooms described below.

- Tele-Lecture Classroom: where a teacher can present real-time vivid and dynamic lectures to remote and distributed learners.
- Tele-Exercise Classroom: where an instructor (a teacher or a teaching assistant) can give instructions on computer exercises or other exercises to a remote learner.
- Tele-Self-Learning Classroom: where a learner can access multimedia on-line course materials in a remote site upon the learners' demands.
- Tele-Seminar Classroom: where a group of teachers, instructors, and learners being resident in several distributed and remote sites can present their ideas and have discussion within the group.

An important feature of the educational system is *high-performance interaction*, by which we mean:

- A learner can ask the teacher questions on the course and get answers presented in various media forms in a real-time manner.
  The medias used in interactive teaching/learning fall into the following two categories: *discrete media* such as text, still image and graphics, and *continuous media* such as voice, audio, video and animation. The high-performance interaction requires real-time exchanges of the continuous media in user-to-server and user-to-user communication. It is the high-performance interaction that can create a truly successful and natural virtual university in the future.
- A teacher can catch the understanding states and requests of a tele-class of learners, quickly, and respond to the requests as many as possible, with the support of provided tools.

- An instructor can monitor a remote learner in real-time by video stream channel, and talk with the learner by audio stream channel to give him/her some instructions and advices. In the same time, the teacher can monitor the learner's operations on the learner's computer, and mark the errors on the display of the computer, and/or demonstrate the correct operations to the learner from a remote site.
- A self-learning learner can ask questions and get some answers and suggestions from remote teachers or other learners asynchronously through Email, Chat, etc., or through video/Audio channel in real-time. Awareness tools provided help the learner to find suitable persons to ask or talk with.
- A group of learner and teachers can exchange their ideas through Shared white board, and Video/audio channel online in real-time. Support tools help the members of the groups to aware each other. And a various of distant floor control are provided to increase the efficiency of discussion.

Another critical feature of this educational system is the capability of personalization, by which we mean:

- – A learner can ask his/her own interested questions freely, and get the answer from the teacher. The learner and the teacher can discuss interactively.
  – Every learner in a tele-lecture room can easily write a memo, a note, a question, and/or an idea on the course material provided online. Such memo etc. will be stored for the personal review use or other purpose.
- A learner can do an exercise on his/her own pace, and get the instruction from the teacher, when the learner has troubles, like face to face personal instruction in physical classroom.
- Personalized course contents are designed for an individual learner, in accordance with the learner's characteristic pattern of behavior, by considering different comprehensive levels, different learning routes, diversified presentation forms, and different learning methods.

Most of the current educational systems for distant learning and virtual universities are based on the Internet, such as Macro University[1], CHEER (Computer-based Hyper-Environment for Educational Reform)[2], SoI[3], and Distance Learning Classroom Using Personal Computers[4]. Although low level interactions by using the discrete media are acceptable over the Internet, its bandwidth is too narrow to support effectively communications continuous media with desired quality to conduct the above high-performance interactions in a smooth and natural way. Moreover, the current educational systems have little consideration on personalized delivery. The emphasis in our system is on the study and development of some key technologies and new online teaching/learning functions that can be implemented only over a high-speed network, the gigabit network, and provide personalized course contents and delivery methods based on techniques which can catch the learners' situations and dynamically create pages and links to suit the learners' situations.

The rest of the paper is organized as follows. Section 2 gives the outline of the environment. Section 3, 4, and 5 presents the tele-classrooms, required tools, and required techniques, respectively. Section 6 is the conclusion.

2   Outline of the Tele-Educational Environment

Fig. 1 shows the outline of the environment constructed by three layers: the top layer (Tele-classrooms), the middle layer (Toolkits), the bottom layer (Techniques).

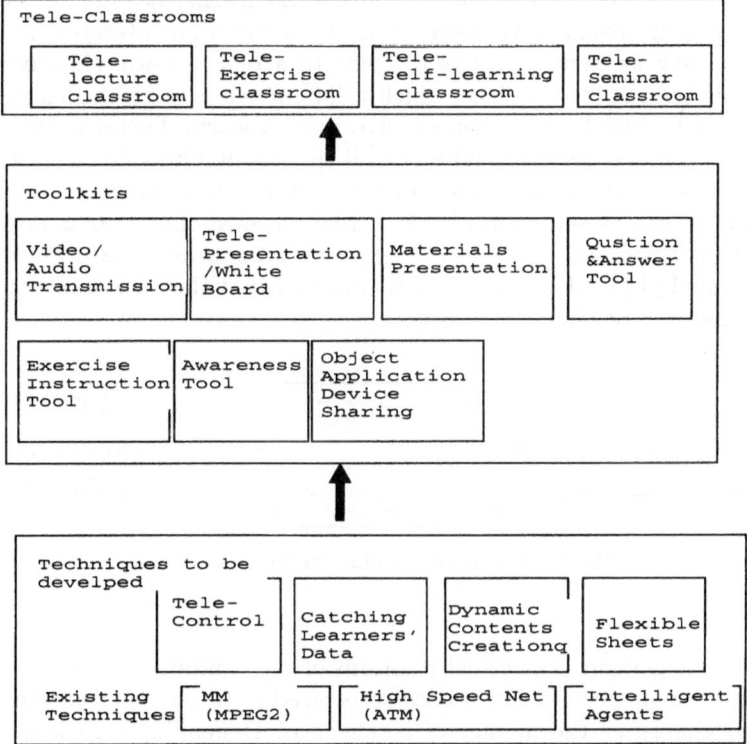

Fig. 1. Outline of the environment

The top layer consists of 4 tele-educational classrooms, each of which is equipped with some support tools. Educational activities, such as a lecture, an exercise, a seminar, or self-learning can be performed in a tele-classroom, by using the tools provided by the tele-classroom.

The middle layer consists of a set of support tools, which provide the basic support for educational activities. Those tools are developed by using existing techniques and newly developed techniques.

The lower layer consists of existing techniques, such as MPEG2 coding/decoding, ATM, and newly developed techniques, such as 1) tele-control platform, 2) techniques for catching learners' situations, 3) dynamic contents creation techniques, and 4) Flexible sheet techniques.

In later sections, we will explain those layers and basic elements in each layer, in detail.

There are many discussions on the relation between a real physical classroom and virtual online classroom. Someone claims the real physical classrooms will disappear, since they will be replaced by virtual online classrooms. Though it may be possible, from technique point of view, to construct home classroom, or desktop classroom, in which every learner has his/her own PC, and can stay in his/her own room to attend a lecture or exercise, we believe it is necessary for some learners to come to a real physical classroom, and meet other learners face to face, which will be much help for the learner to be more sociable, and have stronger motivation to learn. Therefore, we aim at a mixture of real classroom and a virtual classroom. Our tele-classroom consists of several real physical classrooms in distant sites, and connected by the gigabit network, as shown in Fig. 2. A real physical classroom is also called a site of the tele-classroom. Since the tele-classrooms are a natural extension of traditional physical classroom, it is expected that they are easily accepted, and adapted by teachers and learners.

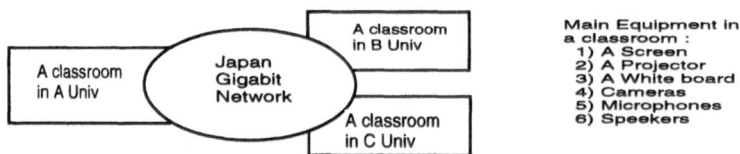

Fig. 2. A Tele-classroom consisting of 3 sites

The arrangement of physical positions of the equipment in a site and the electronic connections between hardwares need to be carefully considered, in order to guarantee the quality of a tele-class. Depending on the type of a tele-classroom, the arrangement is different. More details will be discussed in later sections.

A learner's (or a teacher's) feeling of presence in a classroom can be achieved, only when he/she can participate in interactive and personalized educational activities. The high degree of interaction doesn't only mean the learner can talk with the teacher online in real-time, but also means the teacher can understand the learner's situations of understanding level and psychological state, to make good communication. We provide tools which help the teacher to get feedback from learners easily and to monitor and analyze the behaviors of learners.

3 Tele-Classrooms

3.1 Tele-Lecture Classroom

By tele-lecture classroom, a teacher can give a live lecture to one or a group of distant learners over the gigabit network.

In order to perform the actions in a lecture mentioned above, there are following core issues:

- real-time coding/decoding and processing of voice and video data;
- multicast communication protocols for voice/video; transmissions over the gigabit network;
- synchronizations of inter-locations besides intra-medium and inter-media because learners attending the same lecture may be in remote different sites;
- tele-presentation tool and share white board;
- material presentation tool with synchronization function;
- awareness of learners' questions.

3.2 Tele-Exercise Classroom

By tele-exercise classroom, instructors can give instruction from remote sides.

The core issues in the research and development of tele-exercise classroom are:

- shared editing, execution, and/or debug windows;
- shared memo/note board;
- bi-directional video/audio;
- tools for analysis the patterns of learners.

3.3 Tele-Seminar Classroom

By tele-seminar classroom, a group of members (teachers and learners) take part in interactive synchronous discussions for collaboratively teaching/learning a subject or working on a course related project via the gigabit network. The core issues in the research and development of tele-seminar classroom are

- toolkits for group planning, scheduling and management;
- awareness of other users' states, status, environmental information, behaviors, and intentions;
- control and manipulation mechanisms for shared objects in a group workspace;
- synchronizations among shared objects, devices, and users.

3.4   Tele-Self-Learning Classroom

By tele-self-learning classroom, the teaching/learning materials of courses are stored in the course servers and accessed by each learner over the networks upon demands.

The core issues in the research and development of tele-self-learning classroom are:

- an active course structure and course-bases;
- course contents development based on the course structure and course-bases;
- toolkits for course representation, authoring, and presentation;
- course servers that are used for storing and managing teaching/learning materials which can be accessed simultaneously by many learners;
- real time operations of continuous media such as play, stop, fast forward, reverse and so on.

4   Required Toolkits

- Real-time vedio/audio transmission tools.
  Tools for real time Bi-directional vedio/audio transmission among computers in multiple distant sites. The tools provide learners and teacher(s) with a high degree of presence, and are employed in all tele-classrooms. The tools are built by using Reimay RM200 MPEG2 encoding board and Reimay RD200 MPEG2 decoding board, provided by INS engineering company, and high speed networks. The time delay from one site to another site is less than 0.3 second, by our experience. We can expect that a learner can ask a teacher a question and get a response within 1 second among in most of places, where an access point to Japan Gigabit Network exists.
- Tele-presentation tools
  A tele-presentation tool by which movement of a cursor, changing pages can be co-performed by distant sites of a tele-classroom. The tool is realized based on the tele-control platform A shared White Board with tablet as input equipment is also prepared.
- Course material presentation tool
  Browsers Internet Explorer and netscape are used for presenting course materials, which contain texts, still images, animations and movies. The browsers in distant sites can be co-perform in a synchronous way, by which the same page can be seen by a teacher and learners in the sites, or in an asynchronous way, by which a learner can learn by him/herself. The tools are employed by all tele-classrooms, and is prepared based on the tele-control platform.

- Tools for enhancing questions and answers

  The tools provide functions by which a learner can inform a teacher he/she has a question, and a teacher can point one of learners who have the questions to ask the question. The tools can also let the teacher know on which part(s) of the presentation materials or course material the class of learners have questions, by asking the learners to mark the parts on their screens. The tools are mainly used in tele-lecture classroom, and can also be used in other tele-classrooms. The tools are constructed based on flexible sheet techniques and tele-control platform.

- Instruction tools for exercises

  The tools provide a teacher the functions, by which a learner's operations on his/her computer can be monitored. The teacher can mark any place of the learner computer screen where some problems happen, to give the learner instructions. The teacher can also perform any program, command, or/and applications in the distant computer, in order to demonstrate the correct operations. The tools are employed by mainly a tele-exercise classroom, and are developed based on the tele-control platform.

- Course content construction tools

  The tools help teachers and learners to construct personalized course contents by considering every learner background, etc. The tools are mainly employed by tele-self-learning classroom, and can be used as course materials (handouts) in other classrooms. The tools are developed based dynamic contents creation techniques, and techniques for catching learners' status and situations.

- Objects and/or devices sharing tools

  The tools provide the functions, by which, objects in slides of presentation materials or on white board, and devices such as CD and DVD can be cooperated. The tools are mainly employed in tele-seminar classroom, and based on the tele-control platform.

- Awareness tools

  The tools help a teacher or a learner to be aware of other learners' existence and/or actions in other sites. The tools are mainly employed in tele-seminar classroom, and based on the tele-control platform.

- Other tools

  Besides of above mentioned tools, many others are investigated, and will be developed, depending on the requests of teachers and learners.

5   Tele-Exercises Classroom for Computer Exercises

This is a example of tele-exercisese classroom.

5.1   The Hardware

Fig.3 shows the hardware of the system having 3 sites, each of which is a physical classroom equipped with a remote control camera, a screen and following:

- A local server
  Connected to the JGN exchanging hi-quality video/audio and other data between the sites and controlling the remote control camera.
- Computers for the teacher and learners.
  Each computer has a CCD camera, a microphone and a speaker.

A global server is requested to store the lecture materials and, if necessary, synchronize all the computers. The global server also controls the construction of the network of the system.

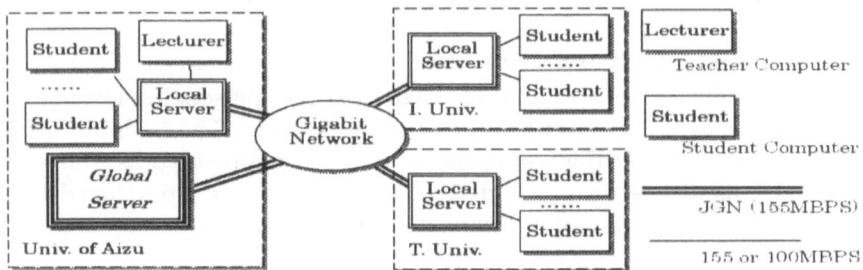

Fig. 3. The construction of the proposed system

5.2   The Software

System Mode The system works under one of following modes:

- **Presenting** Teacher computer synchronizes all other computers to support the teacher to present exercise materials to learners.
- **Discussion** Teacher computer and a student computer selected by the teacher synchronize all other computers to support the teacher to discuss with a learner.
- **Consulting** The teacher talks to a particular learner without bother others. Other learners can decide whether join the conversation or not.
- **Study** Learners learn by themselves without the help from the teacher. If necessary, the teacher can monitor any learner computer.

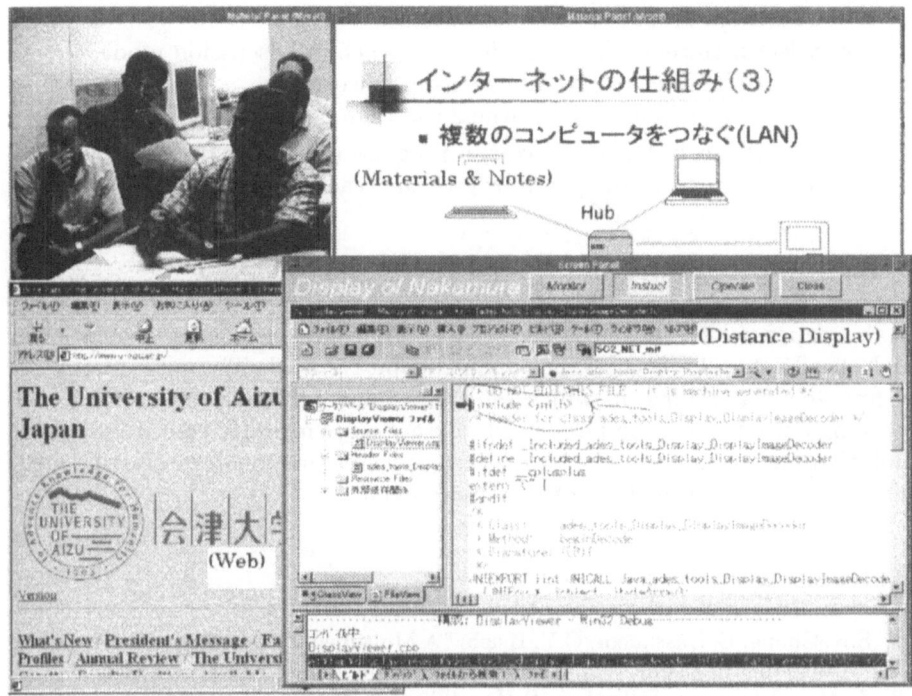

Fig. 4. An image of the main window (teacher computer)

User Interface Fig.4 shows the main window in the teacher computer. There are several sub windows under the control of the main window.

Video Window Transmitting video between the teacher and learners.

Materials Window Showing the materials presented by the teacher. Text or free lines can be written on the window and the materials can be shared by teacher and learners Discussion mode or Consulting mode. This window can be used as white board if no material is shown on it.

Web Window Used to synchronously show the contents to all computers.

Distance Display Window In this window, the screen of a learner computer is displayed and the teacher can do followings:

- **Watch** Monitor the learner computer to catch its status.
- **Indication** Drawing marks or free lines directly on the screen to give the learner more information.
- **Operation** Make remote controls to the compute to solve more serious problems.

Control Window With this window, the teacher can do following:

- Switch system mode.
- Take attendance.

- Check the progress of the exercise.
- Select a learner who wants have a speech in Discussion mode.
- Select a learner to give him/her guidance.

And with this window, the learners can do following:

- Report his/her attendance and progress to the teacher.
- Ask the teacher to speech or give the teacher requests.

6   Conclusion

In this paper, we presented an overview of a tele-education environment over high speed networks, such as the Japan Gigabit Network. The system consists of four tele-classrooms, in which interactive and personalized learning and teaching activities can be performed. We are implementing the environment and planning to deliver several real tele-lectures and tele-exercises in near future, to validate the effect of the environment.

References

1. S.K. Chang, E. Hassanein, C.Y. Hsieh: "A Multimedia Micro-University", IEEE Multimedia Magazine, Vol. 5, No. 3, July-September 1998, pp. 60-68.
2. J. Ma, R. Huang, E.Tsuboi, R.Hayasaka: "A Multimedia Collaborative Environment for Distant Education", in proceeding of the Fifth International Workshop on Distributed Multimedia Systems, Jul., 1998, pp.175-182.
3. K. OKAWA, Y. IJUIN and J.MURAI: "School of Internet – Building a University on the Internet", IPSJ Journal (Vol.40 No.10. Oct. 1999)
4. T.YOSHINO, Y.INOUE, T.YUIZONO, J.MUNEMORI, S.ITO and Y.NAGASAWA: "Development and Application of a Supporting System for Distance Learning Classroom Using Personal Computers via Internet", IPSJ Journal (Vol.39 No.10. Oct. 1998)

"Interactive Multimedia Education at a Distance– Linear Algebra (IMED-LA)": Its Present Status and Special Features of Its Content

Yasuhiko Ikebe[1], DongSheng Cai[2], Yoshinori Miyazaki[3], Nobuyoshi Asai[1], Yasushi Kikuchi[1] and Maha Ashour-Abdalla[4]

[1] The University of Aizu, Japan E-mail: {ikebe, nasai, kikuchi}@u-aizu.ac.jp
[2] The University of Tsukuba, Japan   E-mail: cai@is.tsukuba.ac.jp
[3] Sizuoka Sangyou University, Japan   E-mail: yoshi@ssu.ac.jp
[4] The University of California   E-mail: maha@cdi.ucla.edu

Abstract. The IMED-LA or Interactive Multimedia Education at a Distance - Linear Algebra is the ongoing international joint project by the collaboration of the Japan Team currently consisting of five members and the Center for Digital Innovation (CDI) of the University of California at Los Angeles (UCLA) headed by Director Maha Ashour-Abdalla. The project started in July, 1999. Its goal is the production of virtual university content in linear algebra, intended primarily for graduate students and working students who need a fast-paced study of the basic facts from linear algebra; hence the content can also effectively be used by the beginning college students under a proper guidance from the teacher. Our partially completed content is already available on the Internet at the following URL: http://www.cdi.ucla.edu/linearalgebra.

   This Internet course has several special features worth mentioning: in its approach to the subject matter, the topics selected, the way and style the exercises are supported and the provision of the philosophical or historical notes for encouraging the learners or opening up new horizons for them. At the same time no mathematical rigor is sacrificed and a high level of standard is maintained.

It is our pleasure to state that, thanks to our collaboration, the Japan team mainly providing authoring and the UCLA team the needed IT and project management expertise, the project has been enjoying a steady progress and the both teams are gaining valuable practical experiences. At the present this project is probably only one of its kind as an international joint Virtual University Content Production Project between Japanese and US universities. In this paper we will discuss the content under construction, the needed IT support and the project management technology being employed. For the activities of the CDI/UCLA, see their home page: http://www.cdi.ucla.edu.

Keywords: Interactive Multimedia Education, Content Production, Virtual University, Linear Algebra, Distance Education.

1   Introduction

The IMED-LA or Interactive Multimedia Education at a Distance - Linear Algebra, is the ongoing international joint project by the collaboration of the Japan Team currently consisting of five members and the Center for Digital Innovation (CDI) of the University of California at Los Angels(UCLA) headed by Director and Professor of Physics Maha Ashour-Abdalla.

The project started in July, 1999. Its goal is the production of virtual university content in linear algebra, intended primarily for graduate students and working students who need a fast-paced study of the basic facts from linear algebra; the content can also be used effectively by the beginning college students under a proper guidance from the teacher.

Our partially completed content is already available on the Internet at the following URL: http://www.cdi.ucla.edu/linearalgebra.

It is our pleasure to state that, thanks to our collaboration, the Japan team mainly providing authoring and the UCLA team the needed IT support and project management expertise, the project has been enjoying a steady progress and the both teams are gaining valuable practical experiences. At the present this project is probably only one of its kind as an international joint Virtual University Content Production Project between Japanese and US universities.

This Internet course has several special features worth mentioning: in its approach to the subject matter, the topics selected, the way and style the exercises are supported and the provision of the columns dedicated to philosophical or historical notes. All this is designed in order to allow the learner to grasp the basic structure AND facts of linear algebra at a minimum time without sacrificing mathematical rigor or the level of standard..

Thus, the main structure of the basic linear algebra is neatly summarized in SIX GREAT DECOMPOSITIONS and TWO GREAT CONCEPTS (determinant and inner product). The learner is presented as early as in Chapter 2 TWO GREAT DECOMPOSITIONS on the eigenvalue problem along with four other GREAT DECOMPOSITIONS.

The 80-percent completed Internet course will be tested by the chief author in his graduate course in applied computation in the Fall of this year (2000) at the University of Aizu, for the soundness, integrity and usability of the content and IT support.

In this paper we will detail the content under construction, the needed IT support and the project management technology being employed.

For the general information on the back ground of the Distance Learning and its present status, refer to the following references:[1][2][3][4][5][6][7][8]. The reference [2] is our first progress report (in Japanese).

2   The Organizing Principle.

The source of power of Linear Algebra lies in its abstract approach and generality like in other branches of abstract mathematics. In a word, Linear Algebra is a study of linear transformations from one linear (vector) space to another. The design of our Internet course in Linear Algebra was begun with the determination of the content organization we should take. In Linear Algebra, three distinct but mutually complementary approaches may be employed (in the order of increasing abstractness): Equation-theoretic approach, Matrix-theoretic approach and Operator (Transformation)-theoretic approach.

Example:
The following three theorems are mutually equivalent:
I.   Equation--Theoretic Formulation
An under-determined linear homogeneous system of equations has a non-trivial solution.
II. Matrix--Theoretic Formulation
A matrix equation $\mathbf{Ax} = \mathbf{0}$ has a non-trivial solution $\mathbf{x}(\neq \mathbf{0})$ if $\mathbf{A}$ is $m \times n$ with $m < n$, where $\mathbf{x}$ represents the unknown column vector of order n.
III. Operator--Theoretic Formulation
A linear transformation from an n − dimensional space to an m − dimensional space has its kernel of dimension > 0, if $m < n$.

The existence of three such approaches is the single main source of the existence of varied approaches - and of confusion to beginners - for the study of linear algebra.

For our purpose, that is, the construction of fast-paced presentation of the basic facts from linear algebra for graduate students and working students who wish to study afresh or review the subject matter in a sound way for practical application, we decided to adopt the matrix--theoretic approach as the central guiding principle for our presentation of the Internet course. This choice was a result of the long teaching experience and study of the first author(Y. Ikebe)'s over-the-years.

The net-result: we were able to summarize the main structure of linear algebra in six great decompositions which can be described in terms of matrix multiplication. Most of other basic facts can be derived from these decompositions.

We begin this Internet course by presenting the basic matrix operations(matrix addition, scalar multiplication, matrix multiplication, transpose, conjugation and conjugate transpose). Based on these concepts, we introduce the concepts of vector spaces and linear transformations, where such basic concepts as linear independence/dependence, basis and dimension are explained by using examples of matrices, as well as why they are important and basic. All these are done in Chapter 1.

3   Content Features

3.1   Six Great Decompositions

The six great decompositions are given below. They are presented in Chapter 2 of the Internet course.

(1) THE EQUIVALENCE DECOMPOSITION

Any given $m \times n$ matrix $\mathbf{A}$ can be decomposed into the form $\mathbf{A} = \mathbf{PDQ}$ where $\mathbf{P}$ and $\mathbf{Q}$ are invertible matrices of order m and n, respectively, and $\mathbf{D}$ has the

form $\mathbf{D} = \begin{bmatrix} \mathbf{I}_r & \mathbf{0} \\ \mathbf{0} & \mathbf{0} \end{bmatrix}$, $\mathbf{I}_r$ denoting the identity matrix of order r (the value of

r depends on $\mathbf{A}$ only and is called the rank of $\mathbf{A}$).

(2) THE JORDAN DECOMPOSITION

Any given $n \times n$ matrix $\mathbf{A}$ can be decomposed into the form $\mathbf{A} = \mathbf{VJV}^{-1}$ where $\mathbf{V}$ is an invertible matrix and $\mathbf{J}$, the Jordan normal form of $\mathbf{A}$, is a block diagonal matrix, where each diagonal block, a square matrix known as a Jordan

block, has the form $\begin{bmatrix} a & 1 & & \mathbf{0} \\ & a & \ddots & \\ & & \ddots & 1 \\ \mathbf{0} & & & a \end{bmatrix}$. (Even when $\mathbf{A}$ is real, $\mathbf{V}$ and $\mathbf{J}$ are

generally complex matrices. The diagonal components of $\mathbf{J}$ are the eigenvalues of $\mathbf{A}$ and the columns of $\mathbf{V}$ represent a set of eigenvectors and generalized eigenvectors).

(3) THE SHUR DECOMPOSITION

Any given $n \times n$ matrix $\mathbf{A}$ can be decomposed into the form $\mathbf{A} = \mathbf{QTQ}^{-1}$ where $\mathbf{Q}$ is unitary ($\mathbf{Q}^* = \mathbf{Q}^{-1}$, " $*$ " representing conjugate transpose) and $\mathbf{T}$ is upper triangular. (The diagonal components of $\mathbf{T}$ are the eigenvalues of .)

(4) THE LDU DECOMPOSITION

Any given $n \times n$ matrix $\mathbf{A}$ whose principal sub-matrices (including $\mathbf{A}$ itself) are all invertible can be decomposed into the form $\mathbf{A} = \mathbf{LDU}$ where $\mathbf{L}$ is a unit lower triangular matrix ($=$ a lower triangular matrix with its diagonal components all 1's), $\mathbf{U}$ is a unit upper triangular matrix and $\mathbf{D}$ is a diagonal matrix.

(5) THE QR DECOMPOSITION

Any given $m \times n$ matrix $\mathbf{A}$ where $m \geq n$ can be decomposed into the form $\mathbf{A} = \mathbf{QR}$ where $\mathbf{Q}$ is an $m \times m$ unitary matrix ($\mathbf{Q}^* = \mathbf{Q}^{-1}$) and $\mathbf{R}$ is an $m \times n$ upper triangular matrix whose diagonal components are all real and non-negative. (If $\mathbf{A}$ is real $\mathbf{Q}$ and $\mathbf{R}$ can be taken to be real.)

(6) THE SINGULAR VALUE DECOMPOSITION

Any given $m \times n$ matrix $\mathbf{A}$ can be decomposed into the form $\mathbf{A} = \mathbf{USV}^*$ where $\mathbf{U}$ and $\mathbf{V}$ are unitary matrices of order m and n, respectively ($\mathbf{U}^* = \mathbf{U}^{-1}, \mathbf{V}^* = \mathbf{V}^{-1}$) and $\mathbf{S}$ is an $m \times n$ diagonal matrix of the form

$$\begin{bmatrix} s_1 & & 0 & \\ & \ddots & & 0 \\ 0 & & s_r & \\ \hline & 0 & & 0 \end{bmatrix} \text{ where } s_1 \geq \cdots \geq s_r > 0 \text{ (} r \text{ represents the rank of } \mathbf{A} \text{)}$$

The diagonal components $s_1, s_2, \ldots, s_r, 0, \ldots, 0$ ($\min\{m, n\} - r$ 0's) are the singular values of $\mathbf{A}$.

Note once again that in each of these decompositions the matrix in question is represented as a product of two or three matrices of special type. This makes it possible to present them to the reader early in this Internet course (in fact, in Chapter 2) after introducing the fundamental set of matrix operations.

Thus, the learners get to know such important concepts as eigenvalues, eigenvectors, generalized eigenvectors and singular values early in the course. This should represent a great advantage to the learners not offered by the usual standard texts in linear algebra because the learners get to know early in their study what to study later in the course.

3.2   Two Great Algebraic Concepts

There are two great concepts of utility which are independent of the stated decompositions: the concepts of Determinant and Inner Product.

The determinant of an $n \times n$ matrix $\mathbf{A}$ represents the volume of n dimensional parallelepiped determined by its columns. For $n = 1, 2$ or 3, the geometric interpretation is clear. The main use of determinant is the fact that an $n \times n$ matrix $\mathbf{A}$ is invertible if and only if the determinant of $\mathbf{A}$ does not vanish. Another important use of determinant is the Cramer's Rule for the solution of a matrix equation $\mathbf{Ax} = \mathbf{b}$: The values of each unknown is expressed as the ratio of two determinants constructed $\mathbf{A}$ and $\mathbf{b}$. This is theoretically useful but computationally worthless. The concept of determinant is also needed to establish the fact that the eigenvalues of an $n \times n$ matrix $\mathbf{A}$ are precisely given by the roots of an n − th degree algebraic equation known as the characteristic equation of $\mathbf{A}$.

The concept of the Inner Product introduces the concept of angle and orthogonality. It also gives the concept of length of a vector. A typical example of the Inner Product is given by $(\mathbf{a}, \mathbf{b}) = \mathbf{a'b}$ (the " ' " represents transpose) on the vector space of real column vectors of order n.

3.3   Two Great Analytical Facts

In applications, matrices are mostly real or complex matrices. Hence their analytical properties are important in matrix applications. Among the properties of the real or complex numbers only the following two facts are needed in this course:
(a) The completeness of the real number system and the complex number system.
(b) All norms defined on a finite dimensional vector space are equivalent.
     The proof of these properties is beyond the scope of the course.

3.4   Other Special Features

Let us state that this Internet course includes important facts which are missing from most texts in linear algebra.
(a) Several significant examples of application of the well known dimensional identity $\dim(S \cap T) = \dim S + \dim T - \dim(S + T)$ where S and T are any pair of subspace of a given finite-dimensional vector space.
(b) Presentation of two theorems of functional calculus of matrices: Spectral Mapping Theorem and the Cauchy Contour Integral Representation of a function $F(\mathbf{A})$ where $F(z)$ represents a polynomial or rational function of a complex variable z. The proof is supplied in this Internet Course to demonstrate the power of Jordan Decomposition, the greatest of the six great decompositions.

3.5   The "coffee break"

A set of short stories written for the purpose of sustaining the learner's interest in this Internet course. They are philosophical comments, or helpful technical suggestions or historical notes. For example, "How to write good technical writings in English", "Proofs: Who need them?," historical notes on the founders of matrix theory, etc. Here the first author(Ikebe)'s long teaching experience in the US and in Japan turns out to be the main source of motivation for writing these columns.

4   Technologies for the Creation of Exercises

In IMED-LA, several (approximately 10 or so, at present) exercises are provided in each chapter. Those exercises are designed so that learners can review interactively what they learned. For implementation, we use Java as well as XML to make servlets.

Also, we classified thinkable exercises into 5 types: [A] Multiple Choice type, [B] Fill-In type, [C] Block Diagram type, [D] Free Form type, [E] Visual type (using Mathematica1). We will elaborate in the below:

[A] Multiple Choice type: This is the simplest among five listed, and one of the most frequently used methods to give interactivity on the web. In IMED-LA, this type is implemented to test the understandings of mathematical concepts, rather than letting the learner do the actual computation. Since the structure of HTML to be created is the simplest we, using XML, are not only able to provide pre-made problems, but also to let each individual teacher who will use IMED-LA prepare their own exercises easily, depending, for example, on the level of the students of the class. This cannot be done as for form other four types of exercise (because each exercise will be different in their structures).

[B] Fill-In type: This type is used to check if the learner has mastered the computational skill or can solve the problems with no hints, by requiring their direct "filling in". One example is shown below (Fig. 1 & 2). This exercise is designed to examine how the learner has grasped the concept of "strongly-connected graph". The exercise is implemented as a servlet. In response to the "submission" from the learner, the server returns the correct answer to the problem (sometimes with points).

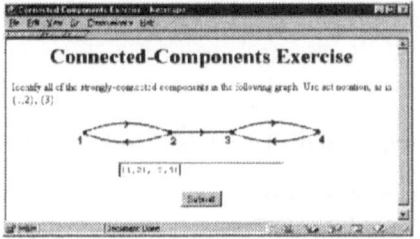 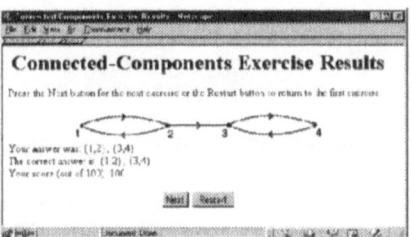

Fig. 1: Example of "Fill-in" Type (For Input)   Fig. 2: Same Example (For its Result)

[C] Block Diagram type: This type of exercise is to foster logical thinking. Each exercise is equipped with finite number of what we call "logical blocks" so that the learner selects some of them which they think are needed to derive the answer. If necessary, one can also provide some "empty" logical blocks in which appropriate notion (or formula) is to be inserted by the learner. The learner has not only to choose or make those blocks but also are required to put a set of links between "Start" button, "Finish" button, and among those selected blocks. For the proof problems appearing very often in the study of linear algebra, "Start" corresponds to the starting point of the proof, "Finish" to the proposition to be proved, and the selected blocks to the conditions given in the problem or some formulas held in linear algebra.

Let us give one example here. The figure below (Fig. 3-5) is the problem asking to prove B=C, given A*B=I, B*A=I, A*C=I and C*A=I, where A, B, C are square matrices of the same size. Thus the problem is to show the uniqueness of an

302   Yasuhiko Ikebe et al.

inverse matrix. In the combo-box [▼], mathematically relevant
axioms, theorems, and some other laws as well as given conditions are ready to be
chosen. If you find some of them appropriate from the box, you select them and
push "Add" button to let them appear in the workspace. If you think that's the
block needed first, put link from Start to the block by clicking "Link" button.
Assume Fig. 5 is the final answer created after several trials. Pushing "submit"
button, the data regarding which blocks were selected and how they are linked are
sent to the server, the learner can see where it went wrong. Of course, one can set
up the option so that those data can be just stored in the database located in the
server, without returning the instant grading to the learner. As one can see, this
type of a series of transaction is very analogous to constructing a flow chart (for
example, of computer programming). The problems of this type are also made as
servelets.

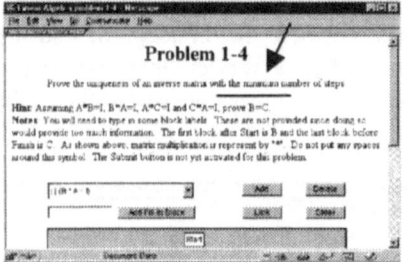 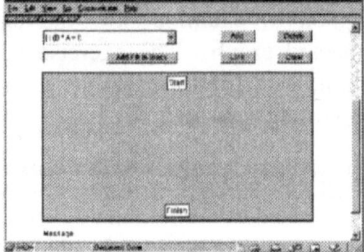

Fig. 3: Example of "Block Diagram" Type   Fig 4: Same Example (WorkSpace)

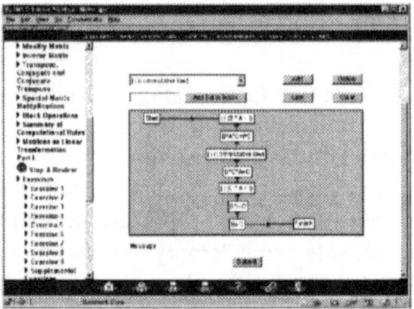

Fig. 5: Same Example (WorkSpace with an Answer Input by a Learner)

[D] Free Form type: The three types mentioned above are, more or less, lacking
in flexibility (in the sense that the learner can only choose from the offered options
(for the type [A] and [C] exercises), and in format (for the type [B] exercises)).
Some type of exercises, however, requires 100% of free input, encouraging the
learner to come up with his/her own ideas. Let this type of problem be called "Free
Form Type". One thing we have to consider, when giving this type of exercise is
that in this subject, linear algebra, many mathematical symbols may have to be

used for proof-writing, although there are no convenient ways on the web to input them. Then, in order to meet such special specification, a prototype, using the IT developed by the CDI, is being built. This type is also aimed to be implemented as servlets.

[E] Visual type: Some examples of real industrial uses or visual examples and their related project type exercises are very important for learners to stimulate their interests in studying the linear algebra. In IMED-LA, we plan to provide a few real visual examples and their related project type exercises in each chapter. In Fig. 6, we show a Mathematica version of visual examples in its note book form. The examples are the image processing problem using the singular value decomposition. The learners can down load the example note books from the web page and run them on their own PCs using their own Mathematica. For the convenience of the learners, in addition to Mathematica, we also plan to provide the same examples and exercises in Matlab and Maple formats.

5   IT and PMT Provided by CDI

The Project Management expertise is mainly supplied by the CDI/UCLA. This IMED-LA Project is the first time CDI/UCLA works with the author from the beginning of the project.

The management aspect is just as important as authoring and IT support. The content development is classified into three stages: CREATION, INTEGRATION and PRODUCTION. The two teams met face-to-face for collaboration in July, August and December, 1999, each time for about one week. The rest of the time we collaborate through the Internet.

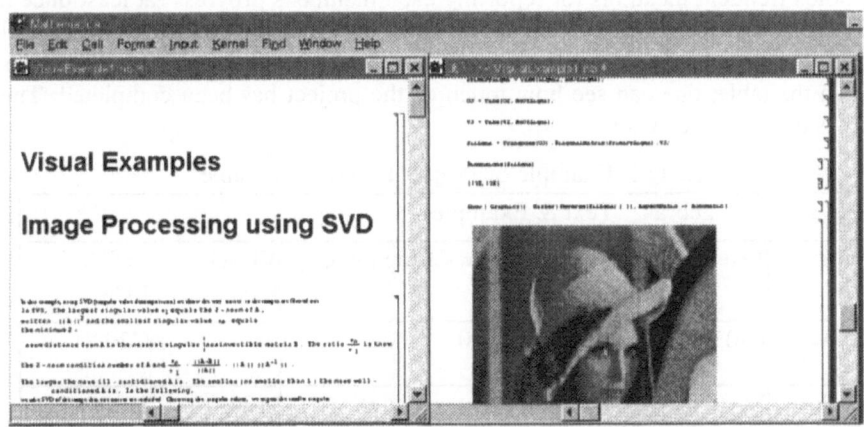

Fig. 6: Visual Example (Image Processing by the Singular Value Decomposition)

The members of the CDI/UCLA include: "Supervisor", who looks over the overall project, "Web page manager", who creates, designs, and manages web-based applications pages, "Digital image creator", who makes both moving and static images, "Editor", who corrects misleading or wrong statements (like a newspaper editor) to make products sound and consistent, "Programmer", who makes interactive contents on the web (mainly Java expert), "Network manager", who provides the best network environment for each of the team members to work together in an as effective way as possible. It also is enlists (experts such as "Video Creator" and "Font Specialist"). For more details on the CDI and its activities, see its home page at www.cdi.ucla.edu.

The IMED includes customized multimedia educational content as well as authoring tools for instructors to build their courses using their own material. The IMED also includes assessment applications and on-line office hours. The next figure (Fig. 7) is a part of the top page of IMED. Most of the functions in the menu are pre-programmed so one can develop web-based course contents with no additional costs.

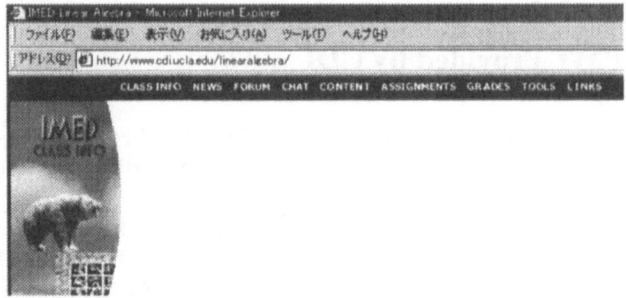

Fig. 7: Top-page of IMED System

PMT shall be explained now. In order to keep track of the status quo of projects, CDI holds frequent meetings for reporting each member's progress (at least once a week, usually twice a week), and makes a table which we shall tentatively call "Project Progressive Table" after each meeting. Since the status of each segment is filled in the table, one can see how much of the project has been completed. The below is the example (Table 1):

Table 1: Example of Project Progressive Table

IMED-Linear Algebra Text & Examples						
Chapter	Text	Image	Flow Chart	Stop& Review	Visual Example	Coffee Break
Chap. 1	P90 I90	I90	I100	I95	na	C20
Chap. 2	X100	I100	na	C0	I100	I100
...	...	...	...	...	...	...
Chap. 9	C80 I80	C80 I80	I100	C100	na	C100
Current as of : Thursday, September 2, 4:30PM Most Recent Meeting: Thursday, September 2						

"I90" means '90% of the Integration stage is done'. Also, this implies that when it comes to "C" and "P" stages, all are done. In contrast, "P90 I90" seen in Text section of Chapter 1 says that "C" stage is done 100% while "P" and "I" stages are only both 90% done". In this manner, which part of the product has to be quickly finished and whose responsibility it is (and sometimes how many extra staff have to be pitched in) is clear. It is considered that this sort of detailed table managing is essential especially to the case where each co-research member is scatteringly situated or each one is tied up with other different projects and cannot concentrate only on one. Our case is really the one.

6   Concluding Remarks

As already stated in introduction, the partially completed content is available on the Internet URL: http://www.cdi.ucla.edu/linearalgebra. The reader's comment or constructive criticism will be welcome. Please address them to imed-la@u-aizu.ac.jp.

References

1. Yasuhiko IKEBE, Dong-Sheng CAI, Yasushi KIKUCHI, and Yoshinori MIYAZAKI, A Status Report on Institutions of Higher Learning in America - with Particular Focus on Challenges from For-Profit Distance Education Universities and Corporate Universities, INFORMATION Vol.3,No.1, 89-95(January, 2000)
2. Yasuhiko IKEBE, Dong-Sheng CAI, Yasushi KIKUCHI, Yoshinori MIYAZAKI, and Maha ASHOUR-ABDALLA, Development of Interactive Multimedia Distance Leaning Program "IMED-LA", Humanity and Computer Science Activity Group Symposium Report 2000-CH-45, 49-56(January 21, 2000), in Japanese
3. R. N. Katz and Associate, Dancing with the Devil-Information Technology and the New Competition in Higher Education, Jossey-Bass Publishers, (1999)
4. J. C. Meister, Corporate University-Lessons in Building a World-Class Work Force, Revised and Updated Edition, McGraw-Hill, (1998)
5. Corporate University Exchange (news service)ARyan@corpu.com
6. Peterson's Guide to 2000 Distance Learning Programs-The Best in Distance Education from Around the World, Peterson's, (2000)
7. The NEA 2000 ALMANAC of Higher Education, National Education Association, (2000) http://www.nea.org/he
8. Y. Miyazaki, D.S. Cai,, N. Asai, Y. Kikuchi, Y. Ikebe, and M. Ahour-Abdalla, An Interim Assessment of Interactive Multimedia Education at a Distance--Linear Algebra (IMED--LA)

Distributed Multimedia Presentation with Floor Control Mechanisms in a Distance Learning System

Huan-Chao Keh, Timothy K. Shih, Lawrence Y. Deng and Teh-Sheng Huang

Dept. of Computer Science and Information Engineering, Tamkang University, Tamsui, Taipei Hsien, Taiwan 251
E-mail: tshih@cs.tku.edu.tw

Abstract. Communication over Internet is growing increasingly and will have profound implications for our economy, culture, society and education. Currently, multimedia presentation technologies among the network are most often use in many communication services. Examples of those applications include video-on demand, interactive TV and the communication tools on a distance learning system and so on .In this chapter, we describe how to present different multimedia objects on a web presentation system with floor control mechanism as a result of the distance learning environment indispensably. The distributed approach is based on an extended timed Petri net model. Using characterization of extended time Petri net, we express the temporal behavior of multimedia objects; on the other hand, we introduce the concepts of user interaction. The main goal of our system is to provide a feasible method to represent a schedule and navigation of different multimedia objects with user interaction. In addition, users can dynamically modify and verify different kinds of conditions during the presentation. To verify the structural mechanism, we implement an algorithm using the Petri net diagram, analyzing the model by time schedule of multimedia objects, and produce a synchronous set of multimedia objects with respect to time duration. Specially, we consider the interactive facilities to support the distance learning requirement. We propose a floor control mechanism, which provides four types of control (free access, equal control, group discussion, and direct contact). These control mechanisms are sufficient to the use of distance learning environment.

Keywords: Petri Net, Distributed Multimedia Presentation, Distance Learning, Floor Control, Virtual University.

1 Introduction

To control and demonstrate different types of multimedia objects is one of important functions in distributed multimedia presentation system. Unfortunately, we saw many "Black magic" compromised multimedia presentation systems; there is little theory to describe the methodologies of such compromised system.

The concept of our model is based on the Petri net [1-3]. Petri net is a graphical and mathematical modeling tool applicable to many systems. Its features can be used with both practice and theory. Thus, it provides a powerful medium of communication between them. Additional extensions have been proposed, and this has led to the following types of Petri nets: the timed Petri net, the stochastic Petri net, colored Petri net, and object-related Petri net.[6-12] The "Object Composition Petri Net"(OCPN) and the "extended Object Composition Petri Net"(XOPCN) were two graphic-based models that proposed synchronous theoretical for multimedia. The OCPN is a comprehensive model for specifying timing relations among multimedia data. The XOPCN can specify temporal relationships for the presentation of pre-orchestrated multimedia data, and to set up channels according to the required Qos of the data [4, 5]. These two models lack methods to describe the details of synchronization across distributed platforms and do not deal with the schedule change caused by user interactions in interactive multimedia systems [13]. However, when considering the network transport issue of multimedia and the floor control with multiple users, OCPN/XOPCN model are not sufficient to deal with those problem.

In this chapter, we use the extended timed Petri net to construct the web operations on a distance learning system. When multimedia objects are represented on the system, we have to consider different situations of multimedia objects such as asynchronous operation, time scheduling, and flow control. In addition to system operations, dynamical operations of users are important issues. Thus, we can apply characteristic of Petri net to implement our mechanism and study the theory.

This chapter is organized as follows. Section 2 defines multimedia objects based on Petri net. Section 3 constructs an algorithm for our web system based on the Petri net and uses an example to verify the algorithm and the group communication mechanism with floor control mode. Section 4 gives the conclusions.

2. Basic Definitions of Distributed Time Petri Nets and Multimedia Specification

We define multimedia objects representation based on the characteristics of the Petri net. As a graphical tool of Petri net, the followings are basic properties of a Petri net [1,2,8] and the description of multimedia objects:

Definition 2.1. A Petri net is a 5-tuple, $PN = (P, T, F, W, M_o)$ where:

$P = \{P_1, P_2, \ldots\ldots, P_m\}$ is a finite set of places,

$T = \{T_1, T_2, \ldots\ldots\ldots, T_n\}$ is a finite set of transitions,

$F \subseteq (P \times T) \cup (T \times P)$ is a set of arcs (flow relation),

$W: F \rightarrow \{1, 2, 3, \ldots\ldots\}$ is a *weight function*,

$Mo: P \rightarrow \{0, 1, 2, \ldots\ldots\}$ is the *initial marking*,

$P \cap T = \varnothing$ and $P \cup T \neq \varnothing$.

The structure of Petri net $N = (P, T, F, W)$ without any specific initial marking is denoted by N. The generic components of Petri net include a finite set of places and a finite set of transitions. Petri net is a finite bipartite graph. Its places are linked with transitions in turn are connected to the output places. For a given place, there are input and output transitions defined.

Definition 2.2. A transition that has no input places is called a *source transition* and a transition that has no output places is called a *sink transition*. Note that a source transition is unconditionally enabled or fired and that the firing or enabling of a sink transition consumes tokens, but cannot produce any.

Definition 2.3. The distribution of tokens over places is called a marking of the net. A transition may enable or fire when each of its input places contains at least one token. The firing of a transition results in removing tokens form its input places and adding tokens to the output places.

Definition 2.4. If a place is both an input and output of a transition, a pair of a place and a transition is called a *self-loop*.

Definition 2.5. If a Petri net has no self-loops, it is said to be *pure*. If all of arc weights of a Petri net are 1's, it is said to be *ordinary*. A marking represents the state of a system, which changes when a transition fired to produce a new marking.

Definition 2.6. Multimedia objects representation specification
- A multimedia object is as a place node including a unique token and a transition node displays an event enabling or conditional sufficiency in the multimedia Petri net.
- A place node holds a token and time duration. It controls a multimedia resource to be played for the time duration. A transition node controls synchronization and it is fired only after each place node adjacent to the transition releases the token. The nodes of place and transition connect via synchronous arcs in a Petri net.
- We add *user transitions* and *user arcs* to our multimedia Petri net. A user transition receives a navigation message form the user before it is fired. A user transition is directly connected to some transitions. The activation of user transition can interrupt the demonstration of an arbitrary presentation window and cause the activation of the connected transitions simultaneously.

As illustrated in figure 1, the followings are components of multimedia objects in a Petri net and an example for multimedia objects based on our multimedia Petri net:

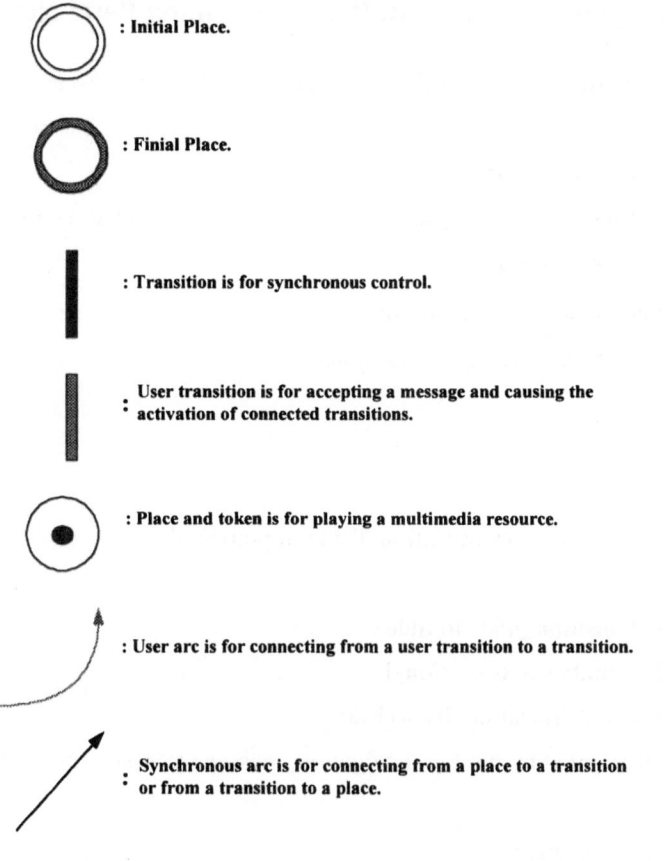

(a) The definitions of multimedia objects by a Petri net

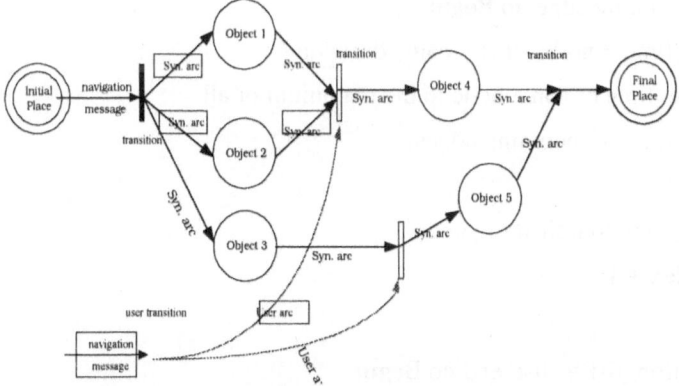

(b) The overview of a multimedia web based on a Petri net

Figure 1. The representation of a multimedia Petri net

3   An Management Algorithm Based on Timed Petri Net

To design the algorithm based on the Petri net [7, 9, 10], we consider two points. The first is the algorithm independent to any operating system. The second is the realization and feasible of our web system.

Algorithm: multimedia objects synchronous set on the Petri net at the run_time

Input: A diagram of a Petri net

Output: multimedia objects synchronous set

Procedure multimedia_objects_synchronous_set

Max: integer;

Index: integer;

Begin

  Sort the transition_node to a transition_list by topological sort

  algorithm;

  Setup the first transition_node to Index;

  Computing the number of transition_list;

  Setup the number of transition_list to Max;

  Initial the node pointed by the first navigation_message to node_time

  = 0;

  For index $\leq$ max do **Begin**

For each incoming edge do **Begin**

  estimated_time = node_time + eage_duration;

  Setup node_time of some node to the maximum of all

  estimated_time of incoming edges;

End;

Setup node_time to transition_node;

Index = Index + 1;

  End;

  For transition_list $\neq$ list_end do **Begin**

Cobegin

  Process 1:

Play the resource concurrently at some transition_node during

node_time;

Process 2:

If user interaction **Then** interrupt;

Wait for instructions;

Coend;

End;

End;

3.1   Implementation by Above Algorithm

We give an example to implement the above algorithm in figure 2. The example is a diagram including multimedia objects such as animation, sound, image, music, text, and video multimedia resources. Transitions "a", "b", "c", and "d" control synchronous operations for the diagram. In addition, we will consider a situation including user transition in the diagram.

There are two cases discussed in the example. Case 1: In figure 2, under the condition that the user transition is not fired, the transition order is "a", "b", "c", and "d" by topological sort of the algorithm. When transition "a" is fired, the synchronous set is {animation, sound, text}. When transition "b" is fired, multimedia objects animation and sound completed. The place named "text" is continuing to play and the places named "music" and "image" begins to play. So the synchronous set is {music, image, text}. When transition "c" is fired, the multimedia resources "text" and "image" complete, and the multimedia object "video" begins to play. So the synchronous set is {music, video}. When transition "d" is fired, all operations completed. The synchronous sets are given in figure (2c) with respect to some transition duration. Case 2: In figure (2d) , If user transition is fired, transition "b" and "c" are fired, but transition "a" is not fired. So the synchronous set is {music, image, video}. The multimedia objects including "animation" and "sound" do not play because the transition "a" is not fired. The operation of the synchronous set is given in figure (2d).

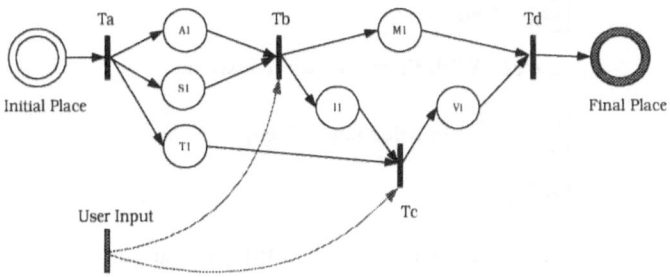

(2a) An example by the above algorithm

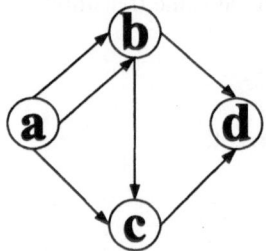

(2b) Topological sort of the transition node

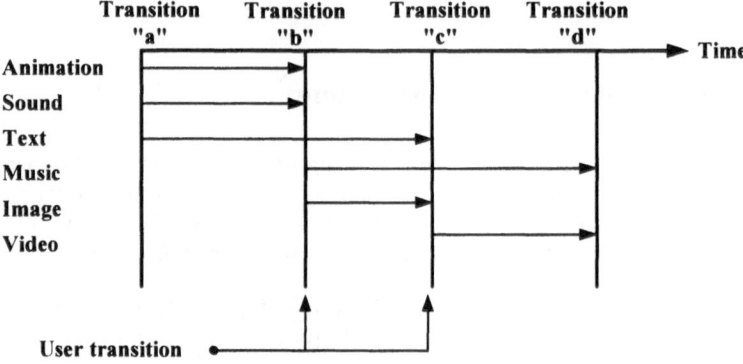

(2c) Time schedule of the example by above algorithm

Case1 : Without firing of user transition

$\boxed{\text{a}}$: {animation,sound,text}

$\boxed{\text{b}}$: {music,image,text}

$\boxed{\text{c}}$: {music,video}

$\boxed{\text{d}}$: End

Case2 : With firing of user transition

$\boxed{\text{b}}$ $\boxed{\text{c}}$: {music,image,video}

$\boxed{\text{d}}$: End

(2d) The synchronous set order of firing of transitions

Figure 2. The description of an example by above algorithm

3.2 Multimedia Presentation In Distributed Environment

The multimedia presentation system in distributed environment can be taken it into a communication tool for virtual conferencing or distance learning. The communication tools need to considerate the group communication and floor control mechanism. In order to achieve these objectives, the distributed multimedia presentation system (DMPS) needed to build a global clock first. The global clock is a standard time in the present period of the client sides. A communication tool which be held "Synchronous" one is because of the bonded delay time. The global clock not only provides the global time frame facility but also control the higher priority of user interaction floor control. For instance, in a group communication case, user need to initial the group first, then every user can set their communication medias of what they needed via our DMPS tools.

The DMPS server build a communication group and initial a global clock when the client side had initialed the communication configuration. The global clock admission control is centralized mode. It has the highest priority to handle the transition enforced to fire immediately or not. If the clock in client side is faster than global clock, the current transition will not fire until global clock arrives. On the other hand, if the local clock in client side is slower than global clock, the transition will be fire without delay. In the presenting period, user can request the floor control and change the presenting media.

The floor control include four modes: (1)Free Access, (2)Equal Control, (3)Group Discussion, (4)Direct Contact. Free access means everyone (ex: including session chair and participant) can send the message to the message-window or whiteboard. This mode is like general discussion with no privacy and priority. We have a limitation of speak in equal control mode. In this mode, there is only one (session chair or participant) can deliver at the same time until the floor control token passed by the holder.

Participants are encouraged to propose their ideas in some time. So, another small group discussion mode is provided. The manner is that a user can create a new group to invite others. For example, user A wants user B receiving his invitation. he can send an inviting message. User B can makes a decision to accept or not. If yes, user B will be chosen as listen group of user A, and the user A will be the session chair in his small group. Everyone can choose whom to receive the message actively. Therefore, all participants in the same group can send message together, we regard it as private communication group. The fourth floor control mode is direct contact. Actually, it is similar to the third mode. It means two people can communicate directly in a private window and communicate with others via free access, equal control, and direct contact at the same time.

The floor control model is managed by group administration of the DMPS server. All the users floor control request inputs are sent to the server, the server will take the messages with their rationality to handle the floor control in group communicating period. If the users floor control requests are permitted, the request will combine with the global clock control and with the same highest priority.

4 Conclusions

The main goal of our multimedia presentation system provides an interactive Petri net model. We suggest a method constructing a web structure on a distance learning system. We hope that the algorithm is independent to any operating system applied different platforms. In addition, we provide a friendly user interface to access multimedia resources on the system. The prototype system was developed on MS Windows 98 or MS Windows 2000 to justify our approach. We provide a model for web multimedia presentation on distance learning by the extension of basic Petri net. With the system, we hope to bring a feasible method including structural design and analysis for the design of the distributed multimedia presentation. Collocating with floor control mechanism, the distributed multimedia presentation system is very suit for distance learning. The model can be used for computer-supporting cooperating work (CSCW), in education, business, and others.

References

1. Tadao Murata, "Petri Nets: Properties, Analysis and Applications," Proceedings of The IEEE Vol. 77, No. 4, 1989.
2. J. L. Peterson, "Petri Net Theory and the Modeling of Systems," Englewood Cliffs, NJ: Prentice-Hall, Inc. 1981.
3. Richard Zurawsi and MengChu Zhou, "Petri Nets and Industrial Application: A Tutorial", IEEE Transactions on Industrisl Electronics, Vol. 41, No. 6, Dec. 1994.
4. T. D. C. Little and A. Ghafoor, "Synchronization and Storage Models for Multimedia Objects," IEEE Journal on Selected Areas in Communications, pp.413-427, Apr. 1990.
5. M. Woo, N. U. Qazi and A. Ghafoor, "A Synchronous Framework for Communication of Pre-orchestrated Multimedia Information," IEEE Network, pp. 52-61, Jan./Feb. 1994.
6. S. Crespi-Reghizzi and D. Mandrioli, "Petri nets and szilard languages," Information and Control, Vol. 33, No. 2, pp. 177-192, Feb. 1977.
7. E. W. Mayr, "An algorithm for the general Petri net reachability problem," SIAM, J. Comput. Vol. 13, No. 3, pp. 441-460, Aug. 1984.
8. Toshinori Suzuki and Sol. M. Shatz, "A Protocol Modeling and Verification Approach Based on a Specification Language and Petri Nets," IEEE Transactions on Software Engineering. Vol. 16, No. 5, May 1990.
9. M. A. Holiday and Mary K. Venon, "A generalized timed Petri net model for performance analysis," IEEE Trans. Software Eng., vol. SE-13, no. 12, pp.1297-1310, Dec. 1987.
10. J. L. Peterson, "Petri nets," ACM Computing Surveys, vol. 9, no. 3, pp. 223-252, Sept. 1977.
11. G. A. Schloss and M. J. Wynblatt, "Presentation Layer Primitives for the Layered Multimedia Data Model," In Proceedings of the IEEE 1995 International Conference on Multimedia Computing and Systems, May 15-18,Washington DC, pages 231-238, 1995.

12. R. H. Thomas and e. a. Harry C. Forsdick, "Diamond: A Multimedia Message System Built on a Distributed Architecture," IEEE Computer, December: 65-78, 1985.

13. Sheng-Uei Guan, Hsiao-Yen Yu and Jen-Shun Yang, "A Prioritized Petri Net Model and its Application in Distributed Multimedia Systems," IEEE Transaction on Computer, Vol. 47 No. 4, April 1998.

14. T. D. C. Little and A. Ghafoor, " Multimedia Synchronization Protocols for Broadband Integrated Services," IEEE Journal on Selected Areas in Communications, pp1368-1382, Dec. 1991.

15. T. D. C. Little, "Synchronization for Distributed Multimedia Database Systems," Ph. D. Dissertation, Syracuse University, Aug. 1991.

Modelling Distant Learning Activities by Agent Task Coalitions

Vadim A. Ermolayev and Vyachyslav A. Tolok

Department of Mathematical Modelling and IT, Zaporozhye State University,
Zaporozhye, 69063, Ukraine
E-mail: eva@zsu.zaporizhzhe.ua

Abstract. Presented is the approach to the design of distant learning facilities for a Virtual/Real University[1] based upon the paradigms of a rational and a benevolent agent, multi-agent system, dynamic task coalition. The particularity of the framework is its capability to perform the tasks without pre-defined task plans. Agents and multi-agent systems inhabit Virtual University Information Space, model real life actors – faculty, technical and administrative staff as well as the users from the outside. Agent coalitions co-operatively provide for the task performance, thus, modelling the processes of university management and distant education. Parametric feedbacks and agents' ability to evolve contribute to the fine-tuning of management routines and to the improvement of teaching and learning. PhD students' recruiting case study provides the illustration of the framework applicability to Virtual University and Distant Education domains.

1 Introduction

Distant Education today is the methodology capable to drastically enhance the effectiveness of various kinds of education both in academic and professional branches. Information Technologies (IT) and the Internet are the means providing the capabilities and the infrastructure to organise the process of distant learning in a rather flexible, adaptable and efficient manner. Emerging Virtual Universities (VU) and Virtual Professional Training Centres (VPTC) provide bright examples of how today's intelligent distributed software systems and underlying ITs educate people.

The paper presents the approach to apply formal agent-based framework for the modelling of the processes of information interchange to the design of a Virtual University Information Space (VUIS) [1] inhabited by agents, that form coalitions to facilitate to the execution of the business processes of distant education.

The very high idea of the presented research was inspired by Angehrn's ICDT model [2] of Internet Business Strategies. The concept of VUIS however differs from that of ICDT Virtual Information Space denoted as simply the channel for displaying and accessing information. In the frame of our research VUIS is understood as a Virtual Medium organised on top of the layered mediator IS unifying the hierarchy of the distributed, heterogeneous, interacting and collaborating functional components (departments) and the wrapped distributed heterogeneous information resources. Human users divine VUIS as the model of

[1] The research presented is run in frame of the Project financed by Ukrainian Ministry of Education and Science, Grant № 0199Y1571.

VU and communicate with it by means of Unified Visual Intranet Interface (UVII) [1]. The concepts of VUIS and UVII are close to the known approaches to Inhabited Information Spaces [3] design. VUIS is inhabited by active functional components (Multi-Agent Systems (MAS) and member-agents) which occupy corresponding organisational cells at different levels. From organisational point of view these components are virtual business objects performing business processes in terms of, say, the Enterprise Framework [4].

The particularity of the approach is the attempt to model the processes of Distant Education as business processes within a VU. Business processes are in their turn modelled as the processes of information interchange among various types of human users and different active functional systems/components presented by MAS/agents possessing appropriate roles and distributed over the Internet. The frameworks, architectures and implementations for business process modelling and management in Virtual Enterprise domain are now emerging high and wide (see [4,5] for some examples). However, the diversity of the processes observed in real life is difficult to be modelled by more or less static means provided by, say, CTL based framework [5], ROOM, OOFRam role models [6], ICRF [7]. Agents' paradigm provides the way out of this world of predefined workflow and role specifications. The presented approach exploits the metaphor of dynamic agent community/coalition[2] in order to provide better means for the modelling of the intrinsic dynamic character of the domain. This approach is close to that used in RETSINA framework [9] for adaptive collaboration among agents' teams facilitating to solve the tasks of decision making and information management. In the frame of the presented approach the agents are the members of various static MAS representing persistent departments of a VU. The departments communicate with each other via the Proxy Agents acting as the executives who are in charge with some external communications/functions. These Proxies in turn form the university MAS on the higher level. On the lower level each member agent of the department MAS may be expanded into a sub-ordinate MAS having the same generic architecture. As far as these department models represent university functional nodes they are pre-designated to perform tasks. These tasks are merely the tasks of information acquisition, integration, mediation and interchange. Agents' roles [10] are more or less static as far as the agents are capable to perform given sets of atomic works. On the other hand agents' capabilities and beliefs change in time due to changing constraints and experience gained. Moreover, the agents within MAS dynamically form the coalitions, denoted as temporal agent communities, to perform one or another task. The approach presented exploits the Diakoptical MAS framework [10], the model of task execution by agents coalition [11,13]. Human user interface designs are based upon the concept of UVII [1].

The focus of this publication is the operational aspects, the evolution model as well as the demonstration of the approach applicability to Distant Education domain.

The contribution is structured as follows: Section 2 outlines the modelling framework; Section 3 presents the approach to cope with VUIS inhabitants' evolution; the contribution of Section 4 is the discussion of PhD students'

---

[2] Business process is for instance viewed by Jennings et al [8] as the Community of negotiating service providing agents in ADEPT project.

recruiting case study; Section 5 summarises the results. This publication is the revised version of [12]

2 Modelling Framework

VIS Functional Face is inhabited by MAS representing functional systems and components at various levels. The member agents dynamically form coalitions for the execution of the tasks of information acquisition, integration, mediation and interchange emerging within the organisation.

The main advantage of the task execution model [11] used in the framework is the absence of statically pre-defined task specifications. The tasks in frame of the presented approach are "summoned" by its Proxy and Facilitator agents and are executed by its middle agents[3]. Middle agents dynamically form coalitions to perform emerging tasks. An agent joins the coalition if and only if it accepts a sensory input containing the (sub)set of atomic works (the part of the task) for the execution. Task execution plan is being developed in more and more details within step-by-step task execution process. The process is conducted by the team of coalition member agents acting in co-operation with each other. Co-ordination agent serves as teams' co-ordinator and monitors the activities of each team. Coalition member agents act as the models of the functional components of the corresponding real world business object performing a business process.

The framework for modelling of the processes of information interchange comprises the following components: functional system/component model [10], process model [11,13], generic agent model [10], communication model [10], co-ordination model and evolution model.

Framework actors are intelligent (rational - Nwana [14]) software agents capable to communicate with each other by means of the defined set of communicative acts with parametric feedbacks [10, 11]. A task is assumed to be the set of atomic works. Each actor (agent) is capable to perform some atomic works from the set of permissible atomic works of the functional system. These capabilities form the role of the corresponding agent. The notion of role used in the framework [10] is close to that of ICRF [7].

At the agent level the framework provides the key agent's characteristics of situatedness, autonomy, rationality and adaptability. Agent accepts external influences, verifies if the incoming influence complies with the agent's role and finally adjusts its behaviour and performs appropriate macromodel program — i.e. executes or rejects the atomic work requested by the input influence. The function of the macromodel is also to rationally form the feedback containing the results. The results may be presented as functions from the parameters of the incoming influence.

Formally [10, 18], the generic agent is reactive, rational, comprises its sensory interface, the cascade of 3 finite-state machines for incoming influence verification local knowledge base and macromodel execution block. Generic agent is thus the

---

[3] Middle agents in frame of this work are understood as those ones facilitating to the task execution inside the department MAS and having no direct interfaces to the outside. The notion used is close to that of RETSINA framework [17].

operational shell providing the skeleton for any framework agent. Agents' specialisations are merely the sets of their role specific macromodel programs. Macromodel programs are thus considered to be agent's policies and are stored in its local knowledge base.

At the community/coalition level it is assumed that the agents taking part in the process of task execution communicate by means of the following communication acts complying with ACL [15] and KQML [16] capabilities (see [10] for the formal specification and for more details): Directive, Determined Query, Determined Query with Results' Analysis, Undetermined Query with Results' Analyses.

At the functional system level the agents are considered to be benevolent. The model of a functional system as well as a functional component model is built upon the idea of "absorption" and "generation" of atomic works from the set of the permissible works $W = \{w_1, w_2, ...\}$ of this functional system. It is considered that the sensory input of the functional component i admits a task $W_i \subseteq W$. A certain part of its works W_i^p may be performed ("absorbed") by the given component and the remaining part of works may be either redirected to another system's components W_i^d in case functional component knows the recipient(s), or rejected W_i^r. Functional component may as well generate additional set of works W_i^g to complete the execution of works W_i^p. W_i^g as well as W_i^d are redirected to another components:

$$W_i \to F_O^i(W) \to \tilde{W}_i, \tag{1a}$$

where: $W_i = \{W_i^p, W_i^d, W_i^r\}$, $\tilde{W}_i = \{W_i^d, W_i^g\}$, $F_O^i(W)$ - macromodel program.

In a special case component i may generate a new set of works W_i^g without been invoked by incoming influence W_i - i.e. may "summon" a new (sub)task:

$$F_O^i(W) \to \tilde{W}_i, \tag{1b}$$

where: $\tilde{W}_i = \{W_i^g\}$, $F_O^i(W)$ - macromodel program.

More detailed presentation of the system/component model is given in [10, 11]. The model extension as well as the routines for negotiating on sub-task placement and on joining the task coalition within the sub-task arrangement phase are discussed in [13].

A process is denoted as the flow of task execution. Process Π_a starts with generation of the new task $W_a \subseteq W$. Task W_a as well as the additional tasks $\tilde{W}_a$ are considered to be linked to process Π_a and labelled with the unique identifier of this process. The component is considered to be *linked to process* Π_a in case it has absorbed the part of W_a, $\tilde{W}_a$, or has generated W_a^g. The agent representing this functional component thus *enters the task coalition*.

Process Π_a is considered to be completed in case all the components stopped to absorb the atomic works of the tasks linked to process Π_a. The set of works $W_{\Pi_a}^z$ not absorbed in the process of Π_a is denoted as the set of *inexecutable* works.

Process Π_a modelling (steady-state mode) is performed by applying (1b) and (1a) to all of the components of the system until the process is completed.

For practice the set of system's permissible atomic works is constrained to a finite: $W = \{w_1, w_2, ..., w_\sigma\}$. Modelling of a functional system (task coalition) performance is organised as a two-level process in a discrete time space $t_n, t_{n+1} = t_n + \Delta t$. Please refer to [11,12] for the details.

3   Actors' and Resources' Evolution

One of the major characteristics of a VU is its inclination to changes. The framework for VU modelling should therefore possess the means to deal with the changes emerging within the real world. The evolution with rrespect to the subject under discussion is understood as the process of proactive self-development and self-adaptability of the intelligent active components (the agents) in response to the changes in the environment they inhabit - the VUIS.

The framework distinguishes and handles the movement in:
- Agents' state constraints — the *capabilities* to execute a work
- Agents' conceptualisations (*beliefs*) about their partners — task coalition members
- Information resources and corresponding metadata.

Capabilities' evolution according to [10] is understood as the process of agent (say, A) transitions from one state s_i to another state s_j. A as an autonomous entity performs these transitions according to its own decisions taken in frame of one or another atomic work execution. Consequently, the "manner" agent A executes policy f, as well as the constraints on policy incoming parameters X_f depend upon the state of agent A. Thus, the evolution of an agent is the evolution of its role.

The set of states of agent A: $S_A = \{s_1, ..., s_n\}$ - is denoted as the set of 3-nested tuples $s_i, i = 1, ..., n$:

$$s_i = \{r(X_A), q(F_A), t(F)\},$$ (4)

where:

$r(X_A)$ - the set of constraints applied in state s_i over the system parameters X_A of agent A (parameter constraints),

$q(F_A)$ - the set of constraints in state s_i over the set of authorised works of agent A (work constraints),

$t(F)$ - the function denoting transitions from state s_i to another permissible states from S_A resulting from the execution of the works $F = \{f_1, ..., f_j, ..., f_m\}$.

Beliefs' evolution is closely tightened to the monitoring of task coalition members' capabilities to perform works. Inter-agent communication and work execution is organised/co-ordinated via parametric feedbacks [10, 11], comprising the information on the current capabilities to execute the certain work. The capability returned by the executor A to the requestor B is, thus, the function from work parameters $c_A^f = c(X_f)$, $c_A^f \in [0,1]$.

An agent monitors the capabilities .of its counter-agents for to intelligently assign works to the executors with probably better capabilities in future tasks. The beliefs on counter-agents' probable capabilities are maintained in the form of matrix $\mathbf{C}$:

$$
\mathbf{C} = \begin{array}{c} \\ A_1 \\ \\ \\ A_i \\ \\ \\ A_n \end{array}
\begin{array}{cccc}
w_1 \quad \cdots & \quad w_j & \quad \cdots \quad w_m \\
\left[\begin{array}{ccc}
c_1^1 & c_1^j & c_1^m \\
\cdots & \cdots & \\
\cdots & c_i^j = c_{A_i}^{w_j}(X_{w_j}) \quad \cdots & \\
\cdots & \cdots & \\
c_n^1 & c_n^j & c_n^m
\end{array}\right]
\end{array} \tag{5}
$$

The dimensions n and m grow in the process of evolution reflecting the income of new knowledge on counter-agents (n) dimensions and the works they are probably capable to perform (m) to matrix $\mathbf{C}$. The upper limit for dimension n is the number of member-agents in the MAS comprising the holder of matrix $\mathbf{C}$. The maximum value for m is the cardinality of the set W of permissible atomic works of the mentioned MAS.

Information resources data and metadata changes are maintained locally by corresponding distributed information systems - resource providers. In frame of the presented research information resource providers are represented by their wrapper agents, which evolve in response to this changes. Wrapper agents are the members (middle agents) of appropriate department MAS.

4   Modelling PhD Recruiting Scenario

PhD recruiting process modelling case has been studied to analyse the applicability of the described approach to distant learning and VU domain. The main reason for to choose this very case was the understanding that a VU needs to be self-regulating to be successful. VU management processes need feedbacks from the processes of distant teaching and learning to adapt to changing students' demands. Otherwise, the routines delivering courses and other knowledge to students should fine-tune themselves grounded on the feedback from improving management facilities. As for the case, PhD students' selection may be considered a management procedure (like hiring personnel). It will be demonstrated below that this process provides new knowledge on the necessity of new courses introduction, thus, feeding back and improving teaching process.

It is assumed that PhD candidates are surfing the VUIS, contacting the departments of their choice via the Proxies and expressing their intents to become students.

It is presumed as well that a Virtual Department is the MAS, comprising at least the following actors:

– Secretary - the Proxy Agent (PA)
– Professors (PRA), Assistants (AA), Course Master (CMA), Librarian (LA) - the Middle Agents

Department MAS also contains utility units providing for scalability, co-ordination and knowledge sharing among its functional actors: Cloning Agent (CA), Co-ordination Agent (COA) with its Shared Data Space (SDS) and Ontology Agent (OA) respectively.

The role of the CA with regard to the case under discussion is to clone a Tutor Agent (TA) each time a new task to process a PhD candidate is "summoned" by the PA in response to the external influence coming from the outer VUIS.

PhD recruiting scenario has been slightly adopted from the real world procedure to highlight the benefits we may obtain from the usage of the modelling approach presented in Section II. The assumptions made here are: participating human actors PhD candidates, Professors, ... are available on-line during the whole scenario; all generated works are accomplished in a reasonably short time.

We presume that the procedure of PhD recruiting comprises the following steps:

– A PhD candidate submits the CV and indicates his/her intention to become a PhD student
– The CV is analysed and the best Professor Match is searched
– Qualified candidate passes the test from the chosen professor
– Successful candidate is interviewed and assigned to a research project
– The professor and his assistant prepare the individual curriculum for the accepted candidate as well as the list of recommended reading

Agents' activities within these phases are as follows.

Phase 1. *Establish connection and submit the CV*: PA accepts the external influence, generates the new task. First atomic works within the task are: CA - to Clone the Tutor Agent; PA - to Pipeline the candidate to TA's human to agent interface, TA - Require CV and Extract Qualification Data)

Phase 2. *CV analysis and search for the best match*: TA submits Candidate's qualifications to Department PRAs. PRAs feed back with their parametric attitudes, having candidate's qualifications as parameters. TA determines the best match in case the feedbacks from some PRAs fit the qualification cluster region. In case the candidate appears to be not up to the level TA generates a work for the proxy to notify the requestor and to recommend him to contact other Departments. In case the best match is found the candidate is recognised to be qualified and TA summons the following Testing Phase.

Phase 3. *Testing:* TA requests the test from PRA. PRA provides the test. TA requests the candidate to fill in the test form and passes it to PRA. PRA evaluates the exercise and replies with the parametric marks (depending from the research project). TA executes the marks' analysis (similarly to Phase 2) and either qualifies the candidate as successful and launches the Interview Phase or entrusts PA to notify the candidate on his failure.

Phase 4. *The interview:* TA generates the task for the PRA to interview the candidate. TA pipelines successful candidate to PRA. PRA arranges on-line communication between his master (human professor) and the candidate. PRA requires his human master to fill in the PhD recruiting form. PRA influences TA to process the PhD recruiting form. TA analyses the PhD recruiting form and either passes it to the Personnel Department's PA to hire the accepted candidate to the project or entrusts PA to notify the candidate on his failure. In case the candidate has successfully passed the interview and thus became PhD student TA launches the Curriculum Phase.

Phase 5. *Curriculum preparation:* TA generates the task for the PRA to prepare the curriculum and the working program for the PhD student for the 1-st semester. PRA redirects the task to his AA adding his course recommendations to the parameters' list. AA prepares the working plan and the curriculum and than requests the necessary electronic courses from CMA. CMA analyses the request and, if necessary, issues the Call for the unavailable courses – see details in [18].

Let's assume that at $t = t_n$ TA initiates the Testing phase and examine the activities of TA, PRA and PA agents within the Phase 3.

At $t = t_n$ TA accepts the set of works $W_{TA} = \{ w_1 = ('Require\ the\ test',\ X_1,\ Y_1) \}$ with the parameters and result descriptions for w_1:

$X_1 = \{ \textbf{\textit{Edu\_Rating}} = <\ structure, \textbf{ontology} = Edu\_Rating >,$

$\qquad \textbf{\textit{Q\_E\_Rating}} = <\ structure, \textbf{ontology} = Qualif\_Exp\_Rating >,$

$\qquad \textbf{\textit{Pub\_Rating}} = <\ structure, \textbf{ontology} = Publication\_Rating >,$

$\qquad \textbf{\textit{Professor}} = <\ Id, \textbf{ontology} = Agent\_Name > \},\ Y_1 = \varnothing.$

Atomic work w_1 is accepted and executed as far as all of the parameters X_1 (obtained as the results of the previous works at previous phases) are available from COA's SDS. While executing w_1 TA, as "subscribed" by its appropriate macromodel, generates the tasks $\tilde{W}_{TA} = \{ W_{TA}^d, W_{TA}^g \}$, where: $W_{TA}^d = \varnothing$ as far as work w_1 is executed and no more works are left for redirection;

$W_{TA}^g = \{ w_2 = ('Provide\_Test', X_2, Y_2),\ w_3 = ('Test', X_3, Y_3),$

$w_4 = ('Evaluate\_Re\,sults', X_4, Y_4),\ w_5 = ('Analyse\_Marks', X_5, Y_5) \}.$

Works w_2, w_4 form W_{PRA} and w_3, w_5 form W_{TA} for the next step $t = t_{n+1}$.

At $t = t_{n+1}$ PRA accepts $W_{PRA} = \{ w_2 = ('Provide\_test',\ X_2,\ Y_2),$ $w_4 = ('Evaluate\_Results', X_4,\ Y_4) \}.$

Work w_2 is executed and the result $\tilde{Y}_2 = \{ Test\_Form = < FILENAME > \}$ are passed to COA for further use. At meantime w_4 is redirected to PRA for the next step – the results of w_3, which form the parameters of w_4, are not yet available from COA. At the same time TA accepts

$W_{TA} = \{ w_3 = ('Test', X_3, Y_3),\ w_5 = ('Analyse\_Marks', X_5, Y_5) \}$

and redirects both works to himself for next steps waiting for the results of respectively w_2, w_4.

At $t = t_{n+2}$ TA executes w_3. At $t = t_{n+3}$ PRA executes w_4 and passes the result vector $\tilde{Y}_{PRA} = \{ \tilde{y}_4^1 = (m_1,\ m_2, ..., m_k),\ \tilde{y}_4^2 = (s_1, s_2, ..., s_k) \}$ to COA. Here, k is the quantity of PRA master's projects with PhD vacancies, m_j is the candidate's mark in case he/she pretends to work on project i, and s_i indicates what the professor thinks about the level, starting from which the mark may be considered to be positive.

At $t = t_{n+4}$ TA accepts $W_{TA} = \{w_5 = ('Analyse\_Marks', X_5, Y_5)\}$

with $X_5 = \{Marks = < \tilde{y}_4^1, \mathbf{ontology} = Mark\_per\_Project >,$

$Scale = < \tilde{y}_4^2, \mathbf{ontology} = Positive\_Mark\_per\_Project >\}$

and decides if the candidate may be successful with respect to one of the project vacancies. In case of success W_{TA}^g will contain

$w_6 = ('Require\_the\_Interview', X_6 = \{X_1, X_5\}, Y_6)$,

otherwise TA generates $w_7 = ('Inform\_on\_Failure', X_7, Y_7)$.

5   Summary

The contribution presents the approach to apply the formal agent-based framework to the design of a Virtual University Information Space and model Distant Learning activities. In the frame of the presented approach the agents are the members of various static MAS representing persistent departments of a VU at different levels of organisation model. Agents dynamically form coalitions to perform the tasks related to the business processes of distant education. The departments communicate with each other via the Proxy Agents acting as the executives who are in charge with some external communications/functions. These Proxies in turn form the University MAS on the higher level. On the lower level each member agent of the department MAS may be expanded into the sub-ordinate MAS having the same generic architecture.

The underlying modelling framework is based upon the paradigms of intelligent software agent, multi-agent system, dynamic agent task coalition. The particularity of the framework is its capability to perform the tasks without pre-defined task plans. The tasks in the frame of the presented approach are "summoned" by Proxy and Facilitator agents and are executed by the coalitions of benevolent middle agents. An agent joins the coalition if and only if it accepts a sensory input containing the (sub-)set of atomic works (the sub-task) for the execution and the mutual agreement on delegating the work to this very executor is gained within the arrangement phase [13]. The task workflow is thus being developed in more and more details within step-by-step execution process and is collaboratively conducted by the coalition agents team comprising co-ordination agent.

The framework provides the model of the agents' evolution to better cope with the diverse changes emerging in real life. Evolution is understood as the process of proactive self-development and self-adaptability of the intelligent functional actors in course of their task execution activities and in response to the changes in the environment they inhabit - the VUIS. Parametric feedbacks and agents' ability to evolve promote to the fine-tuning of management routines and to the improvement of teaching and learning.

PhD students' recruiting case studied provides the illustration of the framework applicability to VU and Distant Learning domains.

References

1. Ermolayev, V. A., Pletsky, S. U., Tolok, V. A. (1998): The Architecture of the Unified Information Space of a Virtual University. Lecture Notes of Zaporozhye State University 1(2), 44-53 (in Russian)
2. Anghern, A. (1997): Designing Mature Internet Business Strategies: the ICDT Model. European Management Journal, 15(4), 361-369
3. I3Net European research initiative. http://www.i3net.org – URL was accessed
    May 8, 2001
4. Papazoglou, M. P., Van der Heuvel, W.-J. (1999): From Business Processes to Cooperative Information Systems: an Information Agents Perspective. In: M. Klusch (ed.): Intelligent information agents: agent based information discovery and management on the Internet. Springer-Verlag, Berlin Heidelberg New York, pp. 10-36
5. Davulcu, H., Kifer, M., Pokorny, L. R., Ramakrishnan, C. R., Ramakrishnan I. V. (1999): Modeling and Analysis of Interactions in Virtual Enterprises. Proc. of the 9-th International Workshop on Research Issues on Data Engineering: Information Technology for Virtual Enterprises (RIDE-VE'99), Sidney, Australia, March 1999
6. OMG Unified Modeling Language. Specification. Version 1.3. June 1999. http://www.rational.com/uml/resources/documentation/ – URL was accessed
    May 8, 2001
7. Lupu, E., Milosevic, Z., Sloman, M.: Use of Roles and Policies for Specifying, Building and Managing Virtual Enterprise. Proc. of the 9-th International Workshop on Research Issues on Data Engineering: Information Technology for Virtual Enterprises (RIDE-VE'99), Sidney,, Australia, March 1999
8. Jennings, N. R., Faratin, P., Johnson, M. J., Norman, T. J., O'Brien, P., Wiegand, M. E. (1996): Agent-based business process management. International Journal of Cooperative Information Systems. 5(2, 3), 105-130
9. Sycara, K., Decker, K., Pannu, A. Williamson, M. and Zeng, D. (1996): Distributed Intelligent Agents. IEEE Expert. Dec. 1996, 36-45
10. Ermolayev, V. A., Borue, S. U., Tolok, V. A., Keberle, N. G. (2000): Use of Diakoptics and Finite Automata for Modelling Virtual Information Space Agent Societies. Lecture Notes of Zaporozhye State University. 3(1), 34-44
11. Borue, S. U., Ermolayev, V. A., Tolok, V. A. (1999): On Diakoptical Approach to Process Modelling in Multi-Functional Information Systems. Proc. of International Conference Knowledge-Dialog-Solution (KDS'99), Katciveli, Ukraine, September 1999, 211-219 (Russian)
12. Ermolayev, V. (2000): Dynamic Agent Communities Facilitating to Distant Learning in a Virtual University Information Space. Proc. of International Conference Emerging Technologies and New Challenges in Information Society (IS2000), Aizu-Wakamatsu, Japan, November 2000, 488-495

13. Ermolayev, V. A., Borue, S. U., Tolok, V. A. (2001): Co-operative Tasks Execution by the Coalitions of Rational Software Agents. Submitted as a regular paper to the 5-th Intl. Workshop on Cooperative Information Agents (CIA'01), Modena, Italy, September 2001
14. Nwana, H. S. (1996): Software Agents: an Overview. Knowledge Engineering Review. 11(3), 205-244
15. Foundation for Intelligent Physical Agents (FIPA) Spec.: DRAFT, Version 0.2, Agent Communication Language, 1999. http://www.fipa/org – URL was accessed May 8, 2001
16. Finin, T., Fritszon, R. (1994): KQML - A language for protocol and information exchange. Proc. of the 13-th DAI Workshop, Seattle, WA, USA, 1994
17. Sycara, K. (1999): In-Context Information Management through Adaptive Collaboration of Intelligent Agents. In: M. Klusch (ed.): Intelligent information agents: agent based information discovery and management on the Internet. Springer-Verlag, Berlin Heidelberg New York, pp. 78-99
18. Borue, S. U., Ermolayev, V. A., Tolok, V. A. (2000): Application of Diakoptical MAS Framework to Planning Process Modelling. Proc. of the 2-nd International Scientific - Practical Conference on Programming (UkrPROG'2000), Kiev, Ukraine, May 2000, 488-500.

Part VI

Emerging Technologies for

the Information Society in the New Century

Tightly Coupled Multiprocessing:
The Super Processor Architecture

Nimrod Bayer and Ran Ginosar

VLSI Systems Research Center, Electrical Engineering Department,
Technion–Israel Institute of Technology, Haifa 32000, Israel
E-mail: {bayer@fuji.ee.bgu.ac.il, ran@ee.technion.ac.il}

Abstract. Due to a number of fundamental hindrances, parallel computing has not yet become a practical general purpose technology comparable to current serial computing technology. Overcoming these hindrances is a major challenge that information society faces in the 21st century.

We advocate and explore a solution that departs from the strong reliance on the locality of data with respect to the individual processor. Under our approach, the multiprocessor is analogous, in fact, to a uniprocessor: The collection of processors acts as a single "super processor", working under fine or medium granularity vis-a-vis a symmetric shared memory. An architectural/physical model of such a system is outlined, and a simple estimate for the clock frequency is given. The main novel part of the proposed "super processor" is a *high flow-rate synchronizer/scheduler*, which coordinates the parallel work. The macro architecture of the synchronizer/scheduler and the micro architecture of its critical component are described. The proposed architectural solution points to secondary, technological, challenges.

1 The Parallel Processing Challenge

1.1 Problem Definition

Massively parallel MIMD systems suffer of three fundamental problems [1]:

1. Memory and communication latency.
2. The software engineering problem.
3. The problem of coordinating parallel work.

Memory and communication latencies, in multiprocessors and multicomputers respectively, result from the facts that data transfer to and from memory is substantially slower than signal propagation inside a processor, and memory access resources are typically in contention. The memory latency problem also spawns the cache coherence problem, when caching is pursued as a solution. Producing effective parallel code turns out to be harder than serial code. Finally, coordinating parallel work means synchronizing multiple instruction streams in a flexible and efficient way, without undue delay in issuing ready to execute work, while maintaining efficient schedule and keeping load balance. These three problems may hinder the fulfillment of promises made in terms of peak rate.

Tight coupling, a common approach to parallel processing, has a dual meaning. Tightly coupled shared memory multiprocessing has emerged as an answer to the software engineering problem: The shared memory programming model, in contrast with message passing, is closer to a uniprocessor's programming model. The second meaning of tight coupling relates to working under fine (or at least medium) granularity: When the granularity is finer, data access tends to be less localized, and the volume of coordination activity increases. The processors work in tighter cooperation with each other and behave as a single large body, a "super processor", vis-a-vis the shared memory. This must be expressed both in the hardware architecture and in the programming model. The motivation for working under finer granularity lies in the need to extract more parallelism out of an algorithm. Yet so far, fine granularity has become a commercial reality only under very small scale of parallelism—instruction level parallelism in superscalar uniprocessors.

We seek an integrated, tightly coupled remedy for the three fundamental problems of parallel processing. Section 2 outlines a novel approach to the architectural side of this problem. This solution, in turn, points on a secondary problem, of a more technological nature, associated with the density of packaging of circuitry at the scale of a large system. This may emerge as a major technological challenge in the near future.

1.2   Comments on the State of the Art

We would like to comment about three characteristics of the state of the art:
a. *Current supercomputers [6] are not oriented towards fine granularity.* First, accessing a remote component is slow, relative to propagation times within a processor. Second, coordination of parallel work is carried out by software, by exercising synchronization or communication primitives alongside other instructions. This may entail too much overhead when working under fine granularity. In addition, "hot spots" and bottlenecks may be incurred, especially when dynamic load balancing is practiced. Moreover, there is a tendency of convergence between the shared memory model and the message passing model—see, for example, Culler and Singh (1999) [2], or Protić et.al. (1998) [3].
b. *Dataflow architectures remain outside mainstream.* The dataflow concept embodies tight coupling in the sense of Paragraph 1.1 by being oriented towards fine granularity, and by the fact that the collection of processors is viewed as a single body by the programming model. However, dataflow architectures have been criticized for low efficiency.
c. *The flourishing of cheap PC clusters.* A cluster of small computers connected through a few off-the-shelf communication switches forms an inexpensive substitute for a supercomputer. And since current supercomputers are not oriented to tight coupling (in the sense of Paragraph 1.1) anyway, why not content oneself with a less expensive substitute?

1.3   Organization of the Paper

Section 2 outlines our proposed architecture of a tightly coupled parallel processor. After describing the overall architecture, we analyze its performance, present the "super processor", discuss the programming model, and go into the details of scheduling and synchronization.

2   A Tightly Coupled Parallel Processor

2.1   The Architecture

Consider the architecture model depicted in Fig.1.

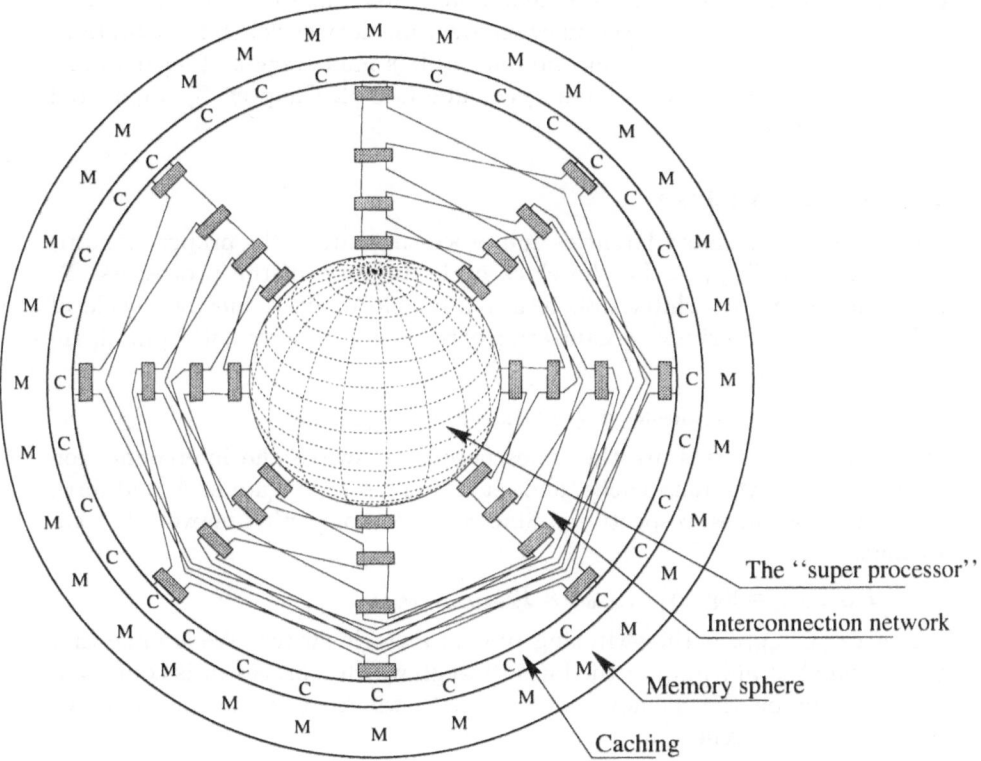

Fig. 1. Architecture and physical model of the multiprocessor. Wiring length inside the baseline interconnection network is bounded by the circumference of the outer circle.

The system comprises three elements: The "super processor", a global symmetric shared memory, and an interconnection network replicated $M_{networks}$

times in parallel. Data are cached at the memory side of the network, whereas instructions are cached at the processor side. (Caching of data at the processor side is possible as well, with the coherency being preserved as a by-product of programming conventions, but the emphasis on tight coupling leads to caching of data at the memory side instead). Input/output paths are omitted from this description.

Memory references are emitted from $N_{\text{processors}}$ different points on the spherical surface of the "super processor"; they are generated by the same number of individual processors. These references reach $N_{\text{processors}} \times M_{\text{networks}}$ different points on the memory sphere, via the interconnection network; From the description of the "super processor" later in Paragraph 2.3, it will follow that the memory traffic does not contain references to synchronization data or to any other type of "hot spots." The entire system is synchronous. This enables the construction of a simple and fast interconnection network, based on circuit switching that is set anew on every memory cycle, and not containing any buffers. The interconnection network is multistage and logarithmic, e.g. a baseline or an indirect binary n-cube (see [4, Chapter 4]) duplicated M_{networks} times.

2.2   Timing Analysis

We now discuss memory latencies and processing rate of the proposed multi-processor. Let $T_{\text{processor}}$ be the clock cycle duration of the processors. To attain a balanced architecture, it is reasonable to fix a memory cycle of $2T_{\text{processor}}$. Under a simple organization of the memory system, without pipelining, we thus have

$$2T_{\text{processor}} = T_{\text{switching}} + T_{\text{cache\_access}} + T_{\text{propagation}},$$

where the three terms are the times needed to switch the interconnection network, access the data cache, and let the signal propagate back and forth on the network lines, respectively. Since the interconnection network is logarithmic,

$$T_{\text{switching}} = \log_2 N_{\text{processors}} \times T_{\text{single\_switch}},$$

where $T_{\text{single\_switch}}$ is the switching time of a single switch. We assume that the maximal total length of the lines through which a processor is connected to any point on the memory sphere is πR, where R is the radius of the memory sphere. Hence,

$$T_{\text{propagation}} = \frac{2\pi R}{\widetilde{c}}, \tag{1}$$

where $\widetilde{c}$ is the speed of propagation through the transmission or optical lines that make up the interconnection network. This value is close to the speed of light. Further, observe that

$$R = \left(\frac{3}{4\pi} \cdot \frac{N_{\text{components}}}{D} \right)^{1/3},$$

where $N_{components}$ is the overall number of components, of various kinds, participating in the architecture, and D is their mean density in the cased system. The components counted in $N_{components}$ are the memory modules, the interconnection network switches, the individual processors, and further components participating in the "super processor" that will be introduced in Paragraph 2.3, and whose number is also about $N_{processors}$. All in all,

$$N_{components} = 2N_{processors} +$$
$$N_{processors} \times M_{networks} \times (1 + \log_2 N_{processors}),$$

where the first term is the number of components in the "super processor" and the second is the number of components in the memory and interconnection network. The above relations give an estimate for $T_{processor}$, i.e. for the speed of operation of the processors, as a function of the architectural parameters $N_{processors}$ and $M_{networks}$, and of the technological parameters T_{single_switch}, T_{cache_access}, and the mean density D. (Note that introducing D does not imply that the components are evenly scattered in space). For example, if T_{single_switch} is 0.4 nanoseconds, T_{cache_access} is 3 nanoseconds, and the mean density D is one component per 10 cubic centimeters, then we can operate $N_{processors} = 1024$ processors with $M_{networks} = 8$ at a clock cycle duration of $T_{processor} \approx 10$ nanoseconds. The radius R would be around 60 centimeters. We do not claim a scalable architecture, since the quantity $\tilde{c}$ appearing in Eq. (1) cannot be scaled up. However, an improvement of the technological parameters, and especially of the crucial parameter D, would allow an upgrade of the system.

2.3   The "Super Processor"

The "super processor" comprises

1. individual processors,
2. A *synchronizer/scheduler* for coordinating parallel work, and
3. Global registers for non-synchronization "hot data", with special networks to access them.

The special networks in (3) are spread out in parallel with a *distribution network* that forms a part of the synchronizer/scheduler. Since the synchronizer/scheduler is far more complex than the registers for non-synchronization "hot data", with their special networks, we concentrate in this paper only on the synchronizer/scheduler.

The synchronizer/scheduler consists of two constituents: The distribution network connects the *central synchronization/scheduling unit (CSU)* and the processors, as shown in Fig.2.

The synchronizer/scheduler allocates computational tasks to processors, while observing dependency constraints of the parallel program, maintaining

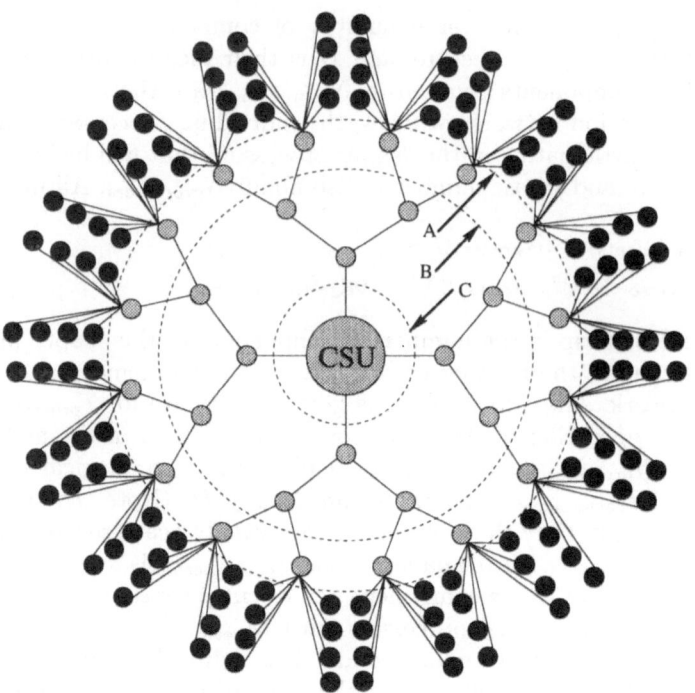

Fig. 2. The "super processor". Black circles are processors. All the rest is the synchronizer/scheduler, comprising the distribution network and the CSU. The arrows marked "A", "B", "C" point to different cross-sections.

efficient schedule, and balancing the load. One of the most important parameters of the synchronizer/scheduler is its flow-rate, namely the amount of traffic that can be transferred through the cross-section that is marked as A in Fig.2. Since the distribution network has a tree topology (with the CSU at its root), it is essential that the traffic via cross sections of ever larger distance from the center will be ever greater. For example, the traffic through cross-section A should be greater than through cross-section B, and the latter should be greater than through cross-section C. Such an amplification effect is indeed attained due to the fact that the traffic in the direction from the CSU to the processors carries chunks of computational work that undergo decomposition as they proceed. These chunks are called *allocation packs*. The decomposition of allocation packs is carried out at each *distribution unit* (node of the distribution network), using the processor availability state pertaining to every sub-tree governed by that distribution unit. Dynamic load balancing is thus accomplished. *Termination packs* flow in the opposite direction, and are subject to unification. The distribution network is somewhat similar to the combining network of the NYU Ultracomputer [5]. Note, however, that here the unification is not accidental, but rather dictated by the allocation packs. Processor availability updates are also transferred from the processors to the CSU, and are also subject to unification, but separately and in a different way.

In order to describe the structure, mode of operation, and properties of the synchronizer/scheduler in more detail, it is necessary to begin with the system's programming model. The very possibility to decompose and unify packs of computational work stems from the programming model. This is the subject of the next paragraph (2.4). Thereafter, in Paragraph 2.5, we briefly describe a possible micro architecture for the most critical unit within the synchronizer/scheduler—the CSU.

2.4   The Programming Model

The program loaded in main memory is essentially a uniprocessor program: It does not contain synchronization primitives. (It may contain references to special registers, however). At the same time, there exists a similarity between this program and a dataflow program: A dependency graph called *task map*, that specifies a parsing of the program into tasks and their interdependencies, forms a part of the representation of the program. The task map is kept by the synchronizer/scheduler, who uses it for scheduling tasks for execution while maintaining the synchronization mandated by the dependencies. The allocation of a task to a processor is attained by transferring the starting address of the task (along with an additional identifier called "instantiation id," explained below). The instructions of the task themselves are fetched from memory. A HALT instruction must be appended at the end of a task. The processor reports on its being in a halted state through a dedicated line, and transmits a *termination condition* bit on another line. The processor may update the termination condition bit during run time as if it were an internal register. When the terminated task is a *conditioning task*, its termination condition is taken into account for the purpose of managing the global conditioning of the program: Such global conditioning is clearly needed, as the intra-task conditioning using the ordinary branching instructions is not sufficient. Conditioning tasks have a special graphical symbol, that serves when one wants to describe the task map graphically. It is one of several symbols serving for graphical description of task maps, which are depicted in Fig.3; the figure also depicts an example task map. The most important feature of the programming model is *duplicable task*. Such a task is in fact a collection, whose average size within an application may be quite large, of tasks arranged in a "parallel do" pattern. We refer to these individual tasks as to the *instantiations* of the duplicable task. The instantiation quota of each duplicable task, although physically kept in the synchronizer/scheduler, can be accessed and modified during run time by any processor as if it were a memory word. All the instantiations of a given duplicable task are implemented by the same code in main memory, with the same start address. But

this code may contain references to the *instantiation id*, that has been transferred to the processor by the synchronizer/scheduler and is kept in a local
register. In this way it is possible to create an effect of code modification.

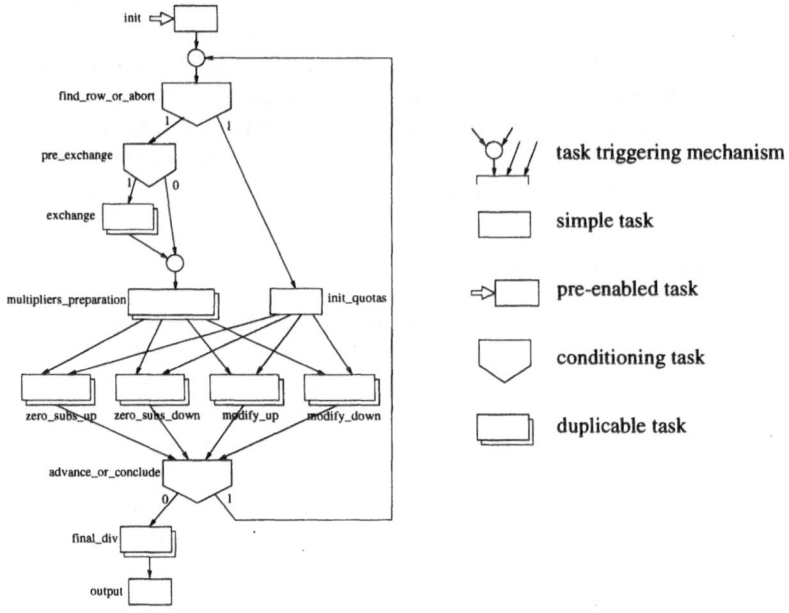

Fig. 3. Some symbols serving for graphical description of task maps (at the right),
and a complete task map (at the left); this example task map belongs to a program
that solves linear equation sets.

This brings us back from the programming model to the implementation:
The duplicable tasks are the key to the architecture, as the packs decomposed
and unified in the distribution network belong to successions of instantiations,
each derived from a single duplicable task. The task map is kept, in fact, by
the CSU.

2.5   The CSU Architecture

The CSU is the most critical component of the entire architecture. To investigate its feasibility, we have implemented a VLSI prototype CSU having the
following properties [7]:

- In every clock cycle, the CSU is capable of issuing allocation packs to four
  branches of the distribution network at once. Every pack may contain up
  to 4K task instantiations (distributed to up to 4K processors known to be
  available at issue time). These packs are derived from up to four different

tasks (which may be duplicable, conditioning, or simple). The generation of the packs is based on full crossing between the tasks ready to execute and the network branches ready to absorb new work. Likewise, in every . clock cycle the CSU is capable of receiving up to four termination packs.

- When a termination pack leads to the issue of a new allocation pack, by *enabling* a new task, the latency between the reception of the termination pack and the issuing of the new pack is one to three clock cycles, provided that there is no contention over ports, and that all the branches of the distribution network are ready to absorb work.

- It is possible to load a map of up to 256 tasks in the CSU, of which up to 128 are duplicable tasks, each equivalent to a "parallel do" structure of up to 2^{20} instantiations.

- The CSU can operate at a clock frequency of $f = 1/2T$, where T is the propagation delay of a 20-bit carry look ahead adder.

- The CMOS implementation of this architecture requires only about a quarter of a million of transistors.

The heart of this CSU architecture is the connection matrix (see Fig.4), in which the task map is coded through programmable connections between columns and rows. Each column is mapped to a task, and the termination of the task leads to an excitation of the column. This excitation may propagate along rows, and affect one or more *enabling cells* (the "e-cells" in the figure, to the right of the matrix), which are also mapped to tasks. An e-cell turns on only when all the conditions necessary for enabling the task for execution are met. If the task is duplicable, the cell turns off at the next clock cycle, but causes the initialization of certain fields in the record belonging to the task within the duplicable task record file. This record file is basically a multiported RAM. The enabling cells in an on state and the duplicable task records with pending instantiations feed, via fast multi-output priority encoders, an allocation pack issue unit. This unit is pipelined, and is assisted by another unit that monitors processor availability state.

3 Summary

Despite the enormous volume of ongoing research, there are still problems that hinder the turning of parallel computing into a practical general purpose technology comparable to serial computing [1]. Contrary to the prevailing trend of distributing the data across the processors and relying on locality, we propose an architectural/physical multiprocessor model that is based on tight coupling in the following sense: The collection of processors behaves as a single "super processor", working under fine or medium granularity vis-a-vis a symmetric memory. The corresponding programming model is similar to that of a uniprocessor, but also, to a certain extent, to that of a dataflow machine.

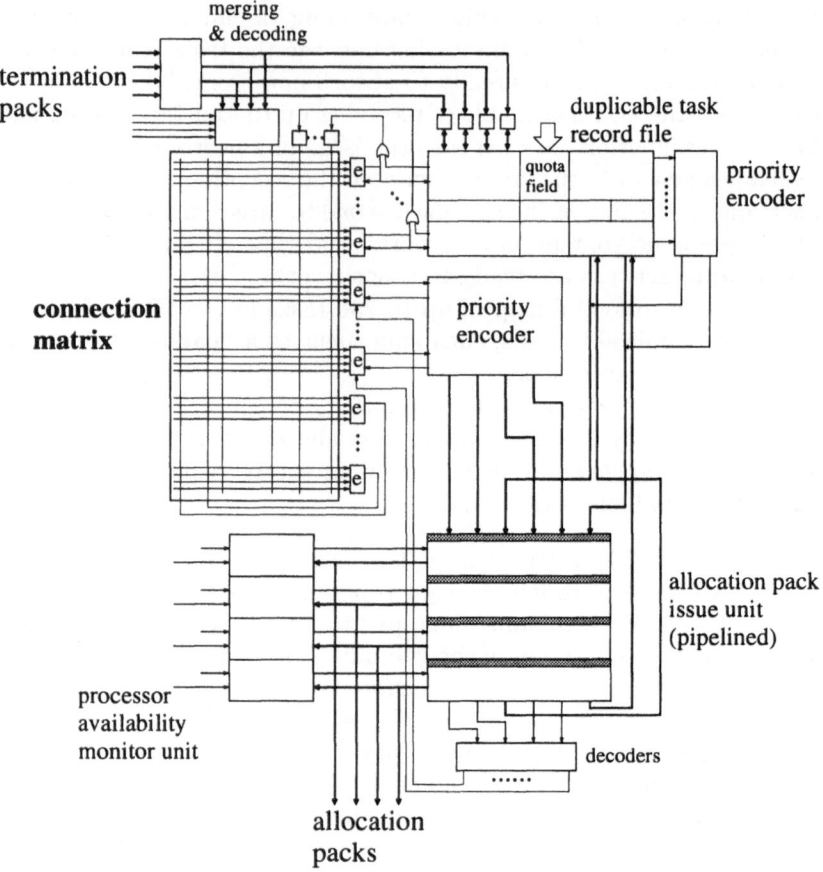

Fig. 4. The CSU architecture

Apart from the processors themselves, the main part of the "super processor" is the synchronizer/scheduler, which is responsible for coordinating the parallel work. The key for the efficient implementation of this apparatus and for preventing it from being a bottleneck is the employment of a decomposing/unifying distribution network, which creates an effect of flow-rate amplification. This relies on the presence of "parallel do" patterns within the dependency web of the program. It is possible to implement the building blocks of the synchronizer/scheduler, in particular its central synchronization/scheduling unit (CSU), as "hot chips": Dedicated, highly optimized, and based on internal parallelism and on pipelining. The CSU can be built around a connectionist structure, slightly reminiscent of a neural network. The synchronizer/scheduler as a whole, with its systolic-like structure, also embodies the traits just listed, despite containing a central unit.

The proposed architecture emphasizes the technological challenges. These seem to be related to the density of packaging circuits at the scale of a large system. They may serve as long term major challenges in their own right, much the same as the miniaturization of circuits on a single chip has served as a major technological challenge in the preceding decades.

References

1. David J. Kuck. *High Performance Computing*. Oxford University Press, 1996.
2. David E. Culler and Jaswinder Pal Singh (with Anoop Gupta). *Parallel Computer Architecture*. Morgan Kaufmann, 1999.
3. Jelica Protić, Milo Tomašević, and Veljko Milutinović. *Distributed Shared Memory—Concepts and Systems*. IEEE Computer Society, 1998.
4. Anujan Varma and C. S. Raghavendra. *Interconnection Networks for Multiprocessors and Multicomputers—Theory and Practice*. IEEE Computer Society Press, 1994.
5. A. Gottlieb, R. Grishman, C. P. Kruskal, K. P. McAaliffe, and M. Snir. The NYU Ultracomputer—designing an MIMD shared memory parallel computer. *IEEE Transactions on Computers*, pages 175–189, February 1983.
6. The "Top 500" web site, http://www.top500.org.
7. Peleg Avieli and Oded Rubenov. *A central synchronization/scheduling unit for multiprocessors*. Engineering project report, Ben-Gurion University of the Negev, September 1999 (In Hebrew, 200 pages).

A Mathematical Theory of NMR Quantum Computations

Tetsuro Nishino

Department of Information and Communication Engineering,
The University of Electro - Communications
Chofu, Tokyo, 182-8585, Japan
E-mail: nishino@ice.uec.ac.jp

Abstract. In this paper, we develop a theory of bulk quantum computations such as NMR (Nuclear Magnetic Resonance) quantum computations. For this purpose, we first define bulk quantum Turing machines (BQTMs for short) as a model of bulk quantum computation. Then, we define complexity classes EBQP, BBQP and ZBQP as counterparts of the quantum complexity classes EQP, BQP and ZQP, respectively, and show that EBQP=EQP, BBQP=BQP, and ZBQP=ZQP. This implies that BQTMs are polynomially related to ordinary QTMs as long as they are used to solve decision problems. We also show that these two types of QTMs are also polynomially related when they solve a function problem which has a unique solution. Furthermore, we show that BQTMs can solve certain instances of NP-complete problems efficiently.

1 Introduction

Current computers are implemented baed on Turing machine introduced by Alan Turing in 1936. Since Turing machine is a very simple and stable model of computation, it is used as a standard model in recursive function theory and computational complexity theory. Many results in complexity theory, however, suggests that deterministic Turing machines cannot efficiently solve hard combinatorial problems, such as NP-complete problems.

In 1985, David Deutsch introduced quantum Turing machines (QTMs for short) as Turing machines which can perform so called quantum parallel computations [7]. Then, in 1994, Peter Shor showed that QTM can factor integers with arbitrary small error probability in polynomial time [22]. Since it is widely believed that any deterministic Turing machines cannot factor integers in polynomial time, it is very likely that QTM is an essentially new model of computation. Many computer scientists are working hard in this area these days, and have obtained a lot of important results [2,12,22,23,28].

On the other hand, many researchers are studying how to physically implement quantum computers based on QTM. In fact, the methods using iron traps, a single photon, or quantum dots are proposed to realize basic elements of quantum computers. Among others, NMR (Nuclear Magnetic Resonance) offers an appealing prospect for implementation of quantum computers because of a number of reasons [3–6,8–11,13–21,24,25,27]. But, quantum computations performed on NMR is slightly defferent from those performed on QTMs as mentioned below.

One tape cell of a Turing machine can contain a symbol 0 or 1, i.e. one bit of information. On the other hand, one tape cell of a QTM can be in an arbitrary superposition of the states 0 and 1, which is called one *qubit* (*quantum bit*) of information. Here, a superposition of the states 0 and 1 is represented by $\alpha|0\rangle + \beta|1\rangle$, where $|0\rangle$ and $|1\rangle$ are state vectors in some Hilbert space representing the states corresponding to 0 and 1, respectively. α and β are complex numbers such that $|\alpha|^2 + |\beta|^2 = 1$, and α (β) is called an *amplitude* of the state $|0\rangle$ ($|1\rangle$).

A computation of a QTM is a sequence of applications of unitary transformations to some qubits on its tape. After the computation, if we observe a tape cell in a superposition $\alpha|0\rangle + \beta|1\rangle$, we will see 0 (1) with probability $|\alpha|^2$ ($|\beta|^2$). Thus, if we observe a tape cell in a superposition $\frac{1}{\sqrt{2}}|0\rangle + \frac{1}{\sqrt{2}}|1\rangle$, we will see 0 or 1 with equal probability $1/2$. Namely, this tape cell is an ideal random bit. But, when we observe this tape cell, the superposition is completely destroyed.

On the other hand, NMR quantum computation can be essentially considered as follows: a large number of QTMs, each of which corresponds to a molecule, execute the same program (i.e. a state transition function). Let a certain tape cell be in a superposition $\alpha|0\rangle + \beta|1\rangle$ after some quantum computation on NMR. Then, if we measure the cell, we are given the real number $|\beta|^2 - |\alpha|^2$. This is the expectation of the value obtained when the cell is observed, because, in NMR, 0 is represented by -1 and 1 is represented by 1. Furthermore, by this measurement, the superposition will not be destroyed for a while. Thus, we can read several times the real values such as above from the superpositon.

For example, if we observe a tape cell in a superposition $\frac{1}{\sqrt{2}}|0\rangle + \frac{1}{\sqrt{2}}|1\rangle$ at the end of an NMR quantum computation, we will obtain the value $|\frac{1}{\sqrt{2}}|^2 - |\frac{1}{\sqrt{2}}|^2 = 0$ with probability 1. Namely, in the case of NMR quantum computation, we cannot implement a random bit by the usual method. Thus, it is quite unclear whether NMR quantum computers can perform ordinary quantum computations defined by QTMs. In this paper, in order to give some insights into this problem, we develop a theory of bulk quantum computations including NMR quantum computation.

2   Polynomial Time Computation

In this section, we first introduce a bulk quantum Turing machine (BQTM for short) as a mathematical model of bulk quantum computations.

Definition 1. A *bulk quantum Turing machine* (*BQTM* for short) is a 7-tuple $M = (Q, \Sigma, \Gamma, \delta, q_0, B, F)$, which is defined in exactly the same way as in [2]. In the case of BQTM, however, axioms for the observation are changed as follows. In this paper, we use the term "measurement" to mean the "observation" for BQTMs in order to clarify our presentation. If a tape cell of a BQTM is in a superposition $\alpha|0\rangle + \beta|1\rangle$, the real number $\theta = |\beta|^2 - |\alpha|^2$ will be measured. Since $|\alpha|^2 + |\beta|^2 = 1$, it follows that $-1 \leq \theta \leq 1$. We assume that this real number θ is represented by a binary number to k places of decimals with a sign, where k is a constant. For example, if $k = 5$, θ may be given by -0.00101.

In the sequel, let $\varepsilon = 1/2^k$.

Then, if we measure a tape cell of a BQTM in a superposition $\alpha|0\rangle + \beta|1\rangle$, we assume that a real number θ such that $|\beta|^2 - |\alpha|^2 - \varepsilon \leq \theta \leq |\beta|^2 - |\alpha|^2 + \varepsilon$ will be read with probability 1.

Furthermore, we assume that we cannot perform a partial observation in the case of BQTM. When we observe several tape cells of a BQTM, only thing we can do is to get a real number θ at each tape cell, independently. Instead, we assume that the superposition will not be destroyed for a while. That is, we assume that we can measure the tape cells in the superpositon some constant times before the superposition is destroyed.

In computational complexity theory, a problem is considered to be a membership problem for a certain languge. Let Σ be an alphabet. A membership problem for a language $L \subseteq \Sigma^*$ is as follows: given a string $x \in \Sigma^*$ decide whether $x \in L$. A language L is in the class EQP (*Exact Quantum Polynomial time*) if there exists a QTM with a distinguished acceptance tape cell and a polynomial p such that, given an arbitrary input string x, whether $x \in L$ is decided with probability 1 by observing the acceptance tape cell at time $p(|x|)$ [2].

We define a bulk quantum analog of the class EQP as follows. Let ε be a constant which is mentioned in Definition 2.1. A language L is in the class $EBQP$ (*Exact Bulk Quantum Polynomial time*) if there exists a BQTM with a distinguished acceptance tape cell and a polynomial p such that, given an arbitrary input string x, whether $x \in L$ is decided with probability 1 by measuring the acceptance tape cell at time $p(|x|)$ in the following fashion: if the value $\theta \geq 1 - \varepsilon$ is obtained then $x \in L$, else if $\theta \leq -1 + \varepsilon$ then $x \notin L$.

On the other hand, a language L is in the class BQP (*Bounded error Quantum Polynomial time*) if there exists a QTM with a distinguished acceptance tape cell and a polynomial p such that, given an arbitrary input string x, whether $x \in L$ is decided with probability at least $2/3$ by observing the acceptance tape cell at time $p(|x|)$ [2].

We define a bulk quantum analog of the class BQP as follows. Let ε be a constant which is mentioned in Definition 2.1. A language L is in the class $BBQP$ (*Bounded error Bulk Quantum Polynomial time*) if there exists a BQTM with a distinguished acceptance tape cell and a polynomial p such that, given an arbitrary input string x, whether $x \in L$ is decided with probability 1 by measuring the acceptance tape cell at time $p(|x|)$ in the following fashion: if the value $\theta \geq 1/3 - \varepsilon$ is obtained then $x \in L$, else if $\theta \leq -1/3 + \varepsilon$ then $x \notin L$.

A language L is in the class *ZQP* (*Zero error Quantum Polynomial time*) if there exists a QTM with a distinguished acceptance tape cell and a halting cell, and a polynomial p such that, given an arbitrary input string x, (1) if the halting cell is observed at time $p(|x|)$, 1 (which means the machine has been terminated)is seen with probability at least $1/2$, and (2) when 1 is observed at the halting cell, whether $x \in L$ is decided with probability 1 by observing the acceptance tape cell.

In order to define a bulk quantum analog of the class ZQP, i.e. ZBQP, we need some consideration. In the case of ZQP, if the acceptance tape cell is observed and 1 is seen, all the configurations in the superposition with a 0 on the acceptance tape cell will disappear. This is because a partial observation is possible in the case of QTM. On the other hand, a partial observation is not allowed in the case of BQTM. Thus, even when the acceptance tape cell of a BQTM is measured and $\theta = 1$ is obtained, no configuration in the superposition with a 0 on the acceptance tape cell will disappear. So, we cannot directly use a ZQP machine as a ZBQP machine as we did in the cases of EBQP and BBQP. But, if we prepare a two acceptance cells called ZERO and ONE for a ZBQP machine, we can define ZBQP as a bulk quantum analog of the class ZQP. The cell ZERO (ONE) is set to 0 (1) before the computation of a ZBQP machine M, and if M decides that $x \in L$ ($x \notin L$) then M writes 1 (0) on both of ZERO and ONE.

Let ε be a constant which is mentioned in Definition 2.1. A language L is in the class *ZBQP* (*Zero error Bulk Quantum Polynomial time*) if there exists a BQTM with a halting cell, and two acceptance tape cells ZERO and ONE described above, and a polynomial p such that, given an arbitrary input string x, (1) if the halting cell is measured at time $p(|x|)$, a value $\theta \geq -\varepsilon$ is given with probability 1, and (2) exactly one of the following two cases will take place : (a) if the cell ZERO is measured, the value $\theta \leq -1 + \varepsilon$ is given with probability 1, or (b) if the cell ONE is measured, the value $\theta \geq 1 - \varepsilon$ is given with probability 1. Then, we obtain the follwing theorems

Theorem 1. *(1) EQP = EBQP, (2) BQP = BBQP, and (3) ZQP = ZBQP.*

3   Function Problems and NP-Complete Problems

Let $R \subseteq \Sigma^* \times \Sigma^*$ be a relation. A *function problem* corresponding to R is the following computation problem : given $x \in \Sigma^*$, find a string $y \in \Sigma^*$ such that $R(x, y)$ if such a string exists, and if such a string does not exist, return NO. For example, the factoring problem may be corresponded to the relation $R(x, y)$ which is defined as follows : for integers x and y, R holds iff $y = p\#q$ for some integers p and q (# is a delimitter), and $x = p \times q$.

In this paper, we only consider the function problems whose underlying relations R satisfy the following Condition A.

Condition A   For every x, there is *at most one* y which satisfies $R(x, y)$.

For example, this condition holds in the case of the factoring problem where it is promised that an input is a prime number or an integer which is a product of two prime numbers. In the case of SAT, it is known that we can introduce this condition without loosing generality [26].

Let us consider the following case : there exists a QTM M and a polynomial p such that, given an arbitrary input string $x \in \Sigma^*$, the unique string $y \in \Sigma^*$ such that $R(x, y)$ is observed on the tape of M with probability at least $2/3$ at time $p(|x|)$ if such a string y exists, and if such a string does not exists, M returns NO.

Then, we obtain the following theorem.

Theorem 2. *There exists a BQTM M' and a polynomial p' such that, given an arbitrary input string $x \in \Sigma^*$, the unique string $y \in \Sigma^*$ such that $R(x, y)$ of above is obtained with probability at least $2/3$ at time $p'(|x|)$ if such a string y exists, and if such a string does not exists, M' returns NO.*

To find a method to solve NP-complete problems efficiently is a challenging problem in computer science. In this section, we show that BQTM can be used for this purpose in some cases.

Let us consider the satisfiability problem (SAT for short) of m-variable logical formula $f(x_1, x_2, \ldots, x_n)$, where $x_i, i = 1, 2, \ldots, m$ are Boolean variables. The BQTM M works as follows:

1. (Preparation of assignments)   The description of the logical formula f and the number m of the variables are given as input on the tape of M. In the sequel, we identify a configuration of M with a description of an assignment to the variables in f and the corresponding value of f. Thus, let $|x_1, \ldots, x_m, x_{m+1}\rangle$ represents a configuration of M, where $x_1, \ldots, x_m$ are qubits corresponding to m variables in f, and x_{m+1} is a qubit corresponding to the value of f, respectively. Let $|0, \ldots, 0, 0\rangle$ is the initial configuration of M.

   There exist 2^m different assignments for m variables of f. M makes a superposition of the 2^m different configurations corresponding to these 2^m different assignments. M performs this by applying

$$V = \frac{1}{\sqrt{2}} \begin{pmatrix} 1 & -1 \\ 1 & 1 \end{pmatrix}$$

   to each qubit from x_1 to x_m. M can execute each application of this transformation in a single step. After this step, we obtain the following superposition:

$$\frac{1}{\sqrt{2^m}} \sum_{x_1=0}^{1} \cdots \sum_{x_m=0}^{1} |x_1, \ldots x_m, 0\rangle.$$

2. (Computation of the values of f)   Now, in each configuration in the superposition of above, an assignment for the variables $x_1, \ldots, x_m$ are specified. Thus, M can evaluate the values of f for these 2^m different assignments simultaneously. M performs this by simulating a deterministic reversible Turing machine [1] which eval uates the value of f under a specified assignment for m variables. After this st ep, we obtain the following superposition:

$$\frac{1}{\sqrt{2^m}} \sum_{x_1=0}^{1} \cdots \sum_{x_m=0}^{1} |x_1, \ldots x_m, f(x_1, \ldots, x_m)\rangle.$$

3. (Measurement of x_{m+1} and output of the result)   Finally, we measure the qubit x_{m+1} and obtain a real number θ. If $x_{m+1} = 0$ in all the 2^m configurations in the superposition of above, $|x_{m+1}\rangle$ is in the superposition $1 \times |0\rangle + 0 \times |1\rangle$. In this case, we obtain $\theta = -1$ and it is concluded that f is not satisfiable. On the other hand, if at least one x_m in the superposition is equal to 1, then $\theta > -1$. In this case, f is satisfiable.

If we can obtain the value of θ with an arbitrary small accuracy, the algorithm of above always works correctly. But, it is assumed that the accuracy of the value θ is 2^{-k} in this paper. Let $h(l)$ be the minimun number of steps of a reversible Turing machine which decides the value of a Boolean expression with the description length l when a variable assignment is given. Then, we obtain the following theorem.

Theorem 3. *Let k be an integer mentioned in Definition 2.1. There exists a BQTM which solves the satisfiability problem for Boolean expressions with k variables within $h(l) + cl$ steps, where l is the length of the given Boolean expression, and c is a constant.*

Theorem 4. *Let k be an integer mentioned in Definition 2.1. There exists a BQTM which solves within $h(l) + cl$ steps the satisfiability problem for Boolean expressions with n variables such that the number of satisfing assignments is $\geq 2^{n-k}$, where l is the length of the given Boolean expression, and c is a constant.*

Notice that, if we simulate the BQTM in Theorem 3.2 by using a deterministic Turing machine in a straightforward fashion, it would require $2^k h(l)$ steps.

The basic idea of the above method is originally mentioned in [6]. In practical situation, it may be useful to apply Grover's algorithm [12] to the qubit x_m before the measurement, in order to increse the amplitude of $|1\rangle$.

4   Concluding Remarks

In this paper, we have shown that BQTMs are polynomially related to ordinary QTMs as long as they are used to solve decision problems. Namely, we have shown that EBQP=EQP, BBQP=BQP, and ZBQP=ZQP.

The function problems solved by the algorithms proposed by Shor [22] and Grover [12] do not satisfy the Condition A in the previous section. But, we can easily show that the both algorithms can be efficiently executed on BQTMs.

Finally, it is easy to see that the method used in Theorems 3.2 and 3.3 can be similarly applied to any problem in the class NP.

References

1. Bennett, C. H. : "Logical Reversibility of Computation", *IBM J. Res. Dev.*, Vol. 6, pp.525-532 (1973).
2. Bernstein, E., and Vazirani, U. : "Quantum Complexity Theory", in *Proc. 25th Annual ACM Symposium on Theory of Computing*, ACM, New York, 1993, pp.11-20. Also in Special issue of *SIAM J. Comp.*, October, 1997.
3. Brun, T., and Schack, R. : "Realizing the quantum baker's map on an NMR quantum computer", quant-ph/9807050, 1998.
4. Chuang, I. L., Gershenfeld, N., and Kubinec, M. G. : "Experimental Implementation of Fast Quantum Serching", *Phys. Rev. Letters*, Vol. 80, Issue 15, pp.3408-3411 (1998).
5. Chuang, I. L., Gershenfeld, N., Kubinec, M.G., and Leung, D.W. : "Bulk Quantum Computation with Nuclear Magnetic Resonance : Theory and Experiment", *Proc. R. Soc. Lond.*, Vol. A 454, pp.447-467 (1998).
6. Cory, D. G., Fahmy, A. F., and Havel, T. F. : "Ensemble Quantum Computing by Nuclear Magnetic Resonance Spectroscopy", *Proc. Natl. Acad. Sci. 94*, pp.1634-1639 (1997).
7. Deutsch, D. : "Quantum Theory,the Church-Turing Principle and the Universal Quantum Computer", *Proc. R. Soc. Lond.*, Vol. A 400, pp.97-117 (1985).
8. Dorai, K., Kumar, A., and Kumar A. : "Implementing quantum logic operations, pseudo-pure states and the Deutsch-Jozsa algorithm using non-commuting selective pulses in NMR", quant-ph/9906027, 1999.
9. Fang, X., Zhu, X., Feng, M., Mao, X., and Du, F. : "Experimental Implementation of Dense Coding Using Nuclear Magnetic Resonance", quant-ph/9906041, 1999.
10. Fu, L., Luo, J., Xiao, L., and Zeng, X. : "Experimental Realization of Discrete Fourier Transformation on NMR Quantum Computer", quant-ph/9905083, 1999.
11. Gershenfeld, N., and Chuang, I. L. : *Science*, Vol.275, p.350 (1997).
12. Grover, L. : "A Fast Quantum Mechanical Algorithm for Database Search, in *Proc. 28th Annual ACM Symposium on Theory of Computing*, ACM, New York, 1996, pp.212-219.
13. Havel, T. F., Somaroo, S. S., Tseng C.-H., and Croy, D. G. : "Principles and Demonstrations of Quantum Information Processing by NMR Spectroscopy", quant-ph/9812086, 1998.
14. Jones, J. A., and Mosca, M. : "Approximate quantum counting on an NMR ensemble quantum computer", quant-ph/9808056, 1998.
15. Jones, J. A., and Knill, E. : "Efficient Refocussing of One Spin and Two Spin Interactions for NMR Quantum Computation", quant-ph/9905008, 1999.

16. Linden, N., Barjat, H., and Freeman, R. : "An implementation of the Deutsch-Jozsa algorithm on a three-qubit NMR quantum computer ", quant-ph/9808039, 1998.
17. Linden, N., and Popescu, S. : "Good dynamics versus bad kinematics. Is entanglement needed for quantum computation ?", quant-ph/9906008, 1999.
18. Luo, J., and Zeng, X. : "NMR Quantum Computation with a hyperpolarized nuclear spin bulk", quant-ph/9811044, 1998.
19. Marx, R., Fahmy, A. F., Myers, J. M, Bermel, W., and Glaser, S. J. : "Realization of a 5-Bit NMR Quantum Computer Using a New Molecular Architecture", quant-ph/9905087, 1999.
20. Pravia, M., Fortunato, E., Weinstein, Y., Price, M. D., Teklemariam, G., Nelson, R. J., Sharf, Y., Somaroo, S., Tseng, C. H., Havel, T. F., and Cory, D. G. : "Observations of Quantum Dynamics by Solution-State NMR Spectroscopy", quant-ph/9905061, 1999.
21. Schulman, L. J., and Vazirani, U. : "Scalable NMR Quantum Computaion", quant-ph/9804060, 1998.
22. Shor, P. W. : "Algorithms for Quantum Computation : Discrete Log and Factoring", in *Proceedings of the 35th Annual IEEE Symposium on Foundations of Computer Science*, 1994, pp.124-134. Also in Special issue of *SIAM J. Comp.*, October, 1997.
23. Simon, D. R. : "On the Power of Quantum Computation", in *Proceedings of the 35th Annual IEEE Symposium on Foundations of Computer Science*, 1994, pp.116-123. Also in Special issue of *SIAM J. Comp.*, October, 1997.
24. Somaroo, S., Tseng, C. H., Havel, T. F., Laflamme, R., and Cory, D. G. : "Quantum Simulations on Quantum Computer", quant-ph/9905045, 1999.
25. Vandersypen, L. M. K., Yannoni, C. S., Sherwood, M. H., and Chuang, I. L. : "Realization of effective pure states for bulk quantum computation", quant-ph/9905041, 1999.
26. Valiant, L. G., and Vazirani, V. V. : "NP is as easy as detecting unique solutions", *Theoretical Computer Science*, Vol. 47, pp.85-93 (1986).
27. Wei, H., Xue, X., and Morgera, S. D. : "NMR Quantum Automata in Doped Crystals", quant-ph/9805059, 1998.
28. Yao, A. : "Quantum Circuit Complexity", in *Proc. 34th Symposium on Foundations of Computer Science*, pp.352-361, IEEE Press (1993).

Quantum Computation Using Artificial Molecules

Nan-Jian Wu

National Laboratory for Superlattices and Microstructure,
Institute of semiconductor, Chinese Academy of Science
P.O. Box 912, Beijing 100083, China
E-mail: nanjian@red.semi.ac.cn

Abstract. Two kinds of quantum computation systems using artificial molecules: quantum computer and quantum analog computer are described. The artificial molecule consists of two or three coupled quantum dots stacked along z direction and one single electron. In quantum computer, one-qubit and two-qubit gates are constructed by one molecule and two molecules, respectively. The coupling between two qubits in a quantum gate can be controlled by thin film electrodes. We also constructed a quantum analog computer by designing a three-dot molecule network and mapping a graph 3-colorability problem onto the network. The ground-state configuration of the single electrons in the network corresponds to one of the problem solutions. We numerically study the operations of the two kinds of the quantum computers and demonstrate that they quantum gates can perform the quantum computation and solve complex problems.

1   Introduction

One of the challenges in nanoelectronics is to develop information-processing systems that are based on quantum mechanical principle and solid-state devices. To construct such systems, one must employ computing paradigms that are suitable for a quantum structure system and whose computational power surpasses that of the classical Neumann-type computation model, and must create feasible quantum devices. This paper gives two novel quantum computation systems that use quantum-dot artficial molecule networks.

We proposed a novel method for implementation of quantum computer gates that use artificial molecules.[1] One-qubit and two-qubit gates are constructed by one molecule and two coupled molecules, respectively.   The method for implementation of the quantum computer has the following features: 1) The structures of the basic quantum gates are simple and can be fabricated by existing technologies; 2) The implementation can be extended to a large-scale quantum computer; 3) Except for the signals that control the quantum computation process, external electric field and magnetic field are not necessary to be applied to the gates so that the coupling of the electrons with external degrees of freedom can be reduced.

A novel quantum analog computer using an artificial molecule network is given.[2] We constructed an three-dot artificial molecule network and mapped a graph 3-colorability problem on it by appling the analog between the problem and the network. We numerically simulated the behavior of the network and demonstrated that analog computation allows us to solve complex problems.

Both of quantum computer and quantum analog computer can compute faster because they perform a computation simultaneously. But, they are quite different from each other in operating principle. Although a superposition of many different numbers can be acceptted by as the iniţial input, but information is processed by different physical means in two kinds of the computers. The computation in quantum computer is not only reversible but also coherent. By contrast, in quantum analog computer the computational process corresponds to the dynamics of physical system with energy dispation and is not reversible. In the following sections, we first present the structures of quantum gates and describe their operations. Next, we present the analog computation system that uses an artficial molecule network. We also discuss issues related to the physical implementation of the quantum computer and quantum analog computer. Finally, we will summarize the main results.

2 Quantum Computer

Although some implementation of quantum gates have been proposed using solid-state strucuture,[3~6] but it is not clear whether these implementations can be extended to large-scale quantum computer or can be fabricated by the existing technologies. We proposed a novel method for implementing quantum gates. Figure 1 shows the schematic structure of the proposed qubit using an artificial molecule. The molecule consists of two stacked asymmetric quantum dots with a disk shape and one single electron. The electron can tunnel between two quantum dots. The dimensions of the asymmetric quantum dots are designed well so that the ground and first excited sates are mainly localized in the dot 1 and dot 2, respectively, as shown in Fig.1(b). The energy states of the artificial molecule exhibit bistable polarization of the charge and can be used to represent |0> and |1> states of the qubit. A resonant electromagnetic wave is used to irradiate and manipulate the qubit through a microstrip line integrated on the substrate. The approach has the following advantages: 1) A qubit can be addressed by a microstrip line connected directly to it; 2) it can be realized by the existing nano-fabrication and large scale integrated circuit (LSI) technologies; and 3) comparing with other kinds of qubits in which the |0> and |1> states are prepared by biasing external electrical field or magnetic field, the coupling of the electrons in our qubit with external degrees of freedom can be reduced.

We can constitute a quantum controlled NOT (CN) gate using two qubits with different resonance frequencies. Figure 2 shows the schematic structure of the CN gate that consists a control qubit and a target qubit. The diameters of the quantum dots in the control qubit are designed to be different from the diameters of the dots in the target qubit, respectively. The coupling between the two qubits are controlled by three metal film electrodes between the qubits: upper electrode, middle electrode and lower electrode. The middle electrode is always grounded. We numerically calculated the electrostatic interaction between the electrons in the qubits. If the upper and lower electrodes are floated, the electrons at two kinds of configurations: 1) occupying dot 1 (dot2) and dot 3 (dot4) and 2) occupying dot 1 (dot2) and dot 4 (dot3) can be coupled by Coulomb repulsion interactions U

and U_1, respectively. But, Coulomb repulsion interaction U is much larger than U_1. Therefore the two qubits are coupled by the dipole-dipole interactions. The electronic state of the target qubit depends on the state of the control qubit. On the other hand, if all of the electrodes between the qubits are grounded, it is found that the interaction energy between the electrons can be controlled to be smaller than 10^{-10} eV. Consequently, Coulomb interaction between the qubits can be turned off, that is, the energy levels of the two-qubit gate can be controlled by turning on/off the electrostatic interaction between two electrons, as shown in Fig. 2(c).

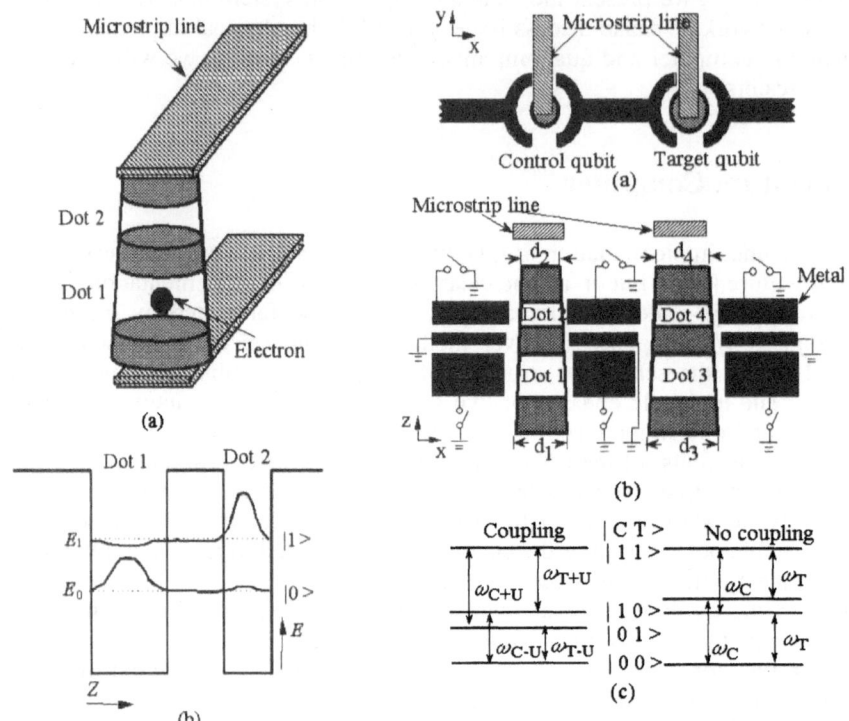

Fig. 1. (a) Schematic structure of a qubit using two coupled uantum dots (an artificial molecule), and (b) electron potential along z direction and two lowest energy levels of the qubit. The structure contains a microstrip line.

Fig.2 (a) a top view of the CN gate; (b) a cross section of the CN gate; (c) energy levels of the gates when the coupling between the qubits is turned on or off. ω_T and ω_c are the resonant frequencies of the control and target qubits.

The quantum CN gate operates as follows. First we turn on the Coulomb interaction between two qubits by floating the upper and lower electrodes. Then we use the resonant electromagnetic wave of the frequency ω_{T+U} to irradiate target qubit for π pulse time. If the control qubit is set to |0>, the target qubit does not change its state, and if the control qubit is |1>, the target qubit change its state from

|0> (|1>) to |1> (|0>). Therefore, the XOR operation is reached. Finally the Coulomb interaction is turned off, the state of one qubit becomes independent on that of the other qubit. The CN gate has the advantages: 1) the coupling between the qubits can simply controlled by floating or grounding the metal electrodes; and 2) even if the length of the metal electrode between two qubits is made longer, the Coulomb repulsion interactions U can be maintained so that the array of the qubits in the quantum computer is designed easily.

We analyzed the operation of the quantum logic gates by the simulation method and demonstrated that the proposed quantum gates can perform quantum computation.[1] We use a box-shaped potential as an analytic model of the quantum dot. The above model is applied to a concrete example of the qubit that is formed by the stacked GaAs/AlGaAs quantum dots. Figure 3 shows the calculated results of the operation of the qubit. The dependence of the probabilities $|\alpha|^2$ and $|\beta|^2$ of the |0> and |1> states on the irradiation of the electromagnetic wave obtained. The dielectric constant was taken to be 10. The effective mass of the electron is $0.67m_0$. The energy difference between the |0> and |1> states of the qubit was set to about 25 meV. The frequency and the amplitude (electric field) of the resonant electromagnetic field is 6 THz and 1.5mV/nm, respectively. As shown in Fig. 3, the qubit changes its states from |0> (|1>) to |1> (|0>) due to irradiation of the electromagnetic wave for the π-pulse time. The operating speed of the gate is very fast(about operation per 4ps). On the other hand, when a π/2-pulse of the electromagnetic wave was irradiated on the qubit, the operation of Hadamard transformation was given.

Figure 4 shows the calculated results of the operation of the two-qubit CN gate. The resonant energies of the control and the target qubits were set to 26 meV and 18 meV, respectively. The Coulomb repulsion interaction energy U was taken to 10meV. As shown in Fig. 4, it was confirmed that if the control and target qubits are set to different states, such as |0>, |1> and α|0> + β|1>, respectively, the XOR operation and the entanglement states were realized by applying intelligently the resonant electromagnetic wave with frequency ω_{T+U}. The above results demonstrated that the proposed gates can be used to construct the quantum computer and perform quantum computation.

3   Quantum Analog Computation

Analog computation is a novel processing method for solving mathematical problems. Figure 1 shows the concept and the basic processes of analog computation. When a mathematical problem is given, we must find an appropriate physical system in which the mathematical relationships between the physical quantities are analogous to those between the variables. We use the physical quantities to represent all the problem variables. Then we operate the physical system and shift it from one non-stable state to a stable one by controlling the dynamic process. Finally, we solve the problem by measuring the quantities of the physical system. Analog computation is quite different from binary-digital computation. In digital computation, one first devises an appropriate algorithm and then executes serially the instructions in the manner of Boolean operation.

Finally, semiconductor integrated circuits (LSI) are used to implement the digital computation. By contrast, in analog computation a mathematical problem is directly mapped to an appropriate physical system and solved by using the natural properties of the physical system. Analog computation is based on the natural properties of physical systems and not on symbolic operations. In analog computation, the dynamics of physical systems correspond to the computational process, and changes in the physical quantities occur simultaneously when the physical system is operated. Analog computation is massively parallel and instantaneous. Thus, it is an approach capable of circumventing the Neumann bottleneck and quickly solving complex problems.

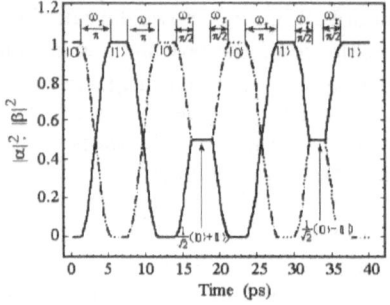

Fig. 3. Calculated basic and Hadamard operations of the qubit. The probabilities of the |0> and |1> states were given. ω_r is the resonance frequency of the qubit.

Fig. 4. Calculated basic operations of the CN gate and an example entanglement state. The probabilities of the |00>, |01>, |01> and |11> states were given.

ω_{T+U} is the resonance frequency of the target qubit.

(Dot 1 : w = 24nm and h = 20nm; dot 2: w = 22 and h = 15nm; dot 3 : w = 29nm and h = 20nm; dot 4: w = 27 and h = 15nm; separation between two dots is 7nm)

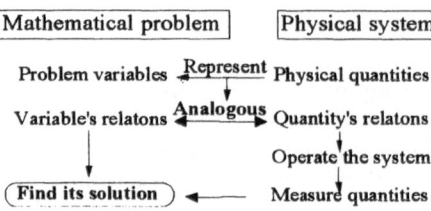
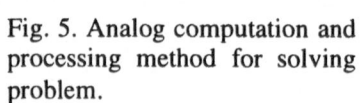

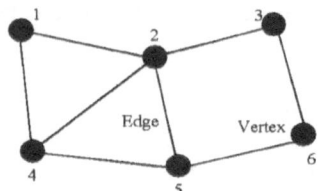

Fig. 5. Analog computation and processing method for solving problem.

Fig. 6. Example of graph 3-colorability problem with six vertices and eight edges.

There are many combinatiorial optimization problems of inherent complexity. These include such as the traveling salesman problem, the graph K-colorability problem, economics, engineering, and very large scale integration (VLSI) design. Most of these belong to a class called nondeterministic polynomial time(NP)-complete problems, and are intractable for Neumann-type digital computation. Solving them requires computational effort that grows exponentially with the size of the problems. However, any NP-complete problem can be quickly converted to another NP-complete problem. In other words, if we found a novel method (or algorithm) for solving one NP-complete problem, we could solve all NP-complete problems by reducing them to the solved one.

Analog computation may be capable of solving this kind of problem.[2] We will describe an NP-complete problem: a graph 3-colorability problem, and look for an analogous physical system. *Given an n-vertex graph G with m edges, the graph 3-colorability problem is defined as the problem:. Can the graph G be colored with three hues such that no two vertices connected by an edge have the same color?* The problem can be considered a planer graph problem with no vertex degree exceeding 4. There are colorable and uncolorable ones in graph 3-colorablity problems. The answer can be obtained by examining all the possible colorings. But, solving the problem by the way requires substantial computation time, and this time grows (3^n) exponentially with the problem size n. Figure 6 shows an example of a graph 3-colorability problem with six vertices and eight edges.

The single-electron configuration in a quantum system is highly complex and changes over time. If we could develop a good design for a quantum structure system and the interactions among electrons, it would be possible to construct an analog computation system to solve such problems. We proposed a quantum artficial molecule network and described a method for mapping a graph 3-colorability problem onto this network. We designed a quantum-dot artficial molecule used to represent three colors. The molecule consists of three stacked quantum dots and a single electron, as shown in Fig. 7. The single electron can tunnel among the three quantum dots. We use the single electron as an information carrier and assign a color to each of the three quantum dots C_{ij} (j=1, 2, 3) at molecule i. The state that the single electron occupies, dot C_{11} represents red, C_{12}, blue, and C_{13}, yellow.

Consider the process of mapping the graph 3-colorability problem onto a artficial molecule network in order to solve it. We must use a network with six molecules (Fig. 7) to solve a graph 3-colorability problem with six vertices (Fig. 6). To ensure that the vertices are connected by an edge, the corresponding molecules are designed to be coupled according to the short-range electron-electron repulsion interaction with image charge effect. The other molecules, corresponding to the vertices that are not connected by an edge, are separated by metal film to prevent interaction.   The single electrons in a pair of coupled molecules tend to occupy the different color dots to lower the electrostatic interaction energy. Consequently, the electron configuration in the ground state of the single-electron configuration of the network can be mapped to solution of the graph 3-colorability problem.   Finding the ground state of the electron configuration in the network is analogous to solving the problem. If the coupled single electrons in the ground state of the network occupy different color dots in different molecules, the graph is colorable, and the single electron configuration gives a possible solution. If not, the graph is uncolorable. Note that although the details of the evolution of the electron configuration in the network are not essential to a correct solution, the dynamics of the electrons in the network correspond to the computing process and determine the computational speed.

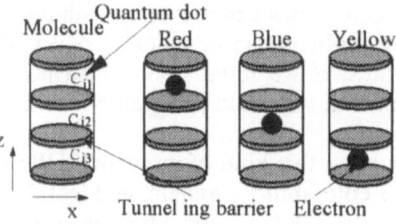

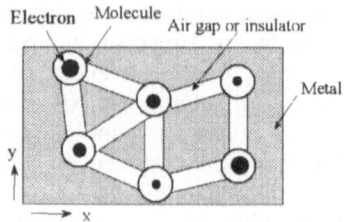

Fig. 7. Schematic structure of artificial molecule consisting of three stached quantum dots and one single election. Dot location in molecul is used to encode one color.

Fig. 8. Network of six molecules analogous to 3-coloring problem in Fig. 6. Molecure corresponding to connected vertices are coupled though air-gap. Other molecules are separated by metal film

We analyzed the ground states of molecule networks using the Hubbard model and used a simulated annealing method[2,7] to obtain the ground states of several networks with n (=4~14) molecules. Figure 9 shows an example: the typical development of the system energy for the network shown in Fig. 8. Figure 10 shows one solution to the graph 3-colorability problem. Initially, we randomly selected an electron configuration in the network, and the system energy decreased as the electron configuration changes. The system finally reached a ground. This ground state provides one solution to the graph 3-colorability problem. The graph is colorable. The result proves that this cell network is capable of performing analog computation.

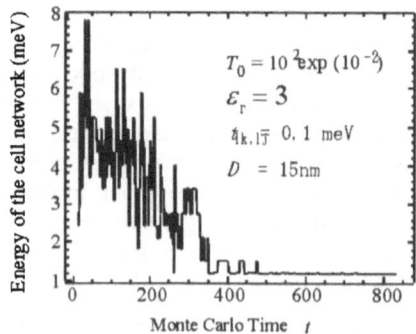

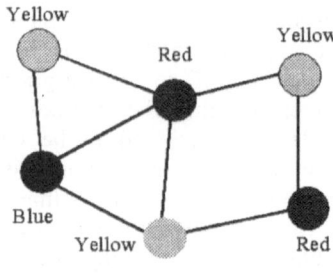

Figure 9. Typical developments in energy in six-milecule network with simulated annealing time.

Figure 10. A solution to graph 3 colorability problem in Fig. 8.

4   Discussion

Here we discuss issues related to the fabrication, computational dynamics process and reading mechanisms of quantum computer and analog computation using artificail molecules. The rapid progress in nanotechnology has made it possible to fabricate fine quantum-dot structures as small as 5-100 nm. Several techniques, such as a mesa etching of multi-barrier heterostructures, and self-organized growth, have been proposed as ways to produce a two-dimension array of stacked quantum dots. Our artificial networks can be produced by combining the techniques above and standard semiconductor processes used in LSI fabrication. After fabricating the two-dimensional array of the molecules, the metal film between the cells can be produced by using a film deposition, lithography and etching process.

There are many physical mechanisms in the quantum system, which contribute to energy dissipation. These include phonon scattering, spontaneous emission and impurity scattering. In quantum computation, the processes induce decohence. Although the impurity scattering results in departures from unitary strucuture of quantum evolution, in principle, impurities can be reduced by improving the crystal growth and nanofabrication technologies. However, the copuling of the elctrons to the phonons is unavoidable. But, if we lower the temperature of the system and design a qubit so that the energy difference between the $|0>$ and $|1>$ states is lager than energies of optical and acoustic phonon, the number of phonons and the electron-phonon scattering rate may be lowered by the well-known phonon bottleneck phenomenon. The quantum computer can work.

By constract, in analog computation, the dissipation processes generally determine computation speed. The faster the dissipation process, the higer the computation speed.   We considered a controlled experimental method for performing analog computation: an annealing method used to obtain a stable state in a crystal lattice. This method has two steps:1) the artificial molecule network is placed in an initial state with a higher temperature or greater energy, and 2) the temperature or energy of the network is decreased carefully(exponentially) until the ideal electron configuration is reached in the ground state. The process is practically parallel simulated annealing and can effectively generate a ground state. Instead of temperature, laser or electromagnetic waves can be also used as the controlling parameter of the annealing process.

The reading of the electron configuration can be done by detecting the voltage potential[7]. We calculated the potential near the upper dot of the cell and discovered that the voltage potential distribution changes markedly when a single electron tunnels among three dots in a molecule. After analog computation, the electron configuration can be detected by using a   single-electron-transistor (SET) electrometer   or SET scanning electrometer to measure the voltage potential distribution.

Reference

1.   N.-J. Wu, M. Kamada, A. Natori and H. Yasunaga, Jpn. J. Appl. Phys. **39**(2000)4642.
2.   N.-J. Wu, K. Satito and H. Yasunaga, Jpn. J. Appl. Phys. **40**(2001)2792.
3.   D. Loss and D. P. DiVincenzo, Phys. Rev. A57 (1998) 120.

4. B. E. Kane, Nature, 393 (1998) 133.
5. Y. Nakamura, Y. Pashkin and J. S. Tsai, Nature, 398(1999)786.
6. A. Barenco, D. Deutsch, A. Ekert and R. Jozsa, Phys. Rev. Lett. **74**(1995)4083.
7. N.-J. Wu, N. Shibata and Y. Amemiya, Jpn. J. Appl. Phys. 37(1998)2433.

Agent-SE: A Methodology for Agent Oriented Software Engineering

Behrouz H. Far

Faculty of Engineering, Saitama University,
255 Shimo-okubo, Saitama 338-0825, Japan
E-mail: far@computer.org

Abstract. Agent-oriented approach to software engineering (Agent-SE) for multi-agent software design is presented. It includes methods to generate organizational information for cooperative and coordinative agents. Agent-SE can be used to design and implement complex, heterogeneous, distributed and networked software systems using dynamic agent coalition structure.

1 Introduction

Software development is a very high risk task. Only about 1/6 of software projects are successful and almost all of the software projects' costs exceed initial estimation. In order to manage such a crisis, software engineering paradigms have been evolved from device oriented assembly languages to procedural and structured programming, to Object Oriented programming, to distributed objects and component-ware and to design patterns. Due to the increasing popularity of the Internet, heterogeneous, scalable and networked software systems are highly needed. However, neither of the software engineering paradigms could make software technology keep up with the current business needs.

Nowadays, an increasing number of software projects are being revised and restructured in terms of software agents. Software agents are considered as a new experimental embodiment of computer programs and are being advocated as a next generation model for engineering complex, heterogeneous, scalable, open, distributed and networked systems.

Agent system development is currently dominated by informal guidelines, heuristics and inspirations rather than formal principles and well-defined engineering techniques. Unfortunately, there has been comparatively little work on viewing agent system design and development as a software engineering paradigm that has the potentiality to enhance software developments in a wide range of applications. There is no standard way of incorporating agent-oriented viewpoint into design and development of agent-based software systems.

In this research we argue that the development of heterogeneous, robust and scalable software systems requires software agents that can complete their objectives while situated in a dynamic and uncertain environment, engage in interactions with other agents or humans and operate within flexible organizational hierarchies. We also argue that agents can be used as a framework for bringing together the components of Artificial Intelligence (AI) and Software Engineering (SE) that are necessary to design and build intelligent artifacts.

The structure of this paper is as follows. In Section 2 we discuss how scalability and complexity can be handled in agent systems. In Section 3 the Agent-SE approach is introduced. In Section 4 a method to derive organizational knowledge is presented. Finally, a conclusion is given in Section 5.

2   Software System Complexity

Business software has a large number of parts that have many interactions (i.e., complexity). The role of software engineering is to provide techniques that make it easier to handle such complexity [6].

2.1   Complexity in SE

Complexity in software systems is structural in nature. As a software system evolves new functions, program modules are added to it and its structure deteriorates to the extent that major effort is needed to maintain its consistency and conformity with the specification. Therefore, hierarchical design is a major way of handling complexity in software engineering. A complex software system is usually composed of many interrelated subsystems, each of which is in turn hierarchic in structure. The relationships among the components are supposed to be dynamic.

Two kinds of relationships can be devised: interactions among subsystems and intra-actions within subsystems. Interactions are between an artifact (or a component) and its outer environment. Intra-actions are the characteristics of the artifact's (or a component's) inner environment.

Contemporary software engineering techniques can manage only the intra-actions using decomposition and abstraction techniques. Decomposition is dividing a large problem into smaller, more manageable units each of which can then be dealt with in relative isolation. Abstraction is to define a simplified model of the system that emphasizes some of the details or properties, while intentionally neglecting the others. Attention can be focused on some aspects of the problem, at the expense of the other less relevant details. All of the contemporary software engineering paradigm, such as: object-orientation, component-ware, design patterns and software architectures provide techniques for decomposition and abstraction.

2.2   Complexity in AI

Complexity in AI is handled via using ontologies and applying synthesis techniques. Ontology in AI refers to a set of concepts or terms that can be used to describe some area of knowledge or build a representation of it. Interest in ontologies has grown due to interests in reusing or sharing knowledge across systems. Developing reusable ontologies that facilitates sharing and reuse is a goal of ontology research [2]. We think that ontologies can play a significant role in identification and design of interactions among software agents (see Section 3). Synthesis works exactly opposite to decomposition. In synthesis, one first defines a subclass of problem to be solved and builds a simplified model or prototype system that will be later incrementally updated to account for additional properties. We think that synthesis is a practical technique for building coalition of software agents.

3   The Agent-SE Approach

In this section we propose a method for multiagent system design, called Agent-SE, based on the abstraction and decomposition (Section 2.1), ontology and synthesis (Section 2.2) and organizational properties. The Agent-SE design steps are as follows:

1. Decompose the problem based on function/ input/ output into an organization of agents.
2. Design the task ontology of the problem.
3. Build an abstraction model and add interactions and signal level organizational relationships using the task ontology.
4. Design each agent and its internal intra-actions using conventional SE techniques (preferably, object-oriented design with UML, etc.) and a predefined agent model, if necessary.
5. Based on the domain ontology, design each agent's knowledge-base using Symbol Structure. (See Section 4).
6. Derive and record symbol level organizational properties based on interactions of pairs of cooperative or coordinative agents. (See Section 4).

These steps are explained in detail in the following sections. Agent-SE offers:

- An effective way of decomposition (partitioning the problem space) and synthesis.
- A means of introducing abstraction to the model.
- An appropriate way of modeling and viewing organizational relationships of complex systems.

Some novel points are:

- Decomposition is based on the function and input/ output rather than conventional data/object.
- Participating agents are described by specifying their input/output and/or functions (interfaces) or their inner environment (classes).
- Organizational properties are derived dynamically.

Organizational formation, maintenance and updating are typical of the dynamic nature of groupings in complex systems. Agent-based systems require computational mechanisms for dynamic formation, maintenance and disbanding of organizations. One such mechanism is presented in Section 4.

4   Organization

Organization is a goal directed coalition of software agents in which the agents are engaged in one or more tasks. Control, knowledge and capabilities are distributed among the agents.

Organizations, of various forms, physical, cognitive, temporal and institutional have been studied in management and computer sciences. The game theoretic approach to study organization focuses on modeling and suggesting computational algorithms for certain aspects of the coalition, such as social welfare, individual rationality, voting consensus, etc. The computational approach focuses on identifying general principles of organization and their exceptions.

The already proposed organizational models for multiagent systems have certain drawbacks. First, they cannot explain the organizational knowledge in terms of its comprising agents without reference to any other intermediary concepts. Second, they cannot provide frameworks for comparing and evaluating different organizations. Third, the organizational knowledge base cannot be updated dynamically, accounting for different configuration of the participant agents. Finally, they cannot explain the need for services of a certain agent in an organization. All of these factors are necessary in organization design and are addressed in our research.

4.1   Assumptions

Intelligence of Pair (IoP) The already proposed theories and formalisms have implicitly assumed that Organizational Intelligence (OI) exists and implemented using a meta-agent (e.g., directory and ontology service agents) (such as [1]). However there are certain difficulties in both logical formulation and actual implementation of such theories. This is mainly due to ignoring the dynamic interactions among the agents when devising the components of OI.

A point in our research is that in a purposeful (i.e., not random) organization, OI is a property of interaction among agents and can only be ascribed to at least a pair of agents. We call this Intelligence of Pair (IoP) assumption.

History of Patterns (HoP) In biological coalitions, participants may have a kind of role or function (during interaction with the other participants), if they show some persistence in their profile of actions over time. The same could be devised for artificial coalitions. As a matter of fact, it is not difficult to find organizations that display non-random persistent and repeated patterns of actions [1].

Agents act and perform in a physical world. Their past experiences can be recorded and explained in terms of their histories, that is, their profile of actions and states that they go through. Intuitively, histories can display certain patterns. A basic feature of state representation is that it assigns a certain characteristic to its reference agent. Therefore it is possible to define OI patterns with reference to agents' history.

Another point is that OI patterns emerge from discovering a persisted state or an ordered pattern in the agent's profile of actions. We call this History of Patterns (HoP) assumption. IoP and HoP assumptions account for dynamic interactions and a computation method based on this assumption is proposed below.

4.2 Modeling

Symbol structure (SS) is used to model individual agent's knowledge structure. SS is a finite connected multi-layer bipartite graph. There are two kinds of nodes in each layer of SS: concepts (c) and relations (r). One source of difficulty when processing concepts, is distinguishing a concept at various levels of abstraction, as well as differentiating between generic concepts and their instances. Function *type* is defined to ease such differentiation. The function type maps concepts and relations onto a set T. The elements of T are called type labels. Type hierarchy provides a means of evaluating a concept at various levels. The type hierarchy is a partial ordering defined over the set of type labels, T.

Flexibility, extendibility and interoperability are three main advantages of knowledge representation and reasoning with SS.

4.3 Reasoning rules

Join rule: Join rule merges identical concepts. If a concept c in symbol structure u is identical to a concept d in symbol structure v, then let w be the symbol structure obtained by deleting d and linking to c all arcs of relations that had been linked to d.

Simplification rule: Redundant relations of the same type linked to the same concept in the same order can be reduced by deletion all but one. If the relations r and s in the symbol structure u are duplicates, then one of them may be deleted from u together with all its arcs.

Generalization/Specialization rule: For two arbitrary levels u and v of any SS, if u is identical to v except that some type labels of the nodes of v are restricted to subtypes of the same nodes in u, then u is called a specialization of v, and v is called a generalization of u.

4.4   Interaction among agents

Now we have a framework for representing and reasoning with the knowledge on an individual agent basis. Knowledge sharing by moving from one agent to another and on an organizational basis requires defining the basic agent interactions, i.e., cooperation, coordination and competition.

Cooperation: Cooperation is revealing an agent's goal and the knowledge behind it, i.e., its symbol structure to the other party. In cooperation both agents have a common goals.

Coordination: Coordination is revealing an agent's goals and the knowledge behind it, i.e., its symbol structure to the other party. In coordination, agents have separate goals.

Loose Competition: Loose competition is revealing only an agent's goals but encapsulating the knowledge behind it to the other party.

Strict Competition: Strict competition is neither revealing an agent's goals nor the knowledge behind it to the other party. Therefore, knowledge sharing is equivalent to merging two or more symbol structures using join, simplification, generalization and specialization rules.

Conventionally, it is believed that for a pair of agents to interact, each should maintain a model of the other agent, as well as a probabilistic model of future interactions [5]. This is totally unnecessary when using SS representation in cooperation and coordination cases.

4.5   Computational OI

Here we propose a method for generating organizational concepts based on the IoP and HoP assumptions and definitions of interaction. In case of *cooperation* and *coordination* the agent's private knowledge is exposed to the other party. In this method, first, a pair of agents are selected and by using join, simplification, generalization and specialization rules their SS are merged. There are finite sets of *actions* and *states* associated with each agent. Given a set of all possible actions, A, an agent's action is a subset $B \subseteq A$. Each agent's state transition is represented by a non-deterministic finite state automaton (NFSA).

Both *actions* and *states* take concepts and relations as their attributes. For each agent, the NFSA state transition model has an initial state *idle* and final state *goal*. A sequence of actions that convert the *idle* state to *goal* is a plan of actions towards a goal. Theoretically, all such sequences form a *regular language (RL)* whose elements are generated by a *regular grammar (RG)* equivalent to the NFSA. Furthermore, there may be various modes of operation (i.e., authority mode, subordinate mode, etc.) each modeled by a different NFSA. The proper mode may be selected by examining the select mode (See Fig. 1).

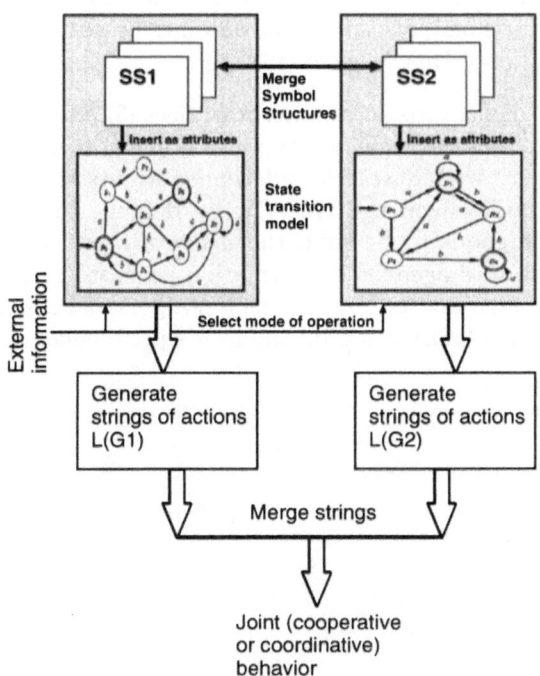

Fig. 1. Deriving organizational knowledge

As both actions and states take concepts and relations of SS as their attributes, in the case of cooperation and coordination, a joint sequence of actions can be generated by matching the actions whose attributes are concepts or relations belonging to the same type hierarchy. Such sequences form the joint plans of actions handled partially by either of the agents pair. The proposed algorithm is as follows:

1. Select an agent pair, Agent (G_1) and (G_2).
2. Merge their SS using join, simplification, generalization and specialization rules.
3. Select mode of operation based on external information.
4. Select the NFSA model and generate sequences of actions for the selected mode.
5. Compare two such sequences $\omega_i \in \mathcal{L}_{G_1}$ and $\omega_j \in \mathcal{L}_{G_2}$ where $\mathcal{L}_{G_1}$ and $\mathcal{L}_{G_2}$ are regular languages of agent (G_1) and (G_2), respectively.

6. For a common action $a \in \omega_i$ and $a \in \omega_j$ check the type of attributes of a. If the attributes belong to the same type hierarchy, merge the sequences from that point on after adjusting the types.
7. Record such joint sequences and check for possible repetition and/or persistence patterns in the future course of actions.
8. When repetition and/or persistence becomes present, add such strings to the *organizational knowledge base*.

Examples of our *electronic commerce* project [3] are presented below. In our *electronic commerce* project 7 types of agents, *customer*, *dealer*, *manufacturer*, *delivery*, *banker*, *search* and *catalog* agents work together and/or compete to do business on the Web [3]. By default, the *dealer* agent only knows about the goods to be sold, the *delivery* agent knows about transporting goods, *banker* agent has information on customers and their credit and/or cash accounts and *customer* agent is a personal assistant agent for a human user and has information on the user's preferences, etc.

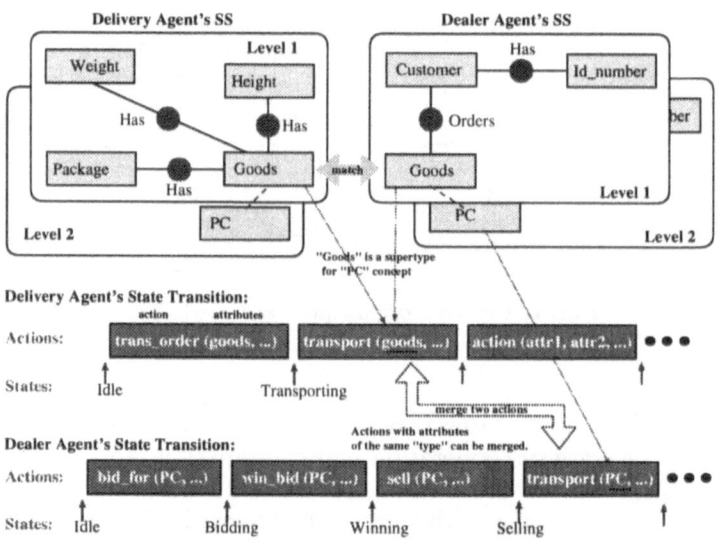

Fig. 2. A portion of SS for dealer agent

4.6   Example: cooperation

Let's consider a case of a *dealer* agent and a *delivery* agent cooperating to sell and deliver an article of commerce, such as a PC to a human user. A portion of SS for *dealer* and a *delivery* agents is shown in the upper portion of Fig. 2. It is visible that the concept Goods is a super-type for PC for both agents. However, based on the agents' roles, the concepts may have different data associated with them. For example, PC in *dealer* agent's SS may be associated with CPU, memory, etc. However, for *delivery* agent the same concept may have weight and size as its attributes.

The lower part of Fig. 2 depicts an example of the sequence of actions for the *dealer* and *delivery* agents. It is shown that the action transport(*Goods,...*) for the *delivery* and transport(*PC,...*) for the *dealer* agents have attributes belonging to the same type hierarchy. Therefore, the strings can be merged by adjusting the type and changing transport(*Goods,...*) to transport(*PC,...*) for the *delivery* agent and let the plan be executed by assigning this action to the *delivery* agent.

4.7   Example: coordination

Let's consider a case of a *dealer* agent and a *banker* agent coordinating their operations in order to exchange information related to a particular human user. Apparently the *dealer* and *banker* agents have separate goals but they coordinate their activities to help each other.

Let's assume that the *dealer* agent already receives a purchase order from a human user through his/her *customer* agent. A portion of the *dealer* agent's SS is shown in the upper right part of Fig. 2.

The *dealer* agent interacts with the *banker* agent by sharing its SS with that of the *banker* agent. By merging the two SS, the customer concept is common between the two SS and in this way the *dealer* agent can verify that the customer has an Account and from the *banker* agent's SS verify that there are either Cash or Credit accounts available. Also it can verify that the user may also use a Cash Card. Therefore, the *dealer* agent can contact the user to get data for Cash or Credit the accounts. It can further verify genuineness of the data supplied by the user by consulting the *banker* agent again. In this simple example, knowledge sharing is used to enable the *dealer* agent to successfully proceed with the selling task in spite of possessing only a limited amount of knowledge about the user without implementing a redundant customer database within the *dealer* agent.

5   Conclusions

In this paper, we proposed a method for multiagent system design by blending AI and SE techniques. We defined agents' interaction problems as cooperation, coordination and competition and devised a method to extract organizational knowledge during cooperation and coordination. These methods are quite useful for designing agent coalitions that are shaped dynamically and defining multiple roles for individual agents when participating in a number of different coalitions.

We have argued that multiagent system design can be achieved at the expense of additional design steps including, design of domain ontology and agents' symbol structure. Actually, designing domain ontology is not a totally new task in software engineering practice. It has been carried out informally in almost all of the contemporary software engineering techniques. For instance, data definition diagrams incorporated with flowcharts and PAD diagrams in structural design and actor definitions in use-cases in object-oriented design are kinds of treatments of this step. We insist on the significance of formalization of this step using task level ontology and the need for tools to support this.

Applications using the framework and techniques described in this paper, such as a multi-agent system for electronic commerce [3,4] have already been developed.

References

1. K.M. Carley and L. Gasser, "Computational Organization Theory," in Multiagent Systems: A Modern Approach to Distributed Artificial Intelligence, ed. G. Weiss, G., pp. 299-330, MIT Press, 1999.
2. B. Chandrasekaran, et al., "What Are Ontologies, and Why Do We Need Them?" IEEE Intelligent Systems and Their Applications, vol. 14, no. 1, pp. 20-26, 1999.
3. B.H. Far, et al., "An Integrated Reasoning and Learning Environment for WWW Based Software Agents for Electronic Commerce," IEICE Trans. Inf. and Syst., vol. E81-D, no. 12, pp. 1374-1386, 1998.
4. B.H. Far, et al., "Formalization of Organizational Intelligence for Multiagent System Design," IEICE Trans. Inf. and Syst., vol. E83-D, no. 4, pp. 599-607, 2000.
5. M.N. Huhns and L.A. Stephens, "Multiagent Systems and Societies of Agents," in Multiagent Systems: A Modern Approach to Distributed Artificial Intelligence, ed. G. Weiss, pp. 79-120, MIT Press, 1999.
6. N.R. Jennings, "On agent-based software engineering," Artificial Intelligence, vol. 117, pp. 277-296, 2000.

Promoting Wearable Computing

Polly Huang

Swiss Federal Institute of Technology, Gloriastrasse 35, CH-8092 Zurich, Switzerland
E-mail: huang@tik.ee.ethz.ch

Abstract. This is a survey on wearable computers consists of a comprehensive introduction and an overview of research activities in I/O interface, searching, communication, and power.

1 Introduction

Wearable computers in a loose sense are computers people can wear *effortlessly*. In a stricter sense [11], wearable computers should run *continuously* and be operated *hands-free*. This stricter definition helps distinguish wearable computers from portable ones. For instance, pocket watches are not wearable computers in a sense that people need at least one hand to hold them and sometimes another hand to open the covers. Wristwatches, in contrast, can be easily flipped over and read when both hands are engaging other activities.

Many small laptops (Figure 1, left [5]), are not wearable computers either. They do not last long enough to meet the continuous run requirement. Wearable computers like MIT's Lizzy [21] (Figure 1, middle left) can run much longer because of carefully selected power-conservative components and efficient batteries.

The wearables and small laptops differ in I/O features as well. To operate hands-free, wearables are usually equipped with head-mount or eyeglass-based displays (Figure 2, left) and one-hand keyboards (Figure 2, middle left) or microphone with speech processing software. Two pictures on the right of Figure 1 show a prototype of IBM ThinkPad 560X shrunk to 10.5 oz (300 gram) and to a size small enough to fit into regular pockets. This prototype, introduced in September 1998, consists of a 233 MHz Pentium CPU, 64 MB DRAM, 340 MB IBM micro hard disk, a micro head-mount display, and a microphone with speech processing software.

Relationship With Ubiquitous Computing. Ubiquitous computers, in the purest form of definition [17], are computers invisibly embedded in the environment and wirelessly communicating with each other. Some may use other terms such as *embedded system* [9], *smart room* [10], and *sensor network* [4]. But in principle, it does not matter if the computers are fixed or migratable, situated in a room or outdoor. They all fall into the broader definition of ubiquitous computing, i.e., *computers in the environment*. By nature, ubiquitous computers have easy access to the resources in the environment, i.e., environment-centric resources. Wearable computers, in contrast, are computers moved with people all the time, i.e., *computers on people*. These computers have easy access to personal information, i.e., human-centric resources.

The wearable and ubiquitous computers, each class has its strength and weakness. It is often that one's weakness is the other's strength. That means ubiquitous and wearable computers can compliment each other, and applications adopting a combination of wearable and ubiquitous computers can take advantage of the both. This avoids the pitfall of putting much effort making one class work for all when in fact a much smaller amount of work is sufficient if cooperating the two. In general, applications involving interaction with the environment are better off introducing ubiquitous computers into the systems. Similarly, when interaction with people are involved, applications are better off using wearable computers.

Fig. 1. (Left): Two Popular Mini-notebooks, Toshiba Libretto 50 (Top) and Sony PCG-C1 (Bottom). (Middle Left): A User Wearing MIT's Lizzy Design. (Middle Right): A User Effortlessly Wearing the IBM Prototype. (Right): Pieces of the IBM Prototype.

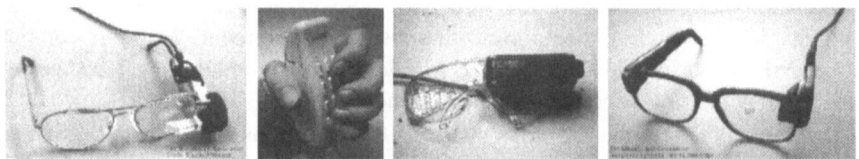

Fig. 2. Typical I/O Devices: (Left) is a micro-display to be clipped onto a eyeglass frame. (Middle Left) shows a twiddler keyboard with integrated mouse functionality. (Middle Right) shows a PrivateEye micro-display mounted on a glass. (Right) shows state of the art integrated eyeglass display.

2   History and motivation

Wearable computers have quite a long history [15] – 732 years to be exact. Eyeglasses considered as wearable computers were first mentioned in literature as early as 1268. Recent proposals show a common trend on improving human abilities beyond our biological limits – so called cyborg applications. Another historical trend is computers being smaller and increasingly accessible. If these trends continue, next generation computers are likely to be worn around our waists and ready to compute anytime.

The first wearable computer [23] was revealed in 1966. It is a roulette wheel predictor. The idea started from 1955 when Ed Thorp was a second year graduate student at UCLA's physics department. In 1960, almost by accident, he described the idea of roulette wheel predictor to'Claude Shannon, a mathematician at MIT. Soon the next year, the two built a wearable computer from scratch in Shannon's basement. It was a cigarette-pack sized analog computer with four buttons. The four buttons were used to indicate speed and the predicted results were transmitted by radio to an ear piece. Thorp and Shannon field-tested their wearable computer in Las Vegas and confirmed the expected gain of 44% obtained by laboratory experiments. Until the end of 1980s, most applications tend to stick to this gambling and gaming theme. However, there is gradually a noticeable amount of medical applications for the hearing and visually impaired. Then there came the blockbuster *Terminator* and the first commercialized head-mount display – *Private Eye* (Figure 2, middle right). The amount of proposals started to bloom in 90s. In the meantime, the theme made a sharp turn towards applications of daily and effortless use, in particular, augmented memory [16], location/context awareness [7], and very small computers capable of running these applications [12]. These proposals were, more or less, driven by the human desire to know – fast, more, anywhere and anytime. As Sir Bacon had nicely put it – knowledge is power.

Another trend we see from the general history of technology is the increasing *accessibility*. Take time computation for example. It has evolved from clock towers, wall clocks, pocket watches, to wristwatches. These time pieces get smaller and more accessible. With the wristwatches now, people can read time anywhere and anytime. Data computers has been following the same trend, evolving from mainframes, mini computers, desktop PCs, to laptops (some of them are really small). The next generation data computers are likely to be even more accessible and wearable, much like the wristwatches. If we think today that wristwatches are indispensable, perhaps one day we will think the same for wearable computers. Or many have already thought so if cellular phones qualify as wearable computers. Strictly speaking, we do not need wearable computers to survive, but like many technologies today they provide convenience and convenience is something difficult to resist. From the history's point of view, we conclude that human desire of knowledge and convenience is the hidden force behind the current wearable computer research.

3   State of research

There are primarily five areas of research – I/O, searching, communication, power, and heat. Some of them deal with higher-level software issues whereas the others deal with lower-level hardware ones. We discuss these topics in a top-down fashion excluding heat, which is rather distant from the computer science and electrical engineering regimes. Example applications are given during the discussion of I/O interface and searching techniques primarily because technologies used are closely related to the nature of applications and showcasing applications helps highlight relevant I/O technologies.

3.1   I/O Interface

We have traditionally relied on text input devices such as keyboard, pointing device such as mouse, and output devices that sit about .5-1 meter away from users' eyes on desktop or laptop. Because of the hands-free and continuous use requirements, these I/O devices do not suit the use of wearable computers. In particular, traditional keyboards are to be operated with both hands. The scale of conventional desktop monitors or laptop LCD panels is too large to carry for a long time and too power consuming. To solve these problems, people have sought alternatives for conventional I/O devices and explore techniques in computer vision, graphics, and speech processing to enable I/O in visual and audio formats.

Input. Solutions for input include one-hand keyboard with integrated mouse functionality, hand writing, video sensor, and speech processors. The integrated keyboard is expected to be used as the main input method and the rest as alternatives.

One immediate solution to replace the conventional keyboards and mouse is to re-arrange keys and to integrate the mouse functionality for one-hand operation. There exist a number of commercial products and lab prototypes. Twiddler [1] (Figure 2, right) is one of the most popular kinds. It consists of 6 function keys and 12 letter keys. The function keys are operated by the thumb. The letter keys are in 4 rows, 3 in each row and operated by one of the other 4 fingers respectively. Twiddler comes with drivers for Windows and Linux, as well as training programs. Some users have reported getting up to the speed of 10+ words per minute within a week [14]. Shortcuts can be pre-set to speed up frequent actions. Operating a Twiddler is pretty much like playing choruses on a guitar.

Hand-writing recognition is used in many palm-top devices. Some of them, e.g., Apple's Newton, recognize characters as they are written naturally, whereas others, e.g., 3Com's Palm Pilot, recognize characters in more cryptic patterns. While hand writing may appear as an intuitive input method, it does not work well for fast and bulk data input [19]. First of all, the recognition software can accommodate hand writing in various forms only to certain degree. For people who never really learn how to form the letters properly, this input method will not be an option. Secondly, to write fast, people tend to scribble. The formations of letters get even worse and become very difficult, if possible, to recognize. Due to these two reasons, hand writing serves well as an alternative but will not be the primary input method.

Visual input is important to applications of more graphical nature. Physical profiles of an object such as size, shape, location, and movement are more direct and precise when obtained through camera-like input devices and analyzed by computer vision technologies. Take the Billiards Assistant [11] (Figure 3, left) for example. A head-mount camera takes a snapshot of the pool table. The computer vision part of the software identifies the white ball, the target ball and the pocket. These data are then fed into the angle calculation part for further processing.

Audio input is inevitable in situations that users' eyes and hands must engage in critical activities, e.g., driving a car. In these circumstances, audio is a nice, natural alternative to provoke simple commands. Microphones are typical audio input devices. They are often used together with speech processing technologies [18]. For instances, *speech recognition* translates analogous audio clips into digital forms that computers can understand or further process. *Speaker identification* helps identify persons or objects by their voice fingerprints. *Noise filtering* enhances the precision of speech recognition and has the potential of discovering context in the background.

Output. Solutions to output include head-mount displays with augmented reality and headphone for synthesized audio. The head-mount displays replace the relatively bulky monitors or LCD panels as primary output devices for wearables. Headphones are, in contrast, a complimentary alternative.

In the wearable paradigm, hardware components tend to be small, so does the display. The next logical solution is to place *micro-displays* in the proximity of users' eyes. There exists a small number of commercialized products and most of the sophisticated ones, with full VGA capability, are still in development. More commonly used micro-displays are composed of 320x240 small pixels within a roughly 12 cm x 8 cm area (Figure 2, middle right). More advanced ones use much smaller and four times more, 640x480, pixels that fit into a 1.2 cm x .8 cm area (Figure 2, left). These micro-displays can be mounted onto a hat, a glass, a helmet, or a custom-made head piece.

Current state of the art (Figure 2, right) is rather a projector than a micro-monitor. The beamer is integrated into one leg of an eyeglass frame. Computer screen is projected onto a small area of the lens. By that, users can see through the display and overlay virtual information with the reality [22]. In the Billiards Assistant example, the exact angle to hit the white ball is overlayed with the real white ball and pool table. This is assuming the users can hold their heads steady and the directions of eyeglasses and eye surfaces coincide completely. In practice, these two factors need to be taken into consideration and used to adjust computation accordingly. For applications that require perception of depth, advanced computer graphics techniques, such as 2D-3D conversions, are necessary.

Audio output is preferable in situations that human eyes must be dedicated to more critical activities, similar to the reasons for audio input. *Speech synthesis* technologies will come in handy as solutions to generate comprehensible audio output.

3.2 Searching

There is a new class of applications unique to wearable computers. They work like personal assistants, handing documents upon request and proactively reminding us of relevant information [16]. Searching techniques are critical to this class of applications. Challenges mainly come from dealing with non-text documents and give *really* relevant reminders. The former problem is equivalent of indexing text, audio, and video archives for easy and fast search – field searching. The latter problem is to imitate association of current context with memories – content matching.

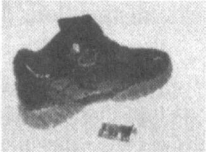

Fig. 3. (Left) plot shows snapshots of the Billiard Assistant before and after angle calculation. (Middle Left) plot is a snapshot of the Remembrance Agent working with Emacs. (Middle Right) depicts the prototype as shoe insert. (Right) depicts the Body Area Network working through hand shakes.

Existing Web searching engines work reasonably well with text-based documents. These searching engines are inadequate in the context of wearable computing where documents are commonly found in more 'cryptic' (or binary) formats – pdf texts, jpg images, and mpg video streams. Indexing and searching these documents poses a non-trivial challenge and is a emerging area of research. Most solutions adopt a 2-tier model. Non-text-based documents are first converted into text formats or smaller audio/video entities. Indexing and searching are done based on these converted texts or smaller entities.

Another desirable mode of searching is to match content and give relevant suggestions to users, much like recalling relevant experience in the memories.. Indexing and searching techniques in this context differ from those used in field searching. Whereas the field searching locates files with exact values in fields specified in the queries, the content matching mode tries to find similar files by matching a significantly wider range of contents. The content matching techniques often break a document into smaller elements, e.g., words, allocate weights to these elements, and compute the relevance combining simple heuristics and user-specified ratings.

MIT's Remembrance Agent [16] (Figure 3, middle left) implements both modes of searches – field- and content-based. The content matching uses a word vector approach. Each document is converted into a vector of unique, meaningful words with corresponding occurrence frequencies. This is referred to as the data vector. Same conversion is done on the text being edited at the moment and resulting in the query vector. A document's relevance is measured a weighted sum of frequencies of words occurring in both the data and query vectors.

3.3   Communication

Communication for wearable computers includes communication between the wearable pieces, e.g., between the eye piece and the computing unit, and communication between the wearable computers to the rest of the world, e.g., between the wireless modem and an ISP dialup pool. We focus our discussion on the communication between wearable pieces, given that the communication between the wearable and the rest of the world is a more general and not specific to wearables. Communication between wearable pieces has a special set of requirements. Due to these requirements, suitable solutions are more likely to be found in short-range low-frequency wireless technologies. In this subsection, we discuss these requirements, review general wireless communication technologies, and finally present a plausible solution called *Body Area Network* [24].

In general, requirements for wearable communication tie back to the strict definition of wearable computer – continuous and intuitive use. For intuitive and easy use, wearable communication should be wireless. For continuous use, it needs to be energy efficient, which often means low frequency transmission. Additionally, due to the high confidentiality of data being communicated among the wearable pieces (often passwords and credit card numbers), it is desirable that the communication method comes with added security features. This usually implies that the wireless transmission needs to be short ranged so it has a lower probability of leaking information. The ultimate solution is to somehow wirelessly transmit signals through human bodies, which avoids leaking important information into the air at all. It is also desirable to reduce interference. However, interference is not specific to wearable communication. It is a general problem that can be solved by signal attenuation and noise filtering techniques. In short, a wireless, low-frequency, body-range communication technology is preferable to connect components of a wearable computer.

Wireless communication technologies can be classified into two classes – far-field and near-field communications. Literally, technologies in the far-field class are more suitable for long ranged communication, and similarly those in the near-field class are for the short ranged communication. Typical *radio frequency* technologies fall into the far-field class whereas *Bluetooth* [6] loosely qualifies as a technology in the near-field class. To be more specific, a typical radio frequency antenna can reach locations that are several hundred meters away. Bluetooth typically covers a region of about ten meter radius. The two classes of communications differ technically in signal degradation ratio and carrier requirement. In terms of signal degradation ratio, the far-field class is proportional to $1/d^2$, where d is the distance to signal source. The near-field class, on the other hand, is proportional to $1/d^3$. In terms of signal carrier requirement, for devices size of a watch or credit card, the far-field class requires carrier frequency in the scale of gigahertz while the near-field class requires carrier frequency in the scale of 0.1 to 1 megahertz.

For wearables, technologies in the near-field class that can cover the human range, roughly a three- to five-meter radius area, is preferable. AT&T Labs Cambridge's *Piconet* [2] is a very low frequency radio network with a roughly five meter range. Piconet meets the requirements of intuitive use and low power consumption. However, due to its radio transmission nature, it is still possible to leak out personal, confidential information in the air. Another promising solution is MIT Media Lab's Body Area Network [24]. Human bodies are used as wet conductor and take part in a circuit connecting a special transmitter, receiver and the earth. When the body is in a steady state, the circuit is balanced with zero potential. When the body moves, the resulting potential carries signals through the current.

It is measured that the carrier strength is 330 kilohertz and the power consumption is as little as 1.5 milliwatts. Middle right picture of Figure 3 shows MIT's prototype as a shoe insert [13]. The prototype is tested with an application exchanging electronic business cards. Right picture of Figure 3 shows two people wearing the Body Area Network transceiver exchange business cards by shaking hands.

3.4 Power

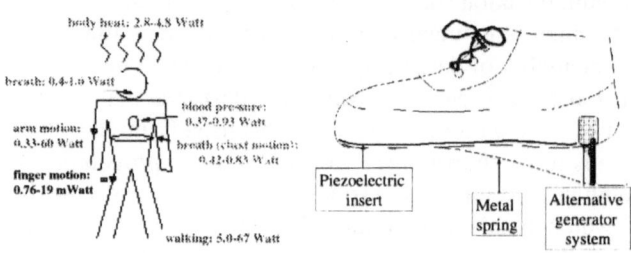

Fig. 4. Human Power: left plot illustrates the theoretical potential of body movements; right plot demonstrates piezoelectric material and mechanical springs can be integrated into shoes to convert walking power.

Power is essential to meet the criteria of continuous run. It also strongly influences a user's decision to use a wearable computer continuously. Unless the computer performs, there is no point of wearing one all the time. Batteries are the conventional solutions. They should be integrated into the wearable computers to provide the last layer of reliability in case that all other power sources fail. However, batteries should not be the sole power source given that wearable computers are supposed to be operated anywhere anytime, including hiking in mountains and standing in queue to get into the German embassy in Switzerland. Next interesting question is how and where to get power. Because wearable computers are with people all the time, it is only natural to seek power generated by people. Below we evaluate the power requirements of wearable computers, provide theoretically figures on human potential, and finally look into some practical power solutions.

To understand better what types of power source are more practical, we first examine the average power consumption of the wearable computers. Traditional bigger wearable computers consume 5 watt energy. A typical configuration includes a head mount display, 2 gigabyte hard disk, 133 megahertz Pentium CPU, and 20 megabyte RAM. More advanced wearable computers can consume as little as 0.7 watt power. This is possible by putting state of the art MicroOptical eyeglass display, flash memory, and StrongArm microprocessor (.3W at 115 MIPs) altogether. A power source that can continuously generate several watts of power is ideal.

According to a theoretical analysis [20], human energy in different forms, body heat, breathing, blood pressure, arm motion, finger motion, and walking, can generate power from milliwatts to several tens of watts. See left plot of Figure 4. Body heat can be converted into 2.8-4.8 watts energy. Blood pressure has the potential of 0.37-0.93 watts. Breathing can generate energy in two ways – facial and chest motions by inhaling and exhaling. They can generate 0.4-1.0 and 0.42-0.83 watt power respectively. These three forms of energy do not require extra actions by the wearable users because people always dispense heat, breath, and have blood pressure.

The next three forms, however, require extra movements. Arm motion energy spans a wider range, from 0.33 to 60 watts. Given that we are more likely to type when using computers, finger motion can be an interesting alternative. Unfortunately, finger motions generate only about 0.76-19 milliwatts of power. The last energy form, walking, has the potential of generating 5 to 67 watt power.

All above figures are theoretically derived. Converting heat and blood pressure to reusable power is technologically difficult. Breathing and finger motion power is almost negligible. Arm motion and walking are both practical. However, walking is preferable for two reasons. The energy converting unit can be easily integrated as shoe inserts, and taking a walk looks much more natural.

There are two ways to transfer the power of walking into electricity. See right plot of Figure 4. One is to use piezoelectric materials that convert pressures of stepping into electrical energy. A 52 kilogram user can generate approximately 5 watts of power. The other is to use more traditional rotary generators that convert heel motions into electricity. The efficiency is determined by the distance of the spring system mounted in the heel, energy storage of the spring system, and the efficiency of the generator. The figure is about 12.5% which means .625 to 8.4 watts energy output. Together, a pair of shoes with both piezoelectric and spring inserts have a realistic potential of 11.25 to 26.8 watts electricity.

4   Summary and outlook

There are in principle six areas of applications for wearables – medicine, military, industrial training, education, entertainment, and daily use. Entertainment and medical applications were proposed early by designers in the pre-1990s. In a remarkable medical application – artificial vision [3], a team of doctors and computer scientists managed to recover a blind patient's eyesight to 20/400 with the help of a wearable computer. During the early 90s, researchers started to exploit practical use of wearables in military, industrial training, and education. Since late 1990s, as wearable hardware getting matured, applications for daily use show up, for example MIT's Remembrance Agent. In [8], we further address speculations among the community about wearable computer's future need and practicality for average and daily use.

We find much work needs to be carried on in four directions: 1) *hardware development*, 2) *AI technique enhancement*, 3) *operating software development*, and 4) *systematic performance evaluation*. In particular, the integrated one-hand keyboard and head-mount micro display are plausible I/O solutions, but related audio and video I/O techniques (computer vision and speech processing) do not seem robust enough for daily use. Communication-wised, Body Area Network and Piconet provide reasonable solutions. However, these technologies are still in development and no systematic evaluation has been done to compare their use. The power aspect is somewhat similar. While piezoelectric and spring system inserts are promising and 'continuous run' seems a reachable goal, no formal experiments are conducted to evaluate their efficiency in practice. Various groups in the Swiss Federal Institue of Technology are pursuing topics in these directions (see [8] for detailed information). We hope, with this article, to encourage contribution from fellow scientists world-wide and thus promote research in the area.

References

1. Handykey corp. http://www.handykey.com.
2. F. Bennett, J. B. Evans D. Clarke, A. Hopper, A. Jones, and D. Leask. Piconet: Embedded mobile networking. *IEEE Personal Communication*, 4(5), 1997.
3. Wm. H. Dobelle. Artificial vision for the blind by connecting a television camera to the visual cortex. *ASAIO Journal*, 35(3 & 4), 2000.
4. D. Estrin, R. Govindan, J. Heidemann, and S. Kumar. Next century challenges: Scalable coordination in sensor networks. In *Proceedings of MobiCOM*, August 1999.
5. X. Feng. Sony pcg-c1 vs. libretto 50. http://www.fixup.net/tips/pcg-c1.htm.
6. Bluetooth Working Group. Bluetooth specification 1.0. http://www.bluetooth.com.
7. A. Harter and A. Hopper. A distributed location system for the active office. *IEEE Network*, 8(1), January 1994.
8. P. Huang. Promoting wearable computing: A survey and future agenda. Technical Report Nr.95, TIK, ETH, 2000.
9. P. J. Koopman Jr. Embedded system design issues (the rest of the story). In *Proceedings of the International Conference on Computer Design (ICCD 96)*, 1996.
10. A. Pentland. Smart rooms. *Scientific American*, April 1996.
11. A. Pentland. Wearable intelligence. *Scientific American*, 9(4), Fall 1998.
12. D. Platt. Hip-pc. The Lap and Palmtop Expo. http://belladonna.media.mit.edu/projects/wearables/timeline.html#1991a, April 1991.
13. MIT Media Lab Personal Area Network Project. Intrabody signalling. http://www.media.mit.edu/physics/projects/pan/pan.html.
14. MIT Media Lab Wearable Copumter Project. Keyboards. http://wearables.www.media.mit.edu/projects/wearables/keyboards.html.
15. B. Rhodes. A brief history of wearable computing. http://wearables.www.media.mit.edu/projects/wearables/timeline.html.
16. B. Rhodes. The wearable remembrance agent: A system for augmented memory. *Personal Technologies Journal Special Issue on Wearable Computing*, 1(4), 1997.
17. B. Rhodes, N. Minar, and J. Weaver. Wearable computing meets ubiquitous computing: Reaping the best of both worlds. In *Proceedings of The Third International Symposium on Wearable Computers (ISWC '99)*, pages 141–149, San Francisco, CA, October 1999.
18. D. K. Roy, N. Sawhney, C. Schmandt, and A. Pentland. Wearable audio computing: A survey of interaction techniques. Technical report, MIT Media Lab, April 1997.
19. T. Starner. The cyborgs are coming. Submitted to Wired. ftp://www-white.media.mit.edu/pub/tech-reports/TR-318-ABSTRACT.html, 1994.
20. T. Starner. Human powered wearable computing. *IBM Systems Journal*, 35(3 & 4), 1996.
21. T. Starner. Lizzy: Mit's wearable computer design 2.0.5. http://wearables.www.media.mit.edu/projects/wearables/lizzy/, 1997.
22. T. Starner, S. Mann, B. Rhodes, J. Levine, J. Heaaley, D. Kirsch, R. W. Picard, and A. Pentland. Augmented reality through wearable computing. *Presence*, 6(4), 1997.
23. E. Thorp. Beat the dealer. *Review of the International Statistical Institute*, 37(3), 1969.
24. T. G. Zimmerman. Personal area networks: Near-field intrabody communication. *IBM Systems Journal*, 35(3 & 4), 1996.

Index